GULF WOMEN

Gulf Women

Edited by
Amira El-Azhary Sonbol

Syracuse University Press

First Syracuse University Press Edition 2012

Syracuse University Press, 621 Skytop Road, Syracuse, NY 13244-5290

12   13   14   15   16   17   6   5   4   3   2   1

First published in 2012 by
Bloomsbury Qatar Foundation Publishing, Qatar Foundation, Villa 3,
Education City, PO Box 5825, Doha, Qatar, www.bqfp.com.qa

Chapters 9 and 10 translated with the assistance of Azza El Kholy.

∞ The paper used in this publication meets the minimum requirements
of the American National Standard for Information Sciences—Permanence of Paper
for Printed Library Materials, ANSI Z39.48-1992.

For a listing of books published and distributed by Syracuse University Press, visit our website at
SyracuseUniversityPress.syr.edu.

ISBN: 978-0-8156-3309-9

Library of Congress Cataloging-in-Publication Data

Available upon request from publisher.

Manufactured in the United States of America

Contents

History books have recorded this battle and the heroism of its leaders and fighters, but the records have not documented the stories told of that day, the memories that have been handed down of those fateful events. Qatar was at total war at al-Wajba, its men, women and children all joining in. While the men stood waiting to fight and then engaged in battle, it was the women who supplied the water, carrying it fifteen and sometimes thirty kilometers, using donkeys when they had them, but mostly walking all the way to supply their sons, fathers, husbands and brothers with water. Having access to water while Turkish troops suffered from the lack of it was critical to the victory at al-Wajba.[1] We do not know for sure that this was part of Shaykh Jasim's strategy, but total war was familiar to Qatar; reliance that all Qataris will stand together and fight is within the spirit and reality of desert life and the history and cultural traditions of Arabia. It is also within the parameters of normative gender relations, as the articles in this book illustrate: the expectation that women would do their part, and dependence on them in critical situations, as in daily life, was natural. That *al-Na'ja* and her sisters are not known by name is less a reflection of the historical truth than of the written historical records popularly used to construct the past. For the Gulf, published records represent the interests and discourses of those who collected and recorded the material in them, rather than the realities of lived experiences. Given the overwhelming focus on political events that is natural to political processes involving struggles of independence, the establishment of ruling dynasties and formation of states, it is not surprising that women rarely appear in historical narratives. Like other players in social history, women's contributions have remained largely unnoted.

That is the first problem encountered by researchers looking for sources and information about women in Gulf history. Very little information on social life, let alone the life of women, has been documented. The impression from reading secondary literature is that women hardly existed in Arabia, or at least that they were concealed and had little to do with the world in which they lived. The fourteen articles in this volume, the result of a project directed to finding sources and studying the history of women in the Gulf, show that in fact there is a very rich history to be researched, discovered and presented as a contribution to a greater understanding of

[1] I am grateful to Shaykh Faysal bin Qassim al-Thani for informing me of this and other important events about Qatar included in this introduction.

Introduction: Researching the Gulf

AMIRA EL-AZHARY SONBOL

She is celebrated as '*al-Na'ja*' (the ewe) for being able to haul two heavy waterskins over long distances. Her real name is not known; it is as *al-Na'ja* that storytellers speak of her, in memory of her strength and courage. The year was 1893, the location fifteen kilometers south of Doha at a place called al-Wajba, where Qataris stood ready to fight for their independence against the forces of the Ottoman *wali* of Basra, who was sent to force Qatar to accept an Ottoman deputy governor, establish post and customs offices in Doha port, and essentially bring Qatar under the direct rule of the Ottoman Empire.

   The approaching forces were significant and Qatar did not have their equal. But Qataris were used to this type of situation, had been in this position before and understood the meaning of independence. This was a situation people of the Gulf had faced many times in their history, threatened by invasions and pressures from covetous expanding empires. In 1893, the inhabitants of the Qatar peninsula became a people at war, the men fighting around their wily eighty-year-old leader, Shaykh Jasim bin Hamad, who knew the terrain and how best to protect it. The story goes that he left the battlefield, let it be known that he was withdrawing his forces, quietly gave orders to poison all the wells in the area, divided his forces into two phalanxes and had them withdraw out of sight. As the Ottomans arrived at al-Musaymir, Shaykh Jasim's fighters attacked them and the battle was won, with heavy Ottoman casualties.

Manat? Though the Prophet Muhammad often consulted women when
making various social rulings, the role women played in the subsequent
development of *Shari'a* was scarcely noted. In fact, there seemed to be
historical amnesia about the role of women in the Gulf and the few references I have found were mainly in poems and oral stories of heroines. In
the colonial and post-colonial periods, this silence was so heavy that it
bordered on a total smothering. Why had women's roles been covered by
a dark veil that cloaked the reality of their dynamic role in the region? My
initial conclusion led me to believe that there had been an avid and even
desperate attempt from the patriarchal societies of the region to protect
women from the colonial fantasies that had punctuated Orientalist interpretations of other Arab societies. This protection, unfortunately, took the
form of erasure and it was a high price to pay for the women of the Gulf.

This book is a call to revisit history – to conduct an excavation of the
Arabian desert for traces that have never been unearthed before. It is a
brave attempt to make what had been erased visible and to arouse the
interest of researchers, historians, and scholars in continuing the search for
the still visible vestiges of our past. It is a plea to break the silence and
critically assess the archive of our history as a critical element in the
construction of our future. To build a future, we need to understand our
past because nations that have lost their memories can easily be molded
into hollow reflections of 'Others' and fall prey to historical revisionism.
This book is a humble attempt to reclaim our memories and a bold call for
others to make this collective memory visible, in our past, and in our
future.

Her Highness Sheikha Moza Bint Nasser

Foreword

Over the years I have often found myself in the precarious position of having to speak on behalf of women in the Arabian Gulf, and to correct many of the misconceptions about us. My own experiences and memories of the women who have populated my own life – my childhood memories and the stories passed on to me by my grandmothers – were in complete contradiction to the stereotypes I often encountered regarding Gulf women. On many occasions I found myself answering journalists and others with history – providing evidence of the prominent roles Gulf women have always played. I realized that the prevalence of numerous misconceptions showed that the Arabian Gulf has been viewed not only as an emerging economy, but also as an emerging society: a motherland that has given birth to a culture frozen in medieval times, peopled by men and women alien to modernity. Indeed it has been tiring and frustrating to find myself in an explanatory and sometimes defensive position.

In my search to find defensive historic tools to counter the stereotypical narrative about women in the Gulf, I was shocked about how little evidence there was regarding the role of our women in history. At times, it appeared that women had been erased from the reconstructed history of our region. How could it be possible that a land of numerous civilizations should contain no references to the women who contributed to its history? A land of Sumerian, Akkadian, Babylonian, Assyrian, and Persian civilizations must have had strong women active in society or else why would pagans have erected three female icons as their goddesses – Al'Uzza, Alat and the history of the Gulf and the Arab world, as well as the history of Muslim women and women everywhere.

On sources and methodologies

At one time, Arabia was studied as '*Arabia deserta*', an empty desert with little to recommend it, described in these terms by Western travelers, who produced an image that, curiously, has remained normative till today. In this context, women were regarded as chattels, the property of their clans and tribes, with little say in their fate or what took place around them. Ironically, this image was confirmed by medieval Muslim historians, who saw nothing worthy in Arabia before the coming of Islam and called that period the *Jahiliyya*, or time of ignorance, with little to offer that Muslims could learn from or be proud of. The fact that understanding the context into which Islam was born is essential for understanding Islam itself was dismissed and replaced by a preconceived image of the context and history of the area. This is problematic, particularly since those who undertook the writing of these early histories and descriptions of life before and during early Islam were not familiar with the world into which Islam was born. Rather, they belonged to peoples of other civilizations, conquered and brought into Islam under the direction of the new state-empires that were establishing their hegemony over wide expanses of territory inhabited by diverse populations.

Establishing a 'legitimate' history and promulgating homogenous laws and uniform moral discourses are a usual part of state-building, and it was no different for the various empires that came to rule over Muslim peoples. Intellectuals play a central role in such processes; it is they who formulate the narratives, discourses, histories and laws. As part of the new hegemonies, medieval Muslim scholars became involved in Qur'anic exegesis (*tafsir*); they traveled widely to collect Prophetic Hadiths (recorded sayings of the Prophet, considered a source of Islamic law) that they could use as sources to further explain Islam and its rules and, as empires need laws by which to rule, scholars were busy formulating homogenous laws that made it easier to rule over and mobilize peoples of very different backgrounds and cultures. Works of *fiqh* (jurisprudence) and *qanun* (law), as well as Hadith collections, were written down as *nusus* (authoritative texts) that would gain legal authority that was sanctified with the passage of time, even though *nusus* consist of words, and words carry their own cultural baggage, intimately connected to the social and political conditions that produce them.

This formulation of Islam's *maqasid* (higher intents and ideals behind the injunctions of the *Shari'a*) into words had some serious consequences: by establishing a particular understanding, supported by and presented through selected traditions, a traditional Islam was constructed out of the thought and experience of the *fuqaha'* (religious scholars) involved in this process. These great thinkers were themselves aware of what they were doing and worried about it, wanting to keep their intellectual horizons open to the exchange and growth of knowledge. As Imam Abu Hanifa al-Nu'man (699–767 CE), founder of the Hanafi school of law, said: 'Our position here is only our opinion. We do not oblige anyone to follow it, nor do we say that it is required for anyone to accept it. Whoever has something better, let him produce it' (al-Andalusi 258).

But what Abu Hanifa feared, an uncompromising interpretation of laws, did happen with the establishment of state-supported laws beginning with the early Caliphate (632–661) and continuing under the other dynasties that emerged through the history of Islam. The modern period (normatively considered to have started with the nineteenth century) has seen a somewhat similar process, although during this time the world of Islam was facing its Western conquerors and the challenges of Westernization and foreign social and cultural dominance. Resisting colonialism requires the purging of foreign culture if true independence and social restructuring are to take place; it was natural to look back to what worked when Islam ruled the world. Faced with disparagement and marginalization by political and cultural imperialism, Muslim scholars focused on formulating ideas of what is 'Islamic' and what is not. Given how acceptable the term has become as a descriptor for all aspects of life in the Muslim world today, and in particular the norms and traditions pertaining to the life of women—from the clothes they wear to marriage and work—it is ironic that the term 'Islamic' is in fact a product of the modern world; it was not used before the modern period to refer to the way Muslims lived, the laws they observed, the history they wrote or any other aspects of their life. There were no lists of what is Islamic, nor was establishing such definitive lists central to Muslim discourses, until the modern period. In other words, 'Islamic' as a term has been coined by modern thinkers to define their heritage in response to what was Western in their attempt to establish independent authentic systems, and has been used by Western scholars to differentiate between what they consider their superior culture and the world of Islam. For them, to label something 'Islamic' is a form of othering.

Focusing on the formulation of what we accept as 'Islamic' from the perspective of law, Sherman Jackson points to the problems that arise from looking at the product of the *fuqaha'* as representing Islam; rather, he sees it as a product of their efforts to reconcile already existing institutions with basic principles of Islam.

> From its inception, Islamic law has often been constituted not by translating scripture or tradition into religio-legal institutions but by simply authenticating and re-inscribing as Islamic pre-existing institutions that were neither dictated nor even inspired by scripture or Muslim extensions thereof. Outside the area of *'ibadat*, or religious observance, this was a basic mode of legalization, where the move was routinely from the reality on the ground to the parameters imposed by the texts, rather than the other way around. On this approach, for an institution to gain induction into the sanctum of law, it need not be dictated or even inspired by scripture. All it need do is show itself – or be shown—not to constitute an irreconcilable contradiction of scripture. (Jackson 178)

Concerning Muslim women, Ziba Mir-Hosseini argues in her contribution to this volume that many aspects of family life today that people take for granted as being Islamic are not in fact so. This includes the hijab, which was no more than a traditional form of dress until the nineteenth century, when it was given prominence in Islamic discourses confronting colonialism and Western cultural hegemony. 'It was then that we see the emergence of a new genre of literature in which the veil acquires a civilizational dimension and becomes both a marker of Muslim identity and an element of faith.'

One further methodological point needs to be added to illustrate why it is imperative that historical realities be presented as a challenge to the history and theology that have been built through discourse and political expediency. Here Ahmed Souaiaia's criticism of Muslim scholars' implicit acceptance of Muslim exegetic writings is that it fails to recognize the role

of orality in the formation of documents and of Islamic civilization, culture
and law. It is in orality that the dynamics of Islam allowed for growth and
change; documented and written laws, while making control and order
possible, at the same time constructed systems that were given permanent
authority, notwithstanding the fact that they were in reality products of the
systems, social relations and cultural-linguistic traditions that gave rise to
them:

> Historically, the adoption of writing as a form of transmission can
> also be explained by political intrusions into religious discourse that
> permitted political rulers to procure some of the growing power of the
> religious establishment. In all cases where rulers announced that they
> would favor the transference of the tradition through written records
> and codes, they justified their decisions by the need to make the law
> accessible to the public. The Caliph's request to Malik[2] that he
> produce a standard book of hadith, and its parallel in the British
> King's order to standardize the Common law in what became the
> Domesday Book, are examples serving to underscore this conclusion.
> (Souaiaia 132–33)

What has come down to us as Islamic history and Islamic law and what we
understand to be the 'order of things' is really the result of intellectual
production based on particular readings and interpretations. The written
word has defined reality even though the written word itself is a product of
orality, of transmission of knowledge and decisions made in consultation
and dynamic interactions.

These thoughts are of particular relevance to the Gulf, given the importance
there of orality in the transmission of knowledge of Arab history and the belief
in the Islamicness of the norms, traditions and laws by which people live. To
be able to conceptualize social history, let alone the history of women, we
need to see actual lived reality beyond *fiqh* moral discourses interpreting what
life for women was like during the lifetime of the Prophet Muhammad. We
also need to look beyond modern political history, which is the period of
interest for historians of the Gulf who use mostly foreign records written by
official representatives of Western countries. These documents, particularly

---

[2]Reference is to Malik ibn Anas (711–795) after whom the Maliki School of Islamic jurisprudence is named.

those from the British Foreign Office have been extensively used by scholars to produce detailed political narratives about the various Gulf dynasties and important families, foreign interests, and invasions by Western empires, such as the Portuguese and the British, local invasions by Ottomans, Persians and Egyptians, and local rivalries between various rulers contending for power in the Gulf. Because trade in pearls was the main economic staple of the Gulf before the discovery of oil, pearl diving and the trade in pearls has also received significant interest, particularly on the part of local researchers, who have used a combination of foreign records and oral histories to begin constructing a picture of Gulf society before and after the discovery of petroleum and the significant changes that accompanied this major economic shift.

Given that it is the recent history of the Gulf that has formed the primary interest of both foreign and local historians, it is easy to see how the past has been constructed from the perspective of the present. As Gulf states proceeded to modernize and create technologically advanced industrial and educational infrastructures, the past began to be regarded as folklore, to be placed in museums and studied in an attempt to preserve a past, albeit a 'conventional' one, that would at once both give it pride of place and ensure that it served as history, thus cementing societies by consolidating preconceived attitudes and conventions. In this construct, women were relegated to a private space, 'imagined' rather than real. The concept of the 'imagined' is not an easy one, since it involves historical construction, strongly held beliefs about self and others, and discourses that are often quite conflicting. Mohammed Arkoun simplifies the concept as he applies it to what he calls the 'imaginary' in Islamic societies.

> The notion of 'Imagining' ... is new; the nonspecialist is not likely to grasp it, for even the experts have not succeeded in mastering the shape, function, and operation of this faculty we call imagination. To be brief, I will say that the 'imaginary' of an individual, a social group, or a nation is the collection of images carried by that culture about itself or another culture—once a product of epics, poetry, and religious discourse, today a product primarily of the media and secondarily of the schools. (Arkoun 6)

In this 'imagining', Gulf women were placed under the full custody of male relatives, their movements constrained, and their presence in the public sphere conceptualized as non-existent; their place was always in the home with other women, with no mixing with males beyond immediate male relatives, such as husbands and brothers, and no traveling except with a *mihrim* (a man related to a woman within the degrees of kinship that make marriage between them impermissibile). This fits well with *fiqh* discourse, and was turned into reality with the formulation of laws and institutions that looked to medieval *fiqh* for answers. The husband's role was to work and provide financial support, while the wife was to be protected and sheltered; as far as women were concerned, work was to be expected only of slave-women, servants, and the very poor, who were forced to earn a living. Over time this image of Gulf women's history became enframed as a reality; it was reinforced by Western travelers, particularly those who were drawn to the mystique of Arabia and its desert tribes, spent time in their company, moved around with them, and wrote down their observations, leaving some of the most copious information about life among the Bedouin. The details they provide of Arab women's lives constitute one of the most useful sources of information for the study of this past. However, this information must be used with care, for the imagery they developed only confirmed the picture of women's seclusion, even when the very stories they tell and incidents they describe show otherwise. Here, applying methodologies that go beyond textual represen-tation, unearthing events and studying photographs or pictures drawn by travelers, produce surprising results, often in stark contrast to the conclu-sions reached by the very traveler who told the story.

The same can be said about missionary records; Fatma al-Sayegh cautions us that missionaries came to the Gulf with the purpose of converting its population to Christianity. They soon realized that women were the heart of Gulf society and the indispensable avenue through which culture could be changed. To reinforce the important educational and religious work they performed in the Gulf, the missionaries constructed an image of the back-wardness and severe oppression of women, which they could sell in the West to gain greater support. While women missionaries visited with Gulf women of the elite classes, their knowledge of the life of Gulf society remained limited and because of this they themselves probably considered this image to be true on the basis of their own preconceptions and perhaps some of the cases that came before them, rather than as a result of their actual knowledge of the lived realities of Gulf society. Nevertheless, these missionary records are an important source of social history and allow us to see an active society with its problems, its dynamics and the central role women played in it.

It is by going beyond traditional concepts, the apparently obvious, and normative discourses and 'imaginings' about the life of women, by using new methodologies and finding new sources, by realizing that *nusus* are the product of discourse and orality, that we begin to acquire an overview of some significance not only for the life of Arabian women, but also for the history of Muslim women. After all, Arabia is the birthplace of Islam and has continued to be the source of inspiration for religion, faith, and the Islamic 'imaginary', in Arkoun's meaning of the word.

Narratives of Gulf women's history

If we were to go beyond what has been written about women and society in Arabia, and take a second look at available sources with new questions and research techniques, we could begin to construct a different Gulf history. Scholars have been making such efforts for some time now, raising new questions about the early foundations of Islam and how Islam changed the life of women. The normative view among Muslims is that women lived in poor conditions before the coming of Islam and that destitution, slavery, and prostitution were rampant in Arabia, impacting in particular the life of women. Islam corrected the situation by establishing inheritance for women and a strict marital system and by controlling extra-marital sexual relations. Most importantly, Islam put an end to female infanticide and the Qur'an spoke in clear terms to men, ordering them not to commit this crime against their helpless young daughters because of their fear of future dishonor. This last has been cherished by Muslim women as the greatest evidence of the honor that Islam bestowed on women and its support for the female gender.

In her controversial and important work, *Women and Gender in Islam* (1992) Leila Ahmed questions these assumptions, asking whether Islam did in fact improve the position of women or whether women in Arabia were better off before Islam. The question touches directly on the authority of *fiqh* moral discourses and the accepted history that accompanies and supports them. The answers lie in historical research into the *Jahiliyya* period, not in Arabia alone, but throughout the world into which Islam spread. Ahmed's   conclusion   that   there   is   no   uniform   answer is plausible—that in some places Islam prevented the deterioration of conditions for women, for example, in Egypt under Greek and Roman patriarchal rule, while it hurt women in parts of Arabia, where matriarchies had predominated. Another question asked by scholars is how much the deterioration or betterment of women's lives was due to Islam itself and how much to political and social systems that perverted what Islam intended. Of course, the question could be reversed to point out that 'deterioration' is a matter of perception and representation rather than a reflection of historical realities.

This collection of articles about the history of women in Gulf countries from ancient times until the present uses diverse sources and methodologies to present an analysis of Gulf women's lives, and discourses and representations of these lives. The articles are presented in a thematic and chronological order, beginning with ancient history, and moving on to the medieval, early modern and contemporary periods. Thematically, the articles present women's history before and after the coming of Islam, discourses regarding the life of women in early Islam and the contrast between those discourses and their lived experiences, women's work and the diversity of jobs they performed as part of their economic contribution to society, the family and how it changed from one period to another, and the legal system and laws dealing with women and the family from the pre-modern to the modern periods. The sources used include written narratives, particularly Western travelers' accounts and missionary records, and oral histories, which have proved to be of particular value in constructing this history, especially when added to archival material, published court records from the Hijaz and unpublished ones from Yemen and Jordan. While the last two countries are outside the modern geographical definition of the Gulf area—which consists of Saudi Arabia, Qatar, Bahrain, the United Arab Emirates, Kuwait and Oman—given the history of Arabia, the nature of tribalism and the connections between the various tribes of Arabia and their extensions into Yemen, Jordan, Iraq, and other countries of the Arab world, sources from these countries can be considered as important references for understanding social systems in the rest of the Arabian Peninsula.

As the volume shows, the story of Gulf women has been dated back to before the third millennium BCE. This comes as a particular surprise, since Eastern Arabia has been dealt with as an area that was almost

women in Arabia, their free associations and the appreciation of their society for their intellectual abilities, learning and intelligence. The same theme was covered by Asma Afsaruddin in her seminal work, *Excellence and Precedence* (2002), about the women of Umayyad Andalucia and the important role they played in the intellectual life of Islamic Spain. The similarities between Afsaruddin's description of women's history in Spain and that detailed by El-Zein is significant, opening doors to a clearer understanding of the life of women under the rule of Islam. Soraya Altorki's contribution extends the discussion to include the early modern Hijaz, where women participated in and held their own public festivities, and were recognized for their intellectual and cultural role, much as in Andalucia and in Umayyad and Abbasid times, as Afsaruddin and El-Zein show.

Even as late as the seventeenth century, women were riding into battle with their men, not only cheering them on with words and tambourines, but also wielding their swords, knowing that they rode to their death. Moneera al-Ghadeer's treatment of the poem by Bint Zi'b and her lamentation for her tribe's destruction by the Sharif of Mecca, tells a story of valor, of women riding into battle with 'their tresses covering their white bosoms', a possible euphemism for the nakedness that was frequent in tribal warfare. Stories of women going into battle are recorded by al-Tabari and other historians; they are found in oral history, in poetry and in recollections of major events. These stories should be seen as cumulative and not as surprising exceptions; they confirm each other and make sense, given the nature of life in desert regions like Arabia and the need for constant vigilance to ward off attacks and to protect life and resources. The poems of lamentation, as exemplified by the poem by Bint Zi'b, give us first-hand historical accounts as events unfolded, as experienced by those who did not live to tell the tale of their tribe's defeat and destruction. In this case, the destruction was at the hands of an Ottoman *wali*, the Sharif of Mecca, who coveted the Zi'b tribe's prized camels—a tale that seems to have repeated itself enough for us to begin to wonder about the possible connections between the actions of Ottoman *wali*s in Arabia during the seventeenth and eighteenth centuries, tribal anger at such arbitrary actions, and the success of Wahhabism in uniting tribes against Mecca.

Love poetry has proved to be an excellent source of social history, giving insight into gender relations and sexuality. El-Zein's reading of medieval Islamic poetry shows that communication between the sexes was natural, that it was normal for women to travel, that going on *hajj* or any other journey did not necessarily require a *mihrim*. While El-Zein's analysis shows how equal relations were between men and women in matters of love and sexuality, Fromherz's different take shows that the defamation of women through *naqa'id* poetry particularly focused on sexual themes, painting women of opposing tribes to be of disrepute. 'Depraved sexuality' became a widely-used accusation with which to defame women who took up arms against 'legitimate' rulers, according to Stowasser. Medieval historians invented stories and wove tales of sexual misconduct and depravity to explain acts of protest and dissent undertaken by women against the state. This was a method by which to undermine any protest movement and reduce it to acts of individual criminality against the legitimacy of powerful rulers. The same method continues to be used up to today, labeling as sexual depravity whatever contradicts moralistic discourses.

By following the same story through the narratives of famous Muslim classical historians, Stowasser shows that stories change with time, and that certain realities documented from the time of the Prophet, such as the woman's *bay'a*, disappear. Over time, pre-Islamic *kahinat* (priestesses) came to be seen as evil, sexually perverted women, and women such as Hind bint 'Utba who fought against Islam before the Muslim conquest of Mecca (630), had stories about sexual misconduct attributed to them. The same can be said of Sajah, who led her people against the efforts of the early Caliphate to extract taxes from the Bani Tamim; she too was turned into a woman of ill repute and a harlot. Then there were the 'harlots of Hadramawt', who gained this description for fighting against control by the Islamic state. Stowasser raises serious questions about how historians have dealt with these women, rather than looking at the political context in which these rebellions took place and asking why women who had accepted Islam took part in the Ridda Wars (632–633 CE). For that matter, why did 'A'isha, the Prophet's beloved and revered wife, ride her camel into battle against the Caliphate? The explanations of her actions have always skimmed the surface, not probing the possible socio-political causes for these rebellions. What about the prominent role that women leaders played in the *Khawarij* and *Qaramita* movements in Eastern Arabia discussed by al-Fassi's article? Dismissing these women as harlots, apostates, or misguided in their rebellion, helps legitimize the actions taken against them by the Caliphate without raising questions as to the purpose behind these acts of rebellion or the causes of such anger among the tribes.

A most curious piece of evidence with regard to women's history in early Islam is the handling of the women's *bay'a* by the Caliph 'Umar (634–644 CE), who totally dispensed with the tradition. The total lack of censure by the sources tells its own story regarding their misogyny. After all, the women's *bay'a* is clearly stipulated in the Qur'an in *Surat al-Mumtahina*, and the Sunna of the Prophet required it. If the *fuqaha'* were concerned to establish 'true' Islam, they should have criticized 'Umar for his actions, but they did not. This tells us that medieval scholars were not really concerned with what 'true' Islam was about, but simply accepted what the state decided and made it part of their repertoire. It is our mistake in the modern period that we have taken the writings of these theologians and exegetes to be a faithful representation of what the Qur'an laid down for believers and what the Prophet practiced among his followers. After all, the Prophet honored Hind bint 'Utba and did not condemn or compel her, but negotiated with followers to pay the *sadaqa* (voluntary alms), which they gave willingly, and he required the *bay'a* from Muslim women followers.

The above discussion leads to an important conclusion regarding sources and the problems they present with regard to the life of Muslim women in general and Arabian women in particular. One of the main problems in trying to write the history of Arabia is that we have to deal with religious sources that construct an image of the formative period of Islamic history through religious discourses rather than through actual lived realities. The predominance of the religious perspective has left its mark on historical literature, which had to 'toe the line', so to speak, or else come up against the religious hierarchy. The various *mihna*s (ordeals, inquisitions) suffered by great thinkers and theologians in Islamic history are evidence of this dilemma. Ahmed ibn Hanbal (780–855 CE) is but one, and his woes are reflected in the experiences of Abu Hanifa al-Nu'man and others like him, who refused to bend to the state's will. The curious thing is that, in the Muslim world, we know all this, and we also know that most of the theology we accept and the constructed history we regard as truth was actually recorded much later than the Prophetic period by non-Arabs, who knew little about Arab life or the context of living in desert environments dotted with towns and oases. Yet we accept their accounts and analysis as reflecting truth and we take the anecdotal representation of characters from early Islam as historically accurate. Women's history has been a victim of these constructed narratives; it is here that we find paradigms dismissing women from public space, paradigms upon which the contemporary life of women continues to be formed, making it essential that this historical image be deconstructed.

Women in the public space

While strict gender segregation existed and continues to exist in certain classes of Gulf societies, the overall economic role of women was extensive in very important ways, both in the home and beyond it. As Hoda al-Saadi illustrates in her contribution to this volume, the spectrum of women's work is broad rather than narrow in Gulf countries. The problem of sources is rather acute when it comes to the economic contribution made by women, but the same applies to men. Even so, by carefully sifting the sources, al-Saadi shows that women were central to the grazing, watering, and herding of the tribal flocks, as well as being active in the marketplace, selling and trading. They worked as house-domestics, slaves, and water-carriers, and served their communities as dress-makers, beauticians, and midwives (*dayas*). Al-Sayegh's careful research in missionary sources finds specific stories of very young girls working as small-time vendors after school hours to make a meager living to support needy families. The picture painted by these articles confirms that, as in the world over, Gulf women's work was essential to the common pattern of life, supporting their families and communities and being indispensable for the welfare of their people.

It is perhaps due to the emphasis on wage labor as a basis for estimating economic contributions that Gulf women's participation has not been given its due recognition, according to Hibba Abugideiri, who points out that women's economic participation is usually judged in financial terms; if few or no wages are received, the conclusion is that the work performed is of little value. This approach leaves out of history large sectors of the population and by so doing denies them recognition as valid producers and participants. According to Abugideiri, a different methodology is needed for studying Arab societies. The differentiation in the wage labor model has 'more often hindered than facilitated the study of Arab women in general and female labor in particular . . . Men's work, in this framework, is more valued since, as skilled wage laborers, they are more fully integrated into modern large-scale industry.' For studies of tribal societies, the emphasis should be 'on the social value of work rather than the wages of work'. When this approach is taken, the contributions of women gain great significance, as Abugideiri shows in her article on Gulf midwives. As elsewhere in the Muslim world, medical services were gender-segregated, but women practitioners, normally referred to as midwives, did much more than deliver babies; they also served the male population in many capacities. In fact, they were acknowledged to be the main source for medications, were experienced in treating common ailments, collected medicinal plants and produced medications from them for various diseases. Although they mainly served their own tribes, their services were offered to the wider community and were widely appreciated and respected. As for compensation, 'Sometimes they were paid in kind or not paid at all, but the work they performed while private, bridged the public and private, and the power they enjoyed as healers had little to do with the wages they earned.'

Pasturing or working the clan's herds, and agricultural labor, all fall within the category of private/public non-waged labor. The same can be said of women selling fish in the marketplace for income rather than wages. Here, the men get the credit because it is usually the men who drive the cattle to market for sale or who go out fishing. But this is the nature of Arabian society; the two genders complement each other for the benefit of the family as a whole. This includes all members of the clan, with fathers, mothers, sons and daughters each contributing within their capacity. For example, daughters work as domestic servants and vendors, or are forced to do odd jobs for a meager income to supplement what their families have. In Jordanian archival records dating from the pre-modern period we find the astonishing tribal practice of fathers and brothers hiring out young daughters and sisters to urban families as what can only be termed indentured workers, since their pay for the period of service is paid to the father or brother in advance. This period of indenture might last for ten years or more, a long time in the life of young eight- and ten-year-olds, during which they were left exposed to all sorts of possible abuse by those who employed them.[3] While this practice can be said to have ended today, it reappears in another general practice in Jordan where father or brother force daughter or sister to take out a bank loan against her future wages. The money is taken

[3] Al-Harbi 1526. Case 1073 dated 17/11/12000. Case 1522, dated 15/11/1200, p 26.

by the male relative to trade or for expenses and the girl is left with the burden of servicing the loan to the bank for long years to come.

Archival records, particularly those dealing with the buying, selling and registration of private property, also show the amount of financial power women enjoyed and how they invested their money. Unfortunately, only a small fraction of the archival records from Gulf countries have been published or made available to scholars; if the records of Medina that have been published are an indication, a wealth of historical evidence is available for social history. For example, pre-modern published records from Wadi al-Fura', an agricultural community close to Medina, where date-palm groves once constituted the most important economic resource, present details of transactions undertaken by women selling or buying palm trees and the 'land and fruit . . . and water-rights' that went with them.[4] Sometimes they delegated a male relative to appear in court on their behalf,[5] but it was more usual for the women to register their own sales, purchases,[6] or other transactions.[7] They came to court regularly to dispute property rights and a woman would 'present and represent herself in her case against . . .'[8] Most interesting is the declaration of *waqf*s (religious endowments) that women set up to benefit their heirs or that were made on their behalf by their mothers or fathers.[9] There are also examples in which the father left his land and property as endowments to his sons and daughters, but to be inherited only in the male line after the death of the daughters. So preference for sons did exist. Al-Saadi goes into some detail regarding *waqf*s and the types of *waqf*s that women endowed. Besides land and palm trees, women endowed mosques with Qur'ans and scholarly books and provided resources for poor students and *kuttab*s (elementary schools).

In the modern Gulf, education is proving to be the most important stimulus for change. State sponsorship of education brought to the Gulf perhaps the most advanced educational facilities and technology available today. This interest is nothing new, as Ramadan al-Khouli shows in his article, but was sought by Gulf leaders early in the twentieth century when teachers

[4]Al-Harbi 1526. Case 1073, dated 17/11/1200. Entry into partnerships (ibid., 1522). Case 1070, dated 15/11/1200.
[5]Ibid., 1497. Case 1049, dated 30/1/1200.
[6]Ibid., 1012. Case 675, dated 19/7/1181.
[7]Ibid., 1513. Case 1064, dated 2/11/1200. Ibid., 1511. Case 1062, dated 8/10/1200.
[8]Ibid., 1475. Case 1030, dated 6/10/1199.
[9]Ibid., 1016–17. Case 678, dated 17/11/1181.

were invited first from the Hijaz, and then from Iraq and other Arab countries, to come and teach in the various countries of the Gulf. Previously *kuttabs*, where the teachers were mostly volunteers, both male (*mutawwi'*; pl. *mutawwi'un*) and female (*mutawwi'a*; pl. *mutawwi'at*) were the main source of education. There, young boys and girls were taught how to read and understand the Qur'an, the Arabic language, rudimentary grammar and some mathematics. The *kuttabs* were supported by the clans, and the women volunteer teachers were usually members of the tribes doing voluntary public service, quite often holding classes within their homes and providing the books themselves. One such teacher from Doha, the respected matriarch Shahah al-Khulayfi,[10] actually used books she had written herself to teach her students and she also held advanced classes for women who wanted to study religious subjects more deeply. Interest in learning, intellectual endeavor and reading was natural in a field where there had always been women intellectuals and teachers. Omaima Abou-Bakr's contribution takes the role of women intellectuals further by showing that, far from being simple recipients of knowledge, women *shaykhat* (religious authorities), *muftiyat* (jurisconsults), *faqihat* (exegetes), and *mutawwi'at* were thinkers in their own rights, produced books and *fatawas* (legal opinions) and acted as teachers to illustrious *'ulama'* (religious scholars). Because of the recognition accorded to their intellectual abilities and the respect and income they received from their work, these women had autonomy of action within their communities and this Abou-Bakr sees as a basis of empowerment that is not usually recognized by historians.

Private lives

Family is central to Arab society. This applies with respect to both the nuclear family that is beginning to predominate today and the clan and extended family, which predominated in former times and continues to be important today. The articles in this volume almost all deal with family in one way or another; some focus specifically on family formation and family law, past and present. The articles also deal with problems within the family, gender relations and the violence that may form part of these relations. The authors' discussions also extend to *fiqh* and other discourses dealing with

[10]Interview in Doha, Qatar, February 2008.

family and personal rights and laws, showing the contradictions between law and discourses and between law and its application. The modern family is of particular interest here: what was the pre-modern family like? How have family structure and relations changed with the move from desert to town, and how have the interests of various family members changed because of modernity? That the family is 'closely related to the overall political, social and economic contexts of society' is an accepted premise of the articles focused on the family in this collection: Amira Sonbol's contribution traces the changing shape of the family from early Islam until today, while Soraya Altorki focuses on nineteenth- and twentieth-century Meccan society. Whether family relations are flexible or rigid is largely dependent on the context in which the family exists. Thus, various forms of family have appeared through Arabian history, emerging in different forms in different places. One major accepted division is between Bedouin who live as nomads in the deserts and those who have settled in towns and have constituted urban populations for many centuries.

Surprisingly, Altorki finds that the more rural the family the more flexible are gender relations and openness to the outside. Less surprising is that the wealthier the family, the more protective and traditional it is. Overall, what Altorki presents us with is a panorama of Meccan society before Wahhabism that is very similar to other Muslim communities such as Cairo, Jerusalem, and Damascus. Women carried on their share of the businesses, endowed *waqf*s and were involved in the spiritual and educational activities of Mecca. They had a good deal of leeway in their marriages and divorces and, even though marital patterns were guided by traditional practices, such as cousin marriage, they were different from what emerged following Wahhabism. Although men and women formerly married and divorced often, polygamy was not widespread and women had certain rights that other Muslim women often did not enjoy. For example, the right to go on pilgrimage at her husband's expense if he was able to pay was a legal right for Arabian women but was unheard of in other Muslim countries. The impact of Wahhabism was to end the flexibility and openness available to Meccans, women and men alike, and to introduce a puritanical attitude towards strict gender relations, which had been much more relaxed before. The Wahhabi rejection of saints and the prohibition of venerating them affected women in particular, since this was an area in which they were very active and held prominent positions.

Basic life in Mecca as described by Altorki can be said to have been reflected to a certain extent in other urban centers of Arabia; but political events in Eastern Arabia were different and the economy differed significantly from that of the Hijaz. The latter was ruled by the Mamluks and Ottomans before the Wahhabis, and experienced both the benefits and disadvantages of being part of an active empire that gathered wealth from commerce and the income generated by pilgrimage. In Eastern Arabia the economy was highly dependent on pearl diving, which was the most important occupation and source of income. It was supplemented by trade, fishing, and small-scale manufacturing to meet the immediate needs of the communities. Life was not easy at the best of times, but during the period between the two World Wars poverty struck the Gulf, partly because of the impact of war on Gulf trade but more particularly because of the successful production of cultured pearls by the Japanese, which hurt the natural pearl industry of the Gulf countries. Memories of that period are still fresh in the oral histories told by Gulf people: the lack of food and resources, the need to engage in piracy and smuggling, and the general fight for survival, which involved all family members. Clans migrated in search of food and work, causing the Shaykh Jassim al-Thani of Qatar, whose population, normally numbering 40,000, is said to have fallen to 6,000 by that time, to salute those who migrated because their departure meant there would be more resources for those left behind, and at the same time to salute those who remained for their perseverance in the face of severe difficulties.[11] These events and the subsequent discovery of oil in the Gulf had a serious structural impact on the Gulf family, which is still experiencing its transformation from a clan-based institution to the type of nuclear family that is familiar in nation-states throughout the world.

This was to be expected, as the articles by Sonbol, Mir-Hosseini and Lynn Welchman show. Nation-state building brings about transformations in all aspects of life, including the economic, social, and cultural. The appearance of the modern patriarchal family is perhaps the most significant development for women, particularly because of the accompanying changes in the legal system brought about through the nation-state building process. The needs of centralizing national governments meant the promulgation of standardized laws and their implementation in a homogenized and equal fashion among

[11]Interview with Shaykh Faysal bin Qassim Al-Thani and three women (names withheld) over 2008–2009.

their peoples. This establishment of justice and the rule of law by the governing power is a normal part of the process of nation-state building. However, establishing new, uniform codes and court systems is no easy matter, particularly when religious differences are serious enough to warrant separate codes, as Welchman shows is the case in Bahrain, which has been reforming its laws and introducing new codes for the Sunni community.

Codification of law is an essential part of legal reform, and all the Gulf countries have been undergoing such reform with the exception of Saudi Arabia, whose laws follow strict interpretations of the Hanbali *madhhab* (school of law). Elsewhere in the Gulf, laws dealing with personal status and family are based on a variety of schools of the Islamic *Shari'a*, but, as Welchman and Sonbol show in their articles, the modern period has witnessed the diffusion of law over international borders and, for the Arab world, this has meant a mixing of local traditional laws (*'urf*), *Shari'a* laws as interpreted by various schools, and Western laws. The last have been introduced through the interpretations of Muslims who have studied in other Arab countries, where modern Western-style codes had been introduced, and in European academies. They have also come in through the influence of colonial institutions and rule, the establishment of Western-style courts, and the process of legal codification, which requires the selection and establishment of standardized codes using modern language. This process brings its own weight to bear on the meaning of Muslim conventions regarding marriage, divorce, child custody and other matters pertinent to personal law. Terms such as *ta'a*, *nafaqa*, and *khul'* (obedience, alimony, divorce) have roots in Islamic laws but the process of modernization in Gulf countries, as elsewhere in the Muslim world, has altered gender relations and the relationship of the individual and the family to the legal system. It is important to note that legal reform in recent years has not been a purely male prerogative; it is true that legal reforms were initiated by state officials, all of whom were men, and it was also men who led the reform efforts. These men came from other Arab countries, particularly Egypt, Syria, and Iraq. A good example is Kuwait's selection of the Egyptian reformer 'Abd al-Razzaq al-Sanhuri to modernize its legal code. Today, however, women are very much involved in the changes being introduced, and these women are Gulf citizens who understand their societies' and families' needs and are pushing for changes in response. As Welchman tells us: 'Women participate as members of legislatures and political parties; as lawyers; as members of governmental commissions of women's (and family) affairs and of non-governmental associations and societies.'

Legal changes accompanied the social changes experienced by individuals, families and the various social institutions. As settings changed with economic transformations, so did people's lives and the norms they lived by. The arrival of oil in the Gulf has been a watershed, bringing about profound structural transformations, the final results of which are still playing out. The family is no longer the same family that existed a hundred, fifty, or even ten years ago. The wider clan living in a single home is becoming a feature of the distant past, although families still try to hold on to the traditions they lived by before, which were a source of security and pride. Modernization and changes are bringing new types of housing more attuned to wealthy nuclear families, and families are not as tightly knit, interdependent, and mutually supportive as before. This is to be expected with increased modernization, consumerism, commercialization, and capitalism. One could speak nostalgically of the pristine desert being polluted with the symbols of commercialism and modernity: signs and symbols of international consumer empires, all mark the landscape. Even the holy Ka'ba has been used in media advertising for real estate in Mecca. Values have changed and with them so have the laws and expectations related to family life, marriage, and other institutions. Ironically, while the material life of women has markedly improved, their lived realities have entailed perceptible changes for the worse with regard to marital and family relations. While the support and backing of a woman's family does continue to protect her from harm or mistreatment by her husband, violence is a living reality faced by women in Gulf society. One is reminded of travelers' observations regarding marital relations in tribal families, which they recorded before these many changes took place. They noted that men who raised their hands against their womenfolk were severely censured. Compare this with the examples that studies by Gulf scholars like Kaltham al-Ghanim or Naji Hilal present of the various forms of abuse that women experience in their everyday life.[12] Physical mistreatment, the violence of polygamy, unilateral divorce, and other forms of abuse are tacitly approved on the basis of interpretations of *fiqh* and a legal system that has yet

[12]Al-Ghanim, "Violence against Women in Qutari Society', *Middle East Women's Studies*, vol. 5, no. 1 (written 2009); and Hilal, al-'Unf al-usari fi al-mujtama' al-Imarati, [Family Violence in Emirates Society]. Sharja: Al-Idara al-'Amma li-Shurtat al-Shariqa, Markaz Buhuth al-Shurta, 2007.

to deconstruct and rethink the *maqasid* (intentions on which Islamic law is based) and apply the true Sunna of the Prophet rather than the patriarchal interpretations that dominate. As Mir-Hosseini puts it, 'assumptions about gender in Islam—as in any other religion—are necessarily social/cultural constructions, thus historically changing and subject to negotiation'.

Many lessons were learned in the process of producing this book but perhaps the most important is the obvious—that it is in the realm of social history that we find the history of people, rich with the realities of lived life experience with all that entails. As we study the specificities of Gulf life and the role that women have played in it, it is at the level of the individual, or social relations, that we begin to see how dynamic that role has been in the past. It is therefore no surprise that we see women playing a very prominent role in the promotion of progress in Gulf countries today. Much research remains to be completed, and primary source material is vital, for it presents society with its good and its evil, exposing relations and participation through actual records of lived human life. There is no better evidence than such records, written and oral; they challenge long-held stereotypical images and paradigms that hinder the progress of women today. The articles in this book, each in its own way, show that women were present in Arabia in a dynamic and effective fashion before Islam, at the time of the Prophet, and the medieval period, about which research is still seriously lacking. They were priestesses, political leaders, warriors, merchants, *waqf* overseers, shepherds, intellectuals, teachers, midwives, vendors, dressmakers, and petty-capitalists, raising funds for their families in various ways. Finally, let it be noted that the picture of a 'womanless' Gulf that the observer encounters in contemporary pictures, whether of weddings or of other ceremonies, is a sign of the growth of a new elitism and the construction of cultural differences rather than a sign of historical continuity.

1. *Women in Eastern Arabia: Myth and Representation*

HATOON AJWAD AL-FASSI

This chapter explores the history of eastern Arabia, looking for traces of women, goddesses, priestesses, *kahinat,* in fact, any female representation. It finds that there are few such traces, but that those that exist, however scarce, are very interesting and telling. Three distinct periods can be identified with regard to women's history in ancient Arabia. First, mythical woman, up to the third millennium BCE; second, historical eastern woman, from the end of the first century BCE; and third, Arabian woman, with evidence from a few decades before the Prophet as part of the survivals of the two ages of pre-Islamic and Islamic—the group of people who are known as *al-mukhadramun.*

Introduction

The history of ancient Arabia is full of gaps that continually stimulate the researcher. When one comes to women's history, the sources are even sparser and eastern Arabia is no exception.[1] Arabian women's footprints

---

[1]Eastern Arabia has been known under various names. One is Bahrain, which includes the western coast of the Gulf between today's Basra and Oman. Some believe that this was the capital of Hajar, while others hold that Hajar was the capital of Bahrain, which included a large area of land and water (Yaqut 1: 23), and the modern Bahrain. It extends westwards to the region of Yamama. Yaqut adds to it al-Khat, Qatif, al-Ara, Hajar, Baynuna, al-Zara, Juwatha, al-Sabur, Darin, and al-Ghaba. The capital of Hajar was al-Safa and al-Mushaqqar (Yaqut 1: 232). This description belongs to the Islamic period

have rarely made their mark. However, it is a historian's task and duty to look for them. Eastern Arabia was a dynamic actor in the making of ancient history as early as the sixth millennium BCE, with stone-age findings of fishermen's and hunters' tools along the west coast, particularly in the Neolithic sites on the Qatar peninsula.[2] In the fourth and early third millennium BCE the material diminishes. One possible explanation is that there was a rise in sea level which led to a transgression that left land two or three meters below sea level. There is evidence that this took place at the beginning of the third millennium BCE (Inizan 173; Potts, 'Eastern Arabia', 124). The historical periods from which we have written records are not very clear in Arabia. Although the Arabian Peninsula's neighbors, the Sumerians, were the inventors of the first attempts at writing, it is not clear what type of writing the people of eastern Arabia used and there is no evidence from before the third century BCE, when we find *musnad*/South Arabian and Aramaic scripts.

The Arabian Gulf, called the 'lower sea' or the 'bitter sea' in the Sumerian records (fourth to third millennium BCE) was the main influence on the history of the people who lived on its western, eastern, and northern coasts. It was the artery that connected eastern Arabia to Sumeria in the north, Iran in the east, and Melluha (Monehjo-Daro and Harappa)—later India—in the south-east, and the inhabitants navigated up and down its waters, trading in everything, particularly myrrh, frankincense, copper, wood, precious stones, dates, pearls, horses, and other commodities that they either produced or imported and exported.

One of the principal sources in which women are presented in the history of eastern Arabia is the myths of Mesopotamia: Sumerian, Akkadian, Babylonian, and Assyrian. They date back to the third millennium BCE onward and a number of these mythological texts refer to Arabia and specifically to parts of eastern Arabia. The most popular and most researched of them all is Dilmun, a civilization and kingdom that flourished in eastern Arabia and today's Bahrain for about 2,000 years. It was first mentioned in mythology of the third millennium as a legendary

---

and probably the late pre-Islamic period, but not all these towns have been identified. More details below.

[2]Most of Qatar's Neolithic archaeological findings come from Khor, in the east of Qatar, which date back to the sixth, fifth and later fourth millennia BCE and are found in over 122 sites in the Peninsula alone (Bibby and Kapel 20). For more details, see Potts, *The Arabian Gulf*, 1:28 ff.

land, but then became a real kingdom almost 1,000 years later, with fleets and trade and kings. It was an important middle power between the Indus valley in the east and southern Mesopotamia in the north and also played an intermediate role with Magan—modern Oman. The first reference to Dilmun and its contact with southern Mesopotamia (Iraq) comes from the Warka (Uruk) period (in Sumer, southern Iraq), i.e. at the dawn of writing, and the central Gulf, at the end of the fourth millennium BCE, around 3200 BCE, where we find the bird-like sign that indicates Dilmun (al-Thani 54). Dilmun then was not limited to the Bahrain of today; it is believed the name referred to the area from present-day Kuwait up to the Strait of Hormuz, and had many coastal centers including Failaka, Tarut, Umm Annar and others (al-Badr, *Mantiqat al-Khaleej al-'Arabi khilal al-'alfayn al-thani wa al-'awal qabl al-milad,* 112).

The island of Bahrain possibly acted as the main center or capital of the state; however, this must have been changeable and the capital would have moved during different phases of history along the western coast of the Gulf.

The reference to Dilmun mentions Umm Annar, in the present-day United Arab Emirates, which was a port for the Magan settlements in inland south-eastern Arabia. Those contacts continued throughout later periods, as is proven by evidence of similar rituals, parallel temple architecture (compare the Barbar temple in Bahrain and the Ninjersu temple in southern Iraq dating to around 2093–2072 BCE (al-Safadi 221), the trade in Dilmuni pearls (al-Badr, *Mantiqat al-Khaleej al-'Arabi khilal al-'alfayn al-rabi' wa al-thalith qabl al-milad,* 141), evidence of Dilmuni ships taking timber to Ur around the mid-third millennium BCE (Kramer, *The Sumerians,* 441; Speece 167) and bringing copper from Magan in exchange for wheat, barley, oil, textiles, cedar wood, and silver (al-Ahmad 269).

Dilmun's relationships with the outside world crossed Sumeria and extended to Syria—some of the items reported to originate from the Lebanese mountains included cedar wood, which was imported by the Sumerians—and Dilmuni influence also extended there. For example, the name 'Dilmun' was given to certain weights that were particularly used in the Ebla weighing system for silver and gold.[3]

---

[3]Ebla was a great civilization in northern Syria, dating from the time of Saragon the Akkadian (2340 BCE). It extended from Emesa in the west, beyond the Euphrates to the north and up to Urfa (Arki 143–4; al-Bunni 7).

Women in mythical eastern Arabia: The Sumerian epics

The mythological Dilmun is referred to in many Sumerian epics. The reading of these texts has shown that Dilmun was portrayed as the Promised Land or the Garden of Eden,[4] the paradise where there is no fear or sorrow, no death or lamentation. It was the land of eternity and immortality. The representation of females in the myths is very strong and telling, even though most of them are goddesses. The world of mythology is full of very vivid signs and symbols that reflect to a certain extent the relationships that existed in the society 'when things began'. It may be suggested that the story of how eastern Arabia (Dilmun) was constructed, with its relationships and images of men and women, during the fourth millennium BCE has much to say about the formation of the history and identity of the people of eastern Arabia. Myths and beliefs have always been important to social structure, as they create relations, identities, and powers and redefine them throughout time. The texts clearly reveal the density of presence, leadership, and the centrality of women in the formation of these myths. The most direct description of the Garden of Eden is found in the myth of Enki and Ninhursag.[5]

Myth of 'Enki and Ninhursag': Paradise myth

This legend is set in legendary Dilmun, a land of sunrise, purity and cleanliness, a land that does not know death or sickness—but that is without water. The water god Enki orders the sun god, Otto, to fill Dilmun with clean water springing from the heart of the earth and this is how Dilmun became a green garden of the gods.[6] In this paradise, the earth and fertility goddess Ninhursag ordered eight kinds of plants to grow and blossom after a complex story of her conceiving from the god Enki and giving birth

---

[4]See the parallel in McKenzie 322.

[5]'Ninhursag' means 'queen and mistress of the hursag', i.e. the foothills. She is identified with the mother-goddess (Frymer-Kensky 15).

[6]It is interesting to note that the issue of water was fundamental. The mythology emphasizes that Dilmun lacks water; however, it also provides a mythical explanation for the abundance of later water in an area famous for its springs. Bahrain is known for its dual flow of both sweet and salt water, with the sweet water flowing in the midst of the salt water of the Gulf. Hasa alone is known to have over 162 springs, not to mention other towns such as al-Qatif and al-Uqair (see al-Badr, *Mantiqat al-Khaleej al-'Arabi khilal al-'alfayn al-rabi' wa al-thalith qabl al-milad*, 111).

in nine days without pain. The paradise myth ends by assigning lords and deities to each part of the body and each important land of the time. Dilmun was given to Enshagag (the lord of Dilmun?). The poem goes like this:

The land Dilmun is a pure place, the land Dilmun is a clean place,
The land Dilmun is a clean place, the land Dilmun is a bright place;
He who is all alone laid himself down in Dilmun,
The place, after Enki had laid himself by his wife,
That place is clean, that place is bright;
He who is all alone laid himself down in Dilmun,
The place, after Enki had laid himself by Ninsikil,
That place is clean, that place is bright.
In Dilmun the raven uttered no cries,
The kite uttered not the cry of kite,
The lion killed not,
The wolf snatched not the lamb,
Unknown was the kid-killing dog,
Unknown was the grain-devouring boar,
The bird on high . . .[7] not its young,
The dove . . . not the head,
The sick-eyed says not 'I am sick-eyed,'
The sick-headed says not 'I am sick-headed,'
Its [Dilmun's] old woman says not 'I am an old woman,'
Its old man says not 'I am an old man,'
Its unwashed maid is not . . . in the city,
He who crosses the river utters no . . .,
The overseer does not . . .,
The singer utters no wail,
By the side of the city he utters no lament.
Her city drinks the water of abundance,
Dilmun drinks the water of abundance,
Her wells of bitter water, behold they are become wells of good water,
Her fields and farms produced crops and grain,
Her city, behold it is become the house of the banks and quays of the
    land,

[7] . . . in this translation indicates that the tablet is broken at this point.

Dilmun, behold it is become the house of the banks and quays of the
   land
. . . .
For the little ones to which I gave birth . . .
Let Abu be the king of the plants,
Let Nintul be the lord of Magan,
Let Ninsutu marry Ninazu,
Let Ninkasi be [the goddess who] sates the heart,
Let Nazi marry Nindar,
Let Dazimua marry Nigishzida,
Let Ninti be the queen of the month,
Let Enshagag be the lord of Dilmun.
O Father Enki, praise! (Trans. Kramer, *Sumerian Mythology*, 82–6)

The Deluge myth

As for the Sumerian Deluge myth, Ziusudra, the king who plays the role
equivalent to that of Noah in the Old Testament, the New Testament and
the Qur'an, saves the population of his town Eridu. At the end of the epic,
he prostrates himself before the gods Anu and Enlil, who give him the
'Breath eternal like that of a god'. The surviving tablet ends with the
following verses:

In the land of *crossing*,
The land of Dilmun,
The place where the sun rises,
They [probably Anu and Enlil] caused to dwell.
[The 39 lines that followed have been destroyed.] (Kramer, cited in
   Pritchard 1: 30)

Myth of 'Enki and the world order'

According to Kramer, this myth is one of the Sumerian story poems, and
one of the best preserved. Its tablets were found in the Nippur excavations
(Kramer, *The Sumerians*, 233). It comprises 466 verses, 372 of them
complete. It starts with an invocation to the god Enki as a deity who rules
the world and has control over the fertility of the land and of human beings.

Enki then describes himself and his relationships with the other high gods, including Anu, Enlil, and Ninhursag, and praises himself. He also describes his temple, Enzu, which is built at Eridu, and his journey, during which Dilmun, Magan, and Melluha send him boats full of gifts to receive Enlil's blessings. The story ends with a declaration of allegiance to Enki as the supreme god who has the principal divine responsibilities (ibid. 280; al-Ahmad 371–2).

The text of this myth refers to the land of Magan and Dilmun as fertile lands. It is possible that the Deluge myth refers to an ethnic historical movement—perhaps to the arrival of the Sumerians in Dilmun after the deluge, and the legitimization of their rule through the description in the myth of the gods enthroning King Ziusudra in Dilmun.

According to Lamberg-Karlovsky, Dilmun was not only the place where immortalized humans were carried for 'breath eternal', but also 'the paradise land to which a significant portion of the Greater Mesopotamian population, including the populations of northern Arabia, came to be buried in order to enter the underworld (the immortal life of the Paradise Land). Only that can explain the over 170,000 tumuli-tombs of Dilmun found in Bahrain, Yabrin and Dhahran' (46–9). Lamberg-Karlovsky's theory is supported by many other researchers; however, it has also been suggested that Dilmun may be extended to include eastern Arabia. In recent decades hundreds of tombs and tumuli have been found in Dhahran and over 200,000 tombs in an area of ten square kilometers in 'Ayn Jawan in the eastern province of today's Saudi Arabia (Zarins et al. 25–6).

Of interest, are the images found on Dilmuni round seals. One common image is of a seated woman drinking from a bottle with a man facing her (see al-Sindi, photo 18, plate I), although Khalid al-Sindi thinks that this seal shows two males, either gods or kings. It seems very strange that, according to archaeologists and analysts such as al-Sindi, there are no seals that definitely depict women, although it is noted that there are many seals in his collection that may possibly represent women, in addition to fertility scenes, which occur in abundance (e.g. ibid., seals 221–6). The seal referred to above shows the seated person with a lock of hair twisted upward in a style usually associated with women. It is therefore very likely that this seal represents a female, either a goddess or a queen, and a slight pointing at the breast and the narrow waist confirm this. This seal is dated late (i.e. between 2000 and 1600 BCE). However, al-Sindi says elsewhere that the libation scenes consist of either two men or a man and a woman sitting facing each other and sucking tubes or drinking together from goblets while servants wait on them, scenes that probably commemorate the New Year (e.g. ibid., seals 10, 11, 13; photo 20). Seals also represent mythological scenes—drinking from the spring of life, sharing life and perhaps love. It is not certain whether these images were of earthly beings or heavenly ones.

The spring of life drinking scenes show a high level of representation, in which the woman as a goddess or queen is seated celebrating the New Year with a man, who is lower in status, and who may therefore be either her vizier or a high priest. Apart from these cases, however, women are not commonly represented in Dilmuni seals. In Failaka, in the north of the Gulf, which was part of the Dilmuni civilization, the Danish Exploration Expedition excavated three sites between 1958 and 1963,[8] and unearthed 427 seals, none of which represented a female, either divine or human, apart from one erotic scene with a nude woman (seal 269). Although this expedition's results do not represent the whole range of Dilmuni seals, the number is significant, as is the absence of women. It indicates that the society was mainly patriarchal, with rare exceptions.

In the centuries that followed, little is known about women except for their assumed normative participation in child-rearing and running the family. No mention is found of women independently, or indeed of men as ordinary individuals. Later, in the final centuries BCE, there are some funerary inscriptions that refer to women on tombs that bear matrilinear inscriptions referring to the interred; these are discussed below.

Women in historical eastern Arabia

From the ninth century BCE onwards scanty references to Dilmun and Magan appear in the royal texts of the Assyrian Empire. The texts refer to an ongoing economic relationship with the Gulf or the Bitter Sea and also imply that Dilmun and Melluha were under Assyrian rule from the time of Tukulti-Ninurta II (891–884 BCE), whose titles included 'King of Dilmun' (al-Badr, *Mantiqat al-Khaleej al-'Arabi khilal al-'alfayn al-thani wa al-'awal qabl al-milad*, 94–5). At that time and up to the sixth century

[8]The report on the seals was not published until 1983; see Kjaerum, *The Stamp and Cylinder Seals, Failaka/Dilmun*.

BCE, Dilmun seems to have been a semi-free state more or less under the tutelage of the Babylonian and Assyrian Empires, but the kingdom was not as famous as before and does not seem to have played a significant role in the Gulf trade (Boucharlat and Salles 74).

Another part of ancient Dilmun emerged in eastern Arabia in the form of cities such as Gerrha, which was a mysterious eastern Arabian kingdom that was at its most advanced in the fourth century BCE. It is still debated whether it was located at Thaj, al-'Uqayr, al-Hufuf (Groom 97), Qaryat al-Faw (al-Ansary) or the salt mine site (Lombard). On the basis of a variety of evidence, mainly Strabo's (d. 24 CE) accounts and some inscriptions, some scholars argue that the Nabataeans originated from eastern Arabia and had some contact with the Gerrhaeans (Milik 264–5). One may add to this some references in the early Islamic sources to Nabataeans who lived in Hajar and then moved elsewhere (see below). This is a plausible view because there is as much evidence for it as there is for other parts of Arabia as the origin of their tribe or group of tribes.

During the first century BCE Gerrha was referred to as a prosperous city and its people, like the Sabaeans, as the richest of all. About their houses, Strabo says: 'They have a vast equipment of both gold and silver articles, such as couches and tripods and bowls, together with drinking-vessels and very costly houses; for doors and walls and ceilings are variegated with ivory and gold and silver set with precious stones' (Strabo 16.4.19). This legendary city-state was renowned for trade in aromatics and spices that came from India to Arabia (Strabo 16.4.18). As for the Gerrhaeans, their caravans reached southern Arabia and it took them only forty days to reach Hadramaut (Strabo 16.4.4). Strabo calls it a 'city', situated 2,400 stadia, i.e. 426.24 km (1 stadion = 177.6 m), from the head of the Gulf, and inhabited by Chaldaeans, exiles from Babylon. The extra details he gives are interesting: 'The soil contains salt and the people live in houses made of salt; and since flakes of salt continually scale off, owing to the scorching heat of the rays of the sun, and fall away, the people frequently sprinkle the houses with water and thus keep the walls firm' (Strabo 16.3.2–4). The fame of Gerrha made it tempting for neighboring powers. The Seleucids tried to conquer it many times, but in vain. In 205 BCE Antiochus III agreed to let the Gerrhaeans buy their freedom, beliefs and peace in return for a large sum of money, frankincense and myrrh (Polybius 13.2.4–5).

To the south of Gerrha there was another kingdom called Omana (or

Suhar or Maka-Makai) on the peninsula of present-day Oman, connecting
the Gulf with the coast of southern Arabia. It was an important port that had
significant relationships with Persia, Karmenia, and northern and south-
western parts of India, from the fifth century BCE (Bin Serai, 'Ancient
Inhabitants', 43, 59). Daniel Potts argues that the present town of al-Dur,
which witnessed minting, is in fact Omana ('Eastern Arabia', 155). It is
situated fifty kilometers west of the Gulf of Oman. In addition to Omana,
there is another town, now called Muleiha, eighty kilometers from al-Dur,
south of al-Quwein emirate, which flourished in the third century CE, while
the surrounding areas date back to Islamic times (Boucharlat and Salles 7).

The memory of the mythical past seems to permeate the ensuing centuries. For example, the second and first centuries BCE yield some social
and religious information. Frequent references to a matrilinear system
have been found in al-Muleiha, al-Ahsa, and Thaj in eastern Arabia.
Tombstone inscriptions in the Hasaean version of south Arabian script
show a number of women using a matrilinear system when referring to
themselves or their descendants. In addition, female fertility figurines also
occur frequently, especially on the site at Thaj. We need here to define
what we mean by matrilinearity, and what the Hasaean inscriptions are.

Matrilinearity involves, first, tracing descent through the mother rather
than the father; second, associating descent with matrilocal residence, in
which the husband goes to the place of the woman's family or tribe in what
is also known as the 'postmarital residence'; third, the authority within the
family belongs primarily to a male representative of the wife's kin (Maciver
and Page 248); and fourth, inheritance follows the female line (Stone 32).
It is important, however, to distinguish matrilinearity from matriarchy.
Anthropologists have dismissed the theory of the existence of a matriarchal society where women are the dominant sex, have control over society
and religion, have a matrilinear descent system and are the major providers.

Since the majority of the genealogies given in Hasaean inscriptions are
patrilinear, it can be accepted that this was the prevailing system used by
the eastern Arabian population. However, this does not exclude the possibility that other types of system existed. Since some matrilinear genealogies
have been found, it can be assumed that matrilinearity might also have
been used in certain cases within a predominantly patrilinear society
without contradicting the norm, which would explain the incidences of
matrilinearity in Hasaean inscriptions.

Putting eastern Arabian society into context, the first cases of matrilinearity in Arabia were mainly among the royal families of northern Arabia. It then spread, I would argue, from the royal house to the elite and people who belonged to that class, such as priestesses. Examples can be found within the Nabataean dynasty, probably in the exogamic marriages of its women (see al-Fassi 56ff.).

In addition to the textual evidence, there is the archaeological. The regular finding in various parts of the ancient world, including eastern Arabia, of terracotta figurines of women with exaggerated fertility parts, such as the breasts, belly and thighs, is significant. It is argued that these figurines do not represent goddesses but were used in fertility rituals, and many other functions are possible (Pomeroy 14).

Probably the main question here is: did the eastern Arabians follow the matrilinear system? Did they have a mother goddess in their pantheon? Did they follow the Sumerian and Akkadian mythological and religious system or they did they have their own? How did this affect the status of women in their society?

In answering these questions we might say that the eastern Arabians, as represented in the Hasaean inscriptions of the third century BCE, did not in general follow the matrilinear system, as the majority of the inscriptions indicate a patrilinear system. There is a question mark as regards the few inscriptions referred to above and we shall now try to investigate this.

The Hasaeans

The history of the Hasaeans is imbedded in the history of eastern Arabian settlements, people and states. Probably the most important site in inland eastern Arabia is Thaj, which is considered the main settlement and largest walled city site in eastern Arabia in terms of size—just over a million square kilometers —in the period between the third century BCE and the third century CE. The history of this period is not very clear, but many coins, shards, inscriptions, and tombs have been found at the site (Boucharlat and Salles 78; Potts, *Arabian Gulf in Antiquity,* 43–4; al-Zahrani 45).

Numerous sites that are not mentioned in any of the ancient records nevertheless produce very important archaeological findings and such sites extend from the north to the south of eastern Arabia. In addition to Thaj, there are 'Ayn Jawan, Tarut, al-Hufuf, al-'Uqayr, al-Dur, Muleiha, and others. They seem to have formed a sort of cultural unity, which can be observed in their language, script, art, religion, and probably also their ethnicity. By the time of the Greek invasion of Mesopotamia in the fourth century BCE, Dilmun was known as Tylus (Arrian 7.20.6) and there are also references to some of the island's inland towns, such as Barbar and the Qal'at.

What concerns us here is the sociological structure of the area, which was without doubt in contact with the rest of the Arabian Peninsula via the land and sea trade and caravan routes that provided one of the main sources of activity for the inhabitants of Arabia. Most studies try to address the issue of the identity of the Arabian Peninsula's people, their language, deities, writings, trade, agriculture, fishing, and the relationship between the members of society in general and between its men and women in particular—very difficult questions when we are discussing a period 2,000–3,000 years ago.

For our purposes, what is interesting in the findings from Hasaean history are the inscriptions (in Hasaitic, a modification of South Arabian script). Two remarkable characteristics of these inscriptions are the high proportion of epitaphs commemorating women, and the reference to a matrilinear system of lineage in at least a couple of the inscriptions. Out of sixteen tomb inscriptions found in Thaj, eight belong to women, and out of fifteen found outside Thaj, six belong to women. This is remarkable, taking into consideration the limited number of Hasaean inscriptions found so far, compared, for example, with the massive archive of south Arabian inscriptions.

Of the inscriptions commemorating women, three give a matrilinear lineage. The first is on a tombstone, probably from Thaj, discovered by an amateur archaeologist. It was published in the 1982 volume of *Atlal: the Journal of Saudi Arabian Archaeology*, and may be read as follows:

Inscription 1

Tombstone and grave
of ghudhayat, daughter

of malikat,
daughter of shabam,
daughter of ahthat,
she of the people
yanukh el.
(Anonymous 139, Pl. 124a; Gazdar et.al.
88, Inscription 16) (Pl. II)

The anonymous commentary in *Atlal* says that Aramaic inscriptions from north-western Arabia tend to give women matronymics (Anonymous 140). In 1986 Jacques Ryckmans wrote a long article about this inscription in which he notes (407) that it is of particular interest in that it presents a matrilinearity going back to the third generation. It is the longest of the matrilinear inscriptions so far found in Arabia, and has particular significance in the discussion about the importance of 'matrilinear system of filiation' in pre-Islamic Arabia. However, two more inscriptions were found later in the area of Thaj or al-Hanat that present a matrilinear system of filiation.

Inscription 2

This inscription goes back to the second generation and of an uncertain provenance of eastern Arabia. It reads as follows:

Grave and tomb
of Karly, daughter
of Garat, daughter
of . . . she of
the tribe . . .
(Gazdar et al. 91, No. 4; no image
provided in the anonymous *Atlal* article)

Inscription 3

Found in Abqaiq, this is an incomplete inscription, but the main reference to a daughter is very clear. It reads as follows:

Tomb and grave

. . . son of

. . . daughter of

. . . he of

the tribe. . .

(Gazdar et al. 91, No. 7)

Although the inscription is damaged and the words cannot be clearly deciphered, the word 'daughter of' is clear and, curiously enough, comes in the second generation after a male is referred to in the first; i.e., a matrilinearity occurs in the second generation, following a patrilineal reference.

Before addressing the question of the significance of these inscriptions, we shall note some cultural points that may be related to these inscriptions.

The figurines

In the ten excavation seasons undertaken in Thaj by the Saudi Arabian Department of Antiquities up to the present, following on from the quick surveys conducted by amateurs since the beginning of the twentieth century, the main findings were terracotta figurines of naked females with a clear emphasis on fertility indicated by the exaggeration of parts such as the breasts and hips. The potter always tries to focus on the area below the belly, in a way that, according to Bibby and Kapel (18), is characteristic of representations of fertility deities as known, for example, among the Greeks. However, they are in fact more similar in appearance to Anatolian and Mesopotamian fertility figurines, although the latter belong to a much earlier date (fourth millennium BCE) (Pl. III). In one season, twenty figurines were found, all of them representing female figures in a squatting position. The nose is of a particular form, and the eyes are mostly unsymmetrical and sometimes more rolled. In some examples, the hands bend to support the breasts, exemplifying the mother goddess. Some of these figurines are decorated with necklaces or belts around the waist. Male figurines were rarely found, but there were numerous camel figurines, and small, square incense burners all made of the same type of mud (Bibby and Kapel 18). Some figurines were found in other parts of the Arabian Peninsula similar to the Thaj figurines in terms of material, form and some other artistic characteristics (al-Zahrani 139–40).

The remaining questions are: what are these figurines, whom do they represent, what role did they play in religion and in society, and is there a link between them and the inscriptions referred to above?

The main feature of these figurines is that they mostly represent women, mainly naked and with exaggerated sexual parts (Pl. IV). Most of the figurines are not complete; usually the head is missing (al-Zahrani 96–9). Many scholars have stressed the religious function of these figurines. Bibby and Kapel suggest that they 'represent a goddess widely worshiped in Thaj, and that probably each house had a shrine group consisting of a figure of the goddess, one or more camels, and an incense burner' (18). It has also been suggested that these figurines were used in human and agricultural fertility rituals and to facilitate giving birth (Gazdar et al. 72). Figurines are found in many cultures and might mean many different things, possibly representing their deities or the animals and birds related to their mythological legends. Some of the figurines were also produced as representing mother goddesses, or figures to scare away strangers, or being used as good luck amulets, healing votive offerings, or simply children's dolls (Hashim 13–14). The abundance of camel figurines also suggests that they had some kind of a ritual importance in either a fertility cult or the worship of a mother goddess in Thaj and its environs. Did the camel figurine represent the god of the caravans, and might it have any relationship to the mother goddess or the fertility goddess?

What I suggest is that these figurines were used as fertility amulets and good luck charms for houses in general and women in particular. They would be related to the special role taken by the female deity in the religious rituals of ancient eastern Arabians, which were presided over by special priestesses responsible for female needs. By following a matrilinear system of filiation, these priestesses followed a distinct custom that distinguished them from the rest of society. It is not clear how much power the priestesses had or to what extent the cult of the female figurines represented a powerful goddess or an advance in women's status in society.

Women in Islamic eastern Arabia

The Islamic period is usually better documented, as we enter a literate period with Arabic established as the script and the language of almost the whole of Arabia. In the east, where we had Dilmun and Magan, the same geographical locations are known as Hajar/Bahrain and Oman in the Islamic period. Just as Dilmun could mean the whole western coast of the Gulf, so it was with the new terms. Hajar, whose identity is confused in many geography books between the region and the city, and with Bahrain which is the name given to the whole of the eastern coast of Arabia in the sixth to seventh centuries CE. Many have addressed the question of how to identify the true location of Hajar or to determine how it differed from Bahrain.[9] I shall refer directly to al-Janbi's findings on the identity of Hajar and its location (al-Janbi 187–238). He has carried out linguistic and geographic field work and literary investigations that have made it possible for him to identify the north-western part of al-Shab'an Mountain (al-Qara) as the location of the great walled city, and to identify its castle and main towns as al-Mushaqqar and al-Safa.[10] This region, Bahrain and Hajar, was under the Manathira of Hira (Iraq) at the dawn of Islam (al-Mulla 2: 30).

Women appear less infrequently in history, but seem stronger in the background, an image that continued in myth as well as in documented history. For example, according to al-Qalqashandi (d. 1418 CE), the Hajar region and town is said in early Islamic sources to have been named after a woman called Hajar, daughter of al-Mukannaf who is reputed to have built it (al-Qalqashandi 5: 52) We have no information about this woman or her identity apart from her name. It seems that this is a remnant of an older tradition of female affiliation to cities as protector goddesses, priestesses or queens.

Dawn of Islam's priestesses

Tradition connects the later settlers in pre-Islamic times with women of influence. For instance, al-Zarqa, daughter of Zuhayr was a *kahina* (shaman/sage) of Quda'a who prophesied where her tribe should settle

---

[9]For a detailed discussion see Bin Serai, *Cultural Relationship*, 52; al-Janbi 232–7; al-Mulla 1:156–8 and others.

[10]Hajar was destroyed by the Qaramita in the fourth century AH/eleventh century CE and Abu Tahir al-Qurmuti built a new town nearby and called it al-Hassa in 314 AH/926 CE (Ibn Khaldun 7:189). However, the name of Hajar lingered as a name for the whole region and al-Hassa then also gave its name to the region in the same way. Bahrain is also a name that many geographers have given to eastern Arabia; some include in Bahrain seven main cities and the island of Awal, including Hajar, Qatif, al-Mushaqqar, al-Khatt, al-Zara, and al-'Uqayr, while others include Juwatha and Darin (al-Ja'fari 26–7).

after losing some battles against the tribe of Nizar, predicting that they would live in Hajar and prosper there. Her people followed her advice, left Tihama on the west coast of Arabia, and moved eastwards to Hajar, in the direction of Bahrain, where they overcame the Nabataeans, who were there, according to the story, and took control. Then, according to Ibn Khaldun (d. 1405 CE), she received another prophecy in rhyme, that they would live in Hajar until a crow cried in a certain way, which would be a sign for them to move to Hira in southern Iraq (Ibn Khaldun 2: 288; al-Asfahani 13: 87). Her tribe trusted in her and believed in her wisdom. It was probably wise advice, since the direction of their migration was in line with the fertile and productive land, in both eastern Arabia and Iraq.

Elsewhere, we find the origin of the term the 'Alliance of Tanukh' tribes of eastern Arabia at the dawn of Islam: this same *kahina*, al-Zarqa, referred in her rhyming prophecy to the place where her tribe would settle as Tanukh; they then became known as the Tanukh tribes and entered into an alliance of various tribes who joined together in order to move to Iraq. A group of them continued to Hira and ruled it, and others stayed in Bahrain and Hajar (Ibn Khaldun 2: 288). This *kahina* had an interesting career, giving prophecies that came to pass each time that were obeyed. What is remarkable is the level of trust that the Arabs gave women, especially with regard to supernatural powers of this kind. Her name poses some questions as to whether it was a proper name or a title related to the color blue. According to the dictionary *Lisan al-'Arab*, the word *zaraqa* means to have either blue eyes, strong eyesight or blind eyes (Ibn Manzur 3:1827–8). The most likely explanation is that the name indicates that al-Zarqa was a blue-eyed woman. It may also be that, because of the rarity of blue eyes in Arabia, a person born blue-eyed was thought to possess some unusual powers, or to be able to see differently from other people — hence the link between blue eyes and strong eyesight. Biologically there is no connection between the color of the eye and sight, but it seems that the rarity may have given it this aura. This may indicate how a *kahina* would be created. Similarly, the renowned Zarqa al-Yamama was another legendary personality with strong eyesight that allowed her to see an army on its way to her town of Jaw (later named al-Yamama after her) in central Arabia, three days before their arrival. Unfortunately, Zarqa was not believed; her people, the tribe of Jadis, were massacred and she lost her eyes (Ibn 'Abd Rabbuh 3:71; al-Mas'udi 2:140–1).

Khawarij

The region of Hajar and Bahrain embraced Islam in 8 AH (630 CE) and the first mosque outside Medina to gather people for the Friday prayer was the Jiwatha mosque, near al-Hufuf in inland eastern Arabia. The Christian tribe of 'Abd al-Qays was the principal tribe residing there that embraced Islam and then resisted the apostate *ridda* uprising against the Islamic state, which took place after the death of the Prophet in 11AH (632 CE). In the following centuries, Hajar and Bahrain continued to be important regions economically, but they experienced religious and political unrest and social revolts because of the Umayyad policy of using one of the main towns, al-Zara, west of Qatif, and Oman, as exile regions (al-Mulla 1: 181). For example, they took part in the fanatical Azariqa-Khawarij movement, which originated after 64 AH/686 CE in central Arabia, most of whose followers were from the tribe of Tamim in the region of al-Yamama. The Tamim expanded into eastern Arabia and so did the Khawarij movement, which lasted until the mid-second century AH/eighth century CE. Some of them moved to Basra in Iraq, where they fought for a long time and then withdrew to al-Ahwaz and then to Makran in Persia (Majid 135ff.). The major Khawarij ruler in al-Yamama in 65 AH/687 CE, Najda al-Hanafi, extended his rule over half of Arabia, including eastern Arabia and Hajar. It is suggested that another leader of the Khawarij, Qatari ibn al-Fuja'a originated in present-day Qatar—hence his name—took the lead after Najda died. He was called Prince of the Believers and ruled over the Azariqa for more than ten years.

In the Khawarij movement, however strict it was in terms of religious doctrine, women were very active in both war and peace. Although the roles these women played were outstanding, reference to them is traced with difficulty in historical annals. Most of the leaders' wives joined in the battles they were waging against the Umayyads and later the Abbasids. They also allowed women to lead the prayers and to be political leaders. We may note Ghazala, the wife of Shabib al-Khariji, one of the Khawarij's main leaders in 76–77 AH/695 CE. She entered Kufa in her husband's absence and went to the main mosque, challenging the merciless governor of Iraq, al-Hajjaj (75–95 AH/ 694–713 CE), where she preached the sermon and then led the morning prayer (al-Baghdadi 113; al-Ikri al-Hanbali 1:83). She also fought with him in battle, when she was killed and her head was brought to al-Hajjaj. Ghazala was a very distinguished personality but it is not relevant to elaborate on this here. Shabib's mother, Juhayza, was also killed in the same battle, fighting alongside his men.[11] Al-Tabari relates that in Qatari's last battle before his death 'fifteen beautiful and strong women were fighting and defending him side by side. It was not clear what relationship these women had to the Khawariji leader' (al-Tabari 3: 606). The only woman's name that has come down to us is Umm Hakim bint 'Amr, who was brave, beautiful, pious, and eloquent, but her relationship to Qatari was not known (Qassab 299). Another of the fifteen women who stood in Qatari's defense, was an elderly woman who attacked one of the Umayyad leaders; bewildered, he told the story of how he had to kill her in self-defense, as she was so unexpectedly strong and her sword reached him so that he found himself retaliating and killed her (Qassab 300). Qatari bin al Fuja'a died in a battle in 77 AH/696 CE (ibid. 296–7).

From greater Bahrain, an uprising was led by al-Rayyan al-Nukari during al-Hajjaj's governship in Iraq. It is said that in the year 79 AH/698 CE al-Rayyan rose against al-Hajjaj in a town called Tab in al-Khat, on the coast of Arabia that includes present-day eastern Arabia, Bahrain and Qatar. He found allies in the Khawarij of Oman and won the town that year. By the following year, al-Hajjaj's troops reached Bahrain and fought al-Rayyan, who was accompanied this time by a woman called Jayda from the al-Azd tribe. They were both killed, but the uprising continued (Ibn Khayyat 1: 278–9). Not much is said about Jayda or her relationship to al-Rayyan, but the general tone indicates that she was a participant in battle on an equal standing. It is possible that she was his wife, as we have seen several cases of Khawarij wives taking part in battles beside their husbands.

In Bahrain again, a few years later, there was Zaynab, sister of Mas'ud al-Muaribi the Khawariji, who fought with her brother in the battle of al-Yamama. Mas'ud rose against the Umayyads in 86 AH/705 CE in Bahrain and ruled it, then went to al-Yamama to fight but lost the battle and he and his sister were both killed (al-Mulla 2: 80; Ibn al-Athir 4: 366).

[11]Imran bin Hattan, a poet and a Khawarij fighter, recited a strongly-worded poem in her praise of al-Hajjaj's satire: 'A lion on me and an ostrich in war. Would you face Ghazala in battle, instead, your heart is in a bird's wings' (al-Asfahani 20: 314). (Showing the humiliation of mighty al-Hajjaj in front of the Khawariji woman is remarkable in the context of the power relationship between the Umayyads and the rest. It gives a glimpse into the position of women within Khariji society.)

It is interesting to note that her brother Mas'ud was called Mas'ud son of
Abu Zaynab (Zaynab's father), i.e. both her father and her brother were
identified in relation to her, a significant sign of the high status given to
Zaynab and probably to women in general in that environment.

Another dramatic Khawariji personality was al-Bathja of the Yarbu'
tribe, who used to criticize Ziyad ibn Abih of the Umayyads (44–53
AH/664–672 CE) for his corruption and fought against him in Mecca.
When the battle was lost and she was killed, he had her stripped and cut off
her hands and feet and hung them up in the market (Ibn al-Athir 3: 517).
The barbaric retaliation to this revolt is significant and telling. How influential and strong was she? Why would a woman threaten one of the
Umayyad's most brutal governors? She was an example of a Khawariji
woman with faith and will stronger than any torture. Many questions arise
as to what motivated such women to resist so forcefully.

Al-Qaramita

In the third century AH/tenth century CE, the east of Arabia was the focus
of a social reform movement named after al-Qaramita (286–378 AH/899–
988 CE). In the view of the Abbasid Caliphate in Baghdad and the Sunni
community, this was a heretical movement and is reported as such in the
historical records. It resisted the Abbasids for about a century and made
some outrageous attacks on pilgrims and on Mecca and the Holy Mosque
itself, killing and burning then removing the black stone from the corner
of the Ka'ba in 317 AH/929 CE and taking it to Hajar. Touching this sacred
part of the Ka'ba was shocking to the Muslim world, but the black stone
nevertheless remained for twenty-three years in Hajar, where the Qaramita
established a community based on equality, sharing and a gentle religion
(Abu 'Izza 213–5).

As with the Khawarij, the women in this community played an important role from the beginning, including accompanying the fighters into
battle (al-Tabari 5: 666). Within the social structure established by the
founder, Hamdan Qurmut, every member contributed to the welfare of the
group in what was called *nizam al-ulfa* (the system of harmony). Women's
contribution came from their income from spinning and from donations of
jewelry and other belongings (al-Maqrizi 1: 46). Part of the ethos that
spread through the Qaramita towns was to value women, respect them,

and acknowledge their contribution to society. A marker of the values of mutual respect was that women went unveiled. That was in resistance to the hypocrisy of the Abbassids' and religious leaders' social values and ethics (al-Laziqani 100–2). This is not the whole story, but Qaramita history was very protected and was rarely revealed in detail. In addition, many controversies and legends govern their social structure and relationships, but this must be left for a later study.

Finally, it must be realized that, in almost every society, women have commonly been regarded as symbols of honor and pride. Arabs were no exception, as their social tradition emphatically indicates. History is full of examples of battles and wars being fought in defense of women's honor. A woman's cry for help was considered to place an obligation on the whole tribe to respond, no matter what the context or the balance of power. In south-eastern Arabia, the controversial movement led by Luqayt ibn Malik al-Azdi in 11 AH/632 CE in Daba, (present-day Oman) within the apostate *ridda* movement against the Islamic state is said to have been provoked by a woman. An elderly woman from the main Azd tribe while paying her *zakat* taxes was not accepted and was treated violently by the tax collectors. She cried out, 'O People of Malik' (of Azd)—a cry recognized as being a call for the defense of her honor, and an uprising immediately broke out in response (al-Amd 106–7). It is not clear whether this story was the main reason for the Omani *ridda*, or whether it was an excuse for the Azd to use the moment of the Prophet's death to regain power over Oman. Many other examples in history show women to be called as the provokers of war or revenge, such as the story of the mother of Amr bin Kalthum, Layla bint al-Muhalhil; she called on her tribe to defend her honor, which resulted in the king, Amr ibn Hind, being killed by her son.[12] There was also the forty-year war of al-Basus (494–534 CE), named after a woman called al-Basus bint Munqith, which took place between the tribes of Bakr and Taghlib (Jad al-Mawla et al. 54). Each of these stories could be rebutted, and many of them are hard to believe, but they are continually used in the Arab imagination and have persisted in the Muslim imagination too. I believe it is interesting to look at the way in which honor is probably used to cover up other motives, such as the desire for power and authority. However, we cannot deny that the honor factor may

[12]However, many scholars do not accept the historicity of this story. Taha Husayn (219–20) is one who doubts many of the pre-Islamic heroic stories related by the poets.

also have been present and have played a role in igniting societal emotions out of respect for women.

Conclusion

It has been noted that eastern Arabia was historically distinct in many ways. First, it was considered by the ancient people of the land of the Two Rivers (Mesopotamia) to be the eternal land, Paradise, and the Garden of Eden. The main character in the presentation of this identity was the mother goddess Ninhursag. The immense number of tombs and tumuli found in Dilmun, on both the island and the mainland, are evidence of the belief in this legendary land. This remained the image of Dilmun until the historical period in the late fourth millennium BCE.

Second, it represented a special type of social structure via the matrilinearity system, as found in the late first millennium BCE. This suggests the presence of an order of priestesses who are the descendants of some kind of marital practice which was related to a cult or a religious ritual that resulted in the formation of a community of women who maintained a matrilinear affinity system that was recognized and accepted in eastern Arabia.[13]

Continuity with the mythological mother goddess may be suggested: Ninhursag extended her representation to the priestesses of the third century CE. It is not clear how long that has lasted or how far it extended. The Islamic period in eastern Arabia seems as distinctive as the pre-Islamic. It was an era when there was a free, independence-seeking spirit. It is debatable whether this was due to the alienation policy with which the caliphs, both Umayyads and Abbasids, treated the region, making it a place of exile for *persona non grata*, or whether such undesirables influenced the locals, or whether this character was inherent in the region and its people, both women and men. This independence of spirit was expressed through a number of revolts and uprisings, giving rise to independent states that were illegitimate from the Abbasid point of view.

---

[13]A system where priestesses were united with either the high priest/king or his representative and donated their descendants to the service of the temple. Similar practices prevailed in Babylon between the high priestess of the goddess Innana and the high priest of the Moon God. Supervising the fertility cult of sacred marriage was one of the tasks of priestesses in Mesopotamia (Frymer-Kensky 64).

They were unlike other states in that they followed a controversial social vision. Two major social groups existed in eastern Arabia or made an impression there: the short-lived Khawarij and the Qaramita state, which broke away from the Muslim community and opposed it in an extreme fashion, and were very literal in their interpretation of the sacred text and the Prophet's practice.[14] This in itself has led to brutal conflict and bloodshed at various points in Islamic history. Whatever may be thought of the Khawarij and the Qaramita themselves, women among them played an important role, showing courage and commitment to their beliefs.

Women in ancient or Islamic eastern Arabia had a distinctive character that was perhaps particular to that region. Is it the periphery psychology, or isolation from the center of political decision, or, possibly, their constant contact with the outside world from ancient times, or may all of these factors together have formed the identity of the eastern Arabian woman? More research is needed and the articles that follow will doubtless make a substantial contribution.

---

[14]There was a third movement, the Zinj, which was a slave uprising. There is no report of women playing a part in this revolt.

2. *Tribalism, Tribal Feuds and the Social Status of Women*

ALLEN FROMHERZ

Jarir and al-Farazdaq, two famed rival poets, were from two different clans of the Tamim tribal confederation, which today includes a large proportion of Arabs in Gulf states such as Qatar. For example, the al-Thani, and al-Kuwari, powerful tribes in Qatar, are Tamimi. The poems that they wrote provide a rich source of information about tribalism, tribal feuds and the social status of women. Indeed, these poets provide one of the first recorded mentions of Qatar and Qataris in Arabic. Although neither of these poets came from the Gulf specifically, they often traveled there in their poems. The Gulf and Gulf tribes were certainly a part of Tamimi geography and the Tamimi poetic realm. A long and bitter poetic rivalry between the Tamimi clans of Jarir and al-Farazdaq lasted for most of the latter half of the seventh century. The *Naqa'id of Jarir and al-Farazdaq*, written in the Umayyad period, was the record of these poetic barbs. The *Naqa'id* also included volumes of extensive footnotes and stories of battles, or *Ayam al-'Arab*, studied extensively by scholars, such as Nabia Abbott and Ilse Lichtenstädter, who are interested in the extensive role of pre-Islamic Arab women in their society. This article examines some of Abbott's and Lichtenstädter's conclusions about the status of women in early and pre-Islamic eras. However, the actual poetry of the *Naqa'id*, the subject on which this article was originally based, has gone largely unnoticed and unexamined despite its fascinating insights into the role of women and women's honor during the *Jahiliyya* and early Islamic period.

Women are mentioned in almost every one of Jarir and al-Farazdaq's *Naqa'id* poems. Indeed, women were a central concern, a central source of pride and of shame for Jarir, al-Farazdaq and other *naqa'id* poets of early Islam. The thesis of this article is that the poetic slander of the women of a rival tribal poet directly threatened the *'ird*, or honor, of the whole accused tribe. It was through this constant use of powerful poetic symbols and accusations that Arab clans constructed notions of modesty and gender roles, making women into symbols not only of a tribe's virility but also of its right to dominate. For example, those male tribe members who did not control their women according to certain norms were accused of being effeminate. The most famous example of this involved al-Farazdaq's sister Ji'thin. Al-Farazdaq had wooed a woman from another tribe. When a man from this tribe discovered this he came to Ji'thin and insultingly touched her on her shoulder. Jarir taunted al-Farazdaq over this throughout the *Naqa'id* by describing Ji'thin as a mere sexual entity (Jayyusi 1984, 411).

This article shows that powerful poetic accusations of gender trouble explained how tribal feuds, whether waged by the sword or by the poet's voice, had a direct impact on the construction of male and female roles in Arab society in a way that was often contrary to Qur'anic norms, which repeatedly condemned the feud and the slanderous use of poetry (Qur'an 26: 221–7). In this sense, the Qur'anic condemnation of slanderous poetry—which almost always included references to women—and the numerous Qur'anic condemnations of tribal feuds were also a condemnation of the use of women as symbols of tribal pride. As Abbott has stated, and as anybody who has read early and pre-Islamic Arab poetry knows, 'In poetry, the major literary passion of Pre-Islamic Arabia, the Arab woman figured large' (Abbott 259).

This article proposes that the position of women as symbolic bearers of honor in pre-Islamic Arab tribal society, including many of the Gulf tribes mentioned in the *Naqa'id of Jarir and al-Farazdaq*, can be at least partially explained by the tribal feud. Islam, by condemning the Arab tribal feud and slanderous poetry, effectively condemned the use of women as passive, symbolic bearers of tribal honor. First, we shall note that the *Ayam al-'Arab* accounts of great pre-Islamic battles contain evidence that women repre-sented tribal honor during feuds, both as 'Ladies of Victory', that is as women who participated in battles, and in their role as the rear guard. This is not to say that women were equated with tribal honor in its entirety or that all of tribal honor was vested in women, but rather that the participation of women in battle, and even the deliberate act of incapacitating one's own women, was a compelling way to induce courage and prevent flight from the battlefield. Second, we shall see that vivid and slanderous passages from the poetic battles of Jarir and al-Farazdaq demonstrate the representation of women in tribal feuds as passive, symbolic representations of tribal honor. This examination of the poetry of the *Naqa'id* will demonstrate how slanderous poetry, or *hija'* which is discussed in greater detail later in this article, enforced assumed tribal gender categories and behaviors. Perhaps much of what is being said in this poetry was not meant to be taken as a reflection of reality. However, and as this article proposes, Arabs believed in the magical properties of *hija'* poetry. Thus, in some ways, the figurative slanders of the *Naqa'id* poetry were even more harmful than the reality. In the *Naqa'id*, women from other clans become less the symbol of a poet's muse—as they are in the classic *qasida,* the traditional Arabic ode, more the symbol of a rival tribe's honor, a symbol that is vulnerable to attack and abuse. They are thus in need of protection from dishonor in the all-important verbal warfare of poetic honor, as in times of actual feud and war. Using passages from the Qur'an that condemn slanderous poetry, this article finally proposes that Islam challenged this tribal notion of women as symbols of tribal honor. After Islam, the symbolization and literal incapacitation of women was challenged, if not replaced, by notions of equality between all Muslims and loyalty to the *umma*, the united Muslim community, as the source and focus of honor. There was a transition from *umma* as symbol, to the ideal of an integrated *umma* or community. Despite the efforts of Muhammad, his wives and some of his immediate successors, however, tribes did not discontinue their feuds after Islam and women have continued to face the consequences of war between men.

Women as symbols of tribal honor: the 'institution' of the 'Lady of Victory'

Draped in finest embroidered robes stitched by the women of the tribe, the 'Lady of Victory', the chief warrior priestess of the Arab tribal god, mounted the portable *qubba*, the sacred pavilion of the local tribal deity, on a bedecked camel.[1] The Lady of Victory usually had the highest social status within the tribe and was accompanied by a number of other women of status affiliated with the sacred cult. As a battle began, this sacred female group stayed in position only a short distance from the fighting, goading their men with chants and songs accompanied by special stringed instruments. The chief Ladies of Victory, one from each tribe, sometimes with their bodies exposed, represented the valor, honor and passion of their respective clans. The battle would rage around these women until the day was decided and the feud was lost or won. The capture of a chief Lady of Victory meant the end of the battle. No man with a vestige of honor would allow a rival tribesman to approach his Lady of Victory without fighting him to the death. Indeed, when the situation was desperate, the leaders of a losing side would cut the hamstrings of the camels of their own Lady of Victory, making retreat impossible for the tribesmen who were bound by honor to stay and defend their sacred female's pavilion to the death.[2] The main motivation for exposing women to the battle was to

[1]Referring to R. Geyer's article on the cult of the Lady of Victory, Nabia Abbott (148) coined the term 'Lady of Victory' in her article, calling it 'a well-recognized institution' (262). As discussed later, early Arabic accounts mentioning the Lady of Victory are found in tales of pre-Islamic tribal feuds: *naqa'id* and *ayam al-'Arab* literature. In a statement that sheds interesting light on her own view of the nature of femininity, Ilse Lichtenstädter is much less dramatic than Abbot in her description of warrior women. 'There is one feature in the Arab woman, according to the *Ayam al-'Arab*, that seems incompatible with European ideas of the female nature and disposition. This is her capacity not only for enduring the hardships incidental to unceasing tribal feuds, but even of taking an active part in the fight itself . . . But their courage and their enthusiasm for military enterprise become intelligible as soon as we recollect that it is just the women who suffered specially in war' (79). The primary source for both Lichtenstädter and Abbott was the *The Naqa'id of Jarir and al-Farazdaq,* which contains both the main text of the poetry and numerous accounts of battles—the *Ayam al-'Arab.* Our focus here, however, is the reference to women in the poetry, that is the main text of the *Naqa'id of Jarir and al-Farazdaq,* not the *Ayam al-'Arab* accounts of battles, which are essentially footnotes to the main poetry text. Perhaps because of the sometimes challenging and lewd nature of the poems, Lichtenstädter does not seem to mention the actual poetry even once in her book, despite the fact that it is full of references to women. It is our purpose here to tackle the poetic material itself head-on, using the tools of modern gender theory and analysis.
[2]As Abbott says, 'On desperate occasions, as, for instance, in the Battle of Dhu Qar, the Arabs either hamstrung the camels carrying the women or severed their saddles and litters so that the women fell to the earth. This device of thus incapacitating the women at a time when they were exposed to extreme danger was meant to banish from the minds of the men any thought of retreat or flight' (263). Lichtenstädter translates a passage from the *Naqa'id of Jarir and al-Farazdaq* that refers to this practice: 'Hanzala ibn Tha'laba turned to his daughter Maria who was the mother of ten (noble) men, one of whom was Jabir ibn Abjar,

make certain the men would not flee. Through their mere presence near the battle, or even in the battle, as Ladies of Victory, women were the guarantors of honor and courage. They clearly symbolized the honor of the tribe. During the battle of Fayf al-Rih referred to in the *Ayam al-'Arab*, 'The Madhhij had their women and children with them so that they might not flee; (they were resolved) to vanquish or to die together' (469: 11;[3] cited in Lichtenstädter 41). Arabs would pour scorn on tribes who fought without their women nearby. Even a great army could not easily defeat a tribe that steadfastly defended its women. One advisor to an Arab king who had sent out a large, probably conscripted army said, 'You have sent forth an army, which is great in number (but which consists of men) whose aims and passions are divergent, against people, who stand up for their women and their flocks . . . my opinion is that they will certainly defeat their army' (67, 9ss; cited in Lichtenstädter 40).

Occasionally, women would take their role as symbols of tribal honor to the extreme and incite their men through nudity and singing.[4] In addition to the battle of Dhu Qar (Lichtenstädter 1), where women uncovered themselves and sang songs, there was even an incident during the battle of Yawm Iyad in the *Ayam al-'Arab*, when the warriors 'saw Umm Darda, a woman of the Banu Salit running along naked' (327).

Although use of the Lady of Victory declined after the destruction of tribal deities and the consolidation of Arab tribes under Islam, the custom of using women as ultimate embodiments of tribal honor in the midst of feuds remained. Lichtenstädter presents extensive evidence for the connection between the woman priestess or *kahina*, and tribal deities. 'The known references to the kahinah in Arabic literature are too numerous to list. These traditions associate one of these women with almost every major move of tribal policy or migration' (260). Clearly, women priestesses had potent roles in the tribe—even more reason to defend them to the death in battle. Even after the tribal gods had been destroyed, it seems reasonable to assume that the custom of the Lady of Victory was still being followed during the great Battle of the Camel (656 AD), when 'A'isha, the

and severed the thongs of her litter so that she fell to earth; then he severed the thongs of the other women, so that they fell as well' (43; cf. Bevan, 643, 5s).
[3]References are given to the poem number and line number, corresponding to both Wormhoudt and Bevan.
[4]On the participation of women in the *Ayam al-'Arab* and other pre-Islamic battles, see Geyer.

headstrong widow of the Prophet Muhammad, directed the battle against the partisans of 'Ali from her camel pavilion. As the followers of 'A'isha were threatened, the last stages of the battle were fought fiercely around her camel, as if she were herself an Islamic Lady of Victory.[5]

As mentioned earlier, evidence for the existence of the Lady of Victory in pre-Islamic and early Islamic Arabia comes from extensive footnotes and glosses to the eighth-century Arabic poems, the *Naqa'id of Jarir and al-Farazdaq*. The term '*naqa'id*' in literature generally refers to folklore, stories and poems about long-lasting tribal feuds. The Lady of Victory was the ultimate symbol of the '*ird* of the tribe during a tribal feud. '*Ird* is an Arabic term referring specifically to the honor of the women in the tribe, an honor that can only be lost by the women or their actions, or through what rival tribes say about them, but still an honor that deeply affects the reputation of the entire tribe. As the historian Beth Baron explains, "'*Ird* can only be lost or redeemed and is mostly connected with a woman's body' (1).[6] Naturally, it was during feuds and battles that the survival of the tribe and the tribe's honor, so embodied by women, was put to the test.[7]

In the popular historical imagination it has often been assumed that war and feuding is a pre-eminently masculine, if not homocentric, activity. Left locked away in the castle while the knights fight for their honor, or left stamped on coins and held up on banners for victory, women are most often seen in Western culture as warriors, national symbols or as prizes of victory only in an imagined way. In Arab society, however, it was during feuds that the honor of the women and the necessity of maintaining the honor of women were explicitly pronounced, even in the midst of battle itself. Women were not merely passive symbols in these feuds but active embodiments of a tribe's virility, pride and identity. While the coming of Islam may have caused the tribal deities so carefully tended by the Ladies of Victory to crumble, the static ideal of women as ultimate living symbols of tribal honor, not simply as equal believers with their brothers in Islam, remained long after the coming of Islam. It would require an entirely new thesis and perhaps

---

[5]For more on the significance of 'A'isha's role in the Battle of the Camel, see Spellberg.

[6]Baron explains that it is public recognition of a girl's involvement in the loss of honor that causes the 'disappearance' of a dishonored daughter. Like the tribe fighting for the honor of its symbolic undefiled priestess or Lady of Victory, the family justifies honor killing as a way of maintaining its '*ird*.

[7]For further discussion of the origins of '*ird* in the pre-Islamic Arabian context, see Fares.

much more new evidence to decipher precisely how the pre-Islamic notions of women's honor and tribal feuds began. All that can be said with any confidence is that women's honor was connected to tribal honor.

After the coming of Islam continuing feuds between Arab Muslim tribes only enhanced the need to create a sacred pavilion of victory for women within an Islamic framework. While women no longer went so boldly into battle, a veiled Muslim woman still represented the ultimate honor of her tribe. The honor being preserved was not the tribal deity but the genuineness of each tribe's claim to Islamic conduct. Poets and leaders of their respective tribes knew that, while battles of honor within and between tribes swirled around them, women, like the Lady of Victory, had little to fight with. As *naqa'id* poetry colorfully illustrates, the status of women in a tribe—their activities, their dress, their roles, their conformity to perceived Islamic standards, standards often determined more by tribal custom (*'urf*) than by Islamic *Shari'a*—was a matter as important as the Lady of Victory before Islam. The status of women in the midst of a culture of tribal feuds became a matter of *'ird*, a matter that could, like the defense of the Lady of Victory, determine the success or failure of a tribe. What led to the construction of restricted symbolic roles for women's bodies as upholders of a tribe or family's *'ird* was the feud, when the honor of the tribe as it related to other tribes was most put to test, not longstanding notions of patrilineal hysteria or the contents of the *Shari'a*. Honor, especially women's honor, was an integral part of early Arab culture.

The tribal feud, not Islam, which was fundamentally against the practice of tribal feuding, was the main motivation for the development of restrictions on women as symbolic bearers of a tribe or a nation's Islamic identity and *'ird*. Neighboring tribes, locked in conflict for shared resources and claiming separate ancestries and identity, would often have drastically different customary rules, or *'urf*, regarding the status of women. In times of conflict between tribes, those that more strictly enforced the segregation and subjugation of women would, as a rule, claim that the rival tribe was effeminate, emasculated, controlled by women, and hence, at least in the eyes of the self-proclaimed 'masculine' tribe, ripe for conquest. When tribal feuding became especially pronounced, those tribes that at one time had a freer attitude toward women could sometimes reverse their previously relaxed approach in order to avoid being labeled effeminate or feminized. Thus, accusations of shameful acts and curses against women of rival tribes could have real consequences in the form of a very strict interpretation of tribal modesty, an interpretation that arises out of a specifically un-Islamic action: the tribal feud.[8] The prominent use of women as representative symbols of honor in the Arab tribe was best described in the works whose mission was to destroy or challenge the honor of rival tribes: the *naqa'id* poets of early and pre-Islamic Arabia.

Poetic slander and the use of women as symbols of tribal honor

Using evidence from *naqa'id* poetry, this article demonstrates how slanderous poetry enforced the notion of women as symbols of tribal honor. *Naqa'id* poets would duel with insults against tribe and person, using the same rhyme and meter. The sign of a good *naqa'id* poet was one who was able to think quickly of the most provocative insult while still respecting the difficult constraints of meter and rhyme. Many of the poems in the *Naqa'id of Jarir and al-Farazdaq* are short, offensive and entertaining barbs directed at the rival. However, there are also much longer poems in the form of a type of modified ode, or *qasida*, that have roughly the same structure as the *mu'allaqat qasida*; these usually evoked the abandoned camp site, the lover muse, the camel trek across the desert and even magical scenes referring to ghosts in the wilderness. Within the *Naqa'id of Jarir and al-Farazdaq*, however, this form was used to strike deeply at the pride and honor of the opposing poet and his clan. It was as if the powerful and highly symbolic power of the *qasida* had been harnessed for the purpose of abuse. Although they presented their own tribes and their own women as paragons of virtue, pedigree and modesty, the poets did not necessarily rebut each other directly and rarely answered or challenged the specific insults of the opposing poet, choosing most often to reply with an offensive statement about the opposing clan's women instead.[9] Scholars of Arabic poetry, such as Salma Jayyusi, have criticized *naqa'id* poetry for

[8]As the Qur'an states, one should turn towards the *qibla* in unity for prayer: 'Turn your face thither: that there be no ground of dispute against you among the people' (Qur'an 2:150).
[9]Gelder claims that the *Naqa'id* poems are almost exclusively offensive rather than defensive in nature: the poets do not defend their women against abuse. However, as this article demonstrates, there were many instances when a poet's own women, such as Jarir's wife Salma, are defended and portrayed as upright examples of virtue.

its repetitiveness and its static nature, calling this its 'gravest artistic fault' (411). Many abusive themes are repeated throughout the poem. Jarir, for example, refers almost formulaically and with tiresome repetition that amounts to incantation to the alleged rape of al-Farazdaq's sister, Ji'thin, and al-Farazdaq's failure to defend her honor. Indeed, Jarir and al-Farazdaq hurled abuse at each other and each other's clans, and especially at each other's women, over some forty years.

In many ways Jarir and al-Farazdaq were like estranged brothers, alike enough to know what could hurt the other. As mentioned above, both were born into the same great tribal confederation of the Tamim some-time during the reign of the Caliph 'Umar ibn al-Khattab (d. 644), only a decade or so after the death of the Prophet Muhammad. Both were from eastern Arabia. Al-Farazdaq was from Yamama, from the clan of Mujashi' of the Darim group of Tamim.[10] Jarir was from north-eastern Arabia and the Mudari Tamim, from the clan of the Banu Kulayb bin Yarbu'.

To the modern reader, the rivalry between Jarir and al-Farazdaq may seem at times like a type of petty game, but it certainly had a much more profound meaning for the tribes of seventh- and eighth-century Arabia. *Naqa'id* poetry is a form of *hija'*—satirical or cursing poetry. In the pre-Islamic and early Islamic period, poetry was often perceived to be magical in nature; poets and poetry were thought to be able to alter the physical and social world. One main purpose of *hija'* poetry was to shame opposing tribes by attacking the *'ird*, or honor of the tribe, an honor, as discussed above, that is most often associated with a tribe's women. *Hija'* was, in effect, a type of poetic, magical warfare. Drawing on the early Arab writer Ibn Qutayba's classical description of Arabic poetry and the *hija'*, scholars have identified the *hija'* as a type of magical curse, an invocation of the spiritual world to serve the purposes of the poet and the poet's tribe. The Hungarian scholar Ignaz Goldziher said, 'The hija' is in origin an incantation, a curse . . . In the primi-tive hija' the poet thus appears with the magic force of his utterance inspired by the jinn'.[11] According to the scholar Maurice Gaudefroy-Demombynes:

[10]His name probably means 'burnt cake' (Wormhoudt, 'Foreword'), or 'a lump of dough' (Blachère). For a study of al-Farazdaq's poetry and his rivalry with Jarir and the poet Akhtal, see Smoor.

[11]Fares disputes Goldziher's explicit categorizations of *hija'* as purely magic, but neverthe-less admits that although 'it is by the very violence of the insult that the enemy is brought low and, in this combination of action in reaction, there is indeed some element of magic . . . Thus, while differing in respect of character and form, the *hija'* and the *kahin* [a kahin was

... [B]y uttering insults according to the inspired rhythmic formulae of
his verse, [the poet] knows that they must produce formidable results. It
is not only his own anger ... that he incorporates in his verse, but also
those of his tribe whose honour (*'ird*), he has in his hands; ... he knows
how to hurl an insult that is at once poetic, virulent and crude and that
brands an individual or group of men for ever. (Gaudefroy-Demombynes
62, cited in Pellat).

Both Jarir and al-Farazdaq seemed very conscious of the potential power
of their words. For instance, when he referred to the judgment of their
poetry by a certain Rabi'a, Jarir said that the 'dreams' or curses of
al-Farazdaq were deemed 'Light, not weighing a grain of mustard' (40:
45–7).

Naqa'id poems often seem crude, and to some extent Jarir and
al-Farazdaq were playing to a crowd, to their patrons, but the abuse they
hurled at each other and at each other's tribes was very serious indeed. The
naqa'id and *hija'* poets were so feared and so vested with power to influence a tribe's fate and enhance or malign its honor, that it is little wonder
that women were so carefully protected in pre-Islamic and early Islamic
Arab tribes, not only to defend them from capture in times of active war,
but also to safeguard them and the tribe's *'ird* from the constant abuse of
hostile poets. Both Jarir and al-Farazdaq accused each other's clans of not
protecting their women effectively during battle. Not only did women
need to be protected on the physical battlefield, as Ladies of Victory or
members of the rear guard, but also, perhaps even more importantly, they
had to be shielded from slander and curses on the verbal battlefield of the
poets. Al-Farazdaq described his clan's battle against Jarir's tribe, the
Banu Kulayb:

> Defenders when the women ride behind
>> for fear captures their camels unsaddled
> When drawn swords defend our women ... (39:10–11)

Likewise, Jarir described warriors defending women in battle as 'defenders
when the women were scattered' (48:20). And in fact, both Jarir and

a tribal soothsayer] formula for imprecation are in agreement from a functional point of
view' (214–8).

al-Farazdaq were defenders of their own women's honor and status, even as they attacked the enemy in verse. This article now examines the various ways in which they both used the power of poetry either to lift up their own women as symbolic paragons of the clan or to demean foreign women as cursed and shamed.

Women in the *Naqa'id*

Although there were a few exceptions, poetry, especially in the pre-Islamic and early Islamic era, was mainly a male preserve. Women in early Arabic poetry were an essential part of the *qasida* as the focus of the requisite romantic interlude but almost always as poetic objects and symbols created in the poet's mind, rather than as independent characters or free agents. When women wrote poetry, it was often in praise of fallen male warriors as in the *Diwan al-Khansa* by Tamadar, in which the poetess bewails the loss of her brothers, even after being reprimanded by the Caliph 'Umar for her endless lamentations. Women poets did sometimes participate directly in the honor feud, but usually in a way that only enforced gender categories.

Women were, as the feminist scholar Ann McClintock has said, 'symbolic bearers' (62). The famed pre-Islamic poets, such as Imru' al-Qays and Labid, portrayed women in the *nasib*, or the love poem section of the typical Arabic ode, the classical *qasida*, in an abstract, idealized way, seemingly unrelated to events or even to time itself.[12] This idea of the *nasib* as an expression of longing for unity and love across tribal boundaries was so strong that according to the *Encyclopaedia of Islam* entry on the *nasib*, 'The basic situation is *always* the same, the separation of lovers belonging to neighboring tribes. In spring the tribes camp together, but when the season of abundant pasture ends, they depart and lovers must separate'.[13] In fact, the situation was not always the

---

[12]There are many excellent studies of the pre-Islamic *qasida* including those by Montgomery and Stetkevych, who introduced a revolutionary new way of interpreting the poems, and, most famously, by Taha Husayn (1889–1973), a former education minister and giant of the Egyptian intellectual scene in the first half of the twentieth century who famously challenged the historical authenticity of pre-Islamic poetry and claimed that most supposedly pre-Islamic poems were compiled centuries after the pre-Islamic period.

[13]See also Lichtenstadter, 'Das Nasib der altarabischen Qaside'. For an academic translation of the *Mu'allaqa* of Imru' al-Qays and his *nasib*, see Jones (239–43), who provides this translation: 'I arrived when she had slipped off her clothes, [ready] for sleep [behind] a screen, all but the covering of a mifdal. She said, "God's oath, you have no way of

same. In the modified *qasida* and *nasib* that make up the the *Naqa'id of Jarir and al-Farazdaq*, women of another tribe were not the poet's personal symbolic muse, but rather the object of scorn and abuse. Instead of the sentiment that love should conquer all, even the fundamental tribal divisions of society, as found in the *nasib* of the *mu'allaqat*, the *nasib* of the *Naqa'id* expressed the sentiment that love for tribe and honor was foremost. While the *nasib* in the *mu'allaqat* was about union, and even possibly an expression of inter-tribal desire written for the great fair of Ukaz near Mecca where the Arab tribes gathered for peaceful commercial exchange, the *nasib* in the *Naqa'id* was one of feud. Jarir and al-Farazdaq praise various women in a type of abbreviated *nasib* at the beginning of their long poems, but only women from their own tribe and family. Jarir's muse Salma, for example, was one of his wives and certainly not the non-clan, foreign beauty of the *Jahiliyya* poets. Jarir praised her as an object of beauty and virtue. He evoked her in a poem written in response to Gassan, the poet designated by the Salit clan to defend them against Jarir and his clan's claim to a watering hole. Her ample body with 'tight anklets' is portrayed as a sign of prosperity in Jarir's clan, the Banu Kulayb.

> Was not Salma up early and her morning happy
>> And her men pulled stakes after assembly
> Then we said already the goal is clear
>> Salma shed tears or drew them forth
> She had plump limbs on which fitted
>> Salma's tight anklets and her bracelets. (7:1–3)

Rather than being a representation of beauty and erotic desire, as in the poetry of the pre-Islamic *mu'allaqat*, those masterpieces of the *qasida* odes written in gold and hung on the Ka'ba, in the *Naqa'id* foreign women and foreignness in general, were an object of scorn. For example, in many of his poems Jarir attacked al-Farazdaq's Mujashi' clan as being the sons of a foreign, red-haired Christian woman:

---

evading them. I see that your ways of error have not left you."' Clearly, unsanctioned relations with the women of other tribes were seen as wrong, as the woman in this *nasib* relates. However, like the other *mu'allaqat* poets, and unlike the *naqa'id* poets, Imru al-Qays often saw beyond tribal conventions.

I was told that you O Ibn Warada[14] were friends
  With the Banu Hudayys sitting and standing
And when I sought you, all of you, you were
  Not Muslims and not generous to me
But you found trouble in our war that
  Settled with you and cast down bodies
Slowly Ba'ith for your mother is our doxy
  Hamra [Red], she overcame with foreign stink
She had experience in weighing with her hand
  The slave purse and playing the games. (26: 7–11)

Jarir and al-Farazdaq hurled abuse at the women of the other clan, even as
they promoted the honor of their own. In the poem above, Jarir manages to
direct a double insult at the matriarch Warada, simultaneously accusing the
Mujashi' line of being corrupted by her 'foreign stink' and by her being a
'slave'. Jarir accuses al-Farazdaq of pouring 'your mother the best wine' and
of having a daughter who wanted to turn the *masjid* into an unholy place of
lust. This was because, according to Jarir, 'A foreigner gave birth to Farazdaq
and Sa'sa' as if their faces were black' (48: 57–8).

In the *Naqa'id*, women from other clans become less symbols of a poet's
muse and more symbols of a rival tribe's honor, a symbol vulnerable to attack
and abuse, a symbol in need of protection from dishonor in the all-important
verbal warfare of poetic honor, as in times of actual feud and war. Women were
mentioned in almost every single *Naqa'id* poem. Indeed, the very first poem in
the *Naqa'id* was recited by Jarir in defense of Bakra bint Malis of the Banu
Muqallad ibn Kulayb, Jarir's tribal faction, against her accusing husband Ibn
'Ulath of the Banu Salit Ka'b ibn al-Harith ibn Yarbu'.

Truly the Salit in rascality is a child
  of folk born to be slaves
Don't threaten me, O sons of stink
  Truly their girls are cursed
Black with lust when they stomach it
  They do the act of leaping she-ass
They want a deal even if tricked. (2: 1–3)

---

[14]Warada had red or blondish hair and was possibly not Arab.

As these first examples of Jarir and al-Farazdaq that use women to shame the tribe demonstrate, women were not simply a side-show, or a secondary part of the poetry of tribal honor and tribal feud, the poetry of the *naqa'id*, but the central concern, the central source of pride and of shame for Jarir, al-Farazdaq and the Bedouin poets of early Islam. Before exploring more examples of how the shame and honor of women are used in the *Naqa'id*, however, an explanation of the history and context of the *Naqa'id of Jarir and al-Farazdaq* and its relevance specifically to Qatar, the Gulf region and Gulf history is in order.

References to the Gulf and Gulf tribes in the *Naqa'id of Jarir and al-Farazdaq*

Although a great many of the places named in the *Naqa'id of Jarir and al-Farazdaq* were in Eastern Arabia, the Gulf and Gulf clans are extensively referred to in the poems. The heartland of the Tamim tribe, the great tribal confederation to which Jarir and al-Farazdaq belonged, was in the Najd and Yamama, but there were also numerous Tamim clans in the Gulf region as early as the seventh century.[15] Indeed, as mentioned previously, great Qatari tribes of today, such as the al-Thani, claim Tamim as their common ancestor. This is to be expected since, before the emergence of modern state boundaries, there was a constant migration of tribes and clans searching for pasture between Eastern and Western Arabia. There may have been a sense that there was a *diyar*, or a tribal area, but it should be remembered that these areas were in flux. The tribal areas of Qatar and the Qatari tribes are mentioned explicitly in the *Naqa'id*. As mentioned at the beginning of the article, Jarir refers to the Qataris as his night-time travel companions. Jarir displays his clan's sense of camaraderie with his Qatari Tamimi relatives. Their presence and their shared burden seemed to comfort him as he refers to the ghost of a woman named Sha'tha who came at night:

> Her ghost comes to us from afar
> It wades the dark of overcast night. (35: 29)

---

[15] Other Tamim lived near Basra and Kufa in Iraq (Lecker).

There are references in the *Naqa'id* to the famed Qatari al-Rayyan water
source and al-Farazdaq refers to the perilous act of pearl diving to describe
the allegedly impossible attempts of the rival Qattan clan to pray and be true
Muslims.[16] It was common for both al-Farazdaq and Jarir to accuse each
other's clans of being completely lacking in religion:

> They went to the house of prayer as if on
> > Sands, their breaks in legs once broken
> Like pearls of a diver aiming in dread of
> > His sin, and a soul whose thought fears
> Deaf guardian of pearls . . . (59: 17–19)

The Rakiyya shores of Bahrain are mentioned by al-Farazdaq when he describes
splitting the heads of Jarir's clan during a feud over a famed horse race:

> Wide the edges of the split as if they were
> > Rakiyya of Liqman . . . (31: 17)

Finally, there are several references to tribes from the large Liwa Oasis,
located today in the United Arab Emirates. Jarir mentions that his clan
camped at the Liwa Oasis:

> Blame the camp after Liwa's rank . . .
> When I remained at the camp at Liwa,
> > My tears spread without any restraint. (46: 2, 5)

It is often hard to decipher the meaning of these sometimes cryptic references to the Gulf and specific Gulf tribes and locations. What they do show,
however, is that the Gulf and women from Gulf tribes, especially nomadic
clans, seem to have been very much a part of the *naqa'id* culture of the
Tamim tribe of Jarir and al-Farazdaq. The *naqa'id* was not simply an Eastern
Arabian phenomenon; it was found throughout the Peninsula and the many
tribes who criss-crossed the great deserts in search of oases and pasture.

Having explained the connection between the Gulf and *naqa'id* poetry
and the association between the honor of women and the honor of the

[16]The reference to al-Rayyan is 'At Tikhfa and Rayyan where over Ja'far, Its eagles and
vultures hovered about' (35: 78).

tribe, this article demonstrates how the Qur'an and Islamic norms were against the tribal use of slanderous poetry—poetry that was often focused on women.

The Qur'an against the poets: prohibiting poetic slander of women

Sura 26 of the Qur'an, called the 'Sura of the Poets', includes a famous condemnation of vindictive poetry in its final verses. It calls on Muslims to 'admonish thy nearest kinsmen and lower thy wing to the believers . . .' (Qur'an 26: 214–5; trans. Yusuf 'Ali). It seems clear that the Qur'an condemns the use of *hija'*, poetic verses used as curses, especially the most powerful of curses—those directed against the women of enemy tribes and groups. However, defensive poetry, such as poetry used in the service of Islam was not expressly condemned. The Qur'an states:

> Shall I inform you on whom it is that evil ones descend?
> They descend on every lying, wicked person,
> (Into whose ears) they pour hearsay vanities, and most
> Of them are liars. And the Poets,
> It is those straying in evil, who follow them:
> Seest thou not that they wander distracted in every valley?
> And that they say what they practice not?
> Except those who believe work righteousness, engage much
> In the remembrance of Allah, and defend themselves only after
> They are unjustly attacked, and soon will the unjust
> Assailants know what vicissitudes their affairs will take!
>
> (Qur'an 26: 221–7; trans. Yusuf 'Ali)

The evil referred to in the verses above is the *hija'* poetry used against the Prophet by certain anti-Islamic poets, who suggested that the Prophet was possessed by evil spirits (Qur'an 26: 210). It was against such curses that the Qur'an eventually responded with its own poetic *jihad*, or purely defensive *hija'*, in response to an 'unjust attack', as sanctioned in the verses above. The most celebrated of the early Muslim poets who defended the Prophet in this verbal *jihad* were Hasan ibn Thabit, Ka'b ibn Malik and 'Abd Allah ibn Rawaha, who devastated the enemy Quraysh and demolished their accusations.[17] Unlike the typical *hija'*, their poetry was seen as defensive; these poets were defending the faith of many tribes, not one. It was a sign of the power of *hija'* and its potential to cause damage that the Prophet had to employ these poetic defenders of Islam.

As demonstrated in the analysis above of the *Naqa'id of Jarir and al-Farazdaq*, a major, if not dominant, feature of the tribal *hija'* poetry condemned by the Prophet was accusations against women. Accusations against the Prophet and against Islam were directed not simply at the origins of the Qur'an but, in a *hija'* or *naqa'id* style similar to the verses of Jarir and al-Farazdaq, against the women of Islam, and often against the Prophet's wives. It was these accusations and the Prophet's response to them that are most interesting, for they show how the Prophet and Islam, in condemning offensive and unjust *hija'*, were in effect defending women, especially Muslim women and the women of the Prophet's household, from the very cycle of tribal feud that turned women into symbols rather than the free and equal members of the *umma* and believers in Allah that Muhammad and Islam intended women to be. Although numerous slanders were hurled at the Prophet's family and wives, the most famous examples are the unjust accusations of infidelity leveled against the Prophet's youngest wife 'A'isha. Sura 66 of the Qur'an, *Surat al-Tahrim*, countered these accusations against the Prophet's household even as the Prophet encouraged his wives to follow the righteous path.

If it was in fact tribal feuds, and the cursing poetry that arose from them, that led to the objectification of women and the formation of customary laws, or *'urf*, to defend the *'ird*, or honor, of women in Arab tribal society, then these customs, including honor killings and the enforced seclusion of women to preserve the tribe from verbal attack, originated in practices resoundingly condemned in the Qur'an and the Sunna. With the coming of Islam there was a transition from the specific, tribal priestess-mother or fertility symbol, to *umma* (the egalitarian Muslim community), an ideal community of believers who were all regarded as equal to each other.

In contrast with the tribal use of women as 'Ladies of Victory' or trophies to be won in war, women who fought during the lifetime of the Prophet engaged in warfare for Islam, not for a specific tribe. They were not symbols of the tribal goddess or tribal honor. Rather, several interesting

---

[17]Apparently, the Prophet even went 'so far as to pledge his supporters the aid of Gabriel' (see Ibn Sallam, *Tabaqat*, 181).

Hadiths pointed to the important role of women on the battlefield as fighters, nurses and supporters of just *jihad*. These Hadiths demonstrate the importance the Prophet and later Hadith narrators vested in the participation of women in warfare. They are portrayed not as passive objects or prizes or as bloody avengers, like Hind bint 'Utba, but as active Muslims struggling for the cause. According to some Hadiths, women were allowed to engage directly in battle, as Umm Haram, daughter of Milhan and wife of 'Ubayda ibn Samit, related:

> One day God's Messenger paid her a visit. She entertained him with food and then sat down to delouse his head. He dozed off, and when he woke up, he was laughing. He was asked what made him laugh. He said, 'Some people from my nation were presented to me who were fighters in the way of God and were sailing in this sea (gliding smoothly on the water). They appeared to be kings or like kings sitting on thrones.' She asked if she would be considered among the warriors. He prayed for her. He then put his head down and dozed off again. He woke up laughing as before. She asked him what made him laugh. He replied, 'People from my nation were presented to me. They were fighters in God's way.' He described them with the same words as he had described the first warriors. She asked him to pray to God that God might include her among these warriors. He said, 'You are among the first ones.'[18]

With the sanction and support of the Prophet, women provided essential comfort, support and food for the Muslim warriors at the base camp. Rubayya' bint Mu'awwadh related, 'They were in the company of the Prophet, providing the wounded with water and treating them and taking the martyred to Madina.'[19] Also, as Umm 'Atiya related: 'She took part with God's Messenger in seven battles. She would stay behind in the camp of the men, cook their food, treat the wounded and nurse the sick.'[20] Yet never in any of these examples of women supporting *jihad* were they expected to become the symbolic bearers of tribal honor or even the honor of Islam on the battlefield. Rather, they were treated as contributors to the effort to spread Islam, able to engage in battle as members of the Muslim

[18]Hadith from *Sahih Muslim* quoted in Kabbani and Bakhtiar 169.
[19]Ibid.
[20]Ibid.

community equal to men. This ran counter to the tribal notions of women as objects to be protected which originated in the tribal feud and tribal customs condemned by Islam. The historian al-Tabari relates that Umm Salama, one of the wives of the Prophet Muhammad, even insisted on allowing women to be fully armed and to join in battle as the equals of male warriors (Mernissi 132).

The Qur'an summarizes the new position of women in an ideal Islamic community thus:

> For Muslim men and women,
> for believing men and women,
> for devout men and women,
> for true men and women,
> for men and women who are patient and constant,
> for men and women who humble themselves,
> for men and women who give in Charity,
> for men and women who fast (and deny themselves),
> for men and women who guard their chastity,
> and for men and women who engage much in Allah's praise,
> for them has Allah prepared forgiveness and great reward.
>
> (Qur'an 33:35)

According to this text, male and female believers are equal before God. The pre-Islamic, tribal notion of women as mere symbols of tribal power, as objects of feud, and of booty, conflicted with the Qur'anic revelation. Islam challenged the objectification of women in the tribal feud. Nevertheless, as the political history of the Middle East attests, the tribal feud and the consequences of the tribal feud for women and women's position in society did not end with Islam.

Conclusion

One final example of the construction of gender identity and gender roles through tribal feuds, taken not from the Arab heartland but from Berber North Africa, demonstrates that the association between tribal feud and the construction of gender roles was not restricted to the Arabs. In twelfth-century North Africa the Almoravid Muslim tribes of the Sahara were traditionally matriarchal. According to Saharan tribal custom, inheritance was matrilineal and women could easily divorce their husbands. In a practice that continues to this day, men would be veiled and women would go unveiled. According to the sources, Saharan women were allowed to command, to ride horses, to wear their hair in elaborate and revealing styles. The Almohad tribes of the Atlas Mountains north of the Sahara, however, were much more patriarchal in nature. Women did not seem to have quite as much freedom in the mountains as they did in the desert. When Ibn Tumart (d. 1130), a charismatic religious reformer who claimed to be the Mahdi, arrived among the Almohad mountain tribes, one of the ways in which he justified the conquest of the Almoravid desert tribes was by identifying them as effeminate, and thus, in his view of Islam, unworthy. For Ibn Tumart, the Almoravids, then the rulers of Marrakech and a vast empire that stretched from the Sahara to al-Andalus, represented decadent and feminized passiveness, while the Almohad mountain tribes were masculine and active. According to Ibn Tumart's writings, especially his book of doctrine or the *A'azz ma yutlab* (c. 1130), the Almoravids were essentially ruled by their women. As a matrilineal society where men were veiled by a blue mouth covering, and women walked freely without covering their faces and divorced their husbands fairly easily, the Almoravids did indeed have a different symbolic approach toward their women. By actively feminizing the Almoravid enemy tribes in his polemics, Ibn Tumart helped rally the Almohad mountain tribes and justified the eventual conquest of their feminized Almoravid desert rivals. According to Ibn Tumart's writings, a good masculine tribe must control its feminine or feminized neighbor.

For Ibn Tumart and the mountain tribes of the Atlas, the fundamentally feminized nature of their Almoravid rivals was most iconically embodied by Sura, the Almoravid princess who rode proudly unveiled on her horse without any regard for what Ibn Tumart and the Almohads viewed as the strict norms and ideals of Islam.[21] Thus, in this distant corner of the Islamic world, al-Maghrib al-Aqsa (the far West) the 'Lady of Victory' of the Almoravids would become symbolic not of honor but of decadence. In the

---

[21]Ibn Khaldun describes how Ibn Tumart reprimanded Sura, the sister of 'Ali bin Yusuf, ruler of the Almoravids. 'One day he encountered Sura, sister of this prince, who was going out in public uncovered, as did all the Almoravid women, and, scandalized by this spectacle, he gave her a vigorous reprimand' (1:325).

midst of tribal feuds and tribal polemics the women of the Almohads and the Almoravids would face the feud as embodiments of the honor of their respective tribes. Whether veiled and secluded as symbols of a tribe's true Islamic standards or decked out like Sura, or flamboyantly dressed as Ladies of Victory, women faced the consequences of war between men.

3. *Women and Politics in Late Jahili and Early Islamic Arabia: Reading behind Patriarchal History*

BARBARA FREYER STOWASSER

This chapter presents a new, comparative reading of old sources. By focusing closely on context rather than polemics and hindsight discursive rhetoric, the older poetic artifacts and historical narratives yield ample information on women's full participation in the political and military activities of late *Jahili* and early Islamic Arabian societies. With the progression of time, this fact is increasingly obfuscated and eventually well-nigh omitted in the historical literature due to the moral-religious nature of these discourses and the prominence of religious authorities in the transmission of knowledge in Islamic literary traditions.

The problematic of women and politics

This chapter is about the Muslim woman's historic right to active participation in public space. I contend that this right was established by Qur'anic revelation and practiced in the Prophet's community in Mecca and Medina. I also contend that this right had historical antecedents in the practices of the *Jahiliyya* period.

To assume a historical link between the two eras, the pre-Islamic and the Islamic, is not a revolutionary notion. Many pre-Islamic political and social, cultural, economic, military and other norms and practices provided the building blocks for the myriad processes of their adaptation and transformation that over time marked the creation of the Islamic order. Historians and other social scientists have come to expect this fact of cultural continuity as one of the 'laws of history'. Religious scholars, on the other hand, are apt to emphasize the newness of all Islamic institutions and practices in opposition to those of the *Jahiliyya* 'other', as their transformation for the purposes of the new world order overrides the fact of their pre-Islamic roots. This binary division holds especially true for gender issues, in particular women's social roles and rights, as the religious discourse formulated by scripturalist experts and other *'ulama'* places an especially sharp delineation between women's status in the *Jahiliyya* and in Islam. By demarcating the two eras against each other in paradigmatic, contrastive mode, politically active women and women in any kind of leadership position all but disappear from the Islamic historical accounts of the pre-Islamic era, replaced by the construct of women's powerlessness, indeed, women as 'chattel' in *Jahiliyya* societies. This construct has remained a prominent theme in the Muslim apologetic literature on pre-Islamic society and culture (echoed in the works of some Western writers).[1]

In the first part of this chapter, I reconstruct some of the areas of women's political activities in the *Jahiliyya* period. In Arabia, this era ended with the spread of Islam during the Prophet's lifetime, but it had a last gasping moment of lingering existence during the Ridda Wars. During these wars, some late *Jahili* women appear to have been politically active against the new Islamic order; unlike the renegade females (who were severely punished or put to death), some of the pagan women rebels survived, joined the new religion, and were active in its service, but their historical images were and remain uniformly negative. One of the dangers of writing about 'women' in the *Jahiliyya* (or any other) period is, of course, that 'women' is not a normative category in and of itself and that *'Jahiliyya'* — or 'Islam', for that matter—is also an undifferentiated catch-all *qua* identifying marker that needs the specificity of chronological, geographic, social, political, and other cultural data to accomplish a meaningful reading (cf. Doumato 177–9). Therefore, to be more specific, in its *Jahiliyya* portion, which mainly covers events of the early seventh century, this

---

[1]This literature has been systematically presented and analyzed by Yvonne Yazbeck Haddad. For a representative sample on the oppression of Arabian women in the *Jahiliyya*, see the Internet essay by the Muslim Women's League.

article presents examples of politically active, pagan and/or renegade, free-born females with strong tribal connections of both sedentary (Hijaz and Yemen) and nomadic background (central plateau and Gulf coastal regions of the Arabian Peninsula), while the examples of Muslim women in politics in the early Islamic period are largely drawn from among the free-born women of the Prophet's community in Medina and Mecca, i.e. the Hijaz, in the early seventh century. In what follows, the term 'patriarchy' refers to a politics of sexual differentiation that privileges males by transforming biological sex into politicized gender, or, in Asma Barlas' words, 'the notion of sexual differentiation that is used to privilege males while Othering women' (Barlas 204, 129).

Islam mandated cultural attitudes and ideals seeking to affect women's status in new ways. Upon accepting the Prophet's call, a woman's political status would transcend tribal affiliation and metamorphose into her full citizenship in the early *umma*. As an egalitarian and inclusive order, Islam would grant rights and impose obligations of citizenship on male and female believers alike; prominent among them was the involvement of both genders in the struggle for the cause and the building of a virtuous society (as legislated, for example, in Qur'an 9:71). The transcendental certainties of the new faith were to transform the quality and purpose of women's political activism. Seen against the backdrop of its historical antecedent—the *Jahiliyya* past—the early Islamic notion of women in politics thus not only continued but was expanded to include all Muslim women, in a politics whose moral compass derived from revelation and Prophetic guidance, and whose focus was the wellbeing of individual and collective alike. For reasons that I hope to argue convincingly below, historical information on the status, let alone the political activities of women in *Jahili* Arabia is hard to find and often difficult to evaluate. This is in large part because the data that we may, indeed, cull from the Islamic sources has been filtered through an ideological elimination process where *Jahili* practices are often negatively weighted and obscured in light of the new Islamic worldview.

But writing about women's political contributions during the earliest Islamic period, while somewhat easier than researching the *Jahiliyya* period, is still not an easy enterprise. Even though the historical records vary as to the scope and detail that they provide on these issues, the data on Arabian Muslim women in politics are rarely highlighted and very often omitted. The main reason for this dearth of information is not, however, that early Muslim women were not active in religion, politics, or war. Rather, the reason lies with the nature of the sources in terms of both chronology (the fact that the earliest among them were recorded a century or two after the Prophet's time) and ideology (the fact that by this time the social, legal, and political norms of Arab Islamic culture, now largely defined in formerly Byzantine or Iranian parts of the Muslim world, had turned to patriarchality); both of these developments determined specific features of traditional historiography. To write women's political history therefore requires reading large amounts of historical texts in the hope of coming across some female actors whose acts just happened to have been recorded (often in an otherwise male-focused context). In very general terms, chronological sequence does bear upon the sources' coverage of women's activism, in that the earlier among them are more inclusive of such information than are the later. Different ideological readings of women's events also exist, both among the various genres of early Islamic historiography (in synchronic terms) and also between the earlier and later texts and compilations (in diachronic terms). Regardless of chronology and genre, however,[2] the material exhibits many instances of textual 'de-coding', where women do and say things that their much later, patriarchally-minded, chronicler has consciously re-shaped to fit with his own aims and criteria.

The historical sources

There exist many different genres of sources that cover the demise of the *Jahiliyya*, the rise of Islam, and the early history of the Islamic community; they include the Sira (biography of the Prophet), Hadith (compilations of authenticated traditions by and about the Prophet), biographical dictionaries (source books about specialists in Hadith learning and their collections of texts), and also histories, chronicles, and some other derivations of one or more of the above. These sources pose some extraordinary methodological

[2]In synchronic terms, the early biographical-dictionary (*tabaqat*) literature is more inclusive here than are the equally early 'foundational'-oriented texts of the Sira (Prophet's biography). In addition, the increased chronological distance of a writer or Hadith compiler from the events under consideration tends to increase his editorial impact on the transmitted texts. These issues are discussed in what follows.

problems for the modern historian who attempts to reconstruct the events of late *Jahiliyya* and early Islamic history,[3] prominent among them being problems of the sources' chronological distance from the described events.

The earliest available account of the Prophet's Sira was written in the eighth century by Ibn Ishaq (d. 767, 135 years after the Prophet's death) edited by Ibn Hisham (d. 834), followed by the works on the Prophet by al-Waqidi (d. 823) and Ibn Sa'd (d. 845). In historiography, there are the historical 'digests' of al-Ya'qubi (d. 897), al-Dinawari (d. 894), Ibn Qutayba (d. 889) and al-Mas'udi (d. 956), and the magisterial, inclusive historical works of al-Baladhuri (d. 892) and al-Tabari (d. 923). Both al-Baladhuri and al-Tabari derived their accounts from previous 'compilations' of materials made around 800.[4] Both also chose for inclusion those past events that they considered carried legal, political, or religious significance and whose accounts could be traced back to reliable authorities (Humphreys 72). Therefore, these histories convey not raw data but 'a consciously shaped literary tradition' in which their authors' aims and criteria—political legitimacy, the nature of right government, Muhammad's mission fulfilled or betrayed—determined the 'names, actions, statements and dates which would constitute the facts of Islamic history' (Humphreys 86). The six authenticated Hadith compilations of al-Bukhari (d. 870), Muslim (d. 875), Ibn Maja (d. 886), Abu Da'ud (d. 888), al-Tirmidhi (d. 892) and al-Nasa'i (d. 915) date to the ninth and early tenth centuries (two and a half centuries after the Prophet's death), which further leaves the modern historian with the question of how fully and accurately the traditions in even these six canonical Hadith collections contain the texts of an original, fluid, oral tradition from which they were culled. The biographical dictionaries (generally titled *tabaqat*) likewise present the problem of how and to what purpose the early Hadith tradition was crystallized, even though one could argue that the *tabaqat* literature (such as the *Kitab al-tabaqat al-kabir* by Ibn Sa'd) is perhaps less selective regarding the Hadith than are the six (authenticated) canonical collections with their emphasis on legal issues. Later biographical dictionaries, which preserve a great deal of otherwise unknown material, are those of Ibn 'Abd al-Barr (d. 1070), Ibn Athir (d. 1233), and Ibn Hajar al-Asqalani (d. 1449). A

[3]This section follows Humphreys 68–98.
[4]Such as the 'compilations' of Hadith materials by Ibn Ishaq (d. 767), Sayf ibn 'Umar (d. 796), al-Waqidi (d. 823), al-Mada'ini (d. 840), Ibn Sa'd (d. 845).

different type of historical source is represented by the monumental *Kitab al-aghani* of Abu al-Faraj al-Isfahani (d. 967), which is 'a history of all Arabian poetry that had been set to music down to the author's time' (Nicholson 347). After quoting the poems and describing the melodies to which they were sung, Abu al-Faraj also introduced vast amounts of historical information, much of it in anecdotal form. While it is primarily a work of belles-lettres and literary history, the *Kitab al-aghani* is also an important source of pre-Islamic and early Islamic lore and cultural attitudes.

The fact that our narrative sources represent a late crystallization of an older, fluid, oral tradition—in other words, that pre-Islamic and early Islamic events are available to us only as seen by Muslims of the late eighth/early ninth centuries or later—poses specific methodological problems for the modern historian who attempts to reconstruct the involvement of 'women in politics' in the late pre-Islamic and early Islamic eras. First, there is the fact that all of pre-Islamic, early Islamic, and later Islamic history was recorded by men; even women's poetry, an important source of women's history especially in Arabia, was recorded and anthologized by men—if, indeed it was recorded and anthologized at all. Second, as mentioned above, Islamic societies (most of them now outside of the Arabian Peninsula) had developed into patriarchal systems by the time when our earliest historical records were first compiled in writing. And third, by this time, the official Islamic position (and that of its historians) toward the *Jahiliyya* was one of contrastive hostility ('the age of darkness overcome'). Even as they suppressed, or altered (often by way of encoding), all manner of *Jahiliyya*-related customs and events, to the biographers, Hadith experts, and other historians of the eighth-tenth centuries, the *Jahiliyya* became *terra incognita*. Thus they chose to forget—indeed, constructed both *Jahiliyya* and Islam in order to forget—the historical fact of cultural continuity where traditional custom persevered even when profoundly reformed and given a new purpose within the new theological context of the Qur'anic revelation and Prophetic Sunna.[5]

[5]Humphreys speaks of 'the profoundly important fact, clearly documented in the Qur'an, that while the Qur'anic revelation and its Prophet came with a new theology, within that new theological context [they] were demanding simply a reform of traditional custom, . . . and the mass of new Muslims . . . continued to direct their conduct according to the values and attitudes of the Jahiliyya' (84–5).

This combination of our scholarly sources' Islamic patriarchality, and their ideologically-based refusal to recognize a modicum of socio-cultural continuation from the *Jahiliyya* into early Islam, has profound implications for a correct reading of historical data that are now hidden under layers of medieval patriarchal Islamic scholarly learning. The sources furnish a few examples of *Jahili* female behavior that follow the pattern of what priestesses and other women of power 'would do', but that often failed to make sense to the much later medieval Muslim historian or to his own sources, so that—even as he recorded them—he would feel justified in altering the import and significance of events, including their rationale and the motivation of their protagonists. In other, post-*Jahiliyya*, contexts, he would judgmentally relegate the political actions of early Muslim women to the realm of 'the exceptional', without considering even the possibility of a socio-cultural continuum between the two eras, or that some forms of previous female participation in Arabian public politics survived well into the Islamic period. Alfons Teipin and others have argued, however, that the Islamic narrative on *Jahiliyya* issues and events, including the public role of women, is not so much based on ignorance of the *Jahiliyya* as on the ideological decision to construct the *Jahiliyya* as the 'other', for the purpose of constructing (a contrastive) Islamic identity. The argument that narrative history creates communal identity stipulates a tight correspondence between negative narratives of *Jahili* women's martial exploits in the Islamic sources, and their tendency to downplay the stories of Muslim women's participation in the wars of the Prophet and his successors (Teipen 453–4).

Women in the *Jahiliyya*

This chapter considers two major political functions that appertained to free-born women in pre-Islamic Arabia. Both were operative within the tribal context of desert nomads and sedentary tribes alike. One was the obligatory, collective role of a tribe's free-born females to participate in their group's wars and battles, to incite the adult males of the ruling warrior class to fight, to mourn the dead, and to call for vengeance. The other was the individual leadership function of the tribal *kahina*, its seer, or priestess, who in an ecstatic, 'inspired' state would transmit messages of knowledge, counsel, or warning that had magical import for the group or one of its members. Both of these functions of female empowerment were operative to the very end of the *Jahiliyya* (or even beyond) and then underwent a transformation.

In what follows, a portrait of Hind bint 'Utba is presented as embodiment of her war-related energies in *marathi* (elegies) and *tahrid* (incitement to avenge) for her pagan, urban clan, followed by her (and her clan's) transformation into elite members of the young Islamic community. In the wars of early Islam, Muslim women soldiers continued to participate as fighters on the battlefield, and women continued to eulogize their dead, even though the rituals of lamentation and wailing were outlawed by the Prophet. By contrast, the tradition of soothsaying waned with the end of the polytheistic universe, together with its many deities and spirits; as the old jinn lost their power, the old *kahinat* lost their functions. But even as the tradition of soothsaying came to an end, women continued to have a role in imparting knowledge and advice, warning and counsel, not as 'inspired' individuals transmitting vaticinations (prophesies) received from a world of the spirits, but as recipients of Muhammad's prophetic knowledge and participants in the communal rites and regulations of the Islamic *umma*. A portrait is presented below of Sajah 'the false prophetess', whose claim to 'individual inspiration' was replaced by her submission to the Qur'anic revelation and her decision to become, and remain, a solid member of the Islamic community in Basra, Iraq.

Women as guardians of tribal identity, honor, and fame: *marathi* and *tahrid*

The free Arabian woman, in desert and city, was a proud and valued member of her tribe whose own lineage was as important to her offspring's noble genealogy as was that of the Arabian male (Lichtenstädter 6–7, 64–86). But this free, pre-Islamic Arabian woman was also ideologically ensconced in her tribe, from which she derived her protection and to which she owed all her public activities. First among these was the obligation to participate in the tribe's military expeditions (*ghazawat*) and wars (*hurub*). Women were a crucial contingent in a tribe's successful presence on the battlefield. Positioning themselves in the midst of battle, they urged the men to fight, 'incit(ing) them with their stirring war songs sung to the accompaniment of their lutes. The leader of the group was the Lady of Victory herself (a woman of outstanding social position) with hair flowing and body partly exposed, embody[ing] an appeal to valor, honor, and passion' (Abbott 262–3). Women on the battlefield watered and nursed their own wounded fighters and on occasion clubbed those of the enemy dead. The most important public service that women were obliged to render their tribe, however, was to perform the ritual obligations of *marathi* (elegies) and *tahrid* (the call to vengeance). Women's public mourning, dirges, and lamentations for the slain, and calls for vengeance were powerful pieces in a tribe's political and poetic legacy (Lichtenstädter 38–45). During the act of wailing, women chanted elegies/dirges (*ritha'/ marathi*; sing. *marthiya*) and wept, tearing at their clothes and hair, scratching their faces and beating their breasts. The call to vengeance (*tahrid*) was an integral part of the *marthiya*. Both were composed in *saj'*, rhymed prose (or, occasionally, the simple and archaic meter of *rajaz*). The elegy celebrated the slain warrior and thus immortalized him, while the call to vengeance exhorted the living to 'revitalize the kin and devitalize the enemy on the battlefield' (Stetkevych 83).[6] In her masterful study of the pre-Islamic *qasida*, *The Mute Immortals Speak*, Suzanne Stetkevych has described the taking of blood vengeance in *Jahili* Arabia as a rite of sacrifice; the imagery and structure of the *Jahili* poetry of blood vengeance are therefore not expressions of personal sentiment but are ritually determined (ibid. 57, 161). Tribal society exists in two opposing ritual states: '*halal* and *haram*, that is, purity (having no unavenged blood) and pollution (having blood awaiting vengeance), the profane and the sacred (or consecrated), or otherwise put, at peace and at war' (ibid 62).

Women had a crucial role in ensuring the tribe's transition from *haram* to *halal* by performing the sacred liturgy of mourning and revenge 'with its carefully condensed and encoded expressions of the ritual concept of sacrifice and redemption' (ibid. 199).[7] Their very appearance on the battlefield—with hair unveiled and parts of their bodies exposed—symbolized that the women were performing a sacred role in 'a typically liminal

---

[6]Stetkevych proposes that women's lamentation/*ritha'* is in perception and expression the inverse parallel of men's blood vengeance/*ritha'* . . . 'both types of *ritha'* are ultimately concerned with sacrifice and redemption: but whereas the male redeems his slain kinsmen by pouring out the liquid soul—the blood of vengeance or his own blood—the kinswoman does so by the shedding of tears, another 'expression' of liquid soul and a metaphor for the composing of *ritha'* itself' (167–8).

[7]'The pre-Islamic elegy, especially that composed by women, can reveal to us that point at which liturgy and literature intersect' (Stetkevych 162).

defiled and yet sacred state' that was ritually prescribed (ibid. 165). Islam would eventually do away with the rituals of female mourning and their call to vengeance. According to Ibn Ishaq's Sira, the Prophet forbade both practices after the battle of Uhud (Guillaume 387–9),[8] but they remained a long-standing issue in the prescriptive literature on gender. In discrediting the pre-Islamic tradition, the Muslim interpreters focused on one specific Jahilite female who would forever embody the individual and communal disorder of the past: Hind bint 'Utba. But even as women's ritual activities of *marathi* and *tahrid* abated with the coming of Islam, Muslim women continued to participate as soldiers in the early struggles of the nascent Islamic community.

Women as 'inspired' spiritual and political leaders: the *kahinat*

The *kahinat* of pre-Islamic Arabia were priestesses, seers, diviners, also sometimes counsellors and judges, or even warriors in their own right. They were prominent actors in their tribe's power structure; the historical records also show that certain *kahinat* were influential well beyond their tribe's enclosure. *Kihana*[9] (divination, soothsaying, prognostication) is the ability to connect with unseen powers to predict the future, solve present problems, confer blessings or curses, or remove curses imposed by others. Certain very special men and women could claim the gift of obtaining mantic knowledge by way of ecstatic inspiration that came to them from their very own *jinni* or *shaytan*, 'demon', and, beyond that demon, from some higher deity. When identifying specific seers by gender and name, the Islamic literature on the spiritual, cultural, and political phenomenon of *kihana* is weighted in favor of the male practitioners.[10] But given the generally patriarchal trend operative in Islamic historiography, which, in some complicated fashion, also appears to project back into the

[8]According to Teipen (445), in the eyes of the later Muslim interpreter, this physical exposure of free women in public symbolically stands for Jahili 'communal disorder . . . resulting from the loss of individual members . . . [that] is ritually inscribed in women's mourning, [while] the Muslim community is in no need of female public mourning, since war and the loss of members do not threaten the divinely instituted communal bond of the *umma*'.
[9]This section of the chapter is based on Wellhausen 130–40; Gibb and Kramers 206–8; and Ali ch. 85 ('On the Wonders of the Arabs'), 830–6; also cf. El-Zein 126–52.
[10]In the *Kitab al-aghani* by Abu al-Faraj al-Isfahani, my research assistant Gilla Camden found that examples of male soothsayers were at least twice as numerous as of females.

Jahiliyya, the fact that we learn less about female *kahinat* than male *kuhhan* (or *kahana*) does not have to be an indication of numerical disparity. There is no way to tell whether there were more female sooth-sayers than male, or less, or whether their numbers were equal.

As was the case with the male *kahin*, the female *kahina*'s demon, male or female, was her companion (*tabi'*), comrade (*sahib*), familiar spirit (*mawla*, or *wali*), sometimes also called her 'seer' (*ra'i, ri'i*), a 'personification of [her] ecstasy' (Gibb and Kramers 207); this alter ego delivered the prophetic messages to her, and through her to her people. Invisible to everyone except the *kahina* herself, the *jinni* had a voice and a physicality that she recognized even from a distance, and at least some of the *jinni*s had personal names. It appears that this personaliza-tion of the demon sometimes introduced a sexual element into the perceived relationship between *kahina* and *jinni*. On one occasion, a *kahina* refused a king's marriage proposal because it would render her *jinni* jealous. On another, the *jinni* of the famous *kahina* Fatima bint al-Nu'man is said to have broken off his regular visits to her house because he knew of the impending rise of 'a prophet who will come to forbid *zina* (fornication)'. The demons' messages were delivered in the form of *saj'*, short sentences in rhythmic rhymed prose full of allitera-tions and parallelisms; frequently they contained oaths sworn by celestial bodies or terrestrial objects or phenomena, sometimes in incomprehensible formulas, followed by symbolic warnings, predic-tions, words of counsel and the like. Thus the *kahinat* were not priestesses connected with a specific place of worship, but holy individuals of tribal affiliation and often, by birth or at least function, considered among the tribe's aristocracy.

Some *kahinat* played important roles in tribal politics as they were interrogated on all important occasions, especially before and during mili-tary enterprises (in which they would often participate, sometimes—as was the case with Sajah—even in a leading role). A *kahina* could direct a tribe's migration pattern over long distances. She could warn of impending enemy attacks or natural disasters. She interpreted dreams of the powerful and ordinary alike. She could prophesy both the death and the manner of death of individuals whom she encountered. A *kahina* predicted that al-Huzayn ibn al-Harith, a poet from Banu 'Amir ibn Sa'sa'a, would die of a snake bite in a remote valley, and this proved to be true (al-Isfahani

15:166).[11] Another passed by a woman named Umm Hudba, who was surrounded by her four young sons, and predicted that the two older would be killed after capture, and the two younger die of grief. This also proved to be true (ibid. 21:191). (The fact that Abu al-Faraj al-Isfahani recorded these and similar facts many centuries later in his *Kitab al-aghani* indicates that belief in the power of these *kahinat* persisted.) Furthermore, the *kahina* would be called upon to name the perpetrators of crimes and misdemeanors (such as murders and thefts), find a stray camel or other missing object, settle paternity issues (such as 'Utba ibn Rabi'a's question as to whether Hind bint 'Utba was his daughter), or decide in all manner of legal disputes between contesting parties. In such cases, the *kahina* would act in the capacity of *hakama*, arbiter or judge, and even though her verdicts were likely often based on knowledge of the specifics of the case and on personal intuition, her decisions were considered inspired and beyond appeal. For such work, the *kahina* received a reward, *hulwan*, that was owed to the *jinni* who had spoken through her and was now demanding remuneration.

Among the *kahinat* famous for their involvement in high-level tribal politics was Tarifa al-Khayr, one of the seers of Yemen, who informed the king of Yemen 'Amr ibn 'Amir that the Ma'rib dam was about to burst and that storm floods would devastate the country. They both left Yemen, together with the people of Qahtan, before disaster struck; then she directed them to settle in the land of Jurhum (Mecca), 'the neighbors of His Holy Sanctuary [the Ka'ba]' (ibid. 15:13). Another was Zarqa' bint Zuhayr, who led her tribe from the Tihama to Hajr in the Yamama and then on to Hira (ibid. 13:52–3), and there was also the (unnamed) *kahina* of the Iyad who predicted her tribe's victory over the Persians, who had pursued them across the Euphrates (ibid. 23:13). The best documented example of a *kahina*'s political career is that of Sajah 'the false prophetess' whose story is presented below.

The multifaceted tale of Hind bint 'Utba

In the early historical literature, most of which is of Abbasid provenance, the Meccan aristocrat Hind bint 'Utba is the embodiment of all that is

---

[11] I owe all *Kitab al-aghani* quotations to Gilla Camden.

repulsive and abhorrent in the *Jahiliyya*. The story begins at the battle of Uhud, where Hind symbolizes the darkest savagery of improper blood vengeance of the pagan past. Yet her literary persona also plays a part in the pledge of loyalty to the Prophet that the women embracing Islam offered to him as a group after he had conquered the city of Mecca and purified the sanctuary of its pagan idols. Even among this large group of women pledging allegiance, Hind stands out by her insolence, but her role in this Islamic part of her story has nevertheless shifted into a positive mode as the Prophet individually welcomes her and also fails to rebuke her for her arrogant remarks about the (Qur'an-revealed!) wording of the oath of fealty.[12] Hind's literary persona serves both to give a history of an Arabian aristocrat (and mother of the much-despised founder of the Umayyad dynasty, Mu'awiya) and also as symbol of the transformation from the darkness of the *Jahiliyya* to the light of Islam. Hind's ritual activities on the battlefield are an essential part of this transformation, as her savagery in the sinful struggle against Islam (Uhud) is replaced by her righteous struggle in the earliest stages of the Arabian Islamic wars of expansion and conquest (Yarmuk).

In Ibn Ishaq's Sira (focused on the creation of the *umma*), the battles of Badr (Guillaume 289–360) and Uhud (ibid. 370–433) are juxtaposed as instances of an archetypal dichotomy between heroic combat (Badr) and sacrilegious abomination (Uhud).[13] The Meccans had taken twelve or more of their high-ranking women with them to the Uhud battlefield to remind their soldiers of the defeat and losses of Badr, stir up their anger, and prevent their running away. Among the women was Hind bint 'Utba, who had lost her father, paternal uncle, brother, and oldest (step)son. While the other women were beating tambourines, Hind recited poems of incitement. The first outrage that occurred at Uhud was that the great Muslim knight Hamza ibn 'Abd al-Muttalib, the Prophet's uncle, died at the hands of an Abyssinian slave named Wahshi (whose name means 'wild', 'savage'), also known as Abu Dasma ('father of darkness') to whom his owner had promised freedom if he killed Hamza; Hind also had incited him to quench her thirst for vengeance and his own. Wahshi pierced

---

[12]Cf. *The women's bay'a* below.

[13]Tabari's accounts of these events are largely dependent on Ibn Ishaq (cf. Watt and McDonald 7:26–80 [Badr] and 105–138 [Uhud]). The following analysis of the story of Uhud in Ibn Ishaq and Tabari is based on Stetkevych 199–205.

Hamza's abdomen with his javelin (not even an Arab weapon, later said the poet Hassan ibn Thabit), mortally wounding him, and then he retrieved his javelin and left the battlefield 'as he had no other business there', a murderer for hire (Stetkevych 202). The second outrage occurred when Hind and the women with her began to mutilate the corpses of the slain Muslims, cutting off their ears and noses to fashion anklets and collars to wear, while Hind had presented her own (precious) anklets and collars and pendants to Wahshi (as a reward). Then Hind split open Hamza's belly, cut out his liver, and sank her teeth into it, but she was unable to swallow any of it and threw it away. In Stetkevych's words, Hind's cannibalism was the perversion of the ancient ritual of blood sacrifice (the slaughter and consumption of an animal); its abomination stands for the sacrilege that the pagan Quraysh enacted at Uhud and, indeed, for the whole depravity of paganism in its last onrush against the righteousness of Islam (Stetkevych 202). Hind then climbed on a rock overlooking the battlefield and shrieked a victory poem at the top of her voice, but in this poem of vengeance accomplished and delivered, she—perversely—declares her undying devotion not to her noble dead but to the black slave who had done her bidding. Her poem is answered by one of the Prophet's kinswomen Hind bint 'Uthatha ibn 'Abd al-Muttalib, who refutes Hind bint 'Utba's claim that vengeance has been achieved (Guillaume 385); on the contrary, their victory at Uhud has brought the Meccans as much disgrace as had their defeat at Badr. And the Prophet's poet Hassan ibn Thabit replies to Hind's boast about her mutilation of Hamza on the battlefield by likening her improper vengeance to fornication and describing her person as bearing the marks of sexual pollution and defilement (Watt and McDonald 7:130–1). (According to the Sira's editor and translator, A. Guillaume (440), much of the poetry in the Sira is forged.)

Ibn Ishaq continues with Hind's story in the context of the Prophet's conquest of Mecca.[14] She reacted with violent rage when her husband Abu Sufyan declared his house a safe haven for all during the fighting, and she strove to stir up the crowds against the Prophet's relative 'Abbas when he proclaimed Muhammad's terms of safety. Accepting the defeat, she vented her wrath on the idols in her house, which she shattered, crying that they had deceived her (Abbott 275). Then follows a summary account of Hind

[14]These events are described in Guillaume 546–54. Tabari's account is in Fishbein 8: 181–3.

bint 'Utba's role in the women's pledge of allegiance to the Prophet, to which she came 'veiled and disguised because of what she had done especially in regard to Hamza, for she was afraid that the apostle would punish her' (Guillaume 553). According to Ibn Ishaq, the Prophet had given orders to kill ten of his old adversaries in Mecca, but Hind is not mentioned among them (Guillaume 550–5), while in al-Tabari her name is included (Fishbein 181–3); neither source, however, reports that the Prophet reacted in any way when he later met her, hale and hearty, and learned of her identity.[15]

In the Sira (an 'edifying' genre by way of its focus on the creation of the *umma* [Teipen 453]) and other similar early historical literature, the Jahilite and the Islamic portions of Hind's story are weighted in favor of the former, as it is her *Jahiliyya* persona that prevails both as to length and emphasis in the narrative. The sources somewhat curiously also report that Hind had early on offered her help to Zaynab, the Prophet's daughter, to get her safely from Mecca to Medina because 'men's quarrels have nothing to do with women', and 'women stand closer together than men' (Guillaume 314–6; Watt and McDonald 7:75; but this story is also told as evidence that she wanted to trick Zaynab, and Zaynab did not believe her.

By contrast, in Ibn Sa'd's biographical dictionary (focused on individual actors in the history of early Islam), the two components of Hind bint 'Utba's life are weighted equally but separately, as they are dealt with in two different contexts: her Jahiliyya past appears in the narration of early Islamic warfare and the death of one of Islam's great knights on the battlefield, while her story in her own biographical listing is largely focused on her genealogy, marriages, and pledge of allegiance to the Prophet. But there are surprising ambiguities in the narration of both parts of her life. In the chapter on 'the Prophet's military expeditions', Hind appears as a battlefield fury at Uhud, calling for vengeance for those fallen at Badr, but her mutilation of Hamza's body is not mentioned (Ibn Sa'd 2:33–40). Her desire to get hold of Hamza ibn 'Abd al-Muttalib's liver is related in the chapter on 'the precedence of Companions in meritorious

---

[15]In Ibn Sa'd (2:126), the story appears within the context of the conquest of Mecca, and Hind's name is mentioned among those to be put to death; however, this detail is lacking in her chapter in Ibn Sa'd's book of personal listings of the women of Islam (which is the last volume of his multi-volume work) where, by contrast, the Prophet personally welcomes her into Islam (cf. below).

service to Islam', which prominently features the heroic struggle and death of this Muslim knight, but it is not she but others who desecrate the slain and then bring Hind a piece of Hamza's liver (ibid. 3:7–17, esp. 11). Ibn Sa'd reports that when the Prophet heard that Hind had not been able to swallow even a sliver of Hamza's liver, he replied that God had forbidden that hellfire should ever consume a piece of Hamza, and then he said: 'this is tough on poor Hind' (hadha shadidun 'ala Hind al-maskina) (ibid. 3:11–12); Abbott (275) translates this phrase as 'these are violent attacks on poor Hind'.

The second, Islamic, persona of Hind bint 'Utba fittingly appears in Ibn Sa'd's volume *On the Women* in the segment on the Prophet's female Companions, sahibat, where her marriage to Abu Sufyan, her destruction of the idols in her household, and her pledge of loyalty to the Prophet are narrated (Ibn Sa'd 10:223–6). Hind was descended from the 'Abd Shams clan of the Quraysh, an aristocrat on both her father's and mother's side. She was married once (or perhaps twice), and there were rumors of her marital infidelity (Abbott 269–70). Eventually her father proposed two suitors for her to consider, and he described them to her in the strictly formal language of rhymed prose (saj') (a literary device that imbues the whole scene with an element of impersonality and epic importance). Of the two, Hind rejected Suhayl ibn 'Amr who, though noble, generous, and kind, was weak-willed, and accepted the aristocratic, vainglorious, stubborn, jealous and cynical Aby Sufyan Sakhr ibn Harb ibn Umayya; she explained her choice as befitting the free aristocratic woman and one that would strengthen and improve her own character. It was as his wife that she participated in acts of hostility against Islam. When Muhammad's day of reckoning with the Quraysh finally came, it was a day of mercy. Hind approached the Prophet wearing a face veil, declared her faith, then took off the veil and identified herself to the Prophet by name, to which he replied: 'welcome' (marhaban biki) (Ibn Sa'd 10:225). Then she joined in the women's pledge of allegiance. This event is analyzed in a separate section below; here it will suffice to say that of all the women pledging loyalty to the Prophet on the day of the conquest of Mecca, only Hind dared to comment on the oath's stipulations in an autocratic, not to say impudent manner, but without incurring any rejoinders on the Prophet's part.

Hind's later life was largely shaped by her son Mu'awiya's rise to power, first as governor of Syria and later, after her lifetime, founder of the

Umayyad dynasty and fifth caliph of Islam. He was hated by both Alids
and Abbasids alike, and is sometimes referred to in the traditions as the
'son of the liver-eater' (Abbott 275). Surely Mu'awiya's and his later
dynasty's unpopularity with the scripturalist experts (who wrote the Hadith
compendia, biographical dictionaries, and similar traditionalist literature)
was in large part responsible for their historical portrait of Hind bint 'Utba,
which in all its facets is the negative mirror image of the Islamic gender
paradigm. During the early years of the caliphate of 'Umar ibn al-Khattab,
Hind and her husband Abu Sufyan fought against the Byzantines at the
battle of Yarmuk, in which the Muslim women as a group fought with
great energy. Hind herself played her leadership role, exhorting the
Muslims to circumcise their uncircumcised adversaries with their swords
(Buhl); her daughter Juwayriyya was wounded. Sometime later, Abu
Sufyan divorced Hind and she took to trading in the land of the Banu Kalb
(in Syria) with capital she had borrowed from the caliph 'Umar. Her sons
Mu'awiya and 'Utba continued to take pride in being the sons of Hind
(Abbott 277–8).

Hind bint 'Utba's portrait may be among the liveliest, most three-
dimensional that the early Islamic biographical literature on female
protagonists has to offer. In the accounts about her, her many *personae*
share in conveying, in a dramatic manner, that a proud woman of Jahili
aristocratic background, no matter how oppositional to the Islamic cause
in the beginning, would eventually be permitted to submit to the new religion and its Prophet and play an active role in its concerns, without
expectations of humility, passivity, invisibility, and the other qualities in
which later pietistic expectations framed women's proper social place. At
the same time we should also recall that historical accounts usually tell
more than a single tale, and that Hind's battlefield atrocities, reputed sexual
exploits, ambiguous domestic role (as the wife who has to 'steal' supplies
from her stingy husband),[16] fearlessly questioning participation in the
women's pledge of allegiance to the Prophet, and military prowess in the
first Islamic war of expansion, add up to a fairly complex package of
messages that span the whole spectrum from censure to embracement. We
would also be mistaken if—beyond the sacrificial dialectic of Jahiliyya
versus Islam—we did not also recognize the mark of the political editor on

[16]Cf. below in the section on *The women's bay'a.*

the whole range of Hind's *personae* in the texts. Her story was first shaped by oral reports that eventually constituted parts of the written historical record. Even its earliest authors, with the exception of Ibn Ishaq (d. 767), were men who worked in the Abbasid period and within its political and sectarian system. The political and ideological, anti-Umayyad sentiments of a number of them are sure to have influenced the telling of Hind's story by presenting it as a tale of both warning and learning. The 'extreme ferociousness attributed to her, reported in works compiled in the Abbasid age, probably owes much of its bloodiness to 'Abbasid hatred of the Umayyad dynasty, founded by Hind's son' (Ahmed 681; cf. Abbott 278). Most lasting in its condemnation of Hind's vengeful outrage at Uhud, as mentioned above, may be Hassan ibn Thabit's metaphoric statement that likens her improper vengeance to fornication, and describes her person as bearing the marks of sexual pollution and defilement (Watt and McDonald 7:130–1).

Women in the Ridda Wars:
the triple taboo of women, rebellion, and sex

Hind bint 'Utba was a freeborn woman, member of the Meccan urban aristocracy, whose participation in the political events of her day was marked both by individual verve and drama, and by the social traditionalism that derived from her role as wife of her aristocratic husband, whose activities—first against the Prophet and later in the service of Islam— paralleled her own. The literature also presents information on several nomadic, tribal women from various parts of the Arabian Peninsula who engaged in political activities against the new Islamic state and sometimes did so in the capacity of military leader in their own right. One of these examples even features a matriarchal duo of battlefield leadership in the persons of Umm Qirfa Fatima bint Rabi'a ibn Fulan ibn Badr, widow of Malik ibn Hudhayfa ibn Badr, and her daughter Umm Ziml Salma (or Jariya) bint Malik ibn Hudhayfa ibn Badr. In a military skirmish that was part of hostilities between the Banu Ghatafan/Banu Fazara and the troops and agents of the Prophet, Umm Qirfa led her party, including her numerous sons and grandsons, against Muslim troops commanded by the Prophet's (formerly) adopted son Zayd ibn Haritha. Both she and her daughter were taken captive and Umm Qirfa was cruelly executed. The daughter was given to the Prophet who gave her to Hazn ibn Abi Wahb; thereafter she was given to the Prophet's wife 'A'isha for a while, and she then returned to her tribe, and apostacized. After the Prophet's death, in a later military encounter in the Najd area against the Muslim general Khalid ibn al-Walid, Salma bint Malik, now a renegade allied with the supporters of the false prophet Tulayha ibn Khuwaylid of the Asad, fought to avenge her mother's death. Like her mother, she led her men in person, riding on her mother's camel. After heavy fighting, she was killed.[17]

In what follows, two further examples of famous (or infamous) episodes of female militancy against the nascent Islamic state are presented. Both exemplify the considerable space that was available for women's political activism in Arabia at the time. In both cases, all of the narrators and reporters of the events are Muslim and unanimous in their condemnation of the events; furthermore, they opt for similar metaphoric language—the language of taboo sexuality—to denigrate the historical actors and condemn their motivation.

Sajah bint al-Harith ibn Suwayd

One of the most significant and least analyzed aspects of the *Ridda*, or 'apostacy,' which occurred in the last years of Muhammad's life and in the caliphate of Abu Bakr (632–634) is the fact that the most adamant opposition to the incipient religious-economic-political system of Islam in all regions of Arabia except al-Bahrayn and 'Uman was directed by the so-called 'false prophets,' four of whom are known by name: al-Aswad (Yemen), Tulayha b. Khuwaylid (B. Asad), Sajah (B. Tamim), and Musaylima b. Habib (al-Yamama). (Eickelman 17)

Sajah's father was of the Banu Tamim, but her mother came from the largely Christianized tribe of Banu Taghlib, a tribe of the Rabi'a group, living between eastern Arabia northward into southern Iraq and the Euphrates fringes. Sajah may have stayed with the Banu Taghlib for some time and was perhaps a Christian, or at least quite knowledgeable about Christianity (Abbott 281–2; Eickelman 40). According to the historian al-Tabari, she declared herself a 'prophetess' after the Prophet Muhammad's

[17]Abbott 279–80; Guillaume 665; Donner, *Tabari* 77–9. Part of the story is also in Ibn Sa'd 2:86–7.

death,[18] while the historian al-Baladhuri asserts that she began her career as a *kahina* (*takahhanat*, 'she claimed to be a *kahina*') (al-Baladhuri 108–9). Whether it was in the capacity of *kahina* or another public role, Sajah must already have achieved some sort of leadership position before the Prophet's death, because otherwise she would not have found sufficient tribal support for her expansionist activities (Abbott 282–4). Sajah burst upon the scene when she attacked the Banu Tamim, recently converted to Islam, whose various clans were divided over the issue of whether to continue sending their *sadaqa* (voluntary taxes) to Medina, where the Prophet had just died and been succeeded by the first caliph, Abu Bakr. Sajah came upon them by surprise with an army that consisted of Banu Taghlib and other splinter groups of the Rabi'a confederation. Sajah's forces began by attacking the Banu Ribab, in obedience to one of her revelations that she claimed to have received in rhymed prose form (*saj'*) 'from the lord of the clouds—who commands you to attack the Ribab' (*'inna rabb al-sihab ya'murukum 'an taghzu al-ribab*) (al-Baladhuri 108). Several divisions of the Tamim apostacized and followed her; this division led to civil war among them, and Sajah lost two minor battles, after which she was forced to make peace on condition that she leave the Tamim territory (Abbott 282–4).

Then Sajah and her army headed for Yamama, core territory of the 'false prophet' Musaylima the Liar of the Banu Hanifa. The Banu Hanifa were part of a larger tribal group, Banu Bakr ibn Wa'il (later known as Rabi'a), that hailed from South Arabia but by AD 503 had become the leading tribal confederation in the central Arabian Kinda empire. Their center was in al-Yamama, where they adopted al-Hajr (near present-day Riyadh) as their core city. The Banu Hanifa among them were primarily a settled group engaged in agriculture; the oases in the area under their control were important agricultural centers, especially for the production of wheat, and al-Hajr was a prominent regional center of commerce and trade, as three caravan routes converged there. The area was also, in some modest ways, culturally and politically linked to the Iran of the Sassanians (Eickelman 28–32). The Banu Hanifa are said to have been one of the most powerful tribes of the Arabian Peninsula on the eve of Islam; their power was also demonstrated by the extremely bitter resistance they offered the Muslims

---

[18]Sajah's story is found in Tabari 10:84–97; Caetani 2/1:628–50; Watt 139–41.

during the Ridda Wars (Donner, 'Tribes and Politics' 19). Data on the
Ridda Wars have been read to mean that Musaylima the false prophet was
active in al-Yamama between 630 and 634, that is, during the last two
years of Muhammad's life and the years of the caliphate of Abu Bakr
(Eickelman 23). He had therefore been well established there when Sajah
arrived upon the scene, but was just at that moment menaced by attacks of
the Muslim army and the insubordination of neighboring tribes who threatened to shake off his authority. Musaylima decided to work out a peaceful
arrangement with Sajah, who is said to have accepted his superior claim to
prophecy and agreed to become his wife; else, they recognized each other's
mission and decided to unify their interests (Gibb and Kramers 485). For
Sajah's dower, Musaylima is said to have offered her and her people
'release' from the last evening prayer and the first prayer of dawn, thereby
reducing the number of required daily prayers to three (Watt and McDonald
10:95–6). This account of Musaylima's offer is curious; was his rebellion,
perhaps, not 'apostasy' as we understand it today? The classical sources
do not quite know what to make of it either; Ibn Ishaq mentions the episode
but is not sure of its veracity, saying that

> He (Musaylima) permitted them to drink wine and fornicate and let
> them dispense with prayer, yet he was acknowledging the apostle as a
> prophet, and Hanifa agreed with him on that. But God knows what the
> truth was. (Guillaume 636–7)

Some accounts mention a treaty between Sajah and Musaylima according
to which she was to withdraw her army in return for a year's revenue of
al-Yamama, half to be paid immediately and the other half to be turned over
later to three of her generals (all of them male), whom she left behind to
receive it. (There were no female generals in her army.) Sajah accepted the
terms and went home, not to the Tamim territory from which she had
recently been ousted, but to the area of the Banu Taghlib in Iraq. The second
installment of Musaylima's payment was never received because he was
defeated and killed at the battle of Aqraba in 634. In time Sajah is said to
have returned to the Tamim. She became a Muslim and settled in Basra, to
where Mu'awiya had transferred most of her tribe at the beginning of his
caliphate. There she died a Muslim and was buried with the proper Islamic
prayers and ceremonies (Gibb and Kramers 486; Abbott 283–4).

Next to nothing is known of Sajah's teachings or the import of her
so-called revelations and doctrines. She is said to have delivered her
messages in rhymed prose form from a *minbar* and employed a *mu'adhdhin*
(caller to prayer) and *hajib* (chamberlain) (Gibb and Kramers 485). One of
the names for God that she is said to have used is 'lord of the clouds'. Her
own career was cut short by the Muslim advances in northeastern Arabia.
Her story survives mainly as part of the accounts on the infamous false
prophet Musaylima; but in the literature, her relationship with this enemy
of God is reduced to a defiling and depraved sexuality. It is as if the reports
did indeed set out to blur what may have been considered a sacrilegious
message and defuse it by systematic ridicule. The historian al-Tabari
describes the encounter between Musaylima and Sajah in grossly obscene
language, where most verbal exchanges are reduced to a series of sexually
explicit pieces of rhymed prose (Watt and McDonald 10:94–5) that meta-
phorically serve as value judgment on the atrocity of the couple's claims.

It is this metaphoric association of Sajah with orgiastic sex that has
garnered her a place in al-Nafzawi's *Manual of Arabian Erotology* (trans.
Burton 20–6; trans. Colville 7–10), whose (otherwise obscure) author is
believed to have lived in Tunisia in the sixteenth century. By contrast, a
secularist, nationalist reading of Sajah's literary persona is presented in an
anonymous posting on the Internet from 'Mesopotamia-Damascus' entitled 'Sajah the woman from Mosul—upon whom the historians have
committed an outrage . . . as an Iraqi and as a woman!!'[19], in which the
author(s) decry that the historical records merely identify Sajah as from
Tamim, or Taghlib, or as a Christian, but not as an Iraqi, and indeed, that
they fail to clarify that her historical roots were in and around the city of
Mosul, as were those of her fellow rebels who fought with her in order to
obtain autonomy. In condensed form, the main arguments of this
'Mesopotamian' statement on Sajah are as follows:

The fact that Sajah was female was an additional factor in her denigra-
tion in the literature. Nobody can tell whether she announced her
prophethood out of sincere spiritual conviction, or with the aim to
exploit the strained political situation of the nascent Islamic state for her

---

[19]*Sajah al-mawsiliyya/ \allati zalamaha al-mu'arrikhuna/ \ka-'iraqiyya wa-ka'imra'a*,
<http://www.mesopotamia4374.com/adad2/sajah.htm> (11 pages, accessed 2009). Many
thanks to Ramadan al-Khouli for sending me this document.

own political purposes. Musaylima, who also claimed prophethood, heard about her army of 40,000 men (*sic*!) and was afraid of her competition. So he opted for peace and alliance, as did she. The greatest defamation of this woman is found in the sneering descriptions of her meeting with Musaylima and their conversation replete with moral depravity and licentiousness.

This (surely Iraqi secularist, nationalist) text, then, questions the veracity of the sexual motifs in the historical accounts on Sajah. It asserts that her many tribal followers were largely driven by opposition to the economic and political demands of the Medinan caliphate, not by motives of apostacy or pagan obstinacy. 'Surely their tribal leaders did not rally to this woman in order to send her forth as lover, or wife-without-dower, in a perfumed night, into the arms of Musaylima. This story merits nothing but a laugh.'

The 'harlots' of Hadramawt

Our second example of women's anti-Islamic activism in politics during the Ridda Wars differs from Sajah's tale in that the protagonists were renegades; a group of two dozen or more women in the Hadramawt, who had accepted Islam during the Prophet's lifetime, publicly rejoiced at the news of the Prophet's death and were ordered severely punished by the first Medinan caliph, Abu Bakr. Yet we could argue that there is a cognitive connector between these (and other) tales of anti-Islamic female rebellion that prompts their Muslim chroniclers to opt for the symbolic language of 'taboos' in their condemnatory writing: enemy women in politics are taboo, as are women's sexual exploits; therefore, women's activities in the former are expressed in metaphors and symbols relating to the latter.

The male protagonists in the story about the harlots are Abu Bakr, caliph of Islam, and al-Muhajir ibn Umayya of the Makhzum clan of the Quraysh (full brother of the Prophet's wife Umm Salama), who had fought in the wars of conquest in Yemen and Hadramawt; Muhammad had appointed him governor of the Kinda territories in Hadramawt (an office he never held), after which he opted to become governor of Yemen under Abu Bakr (Watt and McDonald 10: 20, 53, 105, 153, 165, 173–7, 182, 184–7). In al-Tabari, the events of 'a women's rebellion' (ibid. 10:191–2) (if this is what it was) appear in much foreshortened form: the derogatory label 'harlots' is not applied, and the disturbance is only reported to have involved 'two singing women'. After hearing of Muhammad's death, one of these singing women had sung satirical verses in which she reviled the Prophet. Al-Muhajir cut off her hand and pulled out her front tooth—a punishment which Abu Bakr, in writing, disclaimed as too light (unless she were a Christian), since he himself would have ordered her dead. The wording of Abu Bakr's missive to al-Muhajir here betrays the influence of second- and third-century AH classical Islamic jurisprudence on the difference between legal retribution and illegal mutilation (ibid. 10:192, n. 1166). Furthermore, we never learn what happened to the second singing woman, and why.

A longer and presumably more complete version of the (same?) story is found in the *Kitab al-Muhabbar* by Ibn Habib. This book is very rare, so this writer (like many others) has been forced to derive the data from secondary literature, especially A.F.L. Beeston's 'The So-Called Harlots of Hadramawt'.[20] Ibn Habib (d. 860) was a historian who preceded al-Tabari (d. 923) by almost two generations. Unlike al-Tabari, who in his *History of the Prophets and Kings* meant to establish and verify a Sunni, religious, consensus-based, traditionalist reading of the past, Ibn Habib's approach to history writing appears to have followed the tastes and concomitant methodologies of medieval Islamic humanism, usually referred to as *adab*; the latter, also represented by historians such as al-Mas'udi (d. 956), 'going far beyond Tabari's somewhat timid view of history as accuracy of transmission', combined a universality of historical interest with the love of quotable tidbits of information (Khalidi 63–6). Patricia Crone, decrying the loss of a grand, overall, Islamic (religious or tribal) historical narrative to heaps of 'atomized' (and ultimately irrelevant) historical detail—'the debris of an obliterated past'—has little use for Ibn Habib's *Kitab al-Muhabbar*, 'which must rank with the *Guinness Book of Records* among the greatest compilations of useless information' (Crone 10). In a footnote (ibid. n. 53) to this condemning verdict she adds that 'in it the interested reader will find the answer to questions such as who wore turbans in Mecca to hide their beauty from women . . . , who was the father-in-law of four caliphs . . . , what woman could count ten

[20]Critique of this text, and additional information, is found in Lecker.

caliphs within their forbidden degrees . . . , who had Christian or Ethiopian mothers . . . , what *ashraf* lost an eye in battle, were crucified or had their heads put on a stake.'

On 'peripheral' women's issues, however, it is sometimes the eclectic and anecdotal sources that contain information that the mainstream historians omit. So it is with Ibn Habib and his account of the 'harlots of Hadramawt' (as summarized in Beeston 16–19). There were in Hadramawt six women of the Kinda and Hadramawt tribes who had longed for the death of the Prophet and, when it happened, dyed their hands with henna and played the tambourine in joyful celebration. They were joined by twenty-odd harlots of Hadramawt, who belonged to various villages in Hadramawt: three were of the noble class (*ashraf*), four belonged to the royal tribe of Kinda, and one was a Jewess; furthermore, one was a mother, two were grandmothers, and seven were young girls. Two local notables (who had refrained from joining the rebels) informed the caliph in Medina about the harlots' rejoicing. When Abu Bakr then wrote to the governor, al-Muhajir ibn Umayya, he ordered him to march on the women with his horses and infantry and cut off their hands. Fighting was to take place only if they met with resistance and negotiations proved futile. The Kindites and Hadramis insisted on fighting al-Muhajir, before most of them withdrew and he defeated the rest. Then he captured the women and cut off their hands; the women's partisans were killed, and some of the women emigrated to Kufa.

Assuming that the event occurred as reported, the question arises as to what kind of harlotry was practiced by elderly grandmothers, young girls, members of the nobility and the royal tribe?—or, specifically, why the clapping of tambourines by two dozen women or so in some faraway hamlets of South Arabia was so threatening to the new Muslim order that it commanded its military to intervene? Beeston explains the clash between the women and Islam as the clash between the old religion and the new. He opines that the area (from which the women hailed) had been the center of a pagan cult, and he reads the 'harlot' episode as an act of rebellion by pagan priestesses of the old temples who, in singing and dancing, were attempting to incite their tribesmen to throw off the new religion; they evidently succeeded in gathering support formidable enough for a force to be sent against them. According to Beeston (21–2), the term 'harlot', applied to these largely high-born women, 'could of course be interpreted simply as an opprobrious epithet employed by their political antagonists among the Muslims', but he suspects that the sexual reference may carry echoes of temple prostitution, if indeed the old South Arabian religion paralleled Babylonian practice in this respect.

By contrast, Fatima Mernissi reads the harlots episode as an event of real sexual significance which she places into the process of an early Islamic transition from an Arabian matrilineal to a patrilineal kinship system. Some women of Hadramawt, she asserts,

> opposed Islam because it jeopardized their position. Whatever that posi-
> tion was, it was evidently more advantageous than the one Islam granted
> them. Second, the opposition between these women and Islam was
> clearly in the sexual field. The fact that the caliph labeled his opponents
> as harlots implies that Islam condemned their sexual practices, whatever
> they were, as harlotry. I believe that the Harlots of Hadramawt incident
> is an example of Islam's opposition to the sexual practices existing in
> pre-Islamic Arabia. (Mernissi 33)

To Mernissi, then, at issue was the confrontation of a new, Islamic patri-lineal marriage system with an older, pagan Arabian matrilinear one, where matriliny was characterized by women's sexual autonomy, their sovereignty over the marital household (the tent), and the absence of the concept of male-derived legitimacy.[21]

In yet another reading, Michael Lecker offers ample new details on the women's tribal connections, and their tribes' recent struggles against Medina, on the basis of information gleaned from the genealogies of the Kinda. He opines that the place names where the women were dispersed probably make up 'the map of the Ridda in Hadramawt'; hence he places the 'harlots' report into the context of the Ridda of the Kinda as a whole. The story of untimely rejoicing by women of ill repute and their severe punishment

> probably turns the facts upside down. The amputation of the women's
> hands was an *outcome* of Kinda's total defeat, not a predetermined

---

[21]This notion of a fundamental break in Arab social institutions at the beginning of Islam was first proposed in 1885 by W. Robertson Smith, largely accepted by Watt (388), but rejected by Spencer, and others (cf. Eickelman 22).

target of war. The report plays down and completely trivializes the terrible bloodshed of the *ridda* by bringing the women to the fore and suppressing the role of men. This trivialization (a form of historical apologetics) is the manner in which the tribal or local tradition handles the grievous events of the *ridda*. (Lecker 649)

For our present purposes, the episode on the rebellion and punishment of the 'harlots' of Hadramawt is a prime example of the textual relationship between women's reprehensible political activities and their condemnation by way of sexual defamation. There is no textual or other evidence for or against a connection between these women and the existence and activities of pre-Islamic pagan priestesses. Such connections may of course have existed. Nor is there evidence, for or against, that the women were opposing some tighter gender laws that may have been propagated by the new Islamic authorities in Yemen. (Given the timeframe of the episode right after the Prophet's death, however, this reading is less likely.) To this writer, the sexual 'taboo' in slandering the women's very persons and activities as an expression of hostility against their tribes (in whose rebellion they participated) is the more convincing explanation of the incident.

The women soldiers of early Islam

In 1979, Shaykh Yusuf al-Qaradawi published a small monograph, *Nisa' mu'minat* (Believing Women) that tells the stories of five remarkable women who lived during the Prophet's lifetime. Clearly the issue of gender equality as part of the blueprint of (authentic) Islam was on al-Qaradawi's mind when he wrote this booklet, which describes an era when women were full participants in the Islamic community's spiritual, social, political, and even military activities. Among the five women he chose to include in his primer of female role models at the dawn of Islam, one was the Prophet's wife, Khadija, another their daughter, Fatima, and two were Muslim soldiers whose renown was based on their participation in the Prophet's wars and military expeditions: Umm Salim al-Rumaysa' and Umm 'Umara Nusayba bint Ka'b. Both of these women figure prominently in the biographical literature, such as al-Waqidi's (d. 823) *Kitab al-maghazi* and Ibn Sa'd's (d. 845) *Tabaqat*, as do many others: such as Umm Ayman, Amna bint Jahsh, Safiyya bint al-Muttalib, Umayya bint

Qays, Umm Sinan al-Aslamiyya, Ku'ayba bint Sa'd al-Aslamiyya, and
Umm Kabsha (Teipen 449–52; Afsaruddin 462–6). By their sheer number
and well-recorded political and military activism, these women were
important contributors to the successful rise of Islam as a 'new' community; they watered and nursed the wounded, fought on the battlefield,
inspired the male troops to fight, and eulogized the slain. The women's
struggle, while following the patterns of the past, no longer served to fulfill
the demands of tribal loyalty, but was carried out in service to God and His
Prophet.

Traditional narrative presentation of history is always also interpretation of those facts. It is therefore of interest to investigate how this public
role of Muslim women is dealt with in different genres of early Islamic
writing. In a comparative analysis of women's public activisim depicted in
the early Islamic biographical handbooks (al-Waqidi, Ibn Sa'd) as opposed
to the Sira (Ibn Ishaq, Ibn Hisham) (Teipen 437–59), Alfons Teipen has
shown that, while women warriors are prominently featured in the former
literature (which focuses on individual achievements), their role as
warriors is severely downplayed in the latter. Teipen concludes that the
reason for this discrepancy derives from the basic literary functions of the
Sira, an 'edifying' literature whose focus is on the genesis of the early
Islamic *umma*. *Qua* kerygmatic text, it also comes with a new gender
dichotomy of public versus private, where female public activities on the
battlefield and in mourning, lamentation, and eulogizing are constructed
as violations of female modesty (ibid. 443–53).

While Teipen's analysis focuses synchronically on textual differences
between ideologically divergent early Islamic sources, Asma Afsaruddin
(461–80) has looked diachronically at a specific group of early Islamic
activist women and how they have fared in a series of consecutive readings within the same literary genre, but that span several centuries. Her
main sources are the *Tabaqat* of Ibn Sa'd (d. 845), written during the
Abbasid period, and *Al-isaba fi tamyiz al-sahaba* by Ibn Hajar al-Asqalani
(d. 1449), written during the Mamluk era; both of these works belong to
the biographical dictionary genre.

In the ninth-century biographical literature, we prominently encounter
Umm 'Umara Nusayba bint Ka'b, whose exploits for the sake of Islam are
celebrated by Shaykh Yusuf al-Qaradawi in his primer for Muslim women,
mentioned above. She was among the group of seventy-three men and two

women who first pledged allegiance to the Prophet at Aqaba[22] and also was present at Uhud, al-Hudaybiya, Khaybar, Hunayn, and (after Muhammad's death) al-Yamama. At Uhud she fought in the company of her husband and two sons, and perhaps also her mother. She sustained twelve wounds in her body, which included a deep gash on her shoulder. Initially she had gone to the battlefield to nurse the wounded but was drawn into the thick of the fight when the battle had turned against the Muslims and she rallied to defend the Prophet's life and person with her spear and sword (Ibn Sa'd, ed. Brockelmann 8:301–4; Afsaruddin 465–6). It is probably symptomatic that, while her military prowess at Uhud is celebrated in the biographical literature, Ibn Ishaq in his Sira does not mention her as a participant at Uhud, and it is only in Ibn Hisham's Notes on Ibn Ishaq's Sira that her name appears in relation to this battle (Guillaume 755).[23] Umm Ayman, the Prophet's nurse and freedwoman, later married to his freedman and 'adopted son' Zayd ibn Haritha, was also present at the battles of Uhud, Khaybar, and Hunayn to fetch water, nurse the wounded, and lend psychological support to the troops. Many others appear in the context of the raid on Khaybar (Ibn Sa'd, ed. Brockelmann 8:162–3; Afsaruddin 462–3). A group of women from the Banu Ghaffar, among them Umayya bint Qays (who was a young girl at the time), requested the Prophet's permission to join him in the raid 'to tend the wounded and help the Muslims to the best of their ability', and the Prophet replied 'with the blessing of God'. Due to her participation in the battle, Umayya bint Qays was awarded a share of the booty—a necklace that the Prophet placed around her neck with his own hands (Ibn Sa'd, ed. Brockelmann 8:214; Afsaruddin 464). Umm Sinan al-Aslamiyya requested permission to go to Khaybar in order to 'offer water and tend to the sick and wounded', and the Prophet replied 'go with the blessing of God' (Ibn Sa'd, ed. Brockelmann 8:214; Afsaruddin 464). She stayed in the company of the Prophet's wife, Umm Salama, who was also at Khaybar.[24]

Two curious Hadith narratives concern Umm Kabsha, whom Ibn Sa'd merely identifies as 'a woman from the Quda'a', and Umm Waraqa bint

[22]Cf. the section on *The women's bay'a*, below.

[23]Ibn Ishaq does, however, indicate that Umm 'Umara bint Nusayba and her sister 'went with the apostle' and that she also fought and was wounded twelve times at the battle of al-Yamama against Musaylima (Guillaume 212).

[24]The Prophet's wives drew lots to determine which two from among them would accompany him on his expeditions and campaigns (cf. Stowasser 108).

'Abdallah ibn Harith, usually referred to as Umm Waraqa bint Nawfal. In both cases, the woman requests permission from the Prophet to join him in battle, but he refuses. When this (semi-anonymous) Umm Kabsha asked to attend to the wounded (during a battle that the text also does not identify), the Prophet instructed her to stay behind, 'so that people will not say that Muhammad fights alongside women' (Ibn Sa'd, ed. Brockelmann 8: 225; Afsaruddin 464). Umm Waraqa, on the other hand, is a woman of known ancestry. She is depicted as a woman of Qur'anic learning whom the Prophet commissioned to lead her household in prayer and permitted to employ a private *mu'adhdhin*; he also conferred upon her the honorary epithet of *al-shahida* (the martyred woman). When she requested his permission to attend to the wounded at the Battle of Badr with the words that 'perhaps God will grant me martyrdom', the Prophet denied her request but said that God would, indeed, grant her martyrdom. Eventually she was murdered during 'Umar's caliphate by a male and a female slave of her own household whom she had contracted for manumission after her death; the two murderers fled but were apprehended and crucified under 'Umar (Ibn Sa'd, ed. Brockelmann 8: 335; Afsaruddin 466).

A comparison between Ibn Sa'd's ninth-century information on these women and their entries in the fifteenth-century biographical dictionary of Ibn Hajar al-Asqalani exemplifies 'how societal conceptions of women's agency and proper conduct in the public realm came to be progressively defined and restricted in the late medieval Muslim world, and how these conceptions came to be retrojected onto the lives of the earliest Muslim women' (Afsaruddin 468). One of the established techniques in changing an individual's or a group's historical record, or image, is to omit the information altogether. Thus, in Ibn Hajar's work the military activism of the female Companions is seldom mentioned, and other activities—such as their early pledge of allegiance—are downplayed to a more passive mode. Else, old Hadiths that counter the sensibilities of a later age are reinterpreted to prove the religious rightmindedness of the (re)interpreting authority. This process of editorializing older traditions advanced dramatically during the six centuries separating Ibn Sa'd and Ibn Hajar. To prove this point, Afsaruddin employs the two Hadith clusters on Umm Kabsha and Umm Waraqa, cited above. In Ibn Sa'd, Umm Kabsha (identified only by her tribal affiliation) is refused permission to participate in (an unidentified) battle with the Prophet, 'so that people will not say that Muhammad fights alongside women'; in Ibn Hajar al-Asqalani this episode serves as categorical injunction against women's participation in battle, in whatever capacity, which abrogates all former Prophetic permits for women to do so.[25] And the story of Umm Waraqa, who asked the Prophet's permission to take part in the Battle of Badr in the hope of martyrdom, is altered in Ibn Hajar to read that the Prophet instructed her to 'remain in her house', for God would grant her martyrdom *in her house* (Ibn Hajar 304–5). Afsaruddin clarifies that this addition to the earlier version of the story introduces the element of women's domesticity: women can, indeed, be martyred, but this does not and should not occur on the battlefield (Afsaruddin 472–3, 477). These and similar uses of biographical information on the Prophet's female Companions extend the sexual segregation patterns of later medieval Islamic societies backward into the first generation, a technique that both helps to make sense of the early customs and acts as a legitimizing device for the later age.

Muslim women in early communal politics: the women's *bay'a*

The Qur'anic concept of membership in God's community presupposes the active involvement in communal life of both men and women, 'friends/ guardians of each other' (Qur'an 9:71). To the first generation of Muslims, this membership was obtainable on condition that they swore allegiance to the Prophet in an oath outlining the sins and crimes that defined the 'limits' (*hudud*) of God's law (and thus also the limits of the status of believer). The text of the women's pledge of fealty (*bay'a*) was revealed in Qur'an 60:12. The Sira tells us that males and females swore fealty using the same text, that is, on the same conditions, until the pledge to fight (*jihad*) was later added to the men's oath; and even then, some women were included among the men on several occasions.

Sura 60 of the Qur'an is entitled *Al-Mumtahana* (She who is examined). The Sura has three interrelated themes: severing of relations with the polytheists in Mecca, legal and financial stipulations for cases where the severing of ties involves spouses, and the pledge of allegiance to the Prophet. The oath (in Qur'an 60:12) is worded as follows:

[25]'Or else this becomes a *sunna*' (Ibn Hajar 270–1; Afsaruddin 470–2).

Oh Messenger! When believing women come to you to take the oath of allegiance to you, that they will not ascribe partners to God, that they will not steal, that they will not commit acts of fornication, that they will not kill their children, that they will not utter slander which they have devised between their hands and their feet, that they will not disobey you in what is right (*fi ma'rufin*), then accept their allegiance, and pray to God to forgive them, for God is forgiving, merciful.

The text thus enshrines the conditions of *umma* membership in terms of sins/crimes foresworn that are applicable to all believers regardless of gender: polytheism, theft, fornication, infanticide, slander, and disobedience to the Prophet. Four, or five, of these transgressions were later reckoned among the six, or seven, crimes which the jurists classified as *hudud* offenses (canon law cases with unalterable punishments).[26] Their punishments are decreed in the Qur'an, and are the same for men as for women.[27]

There is nothing gender-specific about the text of the women's *bay'a* in Qur'an 60:12. According to Ibn Ishaq's Sira, men initially pledged their allegiance to the Prophet under the same terms. Of the first pledge at al-Aqaba (that preceded the Prophet's *hijra* to Medina), for instance, a (male) participant reported that

there were twelve of us and we pledged ourselves to the prophet after the manner of women and that was before war was enjoined, the undertaking being that we should associate nothing with God; we should not steal; we should not commit fornication; nor kill our offspring; we should not slander our neighbours; we should not disobey him in what was right; if we fulfilled this paradise would be ours; if we committed any of those sins it was for God to punish or forgive as He pleased. (Guillaume 199)

[26]I.e., canon law cases with unalterable punishments that are 'defined' in the Qur'an as the 'boundaries' or 'limits' (*hudud*) of God's prescriptions. They are: apostasy, theft, fornication, slanderous allegation of unchastity (of a woman), wine-drinking, and armed robbery; the seventh offense, not always included, is rebellion. In Islamic social and legal literature, the term *hudud* signifies the bounds of acceptable behavior.

[27]E.g., theft (Qur'an 5:41–2); fornication (Qur'an 24:2); slander (Qur'an 24:4); infanticide (Qur'an 17:31).

The second pledge at Aqaba contained conditions involving war that were not in the first act of fealty; it was sworn by seventy-three men and two women. One of the women was Umm Umara Nusayba bint Ka'b of the Banu Mazin ibn Najjar; 'she and her sister went to war with the apostle.' The other was Umm Mani' Asma bint 'Amr of the Banu Salama (ibid. 203, 212). The text of the women's *bay'a* was revealed in the time period after the Truce of al-Hudaybiya (AD 628) (some terms of which were superceded and altered by Sura 60) and before the conquest of Mecca (AD 630). After the Prophet had conquered Mecca, he made men and women pledge separately; according to Ibn Ishaq, the men 'paid homage to the apostle promising to hear and obey God and His apostle to the best of their ability', while the women swore fealty using the text of Qur'an 60:12 (ibid. 553–4).

It is said that Hind bint 'Utba was the leader and spokeswoman for the Meccan women as they took the oath of allegiance to Islam. There is a certain air of historic authenticity about this event of her pledge; it conveys a sense of her pride, and also of the weightiness of the oath at hand. The Prophet speaks and Hind responds: 'You shall have but one God.' 'We grant you that.' 'You shall not steal.' 'Abu Sufyan is a stingy man; I only stole provisions from him.' 'That is not theft. You shall not fornicate.' 'Does a free woman fornicate?' (possibly a reference to the looser marriage laws of the *Jahiliyya*, in which no union into which a free woman chose to enter could be termed *zina*, fornication). 'You shall not kill your children' (a reference to infanticide). 'Have you left us any children that you did not kill at the battle of Badr?' 'You shall not slander.' 'Slander is indeed abominable.' 'Do not disobey me in anything that is right.' 'Had we intended to disobey you, we would not be here now' (Ibn Sa'd, ed. Brockelmann 8:4; Guillaume 553; Abbott 276–7; Ahmed 670, 686).

Hadith collections such as the *Tabaqat* of Ibn Sa'd contain large numbers of traditions that identify by name the Muslim women who pledged allegiance to the Prophet. According to Ibn Sa'd, 129 were migrants from Mecca (seventy of Quraysh and their confederates [Ibn Sa'd, ed. Brockelmann 8:161–202] and fifty-nine 'Arab women' not related to Quraysh by blood or clientship [ibid. 8:202–30]), while 349 were Medinan women (sixty-nine of the 'Aus [ibid. 8:230–9, 251–61] and 280 of Khazraj [ibid. 8:261–37]). These women did not take the pledge of allegiance together on a single occasion. As with the men, female conversion and entering-into-Islam was an ongoing process. The large number of women—478—whose pledge of allegiance to the Prophet Ibn Sa'd has recorded may also not all have sworn fealty in the exact words of Qur'an 60:12 because the verse was revealed in the later Medinan period; on the other hand, as indicated above, the terms of the oath are already documented for the first pledge at Aqaba that twelve Medinan men had given to the Prophet while he was still in Mecca. In either case, the oath enshrined the conditions of Islamic citizenship in gender-equal terms as: monotheism; freedom from the transgressions of theft, fornication, infanticide, and slander; and obedience to the Prophet in what is right (*fi ma'rufin*).

The revealed text of the women's *bay'a* does not include a number of features that, in pious opinion in later years, came to weigh heavily in the definition of female righteousness, most important among them being the segregation of the sexes (including women's exclusion from Friday prayers), women's obedience to their husbands, and the cessation of the custom of women's wailing at deaths and funerals and their public recitation of dirges. The Hadith in various ways added these to its accounts of the women's *bay'a*: it was mainly by way of circumstantial riders, and by defining or re-defining the key terms of the pledge of allegiance, that traditionists and exegetes manipulated the meaning of the oath and changed its significance from a gender-neutral into a gender-specific text, embodying such notions as gender segregation and wifely domestic obedience.

Conclusion

The preceding has documented the existence of a long tradition of women as political actors in Arabian culture. The Prophet embraced this tradition, gave it a new purpose, and welcomed women as full participants in the communal politics of Islam's formative phase.

It was consistent with this blueprint that a woman—a member of the highest elite of Medinan females—would decide to play a prominent role in the political and military struggles that would shape the political legacy of her late husband, the Prophet Muhammad: 'A'isha bint Abi Bakr, a major actor in Islam's 'first civil war', the Battle of the Camel, against 'Ali ibn Abi Talib. 'A'isha's story shows that the multiple *personae* of this elite woman in Islamic historiography embody many of the qualities and trends that also mark the historical presentation of other women in politics, both before the rise of Islam and during the years of its political organization and first expansion.[28]

When we attempt to reconstruct history, is it just to excavate some precious remnants of objective data from under the rubble of their subjective transmission, or is it not also to view and employ those precariously excavated data as part of a sacred ancestral legacy that underlies our own identity and cultural authenticity in the here and now? I submit that any effort at reading behind patriarchal history is bound to occur as a two-pronged movement: to gain both an altered (or at least modified) perception of the past, and also a changed understanding of what is authentic in our collective cultural identity.

[28]Cf. the masterly analysis of these issues by Denise A. Spellberg (esp. 1–149).

4. *Love Discourse in Hijazi Society under the Umayyads: A Study in Class and Gender*

AMIRA EL-ZEIN

This research interprets what it terms 'love discourse' in the Hijaz under the Umayyads (661–750 AD). 'Love discourse' refers to a wide range of literature dealing with the theme of love, such as poetry, especially 'Umar ibn Abi Rabi'a's poetry (d. 712), in addition to narratives, anecdotes, stories, and comments that were set down there at that time.

For the Hijazis, love poetry and singing were a communal way of life, almost a necessity of existence. The whole Hijazi population celebrated love and women, and rejoiced in the art of singing. Love was both an individual affair and a collective celebration. Love poetry was recited and sung by the whole society: in their houses, in the streets, and the public gardens. The Egyptian critic, 'Abbas Mahmud al-'Aqqad (d. 1964) described the spread of *ghazal* (love poetry) in Mecca and Medina in these terms: 'It was maybe even a kind of shortcoming for a man to shrink from *ghazal*. No learned man, no *faqih* we know of, did not recite *ghazal* and listen to it' (al-'Aqqad 16).

Love discourse is fascinating not only because it is the lyrical manifestation of souls in ecstasy celebrating the eternal attraction between men and women and the register of their mental and emotional states,[1] but also

---

[1]The lexicographer Ibn Manzur defines *ghazal* as 'a conversation between young men and young women'. He also adds the definition of another lexicographer, Ibn Sidah: 'Ghazal is to take pleasure with women' (14: 4). A contemporary author defines *ghazal* as: 'talking to

because it uncovers how society controls, inhibits, or encourages communication between the genders, thus establishing its own code of behavior that distinguishes it from other societies. It is an especially precious tool for unveiling women's status within society, and a seminal cultural production that sheds light on the level of luxury, opulence, extravagance, and refinement that a particular society has attained. In the context of this study, it is mostly a mirror that reflects class attitudes in Mecca and Medina in the period under discussion.

Although several factors contributed to this unprecedented and unparalleled explosion of love discourse throughout Hijazi society, the focus here will be mainly on the role that the elite class in Mecca and Medina played in producing, disseminating, and determining the shape of this love discourse and how it affected the status of women. By 'elite class' is meant here the class of wealthy, powerful Arabs in these two cities, especially the tribe of Quraysh. This study will attempt to unveil the relation that was created between class, gender, and power under the Umayyads in the Hijaz. This aspect of love discourse is often overlooked by scholars, whether they work in Arabic or Western languages. Critics generally focus more on the innovative aspect of this love discourse, or on its influence on other literatures, rather than on how it depicts class issues in their relation to gender.

Social class is crucial for unveiling the complexities of love discourse, although it is still not given enough attention, as Tillie Olsen (146) maintains: 'Class remains the greatest unexamined factor.' Class is more than a matter of the amount of wealth one possesses. It determines the way one perceives things. It is culture, behavior, attitudes, values, and language. Class can also be distinguished by a combination of social attitudes and manners. In this sense, class differences affected the way in which Hijazi poets perceived women. With regard to love poetry in the Hijaz under the Umayyads, class was undoubtedly a crucial factor.

women and being kind to them' (Abu Rihab 7). The same author adds this seminal striking remark: 'if the man talks and the woman listens to his talk, and there is a dialogue between them, then there is *ghazal* (ibid. 12). This testifies once more to the importance of love discourse, especially poetry, as a bridge between the genders.

The context

An isolated and apolitical Hijaz

During the rule of the Orthodox Caliphs (632–661) and before the Umayyads established their dynasty in Damascus, the Hijaz was rightly considered the center of Islamic government and the heart of the new religion, since it was the place that witnessed the birth of Islam. Hijazis were very proud of this fact, and when the Umayyads took the power and moved the seat of the caliphate from Medina to Damascus, they were outraged, humiliated, and discontented, to say the least. They expressed their dejection through revolutions that were systematically crushed by the Umayyads. 'Abdullah ibn al-Zubayr (d. 692) succeeded, however, in fomenting a rebellion, and established a counter-caliphate in Mecca for seven years. Mu'awiya bin Abi Sufyan (d. 680), founding Caliph of the Umayyad Empire, put an end to 'Abdullah ibn al-Zubayr's rule and killed many of his followers. When Mu'awiya died, his son Yazid (d. 683 CE), took over the caliphate. The people of Medina tried once more to rebel, but they paid a heavy price because Yazid sent Muslim ibn 'Uqba to Medina with 5,000 troops. He killed many, pillaged the city, and compelled people to submit. After that, the Hijaz withdrew from power struggles and turned inward, focusing on interpreting and analyzing the emotions and sentiments of love.[2]

This seclusion had its positive aspect despite the political loss, since it removed the Hijaz from the tribal feuds that were raging in Damascus and Iraq. Poetry in these two provinces of the Umayyad Caliphate continued to invigorate pre-Islamic sectarian politics and ancestral disputes. Poets, such as al-Akhtal al-Taghlibi (d. 710), Jarir (d. 728) and al-Farazdaq (d. 730) recharged the ancestral hostilities and the traditional pre-Islamic style in their verses, while the Hijaz was left to sing of love and enjoy its destiny as a deluxe province. Its poets dedicated their verses to singing the beauty of women, telling their stories and flattering them. Hijazi people learned to prefer love poetry to satire or war poems. We are told, for example, that the 'Udhrite poet Kuthayyir 'Azza (d. 723) composed poems in a satirical vein as well as love poems, but he was known among Hijazis only for his love

---

[2]Hijazis did not produce only love poetry. They excelled in the domain of *fiqh* and other branches of literature too. But *ghazal* was the prevailing literary genre.

poetry. Hijazis were tired of politics and were no longer interested in tribal and sectarian poetry.

A wealthy Hijaz

This isolation was not enough for the Umayyads in Damascus. In order to make Hijazis forget any claim to power, the Umayyads inundated them with money, gold, and silver. Generally speaking, the Umayyads themselves were less concerned with matters of religion than the Orthodox Caliphs who preceded them. They thought that they could enjoy luxury and opulence after the conquests were established (Faysal, esp. 309). They believed that by bestowing wealth, *jawaris* (courtesans), and slaves on the Hijaz, they could separate them from politics and, to some extent, they succeeded.

It is worth mentioning here that, already, under the Orthodox Caliphs, riches were distributed to the Quraysh and the Prophet's wives (see esp. Dayf, *al-Shiʻr*, 25), but these riches were nothing compared with the huge amounts of money that the Umayyads granted to the already wealthy Qurayshis who, little by little, withdrew from political life and turned to a life of pleasure. The Hijaz became a flourishing and prosperous province. Its elite class lived in opulence and luxury. Historical sources speak of hundreds of thousands of dinars, for example, in the possession of ʻAbdullah ibn al-Zubayr, who amassed his wealth from trade (Amin 84–5). Thus the lives of the elite in the Hijaz drastically changed. They now lived in palaces with gardens and canals. Tastes changed. They gradually began imitating the conquered people's ways of eating and dressing, and the way they adorned themselves. Perfumes of all kinds were widespread (ibid. 172).[3] They ate from silver and gold plates and dressed in silk and cotton. Women were decked out with pearls, rubies, silver and gold,[4] and men likewise.

---

[3]Amin refers to a list of the most important perfume shops in Mecca and Medina found in ʻUmar ibn Abi Rabiʻa's poetry (172).

[4]Contrast this luxurious way of dressing with what ʻAʼisha, the wife of the Prophet, said when asked about what she wore when the Prophet was alive: 'By God, it was neither silk, nor cotton or linen. It was made out of camel hair' (ʻAtawi 60). See also the competition between women on the *hajj*. ʻAtawi speaks of hundreds of mules carrying the clothes and jewels that these women took with them (61). He also tells the astonishing story of Sukaynah bint al-Husayn. Once when she was on the *hajj* 'stoning Satan', the seventh pebble fell from her hand, so she took off one of her many rings and threw it instead (ibid.).

Abu al-Faraj al-Isbahani includes many stories in his magnum opus, *Al-Aghani*, about this affluence, which became so habitual with time that it was no longer appreciated. He tells, for example, of Mus'ab ibn Zubayr and his Qurayshi wife, 'A'isha bint Talha. He bought her eighty pearls for 20,000 dinars. She was asleep, so he woke her and scattered the pearls over her. Her reaction was: 'My sleep was dearer to me than these pearls!' ('Abd al-Rahman 81).

*Jawari*s and slaves in the Hijaz

It is true that the Hijaz was cut off from the politics of Damascus, but it was at the same time bustling with people from various parts of the world. The Umayyads provided Hijazis with numerous slaves and courtesans, both men and women, brought from their many conquests.[5] The possession of countless slaves and courtesans made the upper classes more entrenched in their sense of superiority vis-à-vis this subservient population. Some wealthy families had a huge number of slaves, as well as *mawali*s (liberated slaves), and *jawari*s. They were brought to the Hijaz as *sabaya*, or captives, taken during the Arab conquests, and were enslaved. They were from various places, especially from Persia, Byzantium, Egypt, Syria, India, and Africa, to name but a few (al-Babatayn 92).[6] A variety of languages were spoken in the markets and in people's homes, and Persian and Greek began to be spoken alongside Arabic.

Many of the *jawari*s were well educated and talented. They were often from the elite class in their own countries, princesses and daughters of high officials, and became the courtesans who filled the houses of the Hijaz. The modern writer William Shuqayr in his book on the Hejazi poet al-'Arji (d. 738 CE) says we do not have accurate statistics for the number of slaves in the Hijaz at that time. However, he claims that from the sources on the poet, 'Umar ibn Abi Rabi'a, we know that he inherited hundreds of slaves from his father, and that al-Zubayr ibn al-'Awwam had 1,000 female

[5]Some authors mention that Quraysh alone owned 75 percent of the slaves (al-Babatayn 92). The same author says seventy black slaves served the poet 'Umar ibn Abi Rabi'a alone (96).

[6]See also Shuqayr 347. The *raqiq* were the slaves who were not yet liberated. The *mawali* were slaves who had obtained their freedom. Some of them preferred to continue working with their original masters. See in particular al-Babatayn (62–73), who notes, importantly, that Mecca was a hub for the slave trade.

slaves and 1,000 male slaves. He adds that if one of the slaves showed great piety, his master would free him. Shuqayr claims that we may surmise on the basis of the Arabic sources that the number of slaves and non-Arabs easily surpassed the number of native Arabs in the Hijaz (Shuqayr 358–60).

This gives an indication of the overwhelming foreign presence there — especially the female presence, because of the very large number of courtesans. These women deeply affected the way Hijazis thought and acted, especially with regard to the discourse on love. They promptly learned Arabic and excelled in it. They wrote poetry and sang in Arabic and many of them rapidly surpassed Arabs in these fields.[7]

Class, poets, and the authorities

'Umar inherited his father's wealth, which allowed him to dedicate his time to writing love poetry and paying the most famous musicians of Mecca and Medina to set his poems to music. He was thus never compelled to praise princes, caliphs or governors in order to survive. It is reported that the Umayyad caliph Sulayman ibn 'Abd al Malik (d. 717) once asked him, 'What prevents you from praising us?' 'Umar replied, 'I don't praise men, I only praise women!' (al-Isbahani, *Aghani*, 1:90).

Obviously 'Umar was interested in women, as his verse and life demonstrate. However, by replying that he praised women and not men, he was also implying that he did not need or want to praise the authorities in order to survive. Moreover, as a Qurayshi, he was not very eager to praise an Umayyad caliph.

This wealth and noblesse not only allowed the poet to shun flattering the Umayyad caliphs, but also sometimes empowered him to be on the same footing as high-ranking people and, despite his reluctance to be in the shadow of the Umayyads, 'Umar occasionally befriended them. It is said, for instance, that once the Umayyad caliph al-Walid ibn 'Abd al-Malik (d. 715) came to Mecca and wanted to visit al-Ta'if , so he asked if someone knowledgeable about the town could accompany him. 'Umar ibn Abi

---

[7]Al-Babatayn, citing Abu Na'im al-Isbahani, mentions that 'Abdullah ibn Zubayr had a hundred slaves who each spoke a different language (95) and that the poet 'Umar ibn Abi Rabi'a had seventy slaves from Ethiopia alone (96). We may doubt, however, whether these figures are correct. It is difficult to imagine a hundred slaves speaking a hundred languages in one household alone!

Rabi'a was suggested, but the caliph rejected him. He asked twice, and twice was given the same name, so he finally acquiesced. The two men traveled to Ta'if, and had a good time together. They were seen laughing. Al-Walid ibn 'Abd al-Malik was asked, 'What made you laugh so much?' He replied, 'We kept talking about amorous adventures until we returned to Mecca!' (Ghurayyib 83).

In this sense love discourse not only shielded 'Umar from praising the caliphs, but also allowed him to avoid discussing politics with people in power, while other poets were compelled to beg from princes and caliphs in order to survive. One thinks, for example, of poets such as Jarir, al-Farazdaq, and even the 'Udhri poet, Kuthayyir 'Azza,[8] who earned their living by flattering men in authority.

Poetesses as well as poets flattered those in power, who seemed to disregard gender boundaries as long as the poet or the poetess was extolling their qualities. We have a good example in the poetess Layla al-Akhiliyya (d. 700), from the tribe of Banu 'Amir, who eulogized both the caliph Mu'awiya and the emir of the Hijaz, al-Hajjaj ibn Yusuf al-Thaqafi (d. 714). She was a gifted poet and loved a man named Tuba. She used to come to al-Hajjaj's council and he would ask her to recite her poetry, in which she would extol his virtues, and he would reward her with a gift. It is said that once, after she recited her poetry, al-Hajjaj gave her twenty camels. She started to bargain: he offered her forty, she asked for more, he offered her sixty, and so on until he offered a hundred camels, and she was finally satisfied! ('Abbud 3:59–63).

Class and gender in the poetry of the elite class

Love discourse and wealth

Hijazi poets of the elite class often described prosperity in their poems, which led the Egyptian critic, Shawqi Dayf (d. 2005), to write, 'Poetry under the Umayyads reflects economic life in all its aspects and highlights the evolution that took place' (Dayf, *al-Shi'r*, 46).

For example, the poet, al-Ahwas al-Ansari (d. 728), who was, as his name indicates from al-Ansar, described how his beloved Zaynab spent

[8]On the economic situation in Najd under the Umayyads, see especially al-Babatayn 139–70.

winter in Mecca and summer in al-Ta'if (Ruwaqa 324). As for the poet
'Umar ibn Abi Rabi'a, he portrays wealthy Meccan women in lavish
detail. In one verse, he describes his beloved dressed in silk and gold,
glowing with rubies and sapphires (Ghurayyib 155). In another, he says
his beloved, al-Rabab, lives in a palace served by many *jawari*s (Ruwaqa
322).[9] She and her women friends wear satin clothes. In yet another verse,
'Umar's beloved lives surrounded by greenery and water, her husband
meeting all her needs, so that she has no cares (ibid. 323). Several of
'Umar's poems are simply devoted to describing in minute detail the
jewels these women wear, their rubies and coral, and so on. Poetry thus
becomes a means of preserving the standing of these people, decked out
with all the manifestations of their wealth.

Hara'ir versus *jawari*s

Class and gender issues are overwhelmingly obvious in the poetry of the
Meccan 'Umar ibn Abi Rabi'a. Because his father died while he was still
a child, 'Umar was raised by his mother, who was brought captive from
the war in Yemen, and he often spent time among the courtesans of the
household. Nevertheless, 'Umar never devotes a poem to any of his courtesans. His poetry is almost silent on them, which could imply that he
thought these women were not worthy of his poetry. Interestingly enough,
little is written in literary criticism about the poet's interaction with his
courtesans, as if it were taboo to address this topic.

'Umar restricted his poetry to Arab, 'free' women (*hara'ir*) from his
own class. It is known that all the women to whom 'Umar wrote love
poems were either from Quraysh or from one of the prominent Arab tribes.
He praised, for example, the beauty of 'A'isha bint Talha from Quraysh,
and Sukaynah bint al-Husayn[10] from the same tribe. In fact, many women
of this elite class wanted to be acknowledged in his poetry ('Umar ibn Abi
Rabi'a 2:37) and asked 'Umar to mention their names so that they would

[9]On the same page, Ruwaqa says, "Umar often intimates that he does not like life in the
desert with its austerity and difficulties.'
[10]It is interesting to note that while 'Umar's poem on Sukaynah bint al-Husayn was recited
under the Umayyads, this became difficult under the Abbasids. It is said that once the
caliph Harun al-Rashid forbade a singer from pronouncing the name of Sukaynah, considering it blasphemous to sing a love poem about a woman from the Prophet's family. So
singers would replace her name with Zaynab ('Abd al-Rahman 151).

become more famous and influential among their own class, as well as in
order to compete among themselves with all but the caliphs' daughters.[11]
Among the women of the Hijazi elite who sought his attention were
Thuraya bint 'Ali al-Umawiyya and Zaynab bint Musa al-Jumahi, who
asked the poet to write love poetry for them (Dayf, *al-Shi'r*, 98, 229, 263).

The Qurayshi 'Umar was not only very wealthy, but also 'the most
handsome among the youths of his tribe, the tallest, the most elegant, and
the most articulate' (Faysal 316). He was loved and admired by the people
of his tribe as well as throughout Hijazi society, but his poetry was nevertheless restricted to *hara'ir*; he seldom mentioned his *jawari*s in his verse.
In a very rare example, one poem begins with a question that his *jariya* (a
woman educated in poetry and art) asks him about his mood and his
gloomy silence when he returns from an amorous adventure. It is as if the
jariya's presence was only a pretext for starting his poem, no more. Her
appearance is fleeting, her name is not mentioned and she remains anonymous in history.

The critic Georges Ghurayyib says that 'Umar was so elated when he
finished composing this nine-line poem that he decided to free nine of his
slaves, one slave for each line. In this case, the poem takes on a striking
significance inasmuch as poetry here seems to heal the gap between slaves
and their owners. The creation of a beautiful piece of art not only brings
fulfillment to the poet but, more importantly, it gives freedom to nine
slaves in Ibn Abi Rabi'a's household.[12]

'Umar was no exception. Many a poet or a highly placed figure would
do the same—that is, free slaves or courtesans after completing an artistic
work, or when impressed by the artistic performance of a *jariya*. We are
told, for example, that al-Husayn, the grandson of the Prophet, was once
offered a *jariya* by the name of Hawa. The first time she was introduced to
him, she sang beautiful poetry and recited the Qur'an in such a beautiful
voice that she touched him deeply and brought tears to his eyes. He immediately freed her (Ghurayyib 53). The beauty of the verse and the moving
voice of Hawa act as catalyst between classes, abolishing the gap between

---

[11]For example, it is reported that Fatima bint 'Abd al-Malik, the daughter of the then caliph
'Abd al-Malik ibn Marwan (d. 705), asked 'Umar in secret to write a love poem for her
against her father's will. But the caliph had already warned al-Hajjaj ibn Yusuf al-Thaqafi,
the emir of the Hijaz, to forbid the poet from writing any love poems to his daughter on
pain of death. 'Umar did finally write a poem for her, but without mentioning her name.
[12]The story and the poem are found in Ghurayyib 177.

master and courtesan. Reconciliation occurs and restores the woman's lost dignity.

We have another example in the *jariya* Sallama, who was of Persian origin and living in the Hijaz, and whom the caliph Yazid ibn Muʻawiya brought to his court in Damascus. The Hijazi poet al-Ahwas was madly in love with her. Yazid wept when he heard them singing of their passion for each other in poems, for she was a singer and poet too. So he took pity on them, married them, and freed her, and al-Ahwas returned with her to the Hijaz (al-Isbahani, *Qiyan*, 49–52).

Abu al-Faraj al-Isbahani, in his *al-Qiyan*, also tells many touching stories of Arabs falling in love with their *jawaris* not only for their beauty, but also for their talents and intelligence. This love sometimes remained unfulfilled because another master owned the *jariya,* or simply because society would not tolerate a match across the classes. Interestingly, the lover would usually communicate his love to the courtesan through verse, and she would respond likewise. It was almost impossible to talk about love without the language of poetry. It was as if everyone assumed that only poetry could convey strong feelings and the attraction of one soul to the other. We have stories of lovers who would literally die of love for each other, and be buried in the same grave (ibid.).[13]

The elite class as inventors of a new love discourse:
the case of ʻUmar ibn Abi Rabiʻa

There is no doubt that ʻUmar's poetry was very innovative. He ushered in a revolution in form and in content. Although he restricted his verse to the women of his own class, he was also very audacious in opening up the Arab poem to new experiences in form and emotion.

In pre-Islamic times the theme of love was confined to a few lines of a poem. The poet would address his beloved at the beginning of his poem in a section called the *nasib* (love poetry section in Arab poetry). Why would pre-Islamic poets start in this manner? Opinions differ: the medieval literary critic Ibn Qutayba (d. 889), for example, says that beginning the poem in this way appealed to people, who often enjoyed listening to love poetry. Another medieval critic, Ibn Rashiq al-Qayrawani (d. 1064), asserts

[13]See in particular the story of the *jariya* Nafisa al-Sahmiyya and the son of Saʻid ibn al-ʻAs (al-Isbahani, *Qiyan,* 57).

that '. . . the poet considered opening the poem with love as a way to be inspired. The theme of love is stimulating, and the poet was always under the impression that it would spur his creative power' (quoted in Dayf, al-'Asr, 26).

Some modern literary critics, such as Syrian author Shukri Faysal, consider that this pre-Islamic tradition was 'unauthentic because it was compulsive and imperative. The poet was not sincere when he evoked the beloved. He was simply imitating a technique like everyone else' (Faysal 25). Other recent opinions propose that pre-Islamic poets began their poems with a *nasib* not because they wanted to imitate their predecessors, but rather because the *nasib* had become a ritual such that a poem would be deficient without it (ibid. 28). Be that as it may, the theme of love in pre-Islamic times remained a minor part of the poem, confined to the opening (ibid. 193). It was neither creative nor original, but rather repetitive.

Amorous adventures of the elite class

For the first time in the history of Arabic poetry a poet dedicates a whole poem to the theme of love. This was a significant development from the pre-Islamic period. The new poetic genre revealed Arab men's emotions toward women, and showed that they had begun to discern women's subtlety, resourcefulness, and sophistication. It implies a real transformation in Arab male psychology (Dayf, al-'Asr, 108). The relative freedom that this elite class enjoyed was reflected in 'Umar's poetry, where one finds flirtations, intrigues, and adventures. The poet constantly shifts from dialogue to narrative and back again. In fact, 'Umar was the first Arab poet to introduce narrative elements into poetry, which is a modern characteristic, in the sense that today's poetry, at least in the United States, is a story rather than a set of metaphors. This narrative aspect never excluded lyricism. On the contrary it intensified it.

'Umar's poetry is rich in details about women of his own class. He often gives the floor to them, saying *qalat lana*, 'she said to us'. For the first time in Arabic poetry one reads ardent dialogues and affectionate reproaches between the sexes, conversations between women informing us of their amorous escapades, and about *jawari*s, who often acted as messengers between 'Umar and his lovers (Ghurayyib 183). Sometimes they were caught by the husbands or other men of the family, and it was then these *jawari*s who were severely punished, not 'Umar, who was not deterred by these incidents from sending more messages to the women he loved.

One also finds discussions about love between the poet and his male friends. 'Umar's verse portrays scenes of tender, attractive, and sentimental encounters. He even invites men and women to befriend each other beyond love affairs. 'Umar loved women's company and defended them in his verse. As Taha Husayn (d. 1973), nicknamed 'the dean of Arabic literature', affirms:

> I have no doubt that Omar befriended women in the modern sense of the word and wanted freedom for them. He invited them to proclaim their love without guilt or embarrassment. He wanted them to be proud of their beauty the way men are proud of their power and courage. (Husayn 1:292)

'Umar's poetry does indeed reveal a man knowledgeable about the psychology of love in general, and women's feelings in particular. He conveys to us his knowledge of love from within, declaiming it simply and sincerely. For him, the feminine can be better understood and venerated by praising the many women he knew rather than by celebrating one alone. In one of his famous poems about a woman called Nu'm, the poet describes in detail how he escaped the surveillance of his beloved's family by disguising himself in her sister's dress. In a daring move, the poet walks side by side with his beloved and her sisters without being caught. This illustrates the fact that, despite the relative freedom enjoyed by the elite, traditions were still observed. Lovers had to be extremely ingenious and inventive in their subterfuges and tricks in order not to be discovered.

'Umar's poems reflect the discourse of sophisticated love in Mecca and sometimes extend to complex dramatic improvisation. Furthermore, 'Umar is skilled in analyzing jealousy between women, and his poetry thus reveals the feelings of women among the elite of the time.[14] This avant-garde poetical experience caused Taha Husayn to declare:

[14]See in particular Dayf, *al-Tatawwur*, 229.

You will not find anywhere in Arabic literature what is found in 'Umar's *ghazal* with regard to authenticity, sincerity, limpidity, either in the Abbasid period, or in al Andalus, and certainly not in pre-Islamic times. (Husayn 1: 373)

It was not uncommon for these women to invite poets to join their gatherings and share in their poetical discussions. It is related that once, when women in Medina were meeting and reciting poetry among themselves, they decided they would love to have the poet al-Ahwas al-Ansari (d. 728) among them to share their discussion and their singing, so they asked one of their slaves to fetch him. Al-Ahwas came running and they recited poetry to him and he recited his own to them (Abu Rihab 34). This story illustrates the interest of elite women in love poetry in general, and in discussing it in particular, and indicates that poets were in contact with these women, and took their opinions seriously. It also shows that love discourse was a vehicle that allowed elite women and Hijazi poets to interact and exchange thoughts and feelings within the limits of the relative freedom granted to them by their social status.

One finds evidence of a similar interaction between the sexes in the verse of another Hijazi and Qurayshi poet, 'Abdullah ibn 'Umar. He was the grandson of the caliph 'Uthman ibn 'Affan, nicknamed al-'Arji because he was from a place near Mecca called al-'Arj. In one verse, al-'Arji tells the story of five women, who met together in a hidden place, away from the eyes of family and friends, in order to see him. They sent a trusted messenger to the poet advising him to be cautious and avoid intruders (Ruwaqa 325).

This poetry reflects the daily life of the wealthy class in Mecca and Medina that indulged in the amorous exchange. Arab criticism reads this type of verse as an illustration of a society whose money meant that they had the time to analyze their emotions and interpret their love at leisure, 'and who would inhibit them from doing so? They were rich people who wanted to enjoy life and have fun!' (ibid. 81).

There is, however, something else. It is not only a question of wealth. After all, Saudi Arabia is a very rich country and yet communication between the sexes remains, until today, very limited, if not almost impossible. It is also a matter of the relative freedom that existed between men and women *within* the elite class in Mecca and Medina, as well as the refinement and sophistication introduced by the *jawaris*, who were brought from many different parts of the world and helped transform Mecca and Medina into cosmopolitan cities. As will be seen from the example of Sukaynah bint al-Husayn, there was a serious and profound desire to communicate ideas and thoughts between genders within this class. It was not only for fun or out of boredom that poets and singers came to visit Sukaynah, but also out of a true artistic endeavor to evaluate and interpret.

Most importantly for our topic, this poetic success was beneficial not only to 'Umar himself, but also to his class, namely to the tribe of Quraysh to which he belonged. It empowered the tribe and gave it more sway over the Hijaz. Quraysh had been waiting for such success for a long time. As Georges Ghurayyib says, 'We may assert that Quraysh was leading the Arabs in everything except poetry but, with the coming of 'Umar ibn Abi Rabi'a, the control became total' (Ghurayyib 183).

The elite as patron of the arts: the example of Sukaynah bint al-Husayn

Class and the critique of love discourse

The elite class organized literary salons in their homes. The most interesting example of this is undoubtedly Sukaynah bint al-Husayn (d. 735). As her name indicates, she was the daughter of al-Husayn, the grandson of the Prophet. 'A'isha 'Abd al-Rahman states:

> Women of Hijazi high society wanted to emulate her, or at least imitate her. Some thought it was her wit and eloquence that made her so loved. Others maintained it was her unique beauty. Yet others thought it was her noble line and her belonging to the House of the Prophet. ('Abd al-Rahman 43)

Sukaynah started to hold her literary salon when she reached fifty years of age (ibid. 126). This is interesting inasmuch as it indicates that the society considered her then to be a respectable woman and accepted her as such. Sukaynah had a strong personality and a sharp intelligence. She was very articulate and confident. She was not interested in literary criticism per se as much as she was focused and sensitive to the way women were depicted and treated in the poetry of male poets. For example, when asked the reason of her preference of Jarir over al-Farazdaq, Sukaynah said, 'Jarir's poetry is softer, more flowing and lyrical and, most importantly, more attentive to women' (al-Manaa 29).

Sukaynah was beloved and respected by all and used to be addressed as *ya ibnat rasul Allah* (daughter of God's Messenger). She was ahead of her time in her thought and way of life. Sources speak of her courage and independence with regard to her husband, Zayd ibn 'Amr ibn 'Uthman (Shuqayr 241). It is related that when she married him, she set three conditions: not to touch another woman for the rest of his life; not to forbid her from using his money; not to forbid her to leave the house when she so desired (ibid.; cf. 'Abd al-Rahman 124). 'A'isha 'Abd al-Rahman considers that these conditions were in fact a kind of rebellion against Qurayshi society, which was stunned to see Zayd ibn 'Amr ibn 'Uthman accepting them! (126).

She was indeed ahead of her time when we consider that women in Mecca and Medina in the twenty-first century are not allowed to travel without being accompanied by a male family member. Sources speak of her anger when she discovered that her husband was having an affair with a woman well-known in Meccan society, named Dibaja. She left her conjugal home for another she had in al-Ta'if, and she forbade her husband from entering it (ibid. 124).

In the gatherings of poets and singers that used to take place regularly at her home, Sukaynah would discuss the poets' verses as well as try to settle disputes between poets and musicians or between poets themselves. Poets such as Jarir, al-Farazdaq, Jamil Buthayna (born in the latter part of the seventh century), and Kuthayr 'Azza (d. 723), as well as 'Umar ibn Abi Rabi'a, would regularly come to see her, and Sukaynah would discuss one line of poetry or several lines (al-Manaa 18). But how would Sukaynah meet with the poets? 'A'isha 'Abd al-Rahman maintains that she would sit in one room and the poets in another. Her *jariya* would take her questions and give them to the poets, and then bring their replies back to her mistress ('Abd al-Rahman 200–10). However, Suad al-Manaa, after consulting various Arabic sources such as the *Muwashshah* of Muhammad al-Marzubani (d. 994), *Masara' al-'ushshaq* by Ja'far ibn Ahmad al-Sarraj (d. 1106) and *Wafiyat al-a'yan* by Ibn Khallikan (d. 1282), discovered that there are three different versions of how Sukaynah met with the poets. The first version agrees with 'Abd-al-Rahman's proposition, namely that Sukaynah and the poets were not in the same room and there was never any direct contact between her and them. In the second version, Sukaynah deals directly not with the poets, but with their *ruwaat* (reciters). Her *jariya* is not present. In the third version, Sukaynah meets with one poet at a time and discusses his verse with him (al-Manaa 17–18).

It is interesting to note that, in all three versions, Sukaynah is reported to have criticized the poets, using more or less the same words. The disagreement between the texts is over whether she met with the male poets in person, rather than over the content of the discussion. This indicates that interaction between men and women was a sensitive issue for this class in society, especially if it was in the context of criticism of love discourse. All three versions, however, seem to accept the notion of a woman being a critic of love discourse (ibid. 35–9).

In general, Sukaynah seemed to be mainly interested in the content of the poetry rather than in the form. She argued for decent love poetry, and requested that poets not be hypocritical and opportunistic, and not reject women after having pleasure with them. To the poet Jarir, who describes in one poem how his beloved came to him one night and he refused to see her, and asked her to 'return in peace', Sukaynah comments, 'So you came to see her anytime you wished, and she would always welcome you, but when she visited you, you did not receive her?' (al-Sarraj 2: 25–6).

In this reply, Sukaynah is concerned about the treatment of women. Sometimes, she would even suggest that a poet change something in his verse in order to make it fairer to women. She once ridiculed a poet because he boasted of having an affair with a married woman whose husband was jealous. She criticized his ethics and his insensitivity to women's feelings. She condemned another for boasting of his affairs with women and scolded him for singing his own praises instead of the praise of women he pretended to love (cf. al-Manaa 25).

Class and the question of flirtation

Ja'far ibn Ahmad al-Sarraj (1026–1106) mentions in his *Masari' al-'ushshaq* that once 'Azza, a Bedouin woman and the beloved of the 'Udhri poet Kuthayyir, visited Sukaynah. Sukaynah asked her about the meaning of a verse in which the poet sings, 'Every other debtor pays, and his creditor is satisfied; but 'Azza's creditor is put off and remains afflicted.' Asked about the nature of the debt, 'Azza first declined to answer, but Sukaynah pressured her and she then confessed that Kuthayyir had asked her for a kiss a long time ago, but she had never complied. So Sukaynah said, 'Fulfill thy promise, and let the sin of the deed be upon me' (al-Sarraj 2:84).

It is possible to see in this conversation differences between urban and Bedouin societies with regard to gender relations. The urban woman is inclined to let women realize their desires while the Bedouin woman remains withdrawn, fearful, and hesitant. While it is true that Bedouin society was more closed and gossip was more widespread than in urban society, the explanation is not that simple. When one reads Arab sources on this question, one finds that even the relatively free elite society had its limits and was not as free as one might initially believe. 'A'isha 'Abd al-Rahman relates the following story:

> The singer, 'Azza, was once invited to sing in the house of the Qurayshi woman, 'A'isha bint Talha. At a certain point she sang a verse written by the pre-Islamic author 'Imru' al-Qays in which he describes the mouth of his beloved. Women and men were sitting separated by a curtain. 'Azza was sitting with the women singing. The husband of 'A'isha bint Talha, Mus'ab ibn al-Zubayr, was among the men. When he heard 'Azza singing this verse, he stood up very troubled and came close to the curtain and addressed his wife: 'We have tasted your mouth and found it as described! But unfortunately we don't have access to you now.'

> Then he said to his wife, 'Allow 'Azza to come to the men's section to sing this verse to us again.' 'Azza moved to the men's section where she repeated her song several times. ('Abd al-Rahman, 45)

Many things can be inferred from this story:

> First, 'A'isha 'Abd al-Rahman asserts that men and women were sitting separated by a curtain and not together during these meetings, while Abu al-Farj al-Isbahani asserts in *al-Aghani* that they were mixed. He describes one musical performance as follows:

Men and women were sitting together not separated by a curtain,
watching together singers of both genders perform. That is how Jamila
sang in front of 'Abdullah ibn Ja'far and his group. That is how the
singer 'Azza sang at the house of Sukaynah bint al Husayn. (Dayf,
al-Shi'r, 500, quoting from *al-Aghani*)

We have here opposing views on gender interaction.

Second, in the report given by 'A'isha 'Abd al-Rahman, the singer,
'Azza, who was a courtesan of Persian origin, was the only one who was
allowed to circulate between the male and female sections of the audience.
This indicates once more that elite women had restrictions on their freedom
of movement while the courtesans were freer.

Third, it is likely that the advice that Sukaynah gave to 'Azza did not
necessarily reflect the opinion of elite society as a whole but is rather to be
taken as only the author's opinion. After all, being a discourse, it mirrors
the liberal attitude of Sukaynah and her power as a woman of the noble
class ('Abd al-Rahman 87).

Class and the veil: woman aloof versus woman consumed

The discourse of love under the Umayyads in the Hijaz is rich in details
about the veil, and it is in 'Umar ibn Abi Rabi'a's verse in particular that
we find information. He describes how the beloved is dressed, whether or
not she wears a veil, when she takes off her veil, etc. In one verse we read
that a group of unveiled women approached him:

> When we stopped to greet them
> The faces shone that beauty declines to veil.
>   (Quoted in Issa Hilal bin Muhammad 49)

The poet seems here to clearly prefer unveiled women because he can
admire their beauty. When they are unveiled it allows him to follow closely
a glance, a smile, or an expression of sadness or joy on the face of his
beloved. Nevertheless, in many other poems, 'Umar succeeds in discerning
the feelings of his veiled female companions through their voice, their
movements, and the way they laugh. In these poems, 'Umar seems to like
the veil because he likes to be surprised; and, when the beloved unveils, he

is inspired to write a poem dedicated to her (Ibn Abi Rabi'a 1:33). In yet
another poem, 'Umar describes a group of young women approaching:
some immediately veiled themselves out of shyness, while others remained
unveiled and engaged in conversation with him (ibid. 71). 'Umar's verse
seems to indicate that, in general, women from the elite class seem to have
worn the veil, but they would occasionally remove it for their lovers.

We also find in al-Isbahani's *al-Aghani* many stories about how 'Umar's
verse triggered changes with regard to the veil, as well as some information on the segregation of men and women. For example, the poet met
once with the daughter of Muhammad ibn al-Ash'ath. They sat separated
by a curtain. 'Umar recited a verse that pleased her immensely. Out of
enthusiasm and admiration, she spontaneously drew aside the curtain
between them to directly face 'Umar and continue the discussion with him
unveiled ('Abbud 16). In this particular instance, it seems that it is poetry
itself that encourages the woman to remove the curtain. The flow of the
beautiful verse eliminates the distance between genders, allowing face-to-
face dialogue between them. Love discourse induces change and makes
spontaneity thrive between men and women.

In another story, al-Isbahani reveals the attitude of some elite women
with regard to veiling. 'A'isha bint Talha, who was one of the most beautiful and powerful women of her time, didn't veil herself from men. She
would sit unveiled and would ask men to sit in her council (al-Isbahani,
Aghani, 3:25). It is reported that one of the Companions of the Prophet,
Anas ibn Malik, once told her that some people would like to come to visit
her and admire her beauty, and she agreed. Another Companion of the
Prophet, Abu Hurayra, said when he saw her, 'Glory be to God, it is as if
she just came from Paradise' (Issa Hilal bin Muhammad 22). Her husband,
Mus'ab ibn al-Zubayr, once reprimanded her, and she said:

> God, glory be to Him, gave me beauty, so I like people to see it, and see
> I am being gracious to them by showing them my beauty. Why should I
> veil myself? By God, I have no defect to veil. And if I knew of any I
> would have veiled it! (Al-Isbahani, al-*Aghani*, 3:314)

'A'isha argues that it is a disservice to people to forbid them from admiring
her beauty. Her husband cannot reject her proposition unless he wants to
appear to be selfishly keeping her graces for himself alone. 'A'isha was not

only beautiful, but also very intelligent and powerful. Sources on that time inform us that she often dared to contradict her husband in public.

'A'isha was like Sukaynah, a very strong personality. Both were powerful women who made use of their status and wealth to impose themselves on their society. Zaki Mubarak, the Egyptian writer and critic (d. 1952) says that the time of the Umayyads was a time of women's might and sway and gives the example of a line composed by the poet, Ibn Qays al Ruqayyat (d. 704), specifically about 'A'isha bint Talha: 'I wonder how one like her is not in charge of Iraq's expenditure and hasn't the pulpit of power!' (Mubarak 246).

In order to 'distinguish' its own women from the *jawari*s and slaves, whose number kept growing, this class slowly but drastically imposed the veil on the 'free' Arab elite women. By contrast, it strictly enforced a rule that the *jawari*s should be unveiled for pure market reasons. They had to remain uncovered in order to be 'evaluated' by the merchants. The veil was thus a separator of classes, an indicator of the boundaries which both kinds of women could not cross. Elite men required that their wives, sisters, and daughters should be protected, while the rest of the women in Mecca and Medina were 'available' to all and sundry.

Segregation was thus 'invented' in the name of *noblesse oblige*, and Islam thus began to distance itself from its source. A gap started to open up between Muhammad's attitude toward the *jawari*s and how the elite class chose to behave towards them. In a Hadith, the Prophet Muhammad is reported to have said, 'He who teaches a *jariya*, frees her, and then marries her has two rewards.' It should be noted here that Muhammad married Safiyya bint Hayy and freed her after she was taken captive during the Battle of Khaybar. In the same vein, the caliph 'Umar ibn al-Khattab imposed a law on the men of eminent families, limiting the time they could stay away from their wives in order to preserve the rights of 'free' Arab women (ibid. 53). But the men chose to ignore these injunctions, and arrogantly continued to abuse their slaves and *jawari*s.

The rules of the elite class seem paradoxical and created a complex situation in which the notions of freedom and subjugation overlapped. Foreign women regarded the veil as saving them from the market, while 'free' Arab women wanted to unveil in order to compete with the numerous *jawari*s who beguiled their husbands. The houses of this elite class were full of *jawari*s, and their husbands had rights to them. Their wives had to go through the suffering of jealousy and the humiliation of being betrayed every night with their own slaves and *jawari*s in their own houses. The competition was fierce, especially if we bear in mind that these *jawari*s were beautiful, trained in various arts, and competent in several languages, as the sources inform us. They were the daughters of the courts of Persia, Byzantium, Ethiopia, India, the Slavic countries, Syria, and Egypt, to name a few.

As Abdelwahab Bouhdiba rightly states, 'the *jawari*s became veritable anti-wives' (Bouhdiba 106–7). Thus, the houses of the upper classes in Mecca and Medina were divided between veiled 'free' Arab women and unveiled subjugated slaves and *jawari*s, whom the elite women despised, hated, and looked upon as intruders.

Conclusion

Three remarks can be made toward the end of this study.

First, it would be interesting in the future to examine sources on communication between *hara'ir* and *jawari*s within the domestic and public spheres. This would unravel the complexities of interaction between women of different classes and races and would also shed light on Arab men's perspective on the feminine in general and on womanhood in its relation to class and race in particular.

Second, the examination of Arab sources shows differences between writers with regard to gender interaction. As we have seen throughout this study, some authors claim that women and men sat together when listening to a singer or a discussion of poetry, while others maintain that a curtain separated them. This makes the interpretation of texts more difficult. However, it also sheds light on the subjective interference of the author or commentator, and reveals his own preferences and ideology.

Third, Taha Husayn maintains that 'Umar's poetry caused a revolution. It certainly did, both in its content and in its form and the invention of a new literary genre, the poem of love. But at the same time it enhanced the power of Quraysh and consolidated the differences between classes.

5. *Nomadic Histories: Reflections on Bedouin Women's Poetry from the Gulf Region*

MONEERA AL-GHADEER

How can we begin to understand the symbolic representations of the Arabian Peninsula? Is it possible to create a new space for what the region culturally and historically embodies? What is the Arabian Peninsula? Is it still a mysterious desert, calling travelers to a romantic and alluring quest? Or is it the faceless woman shrouded in black, oceans of sand dunes and camels at sunset, captured by the Western media? Regardless of which of these notions is more accurate, the unmistakably prevalent view is that the Arabian Peninsula is a reservoir of oil that keeps the eyes of the world gazing toward the sun. Clearly, the Arabian Peninsula remains obscured and irretrievable in the colossal clichés and stereotypes embedded in the Western discourse on the Middle East. Its evocation conjures up all sorts of phantasms, ironically along with their negations. Throughout the centuries, the Arabian desert, its Bedouin ethos and the imagery associated with its way of life, has fascinated scholars, causing them to ask pertinent questions about Bedouin societies and their oral traditions. Recent debates on the transnational cultural scene have often revolved around questions of traditional culture, oral heritage and folklore, even as the urgent necessity to preserve and celebrate outstanding genres and performances from non-canonical traditions has been increasingly recognized. Without dwelling on mis-representations, this article conjures up a landscape that contrasts with existing clichés and orientalist images. Bedouin women poets do indeed tell of another desert, which is depicted in their poems along with descriptions of Bedouin mores and women's histories. With this in mind, how can we locate and characterize Bedouin women's poetry from the Gulf region?

Despite its exemplary literary and cultural value, Bedouin women's poetry from the Arabian Peninsula has been systematically suppressed in Arabic, English and French literary studies.[1] Even with increasing attempts to preserve world oral heritage and the surge of interest in previously unknown or marginalized cultural production by women, the remarkable poetic compositions of Arabian Bedouin women has so far been ignored and neglected, largely because little was known about it until 'Abdullah Ibn Raddas's *Sha'irat min al-badiya* was first published in 1969.[2] To date, this is the only anthology of Bedouin women's poetry. Modern Western and Arab literary critics, unlike anthropologists, ethnographers and folklorists, have neglected both Bedouin poetry as a body of work and, more importantly, women's contribution to this tradition.[3]

Yet its themes of love, praise, satire, and elegy, interlaced with allusions and techniques, resemble to a great degree those of the classical Arabic poetry that originated in the pre-Islamic era and in the early centuries of Arab history. This poetry exhibits a fascinating continuity of and similarity to the pre-Islamic poetic scores, including their generic concerns: settings, utterances, modes, and, more notably, the unique relationship with desert landscape and its wildlife. This thematic continuity is demonstrated in other articles in this collection. The key difference lies in the language in which Bedouin poetry is composed. It is articulated in the common language, in Bedouin dialects from the Arabian Peninsula, dialects that are derivative of the lofty Arabic style and do not maintain grammatical and linguistic rules identical with those of classical Arabic or Modern Standard Arabic. For this reason, this poetry has been excluded from Arabic literary studies, and gender and vernacular marginality thus converge in this universe. One may well interrogate classificatory categories and

---

[1] For a detailed discussion of the exclusion of Bedouin women's poetry, see my monograph *Desert Voices*.

[2] The first volume of 'Abdullah Ibn Raddas's *Sha'irat min al-badiya* was first published in 1969, and the second volume in 1976. Both volumes have been reprinted a number of times, and I am using the seventh edition throughout this article.

[3] In fact, Arabic literary criticism has shunned Arabian women's oral poetry, and it has been particularly neglected in studies of orality. For example, Sowayan's significant book on Nabati poetry excludes women's poetry, focusing only on male poets in Arabia.

canonization. Nevertheless, there have been many fiery debates about popular poetry in its dialectical variations in a number of Arab countries. Some of these debates have alluded to the risk of contamination and mutation of Arabic and its poetic canon posed by exposure to vernacular expression. Arguments about the superiority and exclusivity of classical Arabic language and poetry can be traced back to the Arab philosopher and sociologist, Ibn Khaldun, and similar sentiments traverse the Arabic literary horizon, resonating in a number of views advanced by the Arab scholars such as Taha Husayn and 'Abdullah Ibn Khamis, among many others.[4] This categorization has contributed to the suppression of Bedouin women's poetry. Though every poem is at risk of being dismissed because of dialectal echoes, this poetry vividly reaches an exalted artistic realm, arranging settings of the ordinary while at the same time evoking the marvelous. The poems discussed in this article are women's oral histories, depicting the desert, and its ethos. Far from the inaccessible terms that pre-Islamic poets eloquently deployed and the historical configurations that create poems of tribal and personal idolization, these women poets echo the oral tradition, with poignant evocations of subterranean feminine historical accounts.

The history of Arabic poetry is one of unrelenting progression from the pre-Islamic to the modern, characterized by a number of literary and epistemological discussions. Other forms of vernacular expression have flourished on the margins of this literary tradition, and these have instigated ongoing debates. One of these forms of expression, Bedouin poetry, has been classified and referred to as Nabati poetry. At this juncture, attention must be drawn to how literary sources have perpetuated the absence of Bedouin women's poetry. A sketch of the beginning of Bedouin poetry in the Arabian Peninsula and its entry into print culture will provide a historical context that is relevant to understanding this crucial oversight. Bedouin poetry from the Gulf region that is available in print was composed between the fifteenth century and the early decades of the twentieth century. It was mostly transmitted by various reciters, then collected and published. Long Bedouin poems, which sometimes extend to 1,500 lines, by well-known Arabian poets from the fifteenth and sixteenth centuries incorporate more classical

[4]For further discussion of this point, see Ibn Khaldun 582. Cf. Husayn 23–84. Ibn Khamis (87) also alleges the linguistically corrupting influence of Bedouin poetry. For further discussion, see Al-Ghadeer.

Arabic fragments, dictions and expressions, showing the proximity of this poetry to literate culture and classical poetic forms.[5] In considering the earliest poems, one cannot assume a clear transition from orality to literacy but can point to the fact that oral Bedouin poetry has found its way into print, allowing the earliest anthologies and collections to produce considerable changes.[6] Printed anthologies of the works of male poets acquired a favorable status and gained the respect of the exponents of this poetic genre, while women poets did not find credibility or attract scholarly attention. Among the first works of vernacular poetry are single-authored collections composed in Arabian dialects and published at various intervals in the first half of the twentieth century. According to Sowayan and Ibn Khamis, *Diwan al-Nabat* (Nabatean Anthology) in two volumes by Khalid al-Faraj (1952) is one of the earliest anthologies of Nabatean poetry to be published (Sowayan 172).[7] Note, however, that *Diwan al-Shaykh Jasim bin Muhammad Al Thani* (Poetical Works of Shaykh Jasim bin Muhammad Al Thani) was published in 1910 in India, Khalid al-Faraj's *Diwan 'Abdullah al-Faraj* (Poetical Works of 'Abdullah al-Faraj) was published in 1920[8] and *al-Badiya* (The Desert) by 'Abd al-Jabbar al-Rawi was published in Baghdad in 1947. 'Abdullah al-Hatim also contributed an important collection of Bedouin poetry (1952), entitled *Khiyar ma yultaqat min al-shi'r al-Nabati* (The Best of Collected Nabatean Poetry). Subsequently, 'Abdullah Ibn Khamis published his study *al-Adab al-sha'bi fi al-Jazira* (Popular Literature in the Peninsula) in 1958, and this was followed by Shafiq al-Kamali's *al-Sh'ir 'inda al-Badu* (Poetry among the Bedouin) (1964), a valuable study that sets out the historical and literary context of Bedouin poetry, citing a number of well-known Arabian male poets. Women poets are almost entirely excluded from these collections and studies.

Among the recent studies of Bedouin poetry in Arabic are Ghassan al-Hasan's (1998) *al-Sh'ir al-Nabati fi mintaqat al-Khalij wa-al-Jazira al-'Arabiyya* (Nabatean Poetry in the Gulf and the Arabian Peninsula) and

---

[5]Sowayan (10) notes that Rashid al-Khalawi was known for his long poems; one consists of 1,500 lines.

[6]Sowayan discusses literacy and its relation to vernacular poetry. He writes (169) '. . . there were a few literate Nabati poets who clearly borrowed techniques and devices from written literature and employed them in their vernacular poetry.'

[7]Ibn Khamis (13) also refers to al-Faraj's anthology as the earliest.

[8]Khalid al-Faraj's *Diwan 'Abdullah al-Faraj* (Collected Works of Abdullah al-Faraj) was published in Bombay in 1920. There is no reference to the publisher.

Sowayan's (2000) *al-Shi'r al-Nabati: dha'iqat al-sha'b wa-sultat al-nass* (Nabatean Poetry: Public Taste and the Power of the Text). These otherwise valuable studies do not consider women's poetry. While al-Hasan cites a number of contemporary women poets, he discards earlier traditional poems by women, most of which were included in Ibn Raddas's collection. This discontinuity deprives the reader of a more comprehensive perspective on women's ongoing contribution to Bedouin poetry. In addition to several texts in Arabic about the cultural and historical significance of Bedouin poetry in the past, there are many books, collected works, magazines, poetry contests, and radio and television programs that focus on contemporary Nabati poetry. Currently, numerous newspapers and magazines in the Arabian Peninsula have weekly sections dedicated to it, and more than 500 Internet sites and blogs publish, discuss, and circulate Bedouin poems. These sites are growing by the day, along with satellite programs and poetry contests.

More significantly, a critical consideration of a number of anthologies demonstrates that even al-Hatim, al-Faraj, and Ibn Khamis, as well as others, perpetuate the omission of women poets from the all-male list of Bedouin poets, which may indicate their opinion that women cannot be compared with their male counterparts and that what they have composed is to be considered an offshoot or 'bad poetry', also denying Bedouin women poets their sophisticated lyrical ability.[9] Some books on Bedouin poetry, such as those by al-Kamali, Ibn Kamis, al-Said, Kurpershoek, and more recently al-Hasan, refer to fragments of women's poetry but without adequate discussion. However, the absence of feminine voices in most anthologies cannot account for the ambivalent attitude toward Bedouin women's poetry, nor does it explain the lack of recognition of it.

A few feminist critics have introduced popular poetry by formulating alternative discussions of the aesthetic discourses to elucidate the articulations of gender and genre as composed by Bedouin women. Most notably, Lila Abu-Lughod has made some fundamental contributions (1986 and 1993) to the study of Bedouin women's poetry in a number of important

---

[9]Ironically, Ibn Raddas refers to this in his introduction (11), where he says he has endured many inconveniences in gathering women's poetry, 'not because of a selective process, since this poetry is not the best of composition nor is it part of a fine poetry'. This unjustified judgment stems from a long patriarchal discourse that has always placed women's poetry in an aesthetically contested space.

texts. She offers some extraordinary insights into these oral poems and stories and develops new considerations of honor, gender and sexuality, among others topics, in studies of oral poetry in the Middle East. Her focus, however, is on the Bedouin Awlad ʻAli in Egypt, and there is no similar investigation of women's oral poetry in the Arabian Peninsula.[10]

Bedouin women poets from the Gulf region

Extensive research shows that Ibn Raddas's anthology is the only book devoted solely to Bedouin women's poetry. These poems were published in two volumes as *Shaʻirat min al-badiya*. About sixty years ago, Ibn Raddas, himself a poet, traveled throughout the Arabian desert listening to reciters and collecting Bedouin women's oral poetry. He does not date his travels, but it appears that he started recording these poems in the 1950s. It must be highlighted that a few poems are cited or included in other poetry collections or on certain internet sites. For example, Talal al-Saʻid included nine women poets in his *al-Mawsuʻa al-Nabatiyya al-kamila* (The Complete Nabatean Encyclopedia), five of whom are included in Ibn Raddas's *Shaʻirat min al-badiya*; al-Saʻid acknowledges that they are quoted from Ibn Raddas. In his introduction to *Shaʻirat min al-badiya* Ibn Raddas writes:

> I spent more than ten years collecting women's poetry yet gained only a few samples because it is surrounded with secrecy and is concealed. Moreover, most of what women compose, they hide, and as a result, it is often forgotten. If it is remembered, it is often attributed to another composer, especially poetry of the sentiments. (11)

Ibn Raddas was the first compiler of Bedouin women's poems. He usually includes a few lines before each poem, containing an acknowledgement of the poet by name, tribal connection, and social status, often adding a few details of the context of the composition, and occasionally a comment on the poet's poetic talent. The arrangement of the poems does not follow any linear method since the date of composition is rarely stated. It often appears as if the few dates mentioned are included at random. He also includes his

[10]There are numerous studies of Arabic oral poetry, and it is important to mention Aida Adib Bamia's insightful analysis of the cultural and political motifs of Algerian folk poetry (cf. Bailey).

uncompromising comments about the implications of the poems. He attempts to arrange the poems by genre, but his approach is not methodical or consistent since some of the poems cross generic borders, so his arrangement does not have a coherent order that allows readers to follow the historical period and the circumstances of the recording, or where and how he heard the poem, leaving many gaps that challenge scholars of folklore and oral cultures. The book does not provide a methodological sequence that can be grasped and commented on without raising other discrepancies. This patchiness could have been avoided if the mediator had been aware of this problematic historical context, which he fails to highlight or incorporate. Hence, Ibn Raddas intervenes as the scribe and editor of the collection by modifying the poems, offering his own comments, explaining obscure and vernacular phrases, and omitting the names of the composers of sensual or erotic poems, all of which attest to his authorial role in assembling and arranging the material. Indeed, there are clear indications that Ibn Raddas's structural organization of this anthology is deliberate.

The language of the poems is of varying obscurity and difficulty. Certain poems are composed in old Bedouin dialects that are not accessible to modern readers. There are also dialectal variations, for this is vernacular poetry; for example, the dialect of poets from the Shammar or Rwala tribes differs from that of a poet from the 'Anaza tribe in Northern Najd. The poems are composed in the feminine first-person, grounding them in self-exploration as they draw on social and cultural models that belong to everyday tribal and Bedouin life. Most of the poems display a rhetorical force and paradoxical tones antithetical to the cultural paradigms. These Bedouin poems have no titles. Some are associated with a particular poet and more than 200 women poets are named, while Ibn Raddas, as mediator, presents other poems as anonymous. Occasionally names are related to the name of the tribe, such as Hissa al-'Anaziyya and Khadra al-Qahtaniyya, but this leads to a certain anonymity since there was more than one Hissa and Khadra in each tribe. Even if we try to establish the authenticity of the names, we are dealing with a crucial element in oral tradition: there are always instances of a single poem being appropriated by more than one oral poet. More specifically, women poets in this anthology appropriate certain lines, frequently the opening lines, by other women poets, imitating the tone and composing the poem in the same metrical pattern. In mediated oral poetry, there is never an 'accurate' version. On the contrary, there will inevitably be different versions of popular poetry in circulation, and some poetic fragments have been attributed to more than one poet. The intertextuality of oral poetry poses a challenge to scholars of orality when discussing the notion of authorship and authenticity, and literary critics have already theorized these concepts. The effect of the correlation between oral poems needs to be taken into account, but their lyrical, transitory nature cannot be accounted for by one explanation of this appropriation.

In Bedouin poetry there are references—for example, to historical events and known personal names or places—that might be read as fictional. These Bedouin poems incorporate a number of historical events, place-names, and names of tribal leaders, thereby creating the correlations between the fictional and historical that have often led to oral poetry being seen as the source of oral history. Jaroslav Stetkevych discusses the poetic implications and referentiality of place-names in classical Arabic poetry:

> These words are names: names of mountains, dunes, rivers, wells, stretches of desert, tribal grounds, regions. There are equally unending insistences on motifs of arrivals at abandoned campsites, of departures from the tribal grounds, of sorrow over such arrivals and departures and over the emptiness that always lies before and after them. (103)

Like pre-Islamic poetry, Bedouin poetry bears equivalent temporal and geographical markers while capturing similar sentiments.

While most of the poems in Ibn Raddas's collection are fairly brief, averaging fewer than fifteen lines each, some are much longer. The shorter poems could be the residue of longer compositions, or their brevity may represent a poetic convention rather than a loss. The anonymous and fragmentary style is related to this poetry's aesthetic strategy, which, as in classic pre-Islamic poetry, involves the progressive unfolding of a succession of evocative images that stand as objective correlatives for the poet's inner states, including desire, melancholy, dispassion, wanderlust, and mystical identification with the desert and its human and animal life. The powerful fragments generated in this fashion are available for appropriation. Certain lines from these poems have become proverbial, while others are borrowed, rearranged and refashioned by other poets.

We do not know whether these women poets recited their poetry publicly or were excluded from performance. There is not a single reference to women performing or any discussion of their participation in public recitation. It is evident that some of these poems were recited and performed by men; however, there are no studies that focus on the differentiation between performing men's poems and performing women's. We have no sound recording of these poems to demonstrate how they were sung. Sowayan (124) indicates that performing and reciting poetry is a habitual activity that occurs when men gather. Ibn Raddas, in his introduction, indicates that he had to seek reciters and bards everywhere, appealing to them to recite for him any women's poems they knew:

> Some of these short poems that we have transmitted are only fragments from long poems that were lost and we were unsuccessful in finding reciters who had memorized them because reciters are unknown and they are not to be found in a specific place. And I used to chase them in *majalis*, social gatherings and on various special occasions, when I collected what I could. We might find someone who had only memorized a few poetic lines that interested him in order to recite them at events. Also, some of the names of the poetesses were not passed down to us because their poetry was memorized as anonymous poetry. (13)

Despite there being numerous anthologies of popular poetry in the Arabian Peninsula that often have wide appeal, women's poetry is not part of these collections. As indicated, Ibn Raddas's text remains to this day the only collection of Bedouin women's poetry and has made women's oral poetry part of print culture, which preserves it and makes the study of it possible. This poetry must be considered part of Bedouin oral poetry, despite its exclusion from other collections.

Vernacular warfare:
women's oral poetry and pre-Salafi history

In this discussion of Bedouin women's poetry as history, it is important to address how these poets destabilize and deconstruct tribal and colonial discourses, testing the limits of their imagination and offering new understandings of the causes of historical conflicts. Emerging from the periphery of the tribe, a feminist reading of the modalities of subversion invokes a critique of history, conflict and their conceptual constructs. The poems discussed in this article might be categorized as historical poetry, concerned with documenting significant events and presenting questions of gender politics and dissent. Yet women poets appropriate these *topoi* not to convey personal grievances, but rather to address conventional views about gender and difference while deploying recollection and poetic imagination. Such *topoi*, however, exemplify the inseparability of poetry from political and social matters, juxtaposing the internal world to the external. By addressing these concerns, Bedouin women poets extend the threshold of the literary and the poetic to include alternative articulations of historical occurrences.

Challenging historians, Hayden White underscores the convergence between history and fiction as enacted in the fictionality of language, indicating 'the historical work as what it most manifestly is: a verbal structure in the form of a narrative prose discourse'. It is 'generally poetic, and specifically linguistic, in nature' (ix). I re-read the other implication of White's observation to demonstrate how Bedouin women's oral poetry preserves, enacts and conceptualizes a number of crucial historical and political events, in addition to embodying traces of past narratives that reflect the encounter between fiction and fact. Moreover, this poetry is, since its documentation, the only textual record of certain historical occurrences, as the poem by Bint Zi'b, which is discussed later in this article, highlights. Furthermore, some of the poems narrate and describe past events; hence Bedouin women's oral poetry, in recounting conflicts between tribal leaders and the Sharifs of Mecca and offering historical accounts of tribal figures such as al-Dawaysh, who resisted the Salafi movement, offers another reading of history. Similarly, this poetry presents a counter-narrative about the Turkish colonial venture in central Arabia. The poems by 'Alya al-Hilaliyya, Bint Zi'b, Muwaydi al-Baraziyya, and Mubaraka bint 'Ali bin Rashad, among others, present many ways of reading history through oral composition, even if some of these poems' dates remain debatable.

However, the possibility of historiography has not yet been fully addressed in this oral context. The main focus of this section is therefore to explore further the role of orality and the concept of preserving history in juxtaposition to what has been documented in historical sources. More importantly, some of these poems can provide historical accounts of certain events in pre-Salafi Najd, that is between the sixteenth and eighteenth centuries, which still pose a number of challenges for historians because of the lack of written evidence, forcing researchers to consider the few texts and accounts by the well-known Najd *'ulama'*, such as Ibn Bassam (d. 1630), Ibn Bishr (d. 1871) and Ibn Mansur (born around 1788), and the chroniclers of the early eighteenth century, al-Manqur (d. 1713) and Ibn 'Abbad (d. 1761), who documented events between 1602 and 1761 (Al-Juhany 5–6). One cannot argue that these writers covered the entire pre-Salafi era, but they provide crucial accounts of important events and conflicts even though 'an entire decade can lapse without mentioning a single event' (ibid. 7). Al-Juhany emphasizes the role of pre-Salafi oral poetry in preserving what has been lost 'whenever historical records are scarce or absent' (21). In his criticism of traditional history for seeking continuity and unity without re-evaluating the recesses of ruptures and shifts, Michel Foucault theorizes a different task for the historian and draws attention to one of the methodological problems facing new history exemplified in 'the specification of a method of analysis' (11). Keeping his proposition in mind, I raise the following questions: What analytical models and gender strategies can be considered in examining orality, gender and conflict together with historical accounts? What type of reading can rethink the discontinuous and examine the otherness of the past? In what ways does oral poetry expose the discontinuities of history? Reflecting on the importance of 'historical discontinuities', Foucault writes:

> The most radical discontinuities are the breaks effected by a work of theoretical transformation 'which establishes a science by detaching it from the ideology of its past and by revealing this past as ideological.' To this should be added, of course, literary analysis, which now takes as its unity, not the spirit or sensibility of a period, nor 'groups', 'schools', 'generations', or 'movements', nor even the personality of the author, in the interplay of his life and his 'creation', but the particular structure of a given *oeuvre*, book, or text. (5)

If we set out to establish a methodical historical account of the events Bedouin women poets evoke, we will realize that their poetry itself and its modes of enunciation embody significant descriptions of past events that historians have moved away from and discarded. Furthermore, one cannot assume or propose that their poetry presents consecutive and uninterrupted descriptions of these events; rather it exposes gaps, breaks and inconsistencies within the conventional historical discourse and reveals the limits of traditional historical documentation. In the passage quoted above, Foucault puts great emphasis on the structure of the text itself and its discursive formation. Instead of proposing a structural analysis, I shall present a comparative reading that will briefly highlight the political modalities and 'reveal several pasts' (ibid.) inextricably interwoven into the contours of Bedouin women's poetry. The constellation of poetic narration and fragmentary historical accounts can be analyzed, re-evaluated and traced within a comparative framework that will allow us to rethink rupture, loss, discontinuity and cultural political influences through a process of translation as reading. This comparative approach attempts to show where oral poetry and history intersect and in what ways they disperse, forming different sites of correlation and mutation while producing a critique of exclusion, discrepancy, and appropriation. In such a space, oral poetry and historical texts will always remain irreducible to one another and cannot be assumed to generate a linear or more truthful narrative. Hence, traces of the historical period in question are only recoverable through a comparative reading of Bedouin women's poetic texts together with historical accounts.

While reading these poems, the frequently asked questions 'Who writes history?' and 'Whose history happens to be recorded?' need to be reconsidered in order to illustrate that women offer oral documentation of significant events in the Arabian Peninsula. For to compose a poem about violent events signals a number of suggestions by which the reader today can understand that each poem includes within its folds a historical testimony by a woman witness, who observes and narrates a historical event while she memorializes her tribe and mediates on conflict and war.

I shall briefly refer to and discuss a few poems included in Ibn Raddas's anthology, along with poems cited in Talal al-Sa'id's book and others, especially what I characterize as the oldest Bedouin oral poem by 'Aliyya al-Hilaliyya, the beloved of Abu Zayd al-Hilali. Scholars of *Sirat Bani Hilal* have quoted various versions of the poem, each of which indicates the region of recitation, whether it is Egypt, Syria, Libya, United Arab Emirates, or what was known as Arabia. In fact, scholars acknowledge that the Banu Hilal originated in Arabia. Accordingly, I suggest that 'Aliyya al-Hilaliyya's poem in its tenth-century Arabian version is one of the most influential oral compositions and that one can trace its intertextual effects in other poems (al-Sa'id 1:317).

Bedouin women should not be perceived as silent, subservient, and passive in the face of political injustice. Rather, they have responded forthrightly in their poetry to authority and tribal hierarchy. An example of political and historical significance is Muwaydi al-Baraziyya, who died around 1850 (ibid. 455). Considered a pioneer in Nabatean poetry, she has influenced other women poets (ibid. 454). According to Ibn Raddas and others, she is renowned for her poetic eloquence. Her poetry particularly raises the questions: When can one speak, and what are the consequences and risks of speaking out? Poetic defiance marks her poetry, which provoked censorship and led to attempts to silence her:

> One day while reciting her poetry, she provoked the anger of some strongly religious people, and they complained of her to Faysal bin Turki Al Sa'ud. The Prince punished her by sending one of his servants, named Salama, who beat her mercilessly and warned her not to sing again. One day she heard a dove singing and advised it not to sing there, but to go to Fira', the land of the Wada'in tribe, who protect their neighbors. (Ibid. 198)

Nevertheless, she resisted and spoke back, and her poem captured the incident:

> How happy you seem with blissful music O dove!
> O you in the greenery of palm branches singing.
> I would grieve for you if Salama knew of you!
> He would make you moan, moan like me, O dove.
> He broke my bones, may God break his.
> See how his stick has bruised and battered my back!
> He came to me saying he was sent by his master.
> May God destroy his town! If you want singing
> And safety, go to Fira', home of the Wada'in.
> Turn to those who guard camels, break up fights.
> Whoever seeks sanctuary will not be harmed,
> And, however poor, he will not be indebted. (Ibid. 198)

The rhetorical and historical characteristics of these poems can be traced in their visual descriptions of warfare, attacks and confrontations, depicting the movement of the enemy's army, the sound of the marching camels or horses, the guns shooting, the glistening swords, and so forth. Each speaker attempts to describe and capture the moment of war while simultaneously attempting to record the temporality of conflict. The moments of confrontation are often conveyed through weather imagery: the army's attack resembles fog mounting up, clouds drawing close, thunder rolling, and rain and hail falling: 'clouds spotted by dark fog, rising from the west with heavy rain clouds' (ibid. 67); 'Those are marching forward and those are retreating like a locust that returns to its nightly dwelling', or 'Like a summery cloud brought by the marching armies, clouds predicted by hail and pouring rain' (ibid. 76). Battle scenes also include striking descriptions of purebred camels, their color and speed: 'The leader of reddish-white camels, the color of white birds' (ibid. 64). In a number of poems, warriors are compared to drunken fighters. In addition, this poetry shows the participation of women in war, in scenes where they uncover their faces and throw off their veils, inciting the warriors of their tribe to confront the enemy. Bint Zi'b relates: 'My cousins tore the canopies' curtains / With copious flowing hair and white of breast / Throughout the day of battle they incite their men' (ibid. 70). This motif can be found in classical Arabic poetry, as discussed by Barbara Stowasser in the present volume. War destabilizes the law and unsettles social conventions, and this ultimately disrupts gender roles. Thus, the veil is lifted and the face is exposed in a number of poems, where there is no rhetoric of victimization, defeat, or lamentation in the face of war or raids. Women poets are not mere onlookers at scenes of warfare, or only lamenting their condition. On the contrary, the prevalent tone is laudatory, recounting the bravery of the speaker's tribe and how the warriors confront the enemy without dread or subjection. These dramatic episodes culminate in the articulation of the heroism of the tribe and its fighters, along with the swiftness of their unrivaled camels.

An ongoing correlation between history and oral poetry is revealed in the longest poem in Ibn Raddas's book, a poem that conveys a 400-year-old historical narrative while highlighting the question of transmission and women's interpretation of the past. Historians cite and refer to this poem since it provides a quasi-documentation of a significant political event, which suggests that history was chanted by bards of oral tradition, though in this context it has never been analyzed. According to a number of historians, the poem provides more fact than fiction. The poem is a testimony to how women preserve history and a claim that their poems are the only source for a significant reading of historical events.

The poet addresses her son and recounts the historical conflict between her old tribe, Zi'b, and the Sharif of Mecca. A historian's perspective indicates that

> ... in 1012/1603, the Sharif of Mecca, who was campaigning in the neighborhood of Bishah, imprisoned the chief of Zi'b, apparently for not sending the annual tribute to the sharif. The dispute with the Sharif of Mecca is also referred to in a boasting poem by a lady of Zi'b, in which she speaks of her tribe's defiance and wars with the sharifs. She refers to her tribe area as lying 'between the Empty Quarter and the Hijaz' . . . The wide area in which Zi'b was roaming indicates the power which this tribal group had up to the end of the 11th/17th century. We do not hear much about Zi'b during the 12th/18th century, by the end of which time it became an inconsequential tribe. (Al-Juhany 62–3)[11]

However, in Turkish sources, we find a number of references to many raids by Bedouin tribes and counter raids by the Sharifs of Mecca which were encouraged by Ottoman rulers, demanding that the Sharifs 'discipline' and 'punish the unruly Bedouin' (Jarshale 111, 155). Bint Zi'b's poem consists of sixty-seven lines and has been anthologized or referred to in several literary and historical sources.[12] It is still recalled and recited in various parts of the Arabian Peninsula, especially Qatar. The speaker presents an eyewitness testimony to what happened. She recalls:

> My memory is prodded by a recollected house:
> Nothing remains but traces of its stones
> Saba', your mother's eyes cry secretly

[11]Al-Juhany remarks on the historical importance of this poem. He adds: 'Since the 10th/16th century, the Sharifs of Mecca, rulers of the Hijaz, launched sporadic expeditions against the Najd towns and nomadic tribes. The *sharifs* were trying to assert their political authority over Najd, but the endless disputes among the large numbers of their clans and factions over the Sharifate of Mecca rendered that objective difficult to achieve' (18).

[12]In addition to the reference cited earlier, al-Thumayri (178–86) cites sixty-nine lines attributed to the woman of Zi'b. Sa'd Ibn Junaydil refers to the places mentioned in the poem and Kurpershoek also cites the poet (19) and translates a different version of her poem (202).

Her streaming tears wound her cheeks
But the blazing flame
Reaches my innermost heart:
Passion is provoked
And God reveals its secrets
The black stone of the eye blazes fire
As if wolves seized it from its socket
I weep like a ruptured waterskin
Carried till nightfall on a jittery camel.

I'm Zi'biya, sister! No lowborn stray!
My lineage is of some renown:
I'm from the Zi'b, and when the Zi'b face war
On horses of swift assault and riposte
Look! When their captive falls
You'll see them bending down
Like panthers over prey
The horse battalion would flee, but it is bound
To advance like gazelles toward a spring
Their pursuit: A flock of sand grouse round a well
Plunging to booty as to fresh cool water
When one with raided stallions cries, they rescue him
I pity the youth delayed by a slowfooted mount
War-horses nourished for affliction and battle
The enemy's valiant fighters flee the rout
O my tribe, don't stud your stallions
For when stallions breed their valor flags
They won't follow you across the flatlands
And they'll shy from the slope
We approached the Sharif in his town
And he confronted us.
The warriors of all the tribes were gathered.
He demanded camels: Our neighbors' herd!
Determined, he wanted the strongest and blackest.
How many horses we offered in their stead:
Ninety white horses, counted and recounted,
Thoroughbreds bound with fancy foreign fetters.

The last was Shaytan, our finest stallion,
He of Mahawis, the famous horseman.

Perish the tribe that doesn't guard its neighbors:
A twist-necked camel writhes to bite the rider.
Our neighbor dwells high on a desert rise
That protects its lowland flanks from the storms of calamity.
My people refused to surrender him,
And protected him with sharp-edged blades.

Our war began when she was in the womb
Continuing until she was a bride
Braids unbraiding from curtained canopies
Black locks draping over breasts
Their faces a towering summer cloud
Pouring forth rain as thunder rumbles
Camels tied together ninety nights
Black-backed beasts, forelegs bound
White ones with glittering ornaments
Unbound, they start swaying
Horses chasing horses
Spears strike spears
Like locusts swelling into swarms
My cousins tore the canopies' curtains
With copious flowing hair and white of breast
Throughout the day of battle they incite their men:
Shields of virgins, lions in combat
Wearers in war of breastplate and metal helmet
In the saddles of fast-converging horses
Fine caftans, booty brought by the panthers of battle
How many they stab with sharpened lance
Whose blazing tips drink blood.

Ninety mares were orphaned in a day
Fit to be tied over the loss of their mothers
Ninety and ninety, and two thousand warriors
Beneath the solid earth are buried

Ninety of my kin, with my father and brothers
Riding ninety horses graced with bridles
Such a tribe! How many rivals it annihilated!
When their generous deeds are tallied
The Zi'b will be praised for their full-hearted valor
Their domain: From the Empty Quarter to the Hijaz
When they head south for hunting, beasts panic and bolt
Led by the deer, ostrich and wild cow
If they head north, the tribes there make hasty flight
When they arrive at camp, the enemy keeps his distance
Wherever they intend, they will surely reach
They exhaust their mounts in pursuit of the enemy
Riding till saddle thongs mark white their hides
Such abundant booty they seize from their enemies!
He who tastes their blows will not come back for more
Tigers in battle, like locusts of Tuháma
They never obey rulers out of fierce hardness
Horizon-bound beasts heading for the land's expanse
My father, the protector, leading night caravans
Riding to the highlands on a white stallion with its mare
He rides awhile, dismounts and walks, then rides again
I am the maiden of this land, daughter to Ibn Gháfil
(How many maidens lost on their errant camels!)
A fine herd, dispersed across a spacious land
You don't want the evil eye of envy falling on them.

I dismounted from my camel, scaled a tree
Making a nest among its highest boughs.
A band of riders came and settled in its shade.
The leader of the troop glanced up and saw me.
He said 'Come down O maid, I'll be your refuge.'
I didn't descend till I trusted his oaths.

A matter ordained by God
An affliction carried by enemies and villains
In a terrible war, unwished-for by the wise
Remembered even by the child in the cradle

I remember a bygone day, a time long since passed
A distant day followed by nights of rejoicing
A glimmering fire seen by shepherds at nightfall
Fire feeding on dry branches of the Artí tree[13]
As if a heap of antlers behind our camp
Were dried Ghadá stalks stoking the heat of its flames
For ninety is the number
Felled in our evening hunt!
Wild cows: We'll make water-buckets from their skins
Our hunter departs at sunrise, then returns
Bringing many an antelope colored by blood
Our water-bearer bends back in a day
With brimming waterskins
Our raiders raid and bend back in a day
With she-camels, udders brimming milk
We have a dwelling between Hibr and Ghiraba[14]
Where we breed the finest camels
And when we settled in al-Hazm ninety nights
Our enemy's fury sought refuge in his spleen
Our wells are deep as chasms, overflowing
With such abundance no-one cares who comes and goes
A well whose depth is eight with eight and four
West of Wásit Mountain, near the desert of Nafúd
A well between the Hádh and Ghadá trees[15]
A land no farmer circles to scatter measured seed
Two thousand dwellers settled round the well
And two thousand desert dwellings frequent that well for drink.

Ninety fought ninety in a day, and all were lost
Because a stranger dared to set foot in Nufúd
Our abode: No place for interlopers
Surrounded by Ramlah with its infinite springs.

(Ibn Raddas 70–7)

---

[13]A tree that grows mainly in the desert of Dahna', with soft leaves that branch into feathery tendrils. It appears numerous times in classical Arabic poetry.
[14]In the Najd region of central Arabia.
[15]The Ghada' grows in sand, the Hadh in solid soil.

In this poem, Bint Zi'b embarked on uncovering the lost ancestral history
that provides the basis for the oral tradition recognized and inscribed in the
written history. Ibn Raddas presents an outline of the poem and para-
phrases the poet's description of the long battle:

> The two parties fought, and the Sharif won the battle, killing most of
> them and wounding the others while a few of the survivors fled. In one
> of their night battles, the daughter of the Emir got lost on her camel, and
> she arrived in a distant land far from her tribe. She thought her people
> were completely destroyed by the war. She continued roaming in the
> desert, until one day she sought shade under a large tree. A group of
> travelers from the Dawasir tribe passed by her and saw her in the treetop.
> They asked her to come down and she did after they took an oath not to
> harm her. So they took her to their people. When they arrived, the son of
> their Emir saw her, admired her and married her. Then she gave birth to
> a son named Saba'. One night a woman from the tribe accused her of
> ignoble ancestry, which injured her feelings. And her creativity was
> aroused, producing this poetic epic. (Ibid. 69–70)

The poem constitutes a critical historical narrative in which the speaker
traces the genealogy of identity and the origin of conflict. Temporal, causal
and factual elements are integrated to demonstrate a sense of lineage. The
speaker recalls her past after a doubting remark about her origin. She calls
attention to her noble ancestry, since she is the only one left to tell the tale.
'I'm Zi'biya, sister! No lowborn stray! / My lineage is of some renown.' 'I
am the maiden of this land, daughter of Ibn Gháfil.' By turning to the past
to uncover an obscure present, she offers a counter narrative that reveals
her identity and traces her history as a descendant of defiant people. Thus,
she aligns herself with her tribe's resistance to absolute power, commemorating the forgotten history of women. The poem reflects the underlying
genre of praise, but of a vanished tribe that survives only in the speaker's
memory. The tribe is not only noble but it adheres to ethics of citizenship
and safeguards its Bedouin ethos. In his introductory remarks to the poem,
Ibn Raddas recapitulates the beginning of the incident and shows that the
Zi'b tribe could have responded to the Sharif's orders by attacking their
neighbor who refused to give up his camels:

They could have taken the camels from their neighbor without his consent, giving him a price instead of going into a destructive war that would shatter their small tribe, since their enemy was better-armed and prepared and had many soldiers. But doing so would humiliate their neighbor, an act unacceptable in Arab culture, which throughout its history has insisted on the ethic of protecting the weaker. (Ibid. 69)

The speaker describes the severity of the battle and the unjust rule of the Sharif and his feudal system, thereby charting a commentary about power and its tacit exclusion, authority and its irrevocable privileges.

She recalls:

> We approached the Sharif in his town
> And he confronted us.
> The warriors of all the tribes were gathered.
> He demanded camels: Our neighbors' herd!
> Determined, he wanted the strongest and blackest.
> How many horses we offered in their stead:
> Ninety white horses, counted and recounted.

Here we have a war that lasted over sixteen years figured and staged in a woman's narration, which, notably, does not embody any rhetoric of passivity or defeat. The 'I' is incorporated in the 'we' to the extent that the poetic act represents an animated presence of the bygone tribe. This rhetorical strategy is an effort to reconstruct the speaker's identity, which has been threatened with extinction.

The speaker insists on counting the tribe, the horses, and the dead, repeating numbers as an attempt to revive the lost and the forgotten. She deploys the compelling numbers 'ninety' and 'ninety-nine'—*tis'in* and *tis'a wa-tis'in*—which reproduce the sharp sounds of consonant phonemes: the voiceless *ta* and *sin*, the voiced *'ayn* and the nasal *nun*, along with their rhythmical effects:

> Ninety mares were orphaned in a day
> Fit to be tied over the loss of their mothers
> Ninety and ninety, and two thousand warriors
> Beneath the solid earth are buried

Ninety of my kin, with my father and brothers
Riding ninety horses graced with bridles

Ninety fought ninety in a day, and all were lost
Because a stranger dared to set foot in Nufúd

The colossal death toll is confronted, with undeniable inscriptions in the story of the speaker's survival. The wounded or captured are not listed in these numbers, and physical injuries are not graphically portrayed but rather implied within the counting of the dead, as if the human body remained integral until the loss of life. Repetitive counting reproduces the effect of injury and loss encompassing both human and animal. As James Dawes notes, 'Counting is the epistemology of war' and war 'is constituted within by the mundane and innumerable calculations' (29–30). Even though the poem documents the destruction of her tribe, the speaker does not deploy or cultivate sentiments of passivity.

Bedouin women's poetry offers a perspective from which we can begin addressing the implications of history in the fields of literary studies. These poets narrate warfare and depict the heroism and courage of their tribe. The speaker, in every poem, offers a tale that provides both the lost past and a critical perspective on conflict and hegemonic history, while including a different understanding of the self in relation to the noble warrior ancestors. There is no disorientation, bewilderment or lamentation. These poems enact a resistance to both power and forgetfulness. Bringing women's poetry to the critical discourse will eventually reinstate it into the topography of poetic debates and canon formation, while repositioning its historical significance and allowing it to become visible, not only as an invaluable aesthetic form but as a metaphysical meditation on history, conflict and justice.

6. *Women and the Economy: Pre-oil Gulf States*

This article attempts to explore the presence of women in the economic and mercantile life of the Arabian Gulf[1] during the pre-modern period, namely the pre-oil era (nineteenth and early twentieth centuries up to World War II).[2] It focuses on the participation of working-class women in the economy and aims to identify patterns in their behavior and activities as both producers and consumers in the market place. The article poses a number of questions: How have women involved themselves in the economic and mercantile life of the time? What were the avenues of participation and investment ventures open to them in the market place? What was the impact of their economic engagement on their social life and gender relations?

The article seeks to reconstruct the historical presence of Gulf women and their activity in the economic arena in order to: (a) highlight their roles as agents and give them centrality; and (b) challenge the patriarchal ideal of female economic dependency, and defy the stereotypical image

---

[1]The Arabian Gulf countries at this time were: Kuwait, the eastern region of Saudi Arabia, Qatar, Bahrain, United Arab Emirates and Oman.

[2]Even though oil was discovered in many of the Gulf states in the 1930s, it was not until the end of World War II that production started and many of the Gulf states began their transformation; and oil revenues prior to 1974 were of little significance. For more information on the significance of oil revenue and how it transformed the Gulf states after World War II, see Nugent and Thomas.

projected by the West that Arabian Gulf societies rendered women helpless and secluded at all times and in all places.

Sources

Social historians have been encouraged to study the economic role of
women in the history of Arab countries such as Egypt, Syria and Iraq in the
pre-modern period as a result of the abundance of sources related to these
countries and the wealth of information they contain. There is scattered
but interesting information about them in various primary sources: chronicles, legal records, papyri, *hisba* (market inspection manuals), treaties and
fatwa collections (juridical opinion/responsa literature), as well as travelers' and geographical accounts. In contrast, the realities of the working
women of the Arabian Gulf in the pre-modern period have not attracted
historians' attention. In general, the period under consideration in the
history of the Gulf is poorly documented. Even though there are plenty of
political records – Ottoman and British archives, as well as national
archives and records, some of which date back to the nineteenth century
– there are no records about the social history of the region. There are
biographical dictionaries and memoirs, either published or in manuscript
form, and newspapers,[3] but these sources only focus on public life. They
fill gaps in our knowledge in terms of the political and intellectual history
of this era, but can prove of very little use as far as women's history is
concerned.

Arabian Gulf women, as such, do not appear in the sources and their
lives are not well documented. The rare information available, is, therefore, rather derived from references to women in *awqaf* records; published
*fatwa*s; judicial writings; personal documents; folk literature; and verbal
and material culture including oral history,[4] art and architecture, songs,

---

[3]The first periodical newspaper in Bahrain was *Al-Bahrayn*. It was established by a well-
known poet and the first edition was published on 7 September 1939. The newspaper
played an important role in cultural and literary circles in Bahrain and the Gulf. For more
information on the development of journalism and newspapers in Bahrain, see al-Muraikhi
280–2.

[4]Haya al-Mughni (18) discusses the problems of oral history, showing the difficulties
facing the researcher when trying to get access to data by interviewing women of the
Arabian Gulf. Some women refuse to be interviewed or to speak about their personal
experiences.

proverbs and dress. However, all such sources are scant and not readily accessible. The only sources that are found in abundance and include interesting information on women are travelers' and geographical accounts. In fact, European travel accounts are widely used in scholarly work as the resource for the history of societies that have not themselves produced a significant body of textual documentation. Such travelogues – helpful inasmuch as they pose almost as the backbone of a knowledge base on Gulf women – are problematic, because they reflect an extraordinary diversity in form and content, which historians and archeologists need to investigate before they can rely on them as primary sources for reconstructing the past.

In addition, there are missionary records in Bahrain, Kuwait and Muscat. Missionaries also set up a series of temporary outposts offering medical services and disseminating Bible literature in major towns and villages in the interior and along the Gulf coast. Western missionaries in the Gulf traveled and lived in places where very few Western men and women had gone before, and provide us with detailed descriptive information about the towns and villages they visited, family life, the life of women, their work, marriage, divorce, celebrations, religious life, education and diseases.[5] The writings of the missionaries, particularly missionary women, are a valuable source for historical inquiry. They had access to ordinary families and to the very intimate world of women. However, despite their richness, both travelers' accounts and missionary records have their biases and problems.

Problems with the sources

This wealth of travelers' literature produced by both men and women who visited the Arabian Gulf in the nineteenth and early twentieth centuries is unique as it gives us an insight into the daily life of the ordinary people: the writings involve the recording of observations of events as they

[5]Descriptive information about the Arabian Gulf by Western missionaries comes in the form of personal and business letters, autobiographies, memoirs, field reports, articles in magazines and journals, and unpublished descriptive materials from missionaries' personal collections. The most important source of missionary writings for the social history of the Gulf is a pamphlet series called *Neglected Arabia,* published from 1892 to 1962. For more information on the literary traces of Western missionaries in the Gulf, see Doumato 43–58.

occurred.[6] However, the observation recorded is that of an outsider. This could be dangerous, as it is an observation of the Middle East by an uninformed Western eye that cannot really understand the cultural context of what it sees, but at the same time has the power to define and construct reality for the Western reading audience. Another problem with travel writings is that they present us with literary snapshots that communicate but a slice of a larger scenario, frozen at a single moment in time.[7] Missionary accounts could also be seen as doubly risky: missionaries were by and large the heirs of the European colonial attitude toward the Middle East and the Arabs, and their writings reflect the views of outsiders on 'people belonging to a closed community in an alien land' (Doumato 58). They were geared to justifying the missionary enterprise by describing how desperately debased the life of Arabian people was and how Arab women were living under miserable conditions.

In general the literature recorded by both travelers and missionaries is burdened by conceptualizations, sources and methodologies that had developed within the framework of Orientalist discourse, which is a

> *distribution* of geopolitical awareness into aesthetic, scholarly, economic, sociological, historical, and philological texts; . . . and *elaboration* not only of a basic geographical distinction . . . but also of a whole series of 'interests', which by such means as . . . landscape and sociological description, it not only creates but also maintains . . . a certain *will* or *intention* to understand, in some cases to control, manipulate, even to incorporate what is a manifestly different world. (Said 12)

Against this larger picture of the textual universe made possible by Orientalist endeavors, travelers and missionaries came to the Gulf carrying their own mental baggage and individual hopes and expectations, and so their writings about Gulf society and Gulf women reflect their own experiences and background. One should recognize that the story being told is thus not only the story of the people depicted, but also a story about the informants whose observations and experiences went into its making.

---

[6]Travel writers whose works are important for studying Gulf society and Gulf women are: Blunt, Burkhardt, Doughty, Dickson, and Palgrave.
[7]For information on the major methodological problems raised by travel accounts as a source of history, see Chouin 53–70.

Arabian Gulf women are usually portrayed in traveler and missionary writings as uneducated, economically inactive and oppressed in ways unknown in the West. The degraded condition of women and their low status became a metaphor for the decadence and backwardness of Gulf society as a whole. Notions of Western superiority were constructed on and around Gulf women, the primary symbol of social decay. Travelers' accounts and missionary records speak of how different and exotic Gulf women were. They were seen as standing outside of history, shackled by unchanging social norms based on a conservative religion and traditional values. Gulf women were studied with the intention of finding ways by which enlightenment could be brought to them. Therefore, even while admitting travel and missionary accounts as a source of information about the experience of women in the Gulf, an expansion of historical writing on Gulf women and an effort to introduce new sources would correct many of the stereotypical images in a significant body of writings by Western writers of the past.

Income-generating activities in the Gulf

Several historical studies have analyzed in detail the economic conditions of the Gulf in the pre-modern era, before the production of oil and the rise of nation states after World War II. These are of course important studies; they monitor the movement of trade and markets, the nature and prices of goods, imports and exports, the classes of people or traders involved in a given trade, the wealth and the profits accumulated by people, and the various professions that dominated in the Gulf.[8] The main economic activities in pre-oil Gulf societies were centered on fishing, pearl diving and trade. Pearl diving was the main industry and employed almost all the able-bodied men of the Gulf throughout the pearl-diving season, which lasted from June to October. Gulf pearls were exported to various parts of the world. In Bahrain, merchants came from places as distant as Paris and New York to transact business in this precious commodity (Anthony 76). Bahrain, Kuwait and Oman were the main commercial centers for trade between Arabia, South Asia and the African coast. Their ports were cosmopolitan and thus removed from the tribal society of the villages and desert.

[8]For more information on the Gulf maritime trade and markets in the pre modern and modern era, see Rice, and Sweet.

They mainly exported pearls, dried dates, date juice, shark fins, mats and imported cotton, silk goods, rice, coffee, tea, sugar, spices, herbs, timber, steel, iron and tin from various countries in Africa and Asia. The bulk of Gulf imports came from India; merchants sailed mostly to the Indian ports to import materials necessary for the daily lives of their people and then re-exported the surplus to other countries of the Arabian Peninsula, Baghdad and Aleppo (al-Khalifa 343). There was also a significant slave trade in the Gulf, especially in Oman, and it was a highly profitable under-taking. Gulf society depended heavily on slaves; they were family retainers and performed menial tasks. Omani merchants brought slaves from eastern Africa and sold them on to other destinations, always retaining some to work in Omani plantations.[9]

Since the main income of pre-oil Gulf societies depended on maritime activities, a major boatbuilding and sail-making industry developed in the region. Gulf countries were renowned for boatbuilding, an industry that required about 200 carpenters and artisans. Bahrain was the biggest boat-building center in the Gulf. Boats were used during the pearl season and when the season was over, they set out as trading vessels. Gulf sailors developed a system for navigating the Indian Ocean that was different from that used in the Mediterranean, using traditional techniques as well as newly introduced European methods to steer their ships throughout the ocean.[10]

Besides boatbuilding, there were other light industries and crafts in which Gulf people were engaged: jewelry making, clothing, palm prod-ucts, pottery and household utensils (al-Mughni 23). With the exception of Bahrain, Oman and the al-Hasa' area in Eastern Arabia, agriculture was not one of the main sources of income. The availability of water and the fertility of the soil played an important role in the agricultural potential of these three places, allowing the cultivation of date palms, fruit trees, and vegetables. Date palms brought a good income and produced a surplus that was exported to Persia and India.

While trade and agriculture were the source of revenue for the people who led settled or semi-settled lives on the shores of the Gulf and in the villages, shepherding represented the only option for the people of the

[9]For more information on Omani control of East African slaves, see Gordon 182–91.
[10]For more detailed information on the system and techniques of navigation developed by the Gulf sailors to help them steer their ships throughout the Indian Ocean, see Brice.

desert, most of whom survived on a subsistence economy, herding animals and raising camels and goats.

There is plenty of material on the economy of the Gulf, and many studies draw conclusions about the economic activity of the region and the professions adopted by its population. In what follows an effort is made to complete the picture by shedding light on the role of women in this context, and by monitoring cases of working women, addressing details relating to their professional lives, trades, financial transactions, and other economic activities. While the material presented may be limited, it is indicative of many other individual women having similar backgrounds.

Gulf women and work

Recording and documenting details about the life of women provides a glimpse of what has been otherwise neglected historically and opens doors for what we may call 'historical imagination' to complete the missing pieces of the puzzle. This is why the examples and models presented in this essay have not been selected according to specific criteria and are not fully representative in a statistical sense. They are nevertheless indicative models, pointing to the 'qualitative presence' of women in various areas of activity, and to the forms of professions, crafts, and financial transactions adopted by women over the ages. As important, the cases presented here are indicators of the relationship of women in pre-modern societies to property, wealth, and commercial and investment activities, and of how women used this wealth and investment as means of empowerment.

Pre-oil Gulf society has been described as a 'women society' (al-Misnad 24) at least for the period between June and October each year, when all the able-bodied men were away from home, pearl diving. The long absence of men from home left women with full responsibility for the family and in charge of its affairs. Women of the Gulf were breadwinners; they were important contributors to sustaining their families in the absence of the male members. Not only were the men away for long periods of time, but they were also unable to secure regular or reliable income from pearling. Furthermore, the very nature of this activity made it an extremely hazardous occupation. Death was always a risk, as was the inability to support a family following the loss of an arm or a leg in a shark attack. In such a society, women's work was needed to support the family, raise the children and cover for the absence or illness of the husband. There are interesting cases of women having to work as pearl divers to ensure the repayment of a debt left by their husbands (Abou Saud 29–30).

Thus, Gulf women worked hard in the past and contributed to their economy and society. The central role of women in the Gulf economy is well illustrated by the public reaction to a decision by the Dubai legislative council in 1931 to ban women from selling fish. Much to the surprise of the legislators, the fishermen protested and immediately called for this decision to be rescinded. They argued that it was impossible for them to catch fish and at the same time sell their goods at market. Fatma al-Sayegh argues in her article 'Women and Economic Changes in the Gulf' that the fishermen's protest had little to do with time and everything to do with money, because women could sell fish at far higher prices than their male counterparts. They simply had a better understanding of the market than their husbands (al-Sayegh 5). Fishermen were not alone in their dependence on women. Bedouin life too would not have been possible in the Gulf region if women had not been capable of assuming direct responsibility for a considerable amount of tribal and commercial business (Foley 172). Women of the desert were engaged in many occupations and served their society in multiple ways throughout the nineteenth and early twentieth centuries. They herded and watered animals, collected water, milked, and processed milk into butter, yoghurt and cheese. They themselves would even sometimes sell these dairy products to traders. They spun and wove camel and goat hair into rugs, bags and tent cloth. They tanned goatskins and made water bags from them. They filled the bags with water, collected firewood, made bread and cooked for their families, and sewed clothes for themselves and for their families. They raised the children and took care of sick family members, as well as sick and injured animals. Doughty logically states: 'virtually all Bedouin men marry in part because of the need for female labour in the pastoral nomadic adaptation' (1:366).

Women living in the towns and villages on the coast of the Gulf were also active contributors to the economy of their communities. They were engaged in various activities and paid occupations, which can be divided into two main categories: gendered occupations, and non-gendered occupations.

Gendered occupations

There is a wide spectrum of occupations that were exclusively for women
or related to female life. They ranged from female teachers to midwives,
wet nurses, hairdressers, beauticians (*'atshafa* or *hawwafa*) and match-
makers (*khatba*). All such services were well regulated and required the
women practicing them to be skilled and rich in knowledge—the kind of
knowledge that was not founded on formal education, but was usually
passed on in the family by mothers and aunts (Rihani 28).

Teaching required great knowledge. There are several cases in the
sources of Gulf women who were known for their expertise in religion and
worked as *muftiyat*, preachers and teachers, teaching young and old
women the Qur'an, *fiqh* and Hadith. They are also variously referred to in
the sources as *murshidat*, *murabbiyat*, *mutawwi'at* and *hajjiyat*. They
earned their living from teaching (*ishtaghalit bi-al-tadris*). Some were
hired by well-to-do families to teach their daughters at home (al-Shaybani
79; Doumato 83–93) and, besides private tutoring, there are many cases of
women in Kuwait, Bahrain and Qatar who worked as teachers in Qur'anic
schools (*kuttab*) or set up their own schools at home to earn an income.
Kuttab teachers were simple, pious women who had a basic knowledge of
the Qur'an, Hadith (Prophetic) tradition and the Arabic language. Their
teaching methods were simple, but they imposed a harsh discipline. The
kuttab teacher or *mutawwi'a* had ten to twenty students in a class and
received a fee of between two and five rupees per pupil. Sometimes she
would take her fee in kind – dates, rice, or fish – depending on each girl's
family income (Doumato 86–8). In Qatar, the first *kuttab* for girls was
established in Doha, by a woman named Moza Selibikhin. However, it
was the *kuttab* of Amna Mahmud, a woman well known in the field of
education that became the most famous in Qatar. Amna established her
kuttab in 1938 and taught both girls and boys there. It was a well-struc-
tured *kuttab* and Amna set the rule that the parents would pay her one
rupee every time their child memorized a chapter of the Qur'an. Amna
exempted poor children from payment or in some cases accepted the fees
in kind, not cash. Amna is a good example of a Gulf woman who was very
interested in her work and succeeded in managing it well, and it was due
to her effort and hard work that in 1956 the *kuttab* became the first girl's
school in Qatar (al-Misnad 36; cf. al-Thani 121–6).

Many of the women who taught the Qur'an succeeded in developing
their *kuttab*s into modern girls' schools, teaching Arabic language, arithmetic, history and geography, as well as religion. In Kuwait, the first
private school for girls that taught non-religious subjects was established
in 1926. It was the private enterprise of 'A'isha Azmir, the wife of a Turkish
schoolmaster. Other women of Kuwait followed her example and opened
private schools so that, by 1933, ten similar private schools for girls, run
by former students of 'A'isha Azmir, were operating in Kuwait. It was
only in 1937 that the state assumed responsibility for educating girls and
established the first state-funded girls' schools (al-Mughni 49–50). Besides
teaching the Qur'an, some women in the Gulf earned their living by
reciting or reading the Qur'an at certain events; these female Qur'an
readers were referred to by the title *mullaya* (Foley 202, n. 42). Professional
women readers in the Gulf always gained recognition and income by
acting as imams for other women, as readers at group religious ceremonies
and as healers who recited sacred texts over the sick. They would sometimes hire themselves out to recite the whole Qur'an from beginning to
end, called a *khatima*, for which the fee varied according to the level of the
reader's piety and religiosity (Doumato 90–1). Many female readers read
other texts too, besides the Qur'an. A woman working with the Bahrain
mission reported that she had met in Bahrain a religious reader who could
recite the New Testament in Arabic, and Shi'i religious readers recited the
poetic histories of the Prophet's life and the Imam Husayn's death. Women
readers were central to Shi'ite religious gatherings and commemorative
events especially 'Ashura on 10 Muharram, the day on which Husayn, the
son of 'Ali and Fatima, was killed at Karbala. Their readings had a great
impact on women attending the event, moving them emotionally and
psychologically. The readings were taken from a book of rhythmic poetry,
not recited from memory (Doumato 116–20). Just as women earned a
living by reciting the Qur'an at religious ceremonies and events, they also
supplemented their income by doing this to relieve people's sorrow or
pain. Every day of the week the woman reader went 'from house to house
to read over a sick baby or to a house for mourning or to read a bad spirit
out of a girl' (Foley 202, n. 42). The readers gained a lot of respect, especially when their interventions were successful.

Besides earning a living from religious work and education, many Gulf
women were engaged in various other interesting occupations and

services, through which they both served other women and made a living for themselves. One such service was preparing brides for their wedding day. The elaborate coiffing and dressing of the bride needed an expert. Some hairdressers specialized in dressing brides and employed an assistant to help them. Beauticians were experts in exfoliation, washing, massaging, depilation and applying henna to the bride's hands and the soles of her feet. Their work was highly skilled, since toxic material was sometimes used in beauty preparations: Harold Dickson reports that a herbal plaster containing arsenic was prepared and used as a depilatory (Dickson, *Arab of the Desert*, 160). Moreover, an artistic sense was always needed for the skillful application of henna (Abou Saud 71–5). In fact, this tradition continues among Gulf women till today. Women who specialize in decorating the hands and feet of the bride are always hired for wedding ceremonies in the modern Gulf states, and Gulf wedding ceremonies still follow many of the old traditions and are influenced by them (Ghunaym, 'al-Mar'a wa-al-zawaj', 198).

The function of the *dallala* (female peddler) was another important occupation through which women served other women. The *dallala* acted as an intermediary between the seller and the buyer; she would visit women in their houses and sell them goods, especially fabrics. The *dallala* did not purchase the goods she offered for sale from a supplier, but was paid a commission by the wholesaler or the manufacturer. Earning commission was an excellent way for any resourceful woman to start out in business on her own account. No capital outlay was needed and she could accumulate capital from commissions, which would grow over a period of time through good will and contacts. In pre-oil Kuwait, there are many cases of female peddlers who played an important role in bringing merchants' goods to upper-class women (Nasharty).

One of the indispensable professions undertaken solely by women was midwifery. Midwives occupied an important position in society; they were usually elderly women skilled in the use of herbal medicines and healing techniques. Their services were considered essential across all classes of society and women sought their help and paid them for their services (al-Shaybani 56). They had a captive clientele, as women would not allow men to come into intimate contact with them. Midwives in pre-oil societies combined two healing functions: curing and caring. They not only assisted with the birth itself but also attended to antenatal and postpartum conditions. They successfully treated a variety of women's diseases, including uterine hemorrhage and infertility. It is interesting that midwives in the pre-modern Gulf used a birth stool so that the mother adopted a squatting position, approved by advocates of natural childbirth today, although the missionary doctors thought it crude and uncomfortable and wanted women to lie on their backs in bed (Doumato 210).

As women were active at weddings and celebrations, caring and healing, they were also present at the time of death. The body of a dead woman was washed by a professional female body washer (*ghasila*), 'who is immediately sent for on a death taking place'. Washing the dead in pre-oil Gulf societies was a paid job and when the family of the deceased was too poor to pay, neighbors would provide the money, or in some cases, washers would give their services free of charge out of kindness and piety (al-'Adli 170). With the discovery of oil and the creation of the modern Gulf states, governments took responsibility for this service, and male and female washers became government employees, earning a monthly salary (al-'Adli 171).

Non-gendered occupations

The second group of women's occupations is that in which services or products are provided to both men and women. A principal example is healing and medicine, a field in which Gulf women were active and earned a living serving both men and women. Elderly women in particular played a vital role in traditional medicine. They usually took responsibility for the sick, and were natural collectors of medical lore and experimenters with it. Women were doctors without degrees, barred from books and lectures, learning from each other and passing experience and knowledge from neighbor to neighbor and from mother to daughter. This role in traditional medicine contributed to female empowerment; control of medicine implies potential power to determine who will live and who will die, who is fertile and who is sterile, who is mad and who is sane.

It is worth mentioning in this regard that in all of the examples of female healers encountered in the sources, the healer is a sole practitioner; there is no mention of a midwife's or healer's apprentice. In spite of the lack of evidence for apprentice training, however, informal instruction was certainly passed on within the family by mothers and aunts. Healing was a craft in which Gulf women were active and much needed. There are interesting cases in the sources of women practicing medicine and midwifery who proudly stated that they did not depend on anyone else for a living but lived solely on the proceeds from their work (al-Shaybani 56).

Being able to support themselves financially through engaging in medical and midwifery practices is not the only source of pride in the history of Gulf women, but as the missionary records of Gulf women show, women who worked as healers possessed specialized knowledge of the healing arts, and succeeded in curing cases where missionary doctors failed. Doughty observes that 'Arabs are cured in the maladies by the harem that have all some little store of drugs, spices and perfumes' (1:255).

Female healers used various techniques and surgical interventions, the most widespread of which were cauterization, phlebotomy and cupping. They diagnosed and treated a variety of diseases, both physical and psychological. They successfully treated eye disease, tonsillitis, severe diarrhea, and intestinal and abdominal problems, as well as epilepsy and psychological problems; they were able to cure cystitis and urinary tract infections, and successfully extracted kidney stones by prescribing a medication made of barley ('Abd al-Rahman 399). Female physicians favored treatment with ointments and medicines they prepared themselves. They were herbal specialists and were believed to have significant knowledge in this area. Many of them had small stores where they prepared and sold drugs, spices and perfumes. They used senna as a laxative and opium as a sedative. Most of the female healers throughout the Gulf region had knowledge of both the Prophet's remedies and Greek medicine.[11]

As such, female healers earned their reputation as widely accepted and respected members of Gulf society. Men and women went to them for treatment for a variety of illnesses and even the very conservative religious scholars in the community visited them and asked for their help. Even after the arrival of missionary doctors in the Gulf around 1909, people would still go to female healers and midwives, whom they trusted more. A leading Kuwaiti in the early twentieth century claimed that he had had an ulcer on his leg that an American doctor in Basra failed to cure. The doctor advised him to have the leg amputated. The man refused this advice and consulted a female healer, who dressed his wound with herbal

[11]Doumato (186) maintains that knowledge about Prophetic and Greek medicine was widespread in Gulf society.

ointment, and within two weeks his leg was healed (Wahba 39). Dickson, in his record of Bedouin medical techniques, describes the treatment given in 1939 by a Kuwaiti village woman who successfully treated a patient diagnosed by the missionary doctors as having a brain tumor. The missionary doctors pronounced the condition hopeless and were surprised to find the man in good health after being treated by the Kuwaiti woman (Dickson, *Kuwait*, 438).

Another outstanding example of such an exceptional female healer is Hamama al-Tiniji, who was a respected practitioner in al-Sharja, and supported herself and her family through the practice of medicine in the 1940s and 1950s. She had a reputation for treating difficult cases that hospital doctors failed to cure, which attracted patients from all over the Gulf region. She treated men, women and children and cured them of various kinds of diseases, both physical and psychological. She successfully treated a young girl who was diagnosed by hospital physicians as having an inflamed appendix that had to be surgically removed. Hamama examined the girl and discovered that she only had an upset stomach. Hamama prescribed an emetic and the girl was cured. The girl's father took her back to the hospital where the physician admitted that he had been mistaken. Hamama also had a good reputation for treating mental and psychological illnesses. She cured an Arabic tutor who was diagnosed by hospital doctors with incurable paranoia. Hamama treated him with medication and eardrops she had prepared herself, the tutor's mental health was restored and he resumed work ('Abd al-Rahman 400).

Women did not draw a clear demarcation line between the scientific and the supernatural traditional medical practices of the Gulf. Some female healers resorted to supernatural practices, such as exorcism of jinn, which were of value for their placebo effect; if the person to be treated believed that the treatment would work, he or she would likely feel that it did. In all the Gulf towns there were societies of women that practiced a form of relief from spirit possession called the *zar*. The word *zar* is commonly used to refer to the ceremony, or exorcism ritual, through which people obtain relief from the symptoms of possession.[12]

Zar sessions to relieve the possessed from the symptoms of possession were organized by a leader. In the Gulf many *zar* leaders were women,

[12]For a detailed description of the *zar*, see the documentary film of the *zar* ceremony in Morocco, made by Elizabeth Warnock Fernea: 'Saints and Spirits' (Granada TV, 1977).

who were referred to as *shaykhat al-zar*. The *shaykha* was usually an elderly woman, a slave or of slave origin. However, despite her origin, *shaykhat al-zar* was held in high esteem because of the belief in her power to heal and relieve symptoms of possession. She was a paid professional, treated with respect by all those who attended her sessions, and consulted whenever someone was believed to be possessed. Ordinary people would consult the *shaykha* at public ceremonies, while wealthy people would host the *zar* ceremony in their homes. The *zar* societies or cults brought together women of different classes and backgrounds, creating a sense of community akin to that of a Sufi brotherhood. The *zar* cults empowered women of the Gulf and provided them with a degree of social power, even among men. The linkage of the *zar* to the jinn made men respect *shaykhat al-zar* and comply with the *zar* demands lest they find themselves on the wrong side of an evil spirit (Foley 172–3).

The above clearly indicates that the participation of women in various medical fields in the Gulf was never restricted, denied or conditioned, even when the methods employed were not grounded on solid evidence-based knowledge (as in the case of healing through the *zar*). While it is true that historians do not give them adequate coverage, there is no explicit tone of disapproval or surprise in the historical discourse. Narrations are free of any sense of amazement when relating stories of female healers treating male patients. Although there are very few specific examples of women practicing medicine, it is more than probable that there were many other successful female healers and physicians beyond the known examples. It is the nature and unavailability of sources that restrict the range of our knowledge.

As much as healing seems to be a domain where women excelled, there were also other shady female-male encounters through occupations that were deemed disreputable, but which did bring income to the women who practiced them. Female entertainers, singers, and musicians were all characters of ill repute and were publicly perceived to be morally suspect, and to some extent socially unacceptable. Singing was taken up as an occupation by poorer classes of Qatari women, who were usually descendents of slaves of African origin. They formed professional groups of singers, dancers and percussionists and performed in public, at gatherings or wedding celebrations, being paid for their services. There were also prostitutes, who were to be found in some Arabian Gulf towns during the pre-oil period. In contrast to the situation in modern Gulf societies, prostitution was then not an illegal occupation, regarded as a necessary evil. Nevertheless, prostitutes were always watched by the authorities and were restricted to unfrequented streets on the margins of towns (Dickson, *Forty Years*, 22).

There were many other occupations in pre-oil Gulf society that brought women into direct contact with men in the marketplace or at home. Fishermen's wives sometimes helped their husbands by mending nets and working as saleswomen in the fish market. Women in the villages worked on the land, marketed the harvest, and sold dairy products such as butter, cheese and yoghurt in the market or to neighbors. Others ground wheat, baked bread and sold it. Poor women, who ranked low on the social scale, could not afford to stay at home. They helped in supporting the family, and had to provide for their children when their husbands were away. They were active in Gulf town markets, selling a wide range of wares. In some markets there were booths for women traders, and there were some women-only markets that specialized in selling products for women.[13] In Kuwait there was an interesting market known as *Suq al-Harim* (the women's market), in which female traders gathered to sell their goods — silk, fabrics, kohl, henna, combs, and many other items brought back by their husbands from trade voyages ('Atallah 239). Gulf women also worked as water carriers (*saqqa*), carrying water skins on their backs to bring water from the springs to people's homes.[14]

The vast majority of Gulf women used to spin thread, and weave and dye textiles, both for themselves and their families and for sale. Spinning was a remunerative occupation. It was the source of income for many widows, spinsters, divorcees and poor women. Women in the cities, towns and desert wove tents, carpets and rugs. The thread was dyed by the women themselves, using herbs that grew in the desert.[15] The Gulf did not import dyed thread or colored cloth until the late nineteenth century. Before then all the work was done by women. It was also women who created textile

[13]Duomato includes in her book interesting photographs of women's bazaars in Unaiza and al-Qatif, two cities in Saudi Arabia on the Arabian Gulf coast.

[14]Muraikhi (164) provides an interesting photograph of a woman carrying a water skin on her back.

[15]The sources do not indicate how these were collected. It may be that women collected them themselves, adding to their responsibilities and jobs in this pre-modern society.

designs, which were usually geometrical (Dickson, *Forty Years*, 209; Abou Saud 135–6).

Sewing and embroidery were also interesting means by which women earned their living. Before the sewing machine became available, all the work was done by hand. Women sewed the long, simple garments worn by both men and women, and made caps for men and shawls for women. They decorated their work with skillful embroidery, using intricate patterns and elaborate designs. Besides embroidering dresses and robes, they also embroidered bed sheets, pillows and cushions. Even though many women of the Gulf sewed for personal and family purposes, there were professional seamstresses who sewed for payment, working in workshops or in their own homes. In fact, some of them were famous around the region for their sewing and embroidery (Abou Saud 136–7; Ghunaym, 'Al-awda' al-iqtisadiyya', 93).

Even though many of the above occupations were directly related to female life and the income derived from them was generally modest, this does not mean that working women had a separate economic world of their own or that they were not in the economic mainstream. Working women formed an integral part of the Gulf economy. They earned wages that were reinvested in the market, not only as they purchased their daily provisions or contributed to the family income, but through investment, no matter how modest, in various ventures. Many women invested part of their income in their business to enable expansion. Women peddlers were a good example of this. Most of them worked on a small, localized scale, earning very little commission on every transaction. However, they invested their earnings by buying new goods or paying for goods that they had taken on credit. Seamstresses would also invest part of their income in the needles and thread they needed; i.e., women invested in keeping their businesses going.

Women's contribution to the economy

From the above, we can clearly see that lower-class Gulf women took up various occupations in the Gulf and contributed to their family's income. Even though many issues linked to the working conditions of women are still not clear, such as the amount they were paid, where they worked, and how they were trained, their presence in the market was a fact of life. No society could function without women and they were active in turning the wheels of the economy. Their income, however modest, and even when it was paid in kind, not in cash,[16] was part of the capital circulating in the economy. Their investment, even on the smallest possible scale, had multiple impacts on economic growth through the creation of new job opportunities and capitalizing on cash turnover. Surplus production, economic rationality and potential profitability are among the main factors for economic growth, and these factors are relevant for all the female workers and investors in the Gulf. Even when women were engaged in unpaid domestic work, they still had an impact on economic growth and were contributing to the family and local economies. Women's own work and contribution maintained the life and livelihood of the Arabian Gulf.

Rich and middle-class women, the wives of Gulf rulers and merchants, were not engaged in any of the above occupations during the pre-oil period, but they participated in the economic life of the region and contributed to it by other means. Some rich women had their own commercial enterprises, such as trading in jewelry. Women took good care of their valuables—gold coins, jewelry and embroidered clothes that they usually received as wedding gifts—and would sell them at times of need to contribute to the family income.[17] These were favored commodities and popular forms of investment, and the sources tell of women buying, selling or loaning such valuables to meet living expenses. Some wealthy women invested in real estate; they owned houses, orchards and jewelry shops.[18] There are also cases of women who invested their money in the pearl business. Shaykha Hussa bint Murr, the mother of the present ruler of Dubai, was a successful pearl merchant; she owned land, was engaged in trade and was widely regarded as a shrewd and formidable businesswoman (Izzard 246).

Many of the wealthy women of the Arabian Gulf invested their money in charitable endowments (awqaf), which are governed by Islamic law. Several Omani women have constructed and endowed mosques, for example. The subject of Gulf women as philanthropists is a very

---

[16]Many women working as domestic help were paid in kind, not in cash (Hay 39).

[17]Women of the Gulf towns invested their money in gold, while in the desert women's jewelry and ornaments were made of silver (see see al-'Izzi 143–4).

[18]Some wealthy women invested in jewelry shops that were managed by male family members on their behalf (Ghunaym, 'Al-awda' al-iqtisadiyya', 97).

interesting one as *waqf* endowments demonstrate the extent of property ownership by women and are examples of wealthy Gulf women enjoying economic independence and power. This type of investment also gave and still gives women a measure of social and economic influence.[19]

The part women played in the economy was not limited to their role as producers and investors; their consumption patterns and purchasing power also had a strong impact on the market and the economy. They were the principle buyers of goods for daily use, so, whether as producers or consumers, Gulf women were active participants in the marketplace. There were, as mentioned above, markets that specialized in selling women's products. In such markets, female traders gathered to sell their goods to other women. However, one should note that most of the women active in the market were women of low social status. Wealthy women usually sent their slaves to buy goods from the marketplace, or would wait for the *dallala* to supply them with what they needed.

The presence of Gulf women in the marketplace and their role in the economy had a significant impact on the standing of women generally. It empowered them and enhanced their position within their families and in their society. The fact that they were wage earners, no matter how modest their earnings, gave them a kind of economic independence that affected all aspects of their lives. Their income meant that they could support themselves and, in many cases, their families. Supporting the family definitely empowered women and gave them authority within the family and in society. It gave them the right to make decisions and take the necessary action in matters concerning the family. Even though the cases of working women discovered in the sources up to now are limited in number, they are indicative that many other individual women would have had a similar background.

A comprehensive historical picture of women in pre-modern Gulf societies thus emerges, which leads to the following conclusions and points to areas for further investigation:

First, women, across the broad spectrum of economic and social classes, were not isolated from public economic life. They interacted in a multifaceted manner in and with society: they moved across the areas of working in handicrafts, offering services, and being actively involved in earning

[19]For interesting information in the sources on *awqaf* established by women of the Gulf, see-Shaybani 124–5, 136, 175.

their living, towards more market-related activities, by way of buying and selling and participating in the cycle of production and consumption. They also had a share in ownership, administration, and investment in property, real estate, endowments, and land. Investments were also used to finance further projects and this, in turn, emphasized the economic status, independence, and empowerment of women.

Second, the research does not paint a rosy picture of a golden, ideal age in the Gulf. Nonetheless, the research calls into question the sacredness of modernity, which is at times imposed as an unquestioned, unprecedented, and un-deconstructible model, in disregard of previous eras, which are not necessarily all backwardness, evil, and darkness. It is more useful to consider history objectively and accurately in order to deduce balanced historical concepts and models.

Third, from this perspective one can say that the Gulf woman has a history that requires much 'archeological' unveiling and analytical study, not as a separate history, but as a history that has been neglected and unexamined. In this way, through the re-construction of history, or through the simulation of history, the woman of the Gulf can be re-integrated into the overall structure of Arab and Islamic history.

Fourth, this history almost always proves that women in pre-modern Gulf societies worked as much as the circumstances permitted them, and were part of public life throughout the pre-modern era and during the formation of the nation states.

7. A Labor of Love: Making Space for Midwives in Gulf History

HIBBA ABUGIDEIRI

Midwifery as a topic of historical inquiry has not figured very prominently in studies of the Arab world. What exists is a handful of scholarly works, almost entirely on modern Egypt, whose discussion of midwives is part of a larger exploration of the social history of medicine.[1] The inquiry is rarely about midwives as women professionals.[2] This is not surprising. Along with the problem of sources, an underdeveloped interest in women's work historically explains this historiographical gap. Indeed, female labor has not enjoyed the same scholarly attention as other gender topics on the Arab world.[3] When it has been considered, scholars have largely focused on the analysis of women's wage labor, with a heavy bias on certain contexts such as Palestine.[4] This trend however is beginning to change.

A materialist approach to the study of women in the Middle East is still very much in the process of formation. We are increasingly aware of the need to address broad questions of social organization and ideology rather than limit discussion to women's participation in the wage labor force. The

[1] See the article by Sharkey and the dissertation by Young. A chapter is dedicated to midwives in the books by Jagailloux and Kuhnke, and a few pages are dedicated to midwives in Sonbol.

[2] See the contributions by Fahmy and by Hatem.

[3] This excludes those works that take a more global perspective on Arab women and development, such as Hijab; Khoury and Moghadam; and Moghadam.

[4] See for example Samed, 'Palestinian Women'; idem, 'Proletarianization'; and Semyonov.

evolution of 'public' and 'private' household social spheres, which differentiated production and reproduction, devalues the activities related to the latter. In brief, the field of inquiry must expand beyond wage labor to encompass the subjects of reproduction, sexuality, social control, household work and casual labor (Tucker 3–4).

As Judith Tucker argues here, only by understanding women's role in reproduction, or the 'private' household, can we truly understand the terms and consequences of women's roles in production (ibid. 4). Her critique rightly points to the inadequacy of studies that situate women's work in production without paying close attention to the constraints that reproduction, as expressed in family arrangements and in the prevailing ideology defining women's spheres, places on women's participation in the wage labor force (ibid.).

Tucker's critique ultimately exposes the limitations that traditional Marxist thinking about labor has historically placed on an analysis of Arab women's work, since this age-old model traditionally privileges production as the most significant index of societal development, and therefore determines the value of men's and women's work based on their respective relationship to 'public' versus 'private' production. Yet the public/private paradigm has more often hindered than facilitated the study of Arab women in general and female labor in particular. Men's work, in this framework, is more valued since, as skilled wage laborers, they are more fully integrated into modern large-scale industry. Because they have typically been less skilled, women, by contrast, receive lower wages—when they are not surplus labor or work inside the household. Because *real* work in this schema is an inherently public activity demonstrated in economic terms, women's labor is valued to the extent that it affects public production and devalued if carried out in spaces deemed to be private.

More and more, however, scholars have attempted to broaden traditional Marxist understandings of the production/reproduction paradigm as it applies to Arab women in order to redress such inadequacies. By paying closer attention to women's work as surplus labor or in the provision of subsistence through work in the home and casual labor outside, the goal of this growing body of scholarship has been to uncover women's contribution to production in its myriad forms (ibid.).

With this goal in mind, this article attempts to diversify scholarly discussions about the organization of labor more generally, and Arab female labor more specifically, by examining the work of midwives in Arabia beginning in the late nineteenth and early twentieth centuries. It demonstrates that the public/private paradigm, as informed by notions of production and reproduction, fails to measure the vital and effective modes through which Arab women's labor mattered in constituting the social organization of their diverse societies. This has been especially true of Arabian women in pre-independence Gulf societies, as their literary image—more so than that of Arab women in other parts of the Middle East—has tenaciously revolved around misconceptions of tribalism, seclusion and the harem, veiling and polygyny. This distorted image not only stems from Victorian cultural attitudes that framed the English travelogues that have been used to write the history of the Gulf, but is also the product of 'the consistent reliance on a model of dichotomous private and public domains in Middle Eastern social systems [which] may typify a more general theoretical bias toward "bounded" models of society' used by anthropologists, among other scholars (Pastner 322).[5] Because they are presumed to be locked away in the privacy of their homes, oppressed, uneducated and dependent on their male kin, the role of women in Bedouin and other pastoral nomadic adaptations has largely been ignored in scholarship—an indication that 'analytical deficiencies persist' (ibid. 310).

By focusing on Arabian midwives, this article illustrates the need for new analytical approaches to Arab female labor, especially within tribal societies, that emphasize not simply the economic, but more importantly the social value of work. It focuses on midwives in Qatar, Kuwait, Saudi Arabia and, to a lesser extent, Oman, as active social agents who helped develop their modern societies through their distinguished roles as women medical professionals. 'Making space for midwives in Gulf history' is not only a much-needed attempt to understand the multifaceted nature of Arabian women's work historically; it also challenges the conceptual scheme of gendered labor that pits women's less valued 'private' work against men's more important 'public' work, as engendered by Marxist thinking. If such 'bounded models of society' problematically obscure Arabian women's productive activities in society, then documenting the roles of Gulf midwives, whose work arguably blurred these boundaries,

[5]Pastner studies the travelogues of Richard Burton and Charles Doughty of the nineteenth century and Harold Dickson of the early twentieth century.

provides an alternative way of tracing the historical imprints that these women left on their societies.

Indeed, the work of midwives defies any clear-cut categorizations determined by the public/private paradigm: while midwifery offered women a skilled trade based on wages, their work very directly affected, and was affected by, reproductive culture, as practiced in the home and out of the public eye. In many ways, midwives occupied both public and private spaces, if we insist on using these categories, and their profession depended on the fluidity, not contravention, of these domains. In fact, the entire public/private paradigm collapses when the nature of these women's work is considered. Studying midwives, in sum, gives scholars access to the interworkings of a female-managed economy as well as insights into sexual behavior, family relations and female medical lifestyles, revealing in a word the 'private politics behind public issues' (Ulrich 33). By uncovering the nature of women's 'private' work through an analysis of midwifery, such insights lead us to question the nature of 'public' space in turn-of-the-century Arabian societies.

Piecing together midwifery in the Gulf

Undoubtedly a key factor in the dearth of scholarship on Arab midwives is the lack of sources. Regrettably there is no equivalent in Arab history of *A Midwife's Tale*, a work that recounts the diary of an Anglo-American midwife in late eighteenth- and early nineteenth-century America (Ulrich). Add to this a general scarcity of archival sources on the Gulf region, and we can quickly begin to appreciate the daunting research challenges posed by a study of Arabian women, let alone midwives. What we do have, nevertheless, are two types of sources. One type is the life histories of midwives, whose oral accounts tell us about the state of medical care, as well as reproductive practices, in Arabian societies. Given the centrality of the spoken word in the region, oral history proves to be an effective methodological approach to the study of Arabian women that partially redresses the problem of written sources (Abugideiri, 'Egyptian Woman').

This article is based on the life histories of three Qatari midwives: Umm 'Abdullah, Umm Fahad and Umm Khalil, as well as Umm Khalid, a Saudi woman who had previously lived in the region of al-Ihsa' in central Arabia, but now resides in Riyadh. All four women are well into their 70s and 80s, are married and have children. Their interviews were conducted in Doha, Qatar, in the spring of 2008. While their life histories provide invaluable insights into how Arabian women were trained and lived as traditional midwives, I also realize that more interviews are needed with women from across the region to both broaden and give texture to the preliminary sketch of midwifery offered here.

Alongside these oral histories is the second type of source, namely the works of Christian missionaries in the Gulf. The nineteenth century witnessed a proliferation of Protestant Evangelical missions to the non-Western world, and, not coincidentally, at a time when European imperialist powers were conquering regions of Africa and Asia in their search for new markets, cheap labor and indigenous resources. In fact, Christian missions were able to spread to foreign lands thanks to path-finding European explorers and imperialists who, after discovering new lands, offered missionaries protection from local Ottoman authorities.[6] Evangelists had been active since the early nineteenth century, mainly in Yemen, through the mission founded in 1885 by Ion Keith-Falconer, which later became the Church of Scotland South Arabia Mission (CSM), and the Danish Church Mission in Arabia (DCM). However, it was the ultimate goal of only one Protestant group 'to occupy the interior of Arabia' (Storm 64).[7]

Missionaries from the New Jersey-based Reformed Church in America (RCA), commonly called Dutch Reformed, officially established a foreign mission, called the 'Arabian Mission', on 1 August 1889.[8] Reverend James Cantine and Reverend Samuel M. Zwemer founded the Mission to address the absence of evangelical work in 'the Mohammedan world'. Early in 1889, the two men undertook reconnaissance trips to Syria, Lebanon, Iraq and Yemen, though it became clear to them that, 'if the Arabian Mission is to be true to its name and purpose, it must occupy Arabia' (Zwemer 16). To choose Arabia out of all the Muslim lands was to focus on a region with a reputation in European traveler, imperialist and

[6]One missionary states: 'It is worthy of note that where the British Government had any sort of control over a locality both the persons and the property of the missionaries and their helpers were much more secure than where this was not the case' (Mason 77).
[7]For more on Ion Keith-Falconer's mission in Yemen, see the books by Robson; and Sinker.
[8]August 1, 1889 marks the approval and signing of the official 'Plan of the Arabian Mission' by its founders, Reverends Samuel M. Zwemer and James Cantine.

evangelical circles of being impenetrable and unexplored, and thus reveals the founders' insistence on conquering the heartland or 'Cradle of Islam' in the name of Christ.[9] Thereafter, opening 'bible depots' in eastern ports along the Arabian Gulf was given the highest priority.

Despite staunch resistance from the Ottoman Sublime Porte,[10] Bedouin tribal wars and the threat of disease, missionary 'chief stations' were established first in Basra (Iraq) in 1891, then Bahrain and Muscat (Oman) by 1893—all three being major ports that were easily accessible by sea, had regular mail delivery and were free of malaria during this period (Mason 79). Amara (Iraq) was added as a center in 1895 and Kuwait by 1900 (ibid. 251). Because Britain became the dominant sea power in the Gulf during the eighteenth and nineteenth centuries and because of its protectorate treaties with certain Arabian rulers, missionaries in Kuwait, Oman and Bahrain especially enjoyed British protection against Ottoman hostilities. The Mesopotamian cities of Basra and Amara, on the other hand, fell under Ottoman rule; it was only after the newly formed Kingdom of Iraq was established as a British mandate a few decades later that these twin stations enjoyed similar protection as their neighboring Arabian centers. Despite these friendly treaties with the British, American missionaries were not shielded from popular resentment as Arabians often called them pejoratively *al-Inglayz*, 'the English'.[11]

The RCA missionaries were active in various efforts to bring the Word of Christ to Muslims in Arabia. Evangelical, educational and medical missions were the three fronts through which they worked. Naturally, they created institutions to address each of these efforts: Sunday schools, a very small number of churches, and Bible shops (where Bibles and other religious materials were sold or distributed to locals) were established; schools for girls and boys were built; and dispensaries and hospitals were created

[9]'There was, however, this essential difference between the Mission to Arabia and those to many other unevangelized lands, in that the land and the peoples to which these young men proposed to go with the Gospel message, was practically an unexplored land and an unknown people' (Mason 64).

[10]'Although it is well known that the Ottoman Government has nowhere and never been friendly to Protestant missionaries, yet the opposition or permission of mission-work depends largely upon the attitude of the local governments' (*Neglected Arabia*, Vol. 1, no. 4 [Oct-Dec. 1892], 3). Typically where there were agreements with the British, as in Muscat, proselytizing was more acceptable.

[11]A treaty tied Bahrain to Britain in 1892 and Kuwait signed its treaty with Britain in 1899, its first British Political Agent being appointed in 1904 (Calverley 12–15).

to treat people *en masse*. Of these, missionaries believed medical missions were the most successful.

> One cannot, and should not, measure one type of work as against another, but it is true that, after forty-two years' experience, medical work has proved to be the key to unlock closed doors, the means of promoting friendships, and the tool for breaking down opposition, fear and superstition ... the medical approach has been undoubtedly the most effective way of preaching the Gospel to Moslems. (Storm 64)

Four major medical stations could be found in the eastern part of Arabia on the eve of World War I: Basra, Muscat, Bahrain, and Kuwait. Of these, Bahrain was the largest, most developed station, most likely due to its historical importance as the first area in the Arabian Gulf to attract the attention of the English East India Company, which in the seventeenth century was looking for new markets outside India (Lorimer 837–8). By the turn of the century, all newcomers of the Arabian Mission were sent to Bahrain to learn Arabic, typically for two years, after which they were dispatched to other stations in the Peninsula (Mason 215; Calverley 23–4).

To justify the missionary campaign to their RCA-based financiers back in the States, 'Arabian missionaries', as they were officially called, kept meticulous records of their evangelistic activities. They penned a rich suite of historical sources (e.g., memoirs, personal letters, official reports and correspondence) that offer insightful yet untapped details about the Gulf, including its cultural habits, health issues and medical practices—details they learned from their extensive trips throughout the region and from treating patients who had traveled to the mission centers from more remote areas in the interior. This is especially true of those memoirs left by missionary women doctors. Indeed, Christian women, and especially the wives of missionary men, contributed significantly to the Arabian Mission. In fact, three years before the formal establishment of the Mission, the wives of Arabian missionaries found their own Christian purpose in the Gulf thanks to the founder's wife and trained nurse, Amy Elizabeth Wilkes Zwemer. She is heralded for beginning 'the first systematic and prolonged effort for the evangelization of the women of Arabia by the women of America' on 1 June 1896 (Mason 89).

To missionaries, and missionary women especially, Islam was the source of Muslim women's oppression, the veil being its most onerous and inhumane mandate. 'Nowhere in the world is the condition of womanhood so pitiful as that found behind the veil in Moslem lands.' By paving the way for 'that brighter day when the light of Christ will penetrate the darkness behind the veil ... nowhere can the ministry of devoted Christian women have hope of greater usefulness or more blessed results' (Storm 65). Women evangelists made this goal central to their missionary work among Gulf women, which to the larger Arabian Mission was considered a welcome and unique contribution, since Christian male 'access to the native women had been rendered impossible by the inviolable customs of ages' (Mason 88).

It was in their service to medical missions in particular that women missionaries prospered the most, a fact they readily acknowledged: 'Women have won for themselves a respectable place in the medical profession, and in no department more assuredly than in the teeming world of foreign missions ... almost everybody is converted to the idea of sending women physicians to the heathen' (Bainbridge 3–4; cf. Allen 26). Strikingly, although American women faced numerous political, economic and social challenges of gender inequality back at home, as Protestant missionaries in 'the Orient', they enjoyed certain freedoms that allowed them to make a name for themselves while also serving Christ (Pruitt). Their sense of medical superiority assumed in their evangelical charge was evident. Often they described midwives as 'terrible' and 'ignorant', and native healers were 'quacks' who brought 'untold suffering upon their ill-fated victims through their misguided methods' (Calverley et at. 58; Allen 19). At the same time and without contradiction, doctors such as Eleanor Calverley and Mary Bruins Allison, having spent decades serving in the Gulf in the early- to mid-twentieth century, viewed the region as 'home' and treated their women patients with respect and even tenderness. 'Many of these [women] are very lovely, and all of them well worth knowing', Calverley recalls during her retirement years (Calverley vii). Similarly, having served as a nurse in Iraq and Oman in the mid-twentieth century, Jeanette Boersma, otherwise known as Khatune Naeema, wrote about her 'beloved Oman': 'Oman was my home for thirty-five years, and my heart still belongs to its people' (Boersma 100–1).

Nonetheless, women doctors and nurses were in short supply in Arabia—a challenge that Arabian missionaries constantly struggled with during their three-decade campaign in the Peninsula. To redress this shortage, the wives of missionaries, and especially of appointed doctors, were often compelled to medically treat native women, even if they themselves were not professionally trained, as the wife of the famous missionary doctor, Paul Harrison, explains.

> It was down in Muscat that I was forced into midwifery . . . Yes, this is Arabia's way. She makes those of us who have had no training do the work of nurses. She forces our nurses to do the work of doctors. That is bad business, of course . . . We cannot tamper with lives. But Arabia cannot wait for our doctors and our trained nurses. There are not enough to go around. Do we realize how large Arabia is? . . . We have taught Arabs to want doctors and nurses and hospital care . . . Do we not owe them something for their confidence in us? Are we not responsible for the trust they give us? Dare any of us turn away from the call of the sick? . . . Healed bodies pave the way for the healing of the soul. Arabia has awakened to her needs. We must answer! (Harrison, 'Arabia Calls'.)

Clearly, Christian women saw in medical missions a sense of religious duty. Their importance to the Mission was secured by the doctor shortage certainly, but also by the region's gender-segregated culture.[12] They saw the all-female contact with Muslim women as their distinguished opportunity to preach the Gospel while also reversing the unsanitary conditions that threatened society at large, since 'access to the homes and to the mothers' gave them 'almost limitless opportunity for improving the healthful condition of the life' (Bainbridge 26). Importantly such access meant that sources written by these women uniquely document Gulf reproductive practices found in no other written sources to date.

With the help of these missionary sources, we are able to piece together some important indicators of Gulf midwifery practices and thus the work of midwives. In fact, these texts offer a contextual framework that helps explain the development of Gulf midwifery by the late twentieth century.

---

[12]Interestingly, such segregation was also practiced in Hindu India, where upper-caste women, such as the Zenanas who refused to frequent British colonially-controlled dispensaries, were not allowed to have direct contact with male doctors. Instead, 'all the conversation being carried on by second parties [were] on both sides of the screen' (Bainbridge 28).

Because of them, we can identify the definitive catalyst of modernizing change to Arabian traditional medicine, and therefore midwifery, not as the discovery of oil in the mid-twentieth century, though oil money certainly helped underwrite state campaigns to modernize Gulf societies, including medical institutions, after independence.

Rather, modernization came earlier in the century, not unproblematically, with the arrival of Christian missionaries, who saw modern medicine as the most effective 'method in disarming prejudice and awakening sympathy in Moslem lands'.[13] This suggests that, at the same time that the advances of European medicine brought lifesaving benefit to a region that suffered from epidemic disease and chronic illnesses, the technology of medicine was also inextricably tied to the ideology of Christian evangelism. This entanglement of medicine with the missionaries' sense of religio-cultural superiority does impede, but does not debilitate, our ability to decode from these sources how illness and treatment were understood and practiced by Gulf natives themselves. After all, missionaries assessed Bedouin societies in most cases with much accuracy, but not much insight.[14]

This study argues that, before the late twentieth century, Arabian societies approached medical care, and midwives approached childbirth, on the basis of local tribal affiliation, with the home, as the exclusive site of childbirth and medical treatment for women, being understood as communal space where kinship bonds and tribal identity were fostered and reinforced through rituals of childbirth. That being so, we can view the 'private' intimate space of Bedouin homes as also invoking notions of 'public' space. That midwives fluidly moved through these domains in order to perform their tasks, not to mention the importance of their work in reinforcing wider kinship ties, says much about the significance of women's work in constituting Arabian societies, as well as mapping out what labor possibilities existed for Arabian women.

Midwives and reproductive culture in the Gulf

To understand the work of midwives, one must frame midwifery in late-nineteenth- and early-twentieth-century Arabia within the larger matrix of

---

[13]'Medical Work', *Neglected Arabia*, Vol. 1, no. 3 (1 July–1 October 1892), 6.
[14]I am borrowing Pastner's critique of English travelogues' romanticized depictions of Bedouin society and applying it to missionary observations of Bedouins (Pastner 310).

an Arabian medical ethos, starting with how illness and medicine more generally operated in the region. Until the late twentieth century, Arabians remained faithful to traditional medicine as the most effective method for treating what they believed to be the two causes of sickness and disease: malign influences ('the Evil Eye') and the hand of God (Dickson 505). As elsewhere, disease was attributed either to 'demons or evil spirits' (Calverley et al. 58), or to God's will and divine punishment for society's spiritual degeneration. Stories of death caused by epidemics served as cautionary tales for society and rulers alike. For instance, when a woman died of plague in Mecca in the early nineteenth century, it was reported that 'the body was washed and put into the coffin; after being dead two days, she suddenly rose, and said, "This plague is on account of our sins; repent, and cease from tyranny!" The Shereef of Mecca proclaimed this marvel over all the country' (Wolff 328).

To combat what were seen as supernatural causes of sickness, there were natural remedies made from God's earthly creation.

> All over Arabia, much reliance is still placed on the medical methods and prescriptions of ancient times. Credit for introducing modern medicine . . . goes to the Americans and British . . . In spite of this, Arabs in general did not greet modern medicine with enthusiasm, except in the sphere of surgery, and that only comparatively recently. They conceded little advantage to modern drugs over ancient ones, and the majority of the population rely on herbs and follow the medical dictates of Avicenna, the famous Bokharan physician of medieval times, and of his disciples, in so far as they are educated enough to understand them. (Wahba 35)

Locals were generally 'happy' with traditional methods to relieve their pain. It was only when a problem, such as disease, infection or a burn, continued or worsened that an Arab '[took] himself off to the doctor in fear or pain' (Moloney 278). Arabians typically avoided surgery. One story relates that when a tutor of Ibn Sa'ud's children had to have an operation on his stomach for a longstanding gastric ulcer, Ibn Sa'ud asked in surprise, 'Has it come to this . . . that men now have their abdomens cut open just as they cut open a sack or an old suit of clothes?' (Harrison, *Arab at Home*, 315). Instead, locals preferred 'to die, be buried and to rise in one piece on the Day of Resurrection', so that human dissection was never permitted and the removal of a portion of the body, such as a gangrened limb, was not readily acceptable (Moloney 278; Harrison, *Arab at Home*, 324).

Although Arabians employed traditional medicine to treat their day-to-day ailments, folk cures increasingly failed to relieve the ravaging effects of epidemic disease due to ignorance of disease causation. The Gulf suffered from the typical illnesses and infectious diseases that riddled other parts of Asia and Africa during the nineteenth and early twentieth centuries. These included cholera, malaria, smallpox, typhoid, and 'fever', which itself encompassed a number of different diseases, such as influenza, typhus, and dengue fever. As elsewhere, when these diseases hit the region, tremendous loss followed (Harrison, *Arab at Home*, 313). Smallpox was particularly deadly and was by far the most dreaded disease of all, as it terrified Arabians 'to an extraordinary degree' (Dickson 510). Alongside global epidemic diseases, local diseases such as trachoma, rheumatism, neuralgia, ulcers, roundworms and especially tuberculosis also threatened the region ('Report from Bahrein' 5; Allison 68).

It was only when traditional medical treatments failed that Arabians increasingly turned to medical missionaries, especially in cases of smallpox, cholera and the plague (Mason 161). Christian medical missions, however, were initially not always welcome in the Gulf. 'Little by little, the desert prejudice thawed and melted' (Dodd 61). Arab reluctance to seek missionary treatment eventually gave way to the region's general acceptance. Missionaries blamed Muslim religious intolerance for their initial reluctance: 'Lacking the polished ways of more civilized regions, where polite words just as often cloak hatred, this rude, rough son of the desert was unable to hide his disgust at having to admit that a Christian doctor was more effective than his own wise men' (ibid.). They also identified religious fanaticism as the reason why Muslims, and especially women, did not at first seek their medical care.[15] For these Christians, healing the bodies of Arab Muslims was the path to converting their souls. 'The native need and appreciation of medical aid ... conclusively proved that by this means even the most bigoted and fanatical natives could be brought into contact with the Gospel message' (Mason 72–3). Native

[15]The text is referring to Miss Mary Van Pelt, a trained nurse stationed in Kuwait, who often took full charge of women's medical work in the absence of a woman doctor. She also served as a dispenser in emergency cases (Van Ess 30).

acceptance of medical services was viewed, in short, as a sign of the mission's evangelistic successes.

To Gulf societies, however, accepting medical services from Christians had less to do with religion and more to do with effective treatment. We know, for instance, that between 1894 and 1924, only sixty-six men and twenty-one women 'native helpers' converted to Christianity, sixteen Sunday schools were established, and five churches were built in the entire region (Mason 251). Those who converted, moreover, often returned to Islam later (Allison xi). Compared with other foreign missions in Africa, India, China, Siam, and Japan, Arabian missionaries were stumped by the failure of their campaign to convert Muslims in the Peninsula: 'Probably no other mission has seen so little result in proportion to the effort expended' (Storm 65).

By contrast, whereas 1,888 Arabs sought medical treatment in 1894, this number swelled to 59,413 by 1924 (Mason 251). In fact, treatment in dispensaries reached 64,128 patients in Bahrain, 66,667 in Kuwait, and 40,091 in Muscat by the late 1930s (Storm 110). Clearly, of the Arabian Mission's activities, medical missions were what locals most utilized, since their advanced treatments yielded obvious and often instantaneous benefit to the body in ways that did not threaten their faith in Islam. In fact, Arabians were very much aware of the Mission's evangelistic aim in dispensing modern medicine and thus differentiated in no uncertain terms between medicine and Christianity: 'Many local people still believe that these Missions have a religious and political bias and that medical missionaries let religion prejudice them when they treat Moslems' (Wahba 38).

Due to the ravages of epidemic disease, medical mission centers prospered in the Gulf where established dispensaries and hospitals offered the advances of Western medicine against these global killers. Furthermore, 'a physician was considered to have some sort of magical insight' (Allison 66). Not surprisingly, missionary sources highlight the extent to which Arabians—Bedouins, villagers, and townspeople alike—came from near and far to seek their treatment, some walking, some by donkey or camel, and still others by steamers 'from the Mikran coast of Beluchistan across the Gulf of Oman' (Mason 156, cf. ibid. 193, 199; Allison 63).

Still, the importance of Western medicine during this period, while significant, should not be overestimated, for Arabians typically sought 'no cure unless in an advanced stage of infection' (Dickson 510) or 'the need

[was] very acute' (Calverley et al. 54). Natives only reluctantly accepted any medical intervention—Western or otherwise—when an illness or the symptoms of disease became too serious for folk cures to relieve. And even when they sought missionary treatment, they did not always appreciate the importance of carrying out the doctor's instructions—a challenge that missionary doctors repeatedly lamented in their memoirs (Harrison, *Arab at Home*, 319; Allison xxi). Accepting more invasive medical treatments of any sort, then, was a last resort; natives preferred natural folk cures to combat their bodily ailments. In sum, the efficacy of Western medicine, as practiced by Arabian missionaries, did gradually change native attitudes toward modern medical intervention; however, the majority of Arabians, until the late twentieth century, understood medicine and its function in everyday life in very traditional terms. Such was the medical ethos that framed the practice of midwifery and therefore the work of midwives.

Midwives were charged with birthing children. In line with traditional medicine, Arabian culture understood childbirth as a natural process that required no outside interference. In the words of one Arabian woman, 'God had ordained that women should bear children. He would see that the process was carried out according to His will without interference by doctors. In fact, it was presumptuous to interfere' (Allison 66). That we find very few missionary reports about normal deliveries evidences local attitudes about childbirth as natural and interference as unnecessary, an outlook that certainly frustrated missionary doctors. For instance, Dr Bruins Allison, who served mostly in Kuwait but also in Bahrain, Oman and Qatar between 1934 and 1975, reported that in four months, out of 9,000 outpatient cases, she only conducted five obstetrical deliveries in 1945 (ibid. 134). Such attitudes about non-interference were based on a broader system of traditional medicine that dictated when medical intervention was deemed necessary. Normal childbirth evidently was no such case and therefore 'midwives allowed Nature to take its course' (Calverley 149).

Still, midwives attended pregnant women to ensure a problem-free birth. The following is a description of a typical delivery in Arabia:

Usually when labor pains began at home, the women would retreat to one of the small back rooms of their house to avoid making a mess in the living rooms. She reclined on a bed of sand with some older woman sitting with her. There were no real midwives. If the case delivered normally, the woman cut the cord of the baby and dressed it in black swaddling clothes. She straightened the legs and bound them and the arms into a compact bundle tied up with long strips like a little mummy. (Allison 66)

Interestingly, this missionary source dismisses the role played by the older woman who very likely was a 'real midwife'. Admittedly, it was customary for women, usually relatives of the birthing mother, to sit with her, offering their company and support, during labor. In the Nejd, as well as Jeddah, for example, close relatives of the birthing mother sat with her to give her company, comfort and prayers, 'not to do anything [birth the child], for what was there to do?'[16] Similarly in Kuwait, 'it is our custom for friends to come and encourage a woman in labor . . . They would be offended if we asked them to leave' (Calverley 89). From this, one could surmise that the 'older woman' in the above quotation was a relative and not a midwife. Yet the postnatal care of the child suggests that the senior woman was there in a professional capacity. For, in references to childbirth found elsewhere, midwives undertook the same series of actions in delivering a child (Dickson 180; Allison 129).

If the life histories of Umm 'Abdullah, Umm Fahad and Umm Khalil are any indication, moreover, midwives were trained in the art of obstetrics through traditional modes of learning. To become a midwife, a girl learned the trade from a senior woman in the tribe, typically her mother or grandmother. In the case of Umm 'Abdullah, she learned midwifery from her husband's mother and grandmother. Thus, midwifery was a trade that was passed on generationally. Two of them, Umm Fahad and Umm 'Abdullah, began their training when they were between eleven and fourteen years of age, whereas Umm Khalil became a midwife after her husband died and left her with a son. This may suggest that midwifery offered vulnerable women a reputable profession to pursue. As young charges, they helped the midwife by preparing the hot water, blankets, medicines (herbal remedies) and the like for the delivery. After some years of apprenticeship, they became midwives when their mothers or grandmothers became too old or, in the case of Umm Fahad, when her

[16]Interview with Umm Khalid (April 2008); Yamani 170.

grandmother died. Typically, Qatari midwives serviced the women of their own tribe as well as neighboring villages. Notably, if a midwife's reputation was outstanding, she was often called to travel to distant areas to birth children in problem deliveries.[17] Not only was midwifery reputable work in Arabia, it also offered women the opportunity to excel within their profession.

Childbirth was only one aspect of a midwife's job. In many parts of the Gulf, such as Kuwait and Saudi Arabia, midwives also had 'a great reputation for treating all sorts of sickness', especially through the common practice of cauterization (Calverley 23). Midwifery, then, was simply one of several medical functions that women local healers performed within their profession. Indeed, the traditional medical system of these tribal societies was based on gender-segregated treatment by local healers: male local healers dominated certain fields, such as bone-setting, male circumcision, and bleeding (practiced more commonly among Bedouin healers), and generally did not treat women patients. Women healers, by contrast, were proficient in midwifery as well as treating common ailments that afflicted their female, and in some cases male, patients. Such expertise raises serious questions about whether 'midwife' constitutes an adequate, or even accurate, label for women whose medical functions were significantly broader than childbirth.

Traditionally, healers often learned the art of healing from family members: grandfathers passed the profession down to their sons and grandsons, while grandmothers did the same with their daughters and granddaughters.[18] Thus, passing the art of midwifery down from one generation to the next, as exemplified by the training of the Qatari midwives, reflected a practice within the wider practice of traditional healing. This was true not only in Qatar.

In Saudi Arabia, specifically in the region of Qasim, we also see that midwifery was carried out by mothers, grandmothers and wise old women as local healers. In an interview with Dr G.E. Moloney, an English surgeon recruited by the University of Riyadh in the 1970s, Umm Ahmad, a

---

[17]Interviews with Umm Khalid, Umm Fahad and Umm Khalil (April 2008).

[18]Moloney suggests: 'Young relatives of local healers who are likely to assist and later take over the practices might also be given a little training' (336). Elsewhere he states, 'We visited three bonesetters, all old, who had all learnt their skills within the family from father to son to grandson' (326).

renowned traditional healer of African origins, explained the midwifery methods she learned from her mother, which she used as late as the 1980s to resolve childbirth complications, including obstructed labor, infections, retained placenta, and hemorrhaging. For instance, she never carried out a vaginal examination and never pulled the baby out during delivery; to remove the placenta she used successive gentle pulls on the cord while gently squeezing the uterus with her other hand; she diagnosed breech presentation by palpation and dealt with it by raising the patient's legs over her back and then shaking her vigorously, claiming that this method, commonly practiced by Bedouin healers, delivered a breech baby; and finally, Umm Ahmad used cauterization for postpartum hemorrhage. Evidently these methods were quite effective, since deliveries admitted at the local hospital were in most instances emergencies that involved too many complications for the local healer to handle. Even Dr Moloney acknowledged these specific midwifery practices as 'useful' (332). That traditional midwifery remained entrenched in certain areas of the Peninsula, even after independence and the discovery of oil, reveals its mass appeal and its effectiveness.

As traditional healers, midwives were also in the business of making and administering folk remedies. For instance, to treat child ailments such as sore mouths, tender gums and mouth blisters, Bedouins in Saudi Arabia crushed a wild flowering plant (*ramram*) into a paste with a pestle and mortar, mixed with *girmiz*, a pink dye, and applied it to the sore place with the finger (Dickson 160). For food poisoning, called *malhus,* they used cauterization, which involved heating a long nail in the fire and then touching the baby's abdomen with it (Allison 74). Umm Fahad and Umm 'Abdullah also mentioned Qatari folk remedies, which they made and administered to their patients, particularly for cases of infertility and insufficient breast-milk production.[19]

Importantly, it was not only midwives who made and administered such remedies. As Soraya Altorki argues, knowledge of medicine, drugs and healing was commonly held and practiced by everyday women, most notably in Saudi Arabia (Altorki 13). Dr Harrison's medical experiences throughout the Peninsula between 1910 and 1948 confirm this: '[Arabia's] only medicine consists of a generally diffused knowledge of certain useful

[19]Interview with Umm Fahad (April 2008); Interview with Umm 'Abdullah (April 2008).

remedies and the kindly ministrations of the Arab women to the sick of their own household . . . It is the common property of every one' (Harrison, *Arab at Home*, 306–7). Harrison later observed, however, that, while drugs that constituted folk remedies were 'generally diffused ideas', it was local healers who excelled at making and dispensing them (ibid. 308). The practice of midwifery, then, should be contextualized within a wider association of Arabian women with medicine and healing. Such female knowledge in general, and the expertise of women healers in particular, must have been vital to maintaining the welfare of society.

While the practice of midwifery included ensuring the safe delivery of a child, what distinguished these women as professionals was their skilled expertise in resolving problem deliveries. Not surprisingly, Arabian midwives were especially needed when the delivery turned life-threatening or birth-related problems arose. A few illustrative examples reveal their professional importance, though regrettably they tell us little about how midwives worked to resolve these problem births. Dr Calverley, who proclaimed herself as the first woman doctor in Kuwait upon her arrival in 1909, was called on by a slave to help her 'Auntie', here meaning slave owner, deliver her baby at home. Apparently the woman had been in labor for four days and nights and the midwives who were called on had done everything they knew, 'but all in vain'. When Dr Calverley arrived, 'someone shouted through the still locked door, "Take the *Englaiziya* [Englishwoman] away! She isn't wanted! Everything is over!"' (Calverley 28).

In another case, Dr Calverley found herself again confronted by the local midwives when she attempted to help another woman in a problem delivery:

> We found Faheema on the floor of a room dimly lighted by a lantern. She was squatting on a pile of sand and two old midwives sat by to support her, one in front and the other behind. Nearby was a pile of sacking and discarded clothing. I heard the old women muttering, 'Why did you call the *Englaiziya*? Leave us alone, and the child will soon be born!' (Ibid. 88)

When Dr Calverley decided to turn to forceps to bring forth the child,

> 'No! No!' the mother intervened . . . 'Wait a little longer!' pleaded the aunt. The two old midwives were more bold now, in their mutterings. 'If

we had been allowed to have our way, the baby would have been here long ago,' they said with black looks in our direction. (Ibid. 90)

There are several such cases when missionary doctors were called to a birthing mother's home, but only after the local midwives 'had exhausted all their methods and given up hope of success' (ibid. 86–7, 150).

While missionaries clearly cited such examples to highlight the superiority of their medical treatments to traditional medicine, more noteworthy is what we can glean from these cases about the work of midwives. First, clearly the birthing mothers' first choice to resolve their birthing emergencies was local midwives, rather than a foreign woman doctor — a preference that arguably reflected the hold traditional medicine continued to have on Arabians, despite the coming of Western medicine.

Second, the basis of the midwives' anger toward Dr Calverley, 'the *Englaiziya*' who had become known for '[cutting] a woman open to deliver her child' (ibid. 89), was due to her invasive and unnatural birthing methods—which evidently clashed with their more natural ones. The local women shared this view as they too found the modern obstetrical encounter intrusive: 'The women resented questioning and felt an examination was too much trouble' (Allison 66). Only reluctantly did they allow foreign doctors to use forceps during problem deliveries in Bahrain in the early 1890s and Kuwait since the late 1930s (Mason 122; Allison 67). Caesarian section, by contrast, 'was usually out of the question' (Allison 67), most likely due to its more invasive nature and to the threat it posed to the natural birthing process. Even when missionary doctors were called to the home to address a problem birth, mothers were still not comfortable with their modern methods. Decades later, women continued to maintain their preference for non-intervention (ibid. 64). Local attitudes toward childbirth did eventually change, but only after the discovery of oil and the spread of modern hospitals, after which women increasingly delivered even 'normal births' in hospital (ibid. 118).

Finally and most interestingly, the above examples afford us a glimpse of the kind of competition midwives must have felt with the coming of missionary woman doctors. While midwives were women's first choice as childbirthers, evidently women doctors, like Dr Calverley and later Dr Bruins Allison, were increasingly called in to help with problem births that midwives could not resolve. These missionary-assisted deliveries clearly

threatened midwives' professional reputation and very likely their livelihood. This would explain the apprehension Dr Calverley felt when she
began her dispensary; instead of welcoming a large number of patients,
she found that the local midwives had 'prejudiced the women against
[her]' (Calverley 23). Clearly the stakes were quite high for midwives in
protecting the legitimacy of their profession from foreign competition—
an indication that these women understood their work as an organized and
respectable trade. In fact, according to Umm Fahad, there was no competition amongst the midwives serving in the same area; they typically helped
each other during difficult deliveries, and 'worked as one family'. If a
midwife from a particular tribe or neighborhood was renowned, she was
called on to help in extremely difficult cases.[20] We can gather from this
type of organization that these women identified as a professional collective who shared a common sense of work.

There are regional differences that are noteworthy. In contrast to
midwife-assisted births that appear most prevalent in the eastern parts of
the Peninsula, some Arabian women delivered their own children, with no
help from a midwife. Umm Khalid, for instance, never heard of a midwife,
for it was a two-century-old tradition that Bedouin women in the central
desert gave birth by themselves. 'Once they felt the labor pains (karab),'
described Umm Khalid, 'they went to an isolated place near their homes,
held on to a tree, delivered the child, and cut the cord themselves.'[21] Self-
managed deliveries were in fact common enough to warrant complaints by
missionaries who, during their travels throughout the Gulf, treated these
women for tearing their bladders during delivery (Allison 70). One
wonders, however, whether women in central Arabia were left to birth
their own children as a result of their remote location, in contrast to the
eastern part of the Peninsula where midwives more commonly practiced.

Midwifery could not be considered a profession if some sort of wage
were not part of their practice. We know that midwives were paid in cash,
which they received for attending a birth. The Qatari midwives, for
instance, received 'what was given to [them] from God [which] was
enough to sustain [them]'.[22] This suggests that wages were expected,
though the three midwives interviewed were quite reluctant to discuss

[20]Interview with Umm Fahad (April 2008).
[21]Ibid.
[22]Interview with Umm Fahad and Umm 'Abdullah (April 2008).

matters of money. Often, however, instead of monetary payment, the Qatari midwives offered their services free, since many families could not afford to pay, stating that they worked instead for God's divine blessings (*ajar*).[23]

Similarly, when Umm Khalid told the story of Umm Muhammad, a respected senior woman in Riyadh who was known for visiting mothers in labor, one wonders whether Umm Muhammad should be considered a midwife. If she were only a visitor, why was she offered money for her 'company', which she consistently refused, believing that her reward was divine blessings (*ajar*) and forgiveness?[24] Had we focused exclusively on money to determine women's work, we surely would have missed out on the social importance midwives themselves placed on the value of their work to their communities. Clearly their recompense held both material and spiritual value for them, though not in equal terms.

Lest we get the impression that midwifery was exceptional as a female profession, it was actually only one of an assorted array of women's work in Arabia. In fact, we learn from missionary memoirs about other types of work available to women, albeit different social value was placed on different types of labor. There were African exorcists, who were hired to beat their tom-toms in the *zar*, or exorcism rites, to rid Arabians of their *jinn*, or spirit possession, which was thought to cause illness. Indeed, 'many a respectable woman, with her coins in her pocket, applied at that hut to be relieved of physical or mental discomfort through the service of the Negroes' (Calverley 151).

We also find women textile sellers and embroiderers who offered their services to the wealthy and aristocratic Arab families. 'All the choice delicacies that the *sook* afforded, or that the ladies themselves had the skill to prepare, were offered to guests in these *hareems*' (ibid. 78). Some local women were known for their business talents. One Kuwaiti woman's husband, for instance, 'owed his prosperity to [her] business ability. He had been poor until after he married her' (ibid. 153). It has also been recognized that Meccan women conducted business in the *suq*, whether by helping their husbands in their business or by working on their own account (cited in Altorki 25). Omani women too were business-savvy shop-owners in some towns (Wahba 30).

[23]Ibid.
[24]Interview with Umm Khalid (April 2008).

As missionaries often hired local women as assistants in the dispensaries and hospitals, their works afford a glimpse of how women contributed financially to their family's income. Take Jameela, a Kuwaiti local, who was hired first as a hospital assistant and later as a nursemaid to Dr Calverley's three daughters; her story as a wage-earner is quite revealing. When Jameela was divorced and asked her oldest sister, Rahma, and brother-in-law to take her in (as their parents had already passed away), she gave the couple her dowry, which she had saved in order to alleviate some of the financial burden she brought to their already strained resources. When she was later employed at the hospital, 'she contributed her wages to the family, and she was helping Yakoob and Rahma even more now by bringing home her wages as a child's nurse' (Calverley 94). Interestingly, when Jameela's ex-husband wanted to remarry her, 'she preferred to stay where she was and continue working for her living' (ibid. 96). When she could no longer work for the Calverleys, they hired a Sudanese woman, very likely a freed slave, as their nursemaid (ibid. 98).

Jameela's case was not unique. We learn from the Qatari Umm Fahad, that during her time as an apprentice midwife, she baked bread for her household and her neighbors, sewed clothes, and sold wood to help with the family income.[25] Umm 'Abdullah, too, supplemented her husband's income and even helped to pay for her son's education with whatever payments she received from able families for her services, although often she took nothing from less fortunate families.[26] Umm Khalil became a midwife after being widowed with a son, suggesting that Qatari women were not necessarily dependent on their male relatives, and in some cases, provided vital sources of family income. Similarly in Oman, and specifically in the extremely poor city of Muscat, it was reported that 'unattached women' earned their own living, although they faced much difficulty in doing so since work such as sewing and basket weaving was difficult to come by and paid little. 'A fair number manage it, though' (Harrison, *Arab at Home*, 109). Dr Harrison recalls a rare but interesting case of four Omani women—a great-grandmother, grandmother, mother and daughter—living together and supporting themselves 'with no masculine assistance . . . The four [were] a happy family together' (ibid. 110).

[25]Interview with Umm Fahad (April 2008).
[26]Interview with Umm 'Abdullah (April 2008).

Missionaries often hired women of diverse ethnic extractions, especially Persians and Indians, mostly from the poorer classes, to act as nurses in hospital wards. In Oman, there are cases where women supported their children after losing a husband by working as nursing assistants in the missionary clinic (Boersma 104–5). Rarely but significantly, it was destitute freed slaves who were hired 'for a small wage' by Kuwaiti patients whose families could not attend them in hospitals (Calverley 137). Strikingly, poor local men and slaves also constituted the hospital staff in the men's wards (Hallock 15–18). While only a glimpse, this rudimentary sketch of female wage labor in Arabia still reveals important economic activity, such as women's participation in their local economies and their ability to supplement, if not generate, their family incomes—areas that certainly warrant further investigation.

Importantly the work of midwives clues us in about Arabian women's sexuality and reproductive culture in noteworthy ways. Certain childbirth practices were common across the Gulf. For instance, after a woman gave birth, midwives or women attending the birth would 'pack the vagina'. Salt was used for its astringent action in place of stitches to repair the birthing lacerations (Calverley 149). Midwives molded damp rock salt into a banana-like shape and inserted it in the vagina. It was kept in place for seven to ten days and replaced as necessary (Boersma 115).

According to missionary practitioners, this treatment dehydrated the vaginal tissues and often reduced the cervix to a hard core. During a following delivery, the cervix would not dilate to allow the baby to be born and the mother would die (Allison 66). While 'packing the vagina' was specifically attributed to Persian midwives in Kuwait, the practice was also prevalent in the wider region as a whole (Calverley 149). Nurse Boersma, for instance, reported that women from the interior also used this treatment (Boersma 114). Dr W. Harold Storm, a missionary doctor who served in all the Gulf mission stations, witnessed its more widespread use: 'In the field of gynaecology and obstetrics a whole book could be written, because in Arabia the common practice of packing the vagina with salt after delivery and the consequent atresias creates a problem not found in other places' (Storm 114; cf. Van Ess 25).[27] Even Britain's

---

[27]Such an observation raises questions about Dr Storm's access to Gulf women, especially during childbirth; however, male doctors did treat women patients through their female nurse or their own wives.

Political Agent in Kuwait, H.P. Dickson, makes reference to this practice among the Bedouin tribes of Kuwait and Saudi Arabia, adding that American missionaries 'never tired of preaching the evil of the practice, but with little result' (Dickson 173).

Umm Khalid, however, disputed that this was the practice in the eastern province of Arabia, although she admitted that a Qatari woman who lived in al-Ihsa' had her very young servant girl collect the salt so that she could 'pack the vagina'. When asked about the dire effects such a practice had on women, Umm Khalid quickly contested the missionary narrative: 'This was imperialism! . . . Those dogs [kilab] wanted to show their superiority, that everything we did was wrong, but we should not imitate them.' '[Packing the vagina],' she continued, 'did not harm the woman . . . it was a genuine attempt to clean the wounds of childbirth.'[28]

Sources differ as to whether or not rock salt packing was also used to shrink and tighten the vagina for male sexual pleasure after childbirth. According to Dr Calverley, 'Mothers were told they would be "ruined" for future marital relations unless this drastic treatment was endured' (Calverley 149). On the other hand, Dickson stated that he and his wife were told by a Bedouin woman that, after childbirth, Bedouin and towns-women resorted to various drugs, such as alum, for this purpose.[29] 'This "pleases the husband", they say' (Dickson 173).

That Bedouin women shared such intimate details with Dickson and his wife, that is, with foreigners including a 'strange' man, is indicative of Arabian tribal society's openness about sexual matters. For, 'interest in sex [was] open and frank', according to Dr Harrison (Harrison, Doctor in Arabia, 98). Dickson similarly observed that, 'Ordinary sexual matters are discussed before small children with a frankness and simplicity . . . which an English person may find at times embarrassing. The bearing of their young by camels, mares and ewes is not only an everyday topic, but mothers will take their children to watch the progress of such events, alongside their menfolk.' Such an outlook explains why 'the birth of a Badawin baby is attended with as little fuss as the birth of a baby-camel' (Dickson 58, 179). Clearly the birthing process, and therefore sexual matters related to birth, were understood by Arabians as divinely ordained and therefore uncontrol-lable and quite natural for humans to discuss openly.

[28]Interview with Umm Khalid (April 2008).
[29]Alum is a common name for aluminum sulfate.

Accordingly, it was not immodest for a Bedouin woman to feed her baby in the presence of her male relatives or even male strangers. 'I have often seen women,' observed Dickson, 'to whom I have been talking, open their front garment and bring out a breast to suckle their infant' (ibid. 180). Strikingly, such practices reveal critical distinctions Bedouins made between a sort of natural sexuality that was openly expressed versus a more culturally derived sexuality, where notions of honor and shame were attached to certain controllable social behaviors — notions that help explain the tribal practice of honor killings, discussed below.

Furthermore, problems of fertility abounded in Gulf societies. Given the importance of producing offspring within Arabian societies, as proof of a man's virility as well as to pass down the patrilineal name, threats to fertility were no small matter, particularly for women. In fact, missionary sources are silent about male sterility, whereas female infertility is more commonly discussed. For women, infertility posed a major threat to their welfare. Arabian women saw pregnancy, among other things, as a strategy for preventing divorce. In Kuwait, 'if [women] were pregnant, they were less likely to be divorced, so they were not interested in family planning. They kept on having many pregnancies even though many children died' (Allison 73: Calverley 150). In Oman, 'having a fruitful wife was very important to a man'; if an emergency hysterectomy was performed, the woman was 'in danger of divorce' (Boersma 115).

Midwives were especially knowledgeable in treating such conditions. Umm Fahad in fact specialized in infertility and saw this as the most important function of a midwife: 'I prepared and helped in giving birth; but I distinguished myself in *al-imsad* [oil massage on the lower abdomen for infertility] . . . We have a lot of midwives from many tribes [who birth children], but the most important thing is *al-imsad* so that [women] can have babies.'[30] *Al-imsad* was equally used by midwives in Saudi Arabia, according to Umm Khalid.[31] Umm Ahmad from Qasim also claimed great success in treating infertility, but by cauterization (Moloney 326).

If a woman did not conceive soon after marriage, she often resorted to various herbal remedies made by midwives. 'The "wise" old women of every tribe are adept in compounding draughts to stimulate fertility and also in preparing of "love philtres", for those who need them' (Dickson

[30]Interview with Umm Fahad (April 2008).
[31]Interview with Umm Khalid (April 2008).

172). Dr Harrison similarly observed that, the 'essences of iron and steel figure prominently in the list of aphrodisiacs which constitute the major stock-in-trade of such quacks' (Harrison, *Arab at Home*, 305). That is, women healers not only formulated medicinal love remedies for female infertility, they also and more notably sold them in the market (ibid. 305–6). This was certainly true of the Qatari midwives.

If they failed to become pregnant and folk remedies proved unsuccessful, women sought the interventionist power of missionary medicine in hopes of deflecting a pending divorce (Calverley 150). Examples of these cases abound. One woman, for instance, confessed to Dr Calverley: 'My husband says he will wait one more year . . . If I can't give him a child in that time, he's going to divorce me' (ibid. 151). In another case, a mother delivered triplets who were small and could only live if they were fed correctly. When it was suggested that she take one child home and leave the other two at the dispensary to be fed properly, the mother confessed that she had been having marital difficulties and thought that if she presented her husband with three babies, she would win him back (Allison 117). In a third example, an Omani woman who had given birth to a two-pound-six-ounce baby, sought the help of Boersma, the missionary nurse who did all that she could, knowing that the mother 'desperately wanted the little child to live—for its own sake and for the sake of her marriage' (Boersma 110).

Such fear of infertility, and by implication divorce, may explain Dickson's comment that, 'An Arab woman is never happy unless she is pregnant. This, one may say, is her permanent state unless she is barren' (Dickson 506). In fact, while 'no disgrace was associated with divorce' (Calverley 154), and it was quite common for women to remarry in Arabia, evidently being married was still preferred to divorce, even if it meant being in a polygamous marriage where the first wife was sterile. This was true in Oman, where occasionally a man would revert to marrying another woman, rather than divorce his sterile wife (Boersma 115). Pregnancy, according to Dr Bruins Allison, safeguarded fertile women from the 'vulnerabilities' of returning to their father's or brother's home a divorcee, though she failed to specify what these 'vulnerabilities' entailed (Allison 73–4). If pregnancy safeguarded fertile women from divorce, this begs the question of what vulnerabilities existed for infertile Arabian women.

In contrast to infertility, missionaries include several cases of young girls becoming pregnant out of wedlock, in Bedouin tribes and towns alike. In one case, a mother brought her pregnant daughter to Dr Bruins Allison to undergo an abortion, very likely because the foreign doctor had no ties to the girl's family or tribe, and so would not expose her shameful behavior. This explains Dr Harrison's comment that, 'Every [missionary] doctor is occasionally approached by some mother in distress, asking that her girl's life be save[d] by the performance of an abortion' (Harrison, *Doctor in Arabia*, 99).Clearly the mother was attempting to protect her child from the tribal punishment for such acts of dishonor: 'It was considered the duty of a brother or father to wipe out the sin by killing the girl. I knew that happened, so I regretted having to refuse. But I promised if they came for delivery, we would keep it a secret and find a mother for the baby, and they could go home immediately' (Allison 72). None of the desperate girls accepted her offer. Although we do not know what happened to girls in cases like this, several instances of honor killings are cited in missionary memoirs (cf. Calverley 74–8; Harrison, *Doctor in Arabia*, 98–9).

As stated earlier, in contrast to more open sexual mores associated with natural childbirth, such as public breastfeeding, other cultural behaviors, especially of women, were associated with tribal notions of male honor and shame. When Dr Calverley intervened in one particular case and sought the aid of a shaykh to intercede on behalf of an accused girl named 'Aziza, he responded, 'It's no use . . . This manner of dealing with immorality in girls has been the absolute right of a family from the beginning of Arab history. I never interfere in these matters touching a family's honor' (Calverley 76). Ultimately 'Aziza's was the only case that missionaries successfully overturned due to the influence of the British Political Agent. Generally, missionaries, like the shaykh, opted to leave cultural matters to tribal law.

In sum, although rudimentary, this historical sketch of Arabian midwives reveals a picture of important social agents who found in midwifery a reputable trade in which they could excel and establish a credible professional reputation. Typically inheriting her trade from her mother or grandmother, an Arabian midwife learned that the art of obstetrics was based not on intervening in the birthing process, but rather in ensuring a problem-free delivery, which in turn meant being prepared for a life-threatening or delivery-related problem. With their expert knowledge of herbal remedies, moreover, midwives also excelled as healers, making them important agents in countering societal illness and infertility. Paid by able families, although they accepted only a spiritual reward (*ajar*) for serving poorer families, midwives used their wages to supplement their family income or support their children, if they found themselves 'unattached'. They were also part of the local economies as they, along with women of other trades, actively participated in the local *suq* as both buyers and sellers. While the economic dimension of midwives' work, that is, their public work, is noteworthy and points to important indicators of women's work opportunities in Arabia, it is not the only factor that explains the significance of female labor in constituting Gulf societies historically. Also important is the social value of their work, which we can identify by uncovering the societal importance assigned to the space they worked in, namely the home.

Labor in the home

Midwives assisted a birthing mother in her home. In fact, Arabian women historically delivered their children and received needed medical attention at home, and preferred the home to the missionary dispensaries and hospitals when they were first established (Allison 64). When asked by a missionary doctor if she would come to the hospital to delivery her baby, one Kuwaiti woman responded with the typical answer heard throughout the Gulf: 'No, that's out of the question . . . the baby must be born in our house' (Calverley 87). This cultural view was pervasive and crossed class and gender lines. A group of women, for instance, called on Dr Bruins Allison for a difficult home delivery of an Iranian woman of humble means, who was a member of the small Shi'ite minority in Kuwait. 'They were not relatives, but in cases like this of real trouble, the women will help each other' (Allison 53). The young girl was in labor for three days and the head of the stillborn fetus was in a position that required the use of forceps. When Dr Bruins Allison declared that the woman needed hospital care, the patient refused: 'She sobbed in her misery, telling us that her husband had gone on a trip to Iran and had told her that if she left the house before he came back, he would divorce her. She had no relatives to help her, this wasn't her country. She wailed, "If you can't help me here, let me die now"' (ibid.). Another Iranian girl, the wife of a carpenter, had similarly been in labor for three days; she too refused to be taken to the hospital despite terrible convulsions, although the men in her middle-class family were willing (ibid. 86).

Medical treatment was also to be dispensed in the home. We know, for instance, that when the wife of the Kuwaiti Amir, Shaykh Ahmad, was diagnosed with a pelvic abscess, the Amir consented to surgery on condition that it be performed in his residence since 'his wife never left the palace' (ibid. 52–3). Yet women of lesser means also insisted that operations be carried out in their homes (Calverley 101). Even the elderly refused medical treatment, some in life-threatening cases, in order to die quietly at home—a point that reiterates the general outlook of traditional medicine as non-interventionist in nature and the home as the exclusive and intuitive site of natural events surrounding birth and death.

Given the centrality of the home to midwives' profession—indeed it constituted their very 'workplace'—it would be easy to dismiss their work as 'private' and reproductive in nature, and therefore less consequential than work conducted in public spaces associated with men and their productive activities. Such a conclusion, however, would be misguided. For, while Gulf societies have historically been organized as sex-segregated systems where men and women occupied certain gendered spaces, their societal notions of 'public' and 'private' do not correspond to the public/private distinctions that developed in Western European societies from the beginning of the seventeenth century and which dominate the scholarly view of gender and spatial boundaries.[32] Namely, those who occupied public space, inevitably associated with the world of high politics and the state, thus men, were viewed as 'empowered'. Women, who occupied the private and intimate world of the family, often symbolized by the domicile, were 'disempowered' since their access to public space was limited to varying and context-specific degrees (Abugideiri, 'Off to Work', 255).

Rather, understandings of 'home', especially in Bedouin tribal settings where many of our midwives practiced, connoted both 'private' and 'public' space due to the ideological meanings assigned to home life. That is, if we are to appreciate the social value of midwives' work, we must understand the cultural meanings attached to the spaces in which they worked. The home essentially was where the communal identity of the

---

[32]For more on the Eurocentric nature of the public-private paradigm to study Arab women, see Abugideiri, 'Off to Work'.

tribe was reaffirmed and reified through specific rituals in which both men and women participated. From this perspective, midwives did more than simply birth children in the home. As childbirth was one of many social rituals designed to foster tribal identity and ties of solidarity, their work had wider ideological implications than birthing children in women's private homes would suggest. To better elucidate this argument, let us briefly examine what the home meant to both tribal and urban Arabian societies.

The home in traditional Bedouin societies was not simply a place of residence. Rather, it offered cultural spaces of exchange based on symbolic ritual acts and a code of conduct that collectively inscribed tribal identity. For many Bedouin societies, we can decode the rich symbolism attached to the home through, among other things, its spatial mapping and the tribal rituals that accompanied coming into or leaving the home. Indeed, the physical construction of the home mattered less than the tribal members' ability to create boundaries for particular types of social interactions. In the case of Arab nomads, their *bayt* [home] referred not to a fixed dwelling, but to small groups, or the nuclear family, that moved from place to place (Altorki 7). Thus, when a Bedouin woman became ill, her devoted family, who traveled with her to hospital, would ask the doctor 'where to pitch their tent and where to tie the camels and the goats' (Calverley et al. 49). As Altorki's study reveals, even the harem—or private quarters reserved for female relatives—was not necessarily a fixed space in homes. Far from the stereotypical image of the secluded harem where countless wives and slaves were reduced to abject servitude, womenfolk of a household in Mecca in the late nineteenth century did not dwell in a fixed area of the home; rather, wherever they were is where the harem was (Altorki 8). In a word, the home in Arabia was not necessarily a fixed physical space that determined how people interacted. While it certainly assumed a physical form, the home should alternatively be viewed as the space in which social, in this case family, interactions took precedence.

Such cultural meanings of the home explain why Bedouins regarded urban houses merely as a substitute for tents and could not understand the point of ceilings, windows or doors to separate rooms. They appreciated that there must be one big door into a house, but did not see why so many internal doors were necessary. In fact, when King Husayn captured Ta'if after the Turks surrendered, his Bedouins removed all the woodwork of roofs, windows, and doors, not in order to sell it, but simply to use it for fuel—for cooking, camp fires or coffee-making. 'Abd al-'Aziz's Bedouins did exactly the same—they removed window-frames and doors and used them for cooking and coffee fires—when they occupied the Hijaz (Wahba 20).

Indeed, urban home layout essentially mirrored how family members interacted, not only with unrelated visitors, but more importantly with each other. The courtyard or harem, which is often described as having numerous windows, was not so much a private female quarter as the center of the home which

> . . . opened into rooms which provided separate domains for each house-hold in an extended family system sometimes consisted of forty or more members. These would be the elderly head of the house, several brothers with one or more wives, unmarried grown sons and daughters, children, widowed and divorced sisters, orphans, and servants. (Allison 29)

For the upper-classes, the harem is similarly described as 'opening' the home due to the numerous rooms belonging to family members. Since there was greater space to accommodate a larger extended family, more-over, 'the whole household [of fifty to sixty persons] would sleep on the flat roof, which was divided into separate enclosures for men and women' in hot weather. Thus, in those spaces where the most intimate daily activi-ties went on, these shared spaces were gendered, if at all, rather than segregated. The symbolism behind the physical structure of urban homes, then, facilitated family interaction by creating central gathering places for its numerous members, both male and female alike.

Turning to the rituals and code of conduct that surrounded entering or exiting a home, these too were assigned symbolic importance, which reveal the 'public' nature of Arabian homes. Such rituals evidence the centrality of hospitality traditions that governed how one entered and departed the home and whose sole purpose was to preserve and honor the kinship ties between tribal members by, among other things, welcoming those outside these bonds into their culture. As Dr Bruins Allison observed, upon entering a Kuwaiti home, 'the exchange of ritual greetings was as involved as a litany. The phrases were formal yet poetic and gave a grace to meetings' (ibid.). More striking were the rituals, especially among women, that involved leaving a home after a visit. After having been served refreshments, tea and finally coffee,

> Custom decreed that we take the cup three times and then shake it to signify that we were satisfied. As a final gesture, one of the women would sprinkle our heads with rose water from brass shakers, then pass around an incense pot containing glowing charcoal and frankincense from Oman . . . We asked permission to leave with the phrase, 'I seek to be cheap,' to which the answer was, 'you are dear'; and '*towa nas*,' which means, 'people are still passing.' (Ibid. 31)

Coffee, importantly, was the general Arab symbol of hospitality.

> All over Arabia the elaborate ceremony of coffee making is the sign the guest is welcome and honoured above all men by his host. From the highest to the lowest this making and offering of coffee is the first duty of a householder, whether he be a town- or tent-dweller, when entertaining a stranger or an acquaintance.' (Dickson 195)

Dickson in fact dedicates six full pages of his travelogue exclusively to the elaborate Bedouin ritual of preparing and serving coffee to guests (ibid. 195–201). In the Nejd and all over the desert, for instance, it was prepared in the guest's presence, and some Kuwaitis who originated from Nejd continue this custom until today (Wahba 31).

Lest we misunderstand the meaning of hospitality rituals as intimate, private interactions between women in the home, we know that the wives of Bedouin shaykhs affected their husbands' prestige through words and deeds and influenced men of the tribe through the use of hospitality and diplomacy in their relationships with other women (Pastner 318; Dickson 53). According to the famous traveler, John Lewis Burckhardt, Bedouin women actively participated with their male kinsmen in showing hospitality to strangers, and in some cases, attended male visitors if their own husbands were away (cited in Altorki 10). Dickson recorded similar practices among Bedouin tribes in Kuwait and Saudi Arabia: 'If an important personage passes by her tent in the absence of her husband, the wife will run out of her tent holding out a frothing bowl of camel's milk or *leben*, as a sign of welcome' (Dickson 55). Even in urban areas, Omani women served in the shops and welcomed guests when their husbands were not at home (Wahba 30). The home, then, should be thought of as communal space where tribal kinship ties and identity were reinforced and presented to outsiders by both women and men alike through specific rituals and behavior. This may explain why Dickson identified the domestic sphere not only with women, but also with the Bedouin as a people. He saw the Bedouin camp as 'an escape into domesticity, a pristine, timeless sphere set apart from the demands of the world beyond the desert' (Pastner 321–2).

Turning back to midwives, given the rich symbolic meanings attached to the home and the cultural code of conduct expected of family members to honor each other as well as outsiders inside and outside the home, it is not far-fetched to view childbirth as one more ritual designed to preserve tribal identity and solidarity. In fact, Mai Yamani's research reveals the importance of childbirth rituals to Saudi family identity. She argues that Saudi Arabians, who increasingly delivered their children in hospital, smoothly transitioned these rituals from the home to the hospital through attempts to 'create in hospital the ambience of the home' (Yamani 175). That is, by transferring rituals and rules of conduct related to childbirth involving, for instance, dress, language, food and gift-giving, from the home to the hospital, Saudis managed to maintain traditions and preserve social identity (ibid. 169).

For, 'the event of child-birth, just as the events of marriage and death, is a time to display family solidarity. A united family is strong, and thus it is respected. The larger the family, the higher its station, and the more loving its members towards one another, as well as the higher the rank obtained and maintained in society' (ibid. 175). Here we see the clearest indication of the home's symbolic meaning to tribal identity, since rituals that traditionally took place there could be accommodated to a hospital setting. What was important was not so much the physical space as the behaviors that fostered communal ties that were associated with the home. Cast in this light, midwives offered a great service to their societies through their reputable work in Arabian homes. By helping mothers to bring their children into the world, and thus ensure the preservation of tribal identity, midwives contributed to the ideological as well as economic makeup of their societies.

Conclusion

The story of Arabian midwives is not a simple narrative of women's reproductive work in other women's private homes. Rather, it reveals how these professional women navigated through, but also helped constitute, the complex socio-economic organization of Gulf societies themselves. As women whose very trade required them to be in public and whose daily work organically wove their lives into the intimate lives of others, their profession uniquely narrates the collective history of their society at the same time as it tells us about what possibilities, both economic and social, existed for Arabian women in the Gulf's historic past.

8. *Women's Religious Activities in the Arabian Peninsula: A Historical Outlook*

OMAIMA ABOU-BAKR

Introduction

This study aims to shed light on the role of women as religious educators and scholars, for two main purposes: (a) to prove women's continuous presence in this arena within the Arab/Islamic tradition; (b) to analyze this historical information in terms of the extent of empowerment and autonomy that this activity afforded women within their societies. An attempt is made to investigate women's relation to orthodoxy and male religious authority, as manifested in the historical accounts by male historians or biographers.

In terms of the time period covered, the available information on the following types of women: *shaykhat, muftiyat, faqihat,* and *mutawwi'at* (feminine of Shaykhs, jurisconsults, exegetes and teachers) falls into two main, broad time periods: pre-modern until the Ottoman era (sources are mainly biographical dictionaries and other historical data), and twentieth-century pre-oil times in the Gulf region. The gap or absence of data relating to the period between the two eras, although usually noted by scholars and sometimes attributed to the lack of historical documentation itself rather than the disappearance of women from history, should not lessen the significance of the phenomenon or deter attempts to re-instate the continuum, albeit in different forms, as will be presented. This general lack of specific documented information on women's history from Arab sources is a continuing problem that has had an impact on the production of knowledge on Arab women—especially their role in religion. Hence, researchers in this area have also relied on the power of the imagination to re-construct the missing parts of the historical picture.

Besides making deductions about the lives of women and the practice of religious education itself, this article also relies on the methodology or approach of discourse analysis of sources to probe social and cultural attitudes toward women scholars and teachers of religion as reflected in the historiography of this subject. A distinction must be made here, however, between how society views women and what Islam intended; the first is not usually an indicator of the latter. Discourse analysis usually provides textual evidence of changing concepts of gender relations within societies. This article also makes use of the theoretical framework of medieval feminist historians and cultural critics who have studied the European history of nuns, women mystics, and ascetics, and produced interesting scholarship on issues such as religious patriarchy, male authoritarianism within the Church, medieval misogyny, and female spirituality as a form of empowerment. Christian feminist theologians have also asked important questions regarding the relation of women to religious practice, the interpretation of scripture, and the construction of symbols and images (see, for example, the works of Rosemary Reuther, Caroline Bynum, and Eleanor McLaughlin).

Religious knowledge and empowerment

Any comprehensive study of the cultural history of women in the Gulf region should investigate the role of religion as a primary factor in shaping and structuring society in the Arabian Peninsula, itself part of the wider Arabo-Islamic civilization. More pertinently, researching the complex relationship between women as historical agents and Islamic orthodoxy may not only yield forgotten information about Muslim women, but also suggest a new analytical and interpretive lens.

By asking previously unasked questions about women, men, and religion, employing methods of social history and historical-critical discourse analysis, and focusing on the significance of women's presence and absence, participation and exclusion in religion and society, we can generate new questions and new findings. Scholars in the field of women's studies and religion have grouped such inquiries and their epistemological outcomes in terms of three 'Rs': rereading, re-conceiving, and re-constructing religious history (O'Conner). 'Rereading' is re-examining religious materials and traditions, paying attention to women's roles, words, participation, presence or absence, voice or silence, recognition or denial. 'Re-conceiving' requires the retrieval of lost sources and reclaiming women's heritage for the purpose of remembrance of the original liberating message, as opposed to the dominance of patriarchy. Finally, 'reconstructing' the past is based on new information and the use of historical imagination to re-establish women's contributions and visibility within their religious traditions. The above-mentioned theoretical reflections can be applied to the situation of Arab Muslim women in the Peninsula when considering their specific religious experiences and activities in medieval times, as well as in the decades immediately preceding the economic and social changes brought about by oil. How did Muslim women in the Gulf region participate in religious life and in what capacity? Were they part of Islamic orthodoxy and formal, official practice, meaning associating with the religious elites (judges, 'ulama', tribal chiefs) of the time? Or did they experience and practice Islam differently, and did they voice these experiences and describe them? Did they frequent mosques, and what religious roles, rites, and communities did they create? What kind of religious authority did women hold, and what influence did they have in the transmission of Islamic knowledge and education?

Two works of scholarship that argue a re-conceptualization of the notion of empowerment in relation to women and religion in Muslim societies are Sherine Hafez's *The Terms of Empowerment* and Saba Mahmood's *Politics of Piety*. Although both take the social science approach and aim at interpreting contemporary activist women in Egypt, their theoretical framework constitutes a paradigm shift from the strictly Western liberal understanding of 'empowerment' as absolute power to the individual self, isolated from the collective entity, to alternative forms of self-empowerment, embedded within indigenous structures (Hafez 80). Rather than the analyst looking for a direct confrontation with patriarchy from an external position, one can see that indigenous religiously active women usually realize their empowerment from within the relations of power, as Hafez suggests, evoking Foucault's theory of the 'relational individual' (ibid.). In this sense, women religious scholars, teachers, educators, or preachers, in

Muslim contexts, in their pursuit of high achievement in this vocation, are challenging the patriarchal exclusivity of the religious domain. This kind of 'feminist contestation or resistance of male authority' is considered 'unintended after-effects' of women's professions and activities (ibid. 2). Similarly, in her extensive study of the contemporary Egyptian women's 'piety movement' or 'mosque movement', Mahmood challenges the liberal assumptions and interpretations of human agency, as well as secular feminist attitudes toward the issue of religious difference and cultural specificity. She argues that this newly developed and newly spread activity has led women preachers and learners of religion to alter 'the historically male-centered character of mosques as well as Islamic pedagogy' (ibid. 2). Although this view in itself carries an inaccurate assumption about women's complete absence from mosques, specifically in pre-modern times, as we shall see in considering women *faqihat* (legal scholars) and *muhaddithat* (instructors in Hadith), Mahmood's redefinition of notions of agency, autonomy, and resistance in application to women's religious instructional activities is definitely beneficial.

One methodological issue to be considered in the act of 'reading' classical or modern historical sources documenting women's history/biographies is the subtle differentiation between, on the one hand, the actual lives of women that these works illustrate and the social reality that we are able to re-construct, and, on the other, the historicizing discourse itself or re-presentation (imaging) by male biographers/historians. Both can be analyzed using the historian's approach *and* the feminist, textual critic's tools, showing at times — what New Historicists call — a 'fissure' or 'cracks' in the text. This is exemplified when classical biographers and hagiographers comment on and interpret women's lives and achievements in a manner that ironically confirms the very patriarchal social attitudes that the women were challenging, or when a narrator contradicts his own high esteem of a woman figure by paradoxically measuring her historical achievement against the normative criteria of 'men'. One critic describes this phenomenon as 'the fissure between the represented object and the representing agent' (Weimann 190). Similarly, modern, twentieth-century male historians tend to misread and misinterpret women's histories by imposing 'modernist' discourses and conceptions of gender roles (see Abou-Bakr 1999).

Women scholars in the classical period
up to the Ottoman era

Women's participation in the field of religious sciences in pre-modern or classical Arab/Muslim history included their roles as learned scholars (*faqihat, muhaddithat,* and *muftiyat*), mystics (*sufiyyat, 'abidat,* or *musta-fayat*), preachers (*wa'izat*), and managers of hostels/teaching institutions (*shaykhat rubut*). In other words, whether in the domain of orthodox religious knowledge, spirituality, or social services, women played the prominent role of teachers and guides in a mixed environment and so contributed extensively to education and the dissemination of Islamic learning and Sufism. Mamluk sources (mainly biographical dictionaries) provide us with a huge body of very significant information about women's specific religious teaching activities in learning circles in homes or lecturing and preaching in mosques. In previous works I have presented detailed information on *muhaddithat* (women teachers of the Hadith tradition) and *'abidat* (women mystics) across the Muslim world (Abou-Bakr 2003, 1998); hence, I will focus here on selected representative cases from the categories of *faqihat, muftiyat,* and *wa'izat* in the Arabian Peninsula in particular.

Classical sources overall manifest the presence of women in these societies as early as the first generations of the *sahabiyyat* (Prophet's Companions) and the *tabi'iyyat* (Followers) around the eighth century, showing participation in the field of theology, religious knowledge and scholarship, as well as the teaching of these sciences. The earliest case on record is Zaynab bint Abi Salama al-Makhzumiyya (d. CE 692) who was 'one of the best *faqiha* of her time in Medina' (al-Dhahabi 200). Al-Dhahabi also documented the biographies of Hajamiyya bint Hayy al-Awsabiyya, known by the name of Umm al-Darda' (d. 700 CE), who was a 'great *faqiha* well read and well versed, as well as fully wise and intelligent' (ibid. 207). As for Hafsa bint Sirin (d. 718 CE), her scholarly reputation in relation to classical sources is overwhelming and worth observing in terms of the discourse used by biographers and historians. Hafsa, the *ansariyya* (originally from the early generation of the Medinans who supported the Prophet), is referred to by contemporary male *'ulama'* as a 'trusted and capable *faqiha'* — the exact word being used to describe her is *'hujja',* meaning her knowledge is a 'proof' and source reference. Another says, 'I have not seen any more intelligent or wiser than Hafsa' (al-Jawzi 247). Again the adjective used in the comparative (a'qal), from 'aql (mind), is the same term that appears later in the canonical works of *fiqh*, *tafsir*, and interpretations of Hadith to essentialize women as lacking (*naqisat*) in mental and rational capacity. This is one small, but telling, example of clashing discourses, between the prescriptive/normative approach espoused in male *'ulama'*'s interpretations, and the historical or hagiographical mode of historians and biographers, which points more to lived reality and to social attitudes to women. This problematic issue prompts us to avoid the tendency to historicize in relation to the 'Muslim woman' in this essentialist manner through the prescriptive, theoretical literature of *fiqh*, *tafsir*, and interpretations of Hadith. Moreover, Hafsa's brother, Muhammad bin Sirin, himself a contemporary scholar, if puzzled by a reading problem in the Qur'an, used to advise people to go and ask his sister.

'Amra bint 'Abd al-Rahman (d. 716 CE), also from Medina, was also a renowned *faqiha,* with documented juristic precedents which scholars referred to and used as legal source references. Major classical historians and biographers, such as al-Dhahabi and Ibn Sa'd, described her as a *faqiha* and *'alima*. Another source, al-Suyuti, who produced a major explication of Imam Malik's master legal source reference, the *Muwatta'*, recorded a few of 'Amra's juristic opinions on the issue of selling fruit before it was fully grown and a case of implementing *hadd* (legal punishment) (51, 177), precedents that Imam Malik followed. An example that can be included here, although she was a scholar of Hadith specifically, is Fatima bint al-Mundhir al-Qurayshiyya (b. 668 CE), from the generation of *tabi'in* in the Medina, who was her husband's *ustadh*, his authoritative teacher in this field (Jum'a 96).

While mention of other *faqihat, mutafiqqihat, muftiyat,* and *wa'izat* of the following decades and centuries abound in the available sources, this article covers only those known to have come from the Hijaz area. These include women scholars who are said to have learned and practiced diverse branches of the Islamic sciences: *tashtaghil bi-al-fiqh* (worked in jurisprudence) or *kanat tafti* (used to pronounce legal judgments) in certain religious matters or *tufassir ayat al-Qur'an* (interpreted Qur'anic verses). Zaynab bint Mu'bad bin Ahmad al-Murwazi (d. 1148 CE), known as 'the best of all women', held preaching circles or sessions in both Baghdad and Mecca (Safadi 64), and Taj al-Nisa' bint Rustum bin Abi al-Raja' al-Asbahani (d. 1214 CE) was a famous preacher in Mecca known as *shaykhat al-haram*, meaning the main scholar of the Holy Mosque of the Ka'ba (Safadi 374). As late as the twelfth Islamic century (eighteenth century CE), we find mention of women scholars such as the Meccan Quraysh bint 'Abd al-Qadir al-Tabariyya (d. 1694 CE), whose students used to 'recite to her *hadith* books at her house' (Kahhala 92).

Three points should be considered in the overall history of such women religious scholars: first, these activities were considered professional in the sense that the women had to receive rigorous scholarly training, read up-to-date *fiqhi* scholarship, and interact with peer *'ulama'* in order to gain the necessary expertise and the learned community's sanction to issue religious opinions. Furthermore, the sources document several titles of books written by some of these *'alimat* (feminine of *'ulama'*), who are said to have either compiled certain legal information/opinions or written explications and analytical tracts on works by other *'ulama'* (al-Sa'di and Abou-Bakr 13). Unfortunately, no full first-hand texts or extant manuscripts of these works have been found, but the clear references to the titles and descriptions of these works point to the existence of a 'textual' legacy of these professionals.

Second, a large number of these *faqihat* seem to have specialized in the subject of the science of inheritance laws and its computations (*'ilm al-fara'id wa-al-hisab*), not necessarily the expected domain of issues related to women's purification rites, menstruation, nursing . . . etc. This confirms the professionalism of the practice and how scholarly specialization within the field was taken seriously. In confirmation of this, some women scholars were referred to in biographies by their subscription to and expertise in one of the four major juristic schools. A certain *shaykha* would be referred to as a *Shafi'iyya*, or a strict follower of the *Hanafi* doctrine, for example, despite the fact that her father or husband was known to have been a *Maliki* or a follower of another school. One *shaykha* is said to have raised four sons, bringing up each to be a follower of a different one of the four schools.

Third, women practiced *ifta'* (delivering legal opinions) when it was in the informal domain of independent muftis. The historical development of *ifta'* shows that it began spontaneously and informally during the first and second generations of the Companions in Hijaz; it was not connected to official or political authority, but was a kind of open freelance task, permitted to the qualified and knowledgeable. Thus, during those decades and centuries, we find a large number of women scholars who were author-ized to issue *fatawa* based on their knowledge and the community's trust, not on their official appointment by rulers or states, and to whom people went to pose questions and legal problems and *yastafti* (seek a legal opinion from a scholar). As time passed, the *ifta'* became more linked to political authority, especially judges and the court system, and women were not officially appointed as judges or muftis in the court (although they were sometimes appointed as court expert witnesses, as proven by Muhammad Fadel, 'Two Women, One Man: Knowledge, Power, and Gender in Medieval Sunni Legal Thought', IJMES, 29 (1997), 185–204). Around the seventeenth century, *ifta'*, became institutionalized and centralized when the Ottoman state created the post of *Fetwa Emini* in Istanbul, an official who would supervise and centralize fatwas. He owed allegiance to the Shaykh al-Islam at the head of the religious hierarchy created by the Ottomans (Masud 11–12).

Women educators in the Gulf in the nineteenth century

Two representative sources, in particular, were examined for this study with regard to the role of women educators in the second half of the nine-teenth century and the beginning of the twentieth. In contrast to the preceding time frame, these cases represent the modern, 'pre-oil' state of affairs in the Gulf region. The focal economic activity of these societies was *al-ghays* (diving for pearls), followed by journeys to India and other Asian regions for trade. Such sea and land excursions were undertaken by men, who left the women behind for months to manage affairs at home. Interestingly, playing a significant public role in the primary religious education of girls and boys of the community seems to have been a respon-sibility shouldered by a large number of women educators—called *mutawwi'at*.

A *mutawwi'a* (masc. *mutawwi'*) is defined in one source as 'a religious woman who teaches young girls and boys Qur'an, reading, and writing in a small room or house called a *kuttab*' (al-Khurafi 13). The author relates the term to its lexical origin as a Qur'anic word (*al-mutawwi'in*) in *Surat al-Tawba* (Qur'an 9:79), where it means those who 'volunteer' to strive in the path of God. These *kuttab*s, which were prevalent in Kuwait, for instance, until the mid-twentieth century, played a major role in the foundational education of the younger generation before the establishment of modern, structured schools in 1926. Despite the sociological indication that such Gulf societies at that time were characterized by pre-urban simplicity, uncomplicated modes of living, and the absence of luxurious or materialistic lifestyles, communities emphasized the importance of religious education for both boys and girls. Receiving an education in the *kuttab* was culturally prestigious. In the words of one elderly man: 'As boys, we used to drop ink purposely on our clothes, to show that one was a *katib,* that is a writer' ('Abd al-Rahman 62). Besides the *mutawwi'a,* the sources indicate the existence of the *mullaya* (masc. *mulla*), who is sometimes differentiated from the *mutawwi'a* with regard to the content of the education she gave—adding principles of dictation and elementary mathematics to oral Qu'ran recitation. The *ustadha* (masc. *ustadh*) was a 'cultured' woman who taught in a private or public school (al-Salih, cited in al-Khurafi 452). It is noticeable that, as far as these titles and the occupations they signified are concerned, gender equivalence was maintained; that is, both men and women worked under these titles and are referred to equally in the histories. Women practiced these occupations in a similar way to male teachers and clearly enjoyed the same social status and authoritative positions. It is also worth noting that there were women teachers in Qur'an schools (*kuttab*s) only in this region; *kuttab*s in other areas of the Arab Muslim world, such as rural Egypt, were run entirely by male imams or *shaykh*s, who may in rare cases have taught young girls up to a certain age before puberty.

The conditions under which the *mutawwi'a* worked are interesting and important to bring into focus. Whether in her home or in another house or place allocated to be the *kuttab,* she would sit in a prominent position in the *halaqa* (circle) on a cotton-upholstered seat with a long stick at her right side called a *khayrazana,* which she used as a ruler or to point at the students. At her left side, there would be a bag of sweets to distribute as rewards. As teachers of difficult and important subjects, such as learning, memorizing, and reciting the whole of the Qur'an, which is one of the foundational Islamic sciences (*'ulum al-qira'a wa-al-tilawa*), such women educators had undoubtedly mastered the necessary knowledge of the intricacies of the Arabic language and rules of recitation, as well as the skills needed to transmit and disseminate this specialized knowledge to the younger generation. One should point out that this activity is a positive indication in itself of the continuing tradition (up to this time under consideration) of an uncomplicated and taboo-free relationship between women and scripture, women and the socio-cultural empowerment that ensues.

One source describes outdoor places used as *halaqa*s or classes. In summer it was a bower made of palm leaves with mats below, and in winter it would preferably be some sort of walled room spread with a kind of mat known as a *manqur*. The girls sat in semi-circular rows around their teacher, each with a wooden stool (called *bashtakhta*) in front of her on which to place her book or *mushaf* (copy of the Qur'an). This particularly indicates the public nature of the space and, hence, the 'public' visibility of both teacher and female students. Great attention was given to the time of a girl's graduation, specifically the *khatma*—the successful completion of learning and memorizing the whole Qur'an. On that day, the girl's family would send the *mutawwi'a* bowls of sweets, nuts, incense, and rosewater, and accompany the girl in a procession to be formally received. A decorated seat was prepared for her in a prominent place beside her teacher, who blessed this special event by reciting verses from *Surat al-Baqara* and the *Fatiha*. Next, a boy would stand and recite the *tahmida* (a standard formula of praises to God followed by the listeners' response with 'amen') (al-Khurafi 453). Again, this seems to have been very much a public event, with its own celebratory rituals at which boys were also present. The cultural significance of this kind of emphasis on a girl's completion of her Qur'anic education lies not so much in the act of memorizing scripture as in the subsequent status transformation that the girl acquires—becoming officially a *hafiza* or *hamila* (literally a carrier) of the Qur'an. Once more, an association is freely made between female personhood or identity and the Word of God.

Because of the informal and flexible nature of this educational process, the fees or wages for the *mutawwi'a* varied from unspecified sums of money, depending on each student's financial ability, to payment in the form of goods and food. The manner of payment also varied. Some students paid monthly, and others after the completion of each section (*juz'*) of the Qur'an, or at the very end, at the *khatma*, the completion of the reading the Qur'an. In the rare cases when a student was completely unable to provide even a minimal payment, the families of other girls would collect the fees and donate them jointly. This would be carried out through a traditional procession known as the *zaffa*, when the girl went around the houses in the neighborhood to collect the amount required. If this was not done, the girl's father would be committed to pay the teacher out of the money saved for his daughter's dowry (*mahr*), which was an accepted custom. In a few cases, a *mutawwi'a* would decline fees to maintain her 'volunteer' position. Despite this unstructured system of pay and the spirit of charitable achievement, one can still argue for the professional status of the women. As stated above, they had a set job title with a defined occupational task that their communities relied upon and trusted.

Women *mutawwi'at* established their Qur'an schools essentially for girls, although occasionally and only up to a certain age, mixed-gender *kuttab*s also existed. In Kuwait, the first such *mutawwi'a* with such a *kuttab* on record is Habiba 'Abdullah al-Dhawadi (born in Bahrain in 1810), who bought a house to use both as her place of residence and as a Qur'an school for boys and girls. She established her *kuttab* in 1850. In addition to her teaching, she was known for a traditional kind of religious chanting—recitation of mystical poems and lyrics in praise of the Prophet's blessed birth—which she performed at the community's various occasions and celebrations, such as the *mawlid* (celebration of the Prophet's birth). The combination of the serious, respected vocation of the teacher and the practice of a form of public entertainment for the community is interesting. A large number of these women teachers, such as Fatima bint Husayn al-Shihab (b. 1870) and Moza bint Hamada (b. 1836), who will be referred to later, were also known for their group *inshad* (chanted recitations) and their 'soft, moving' voices (al-Khurafi 477). Even if this singing activity probably took place within exclusively female gatherings, it seems that their reputation for skill and good voices circulated freely throughout the community without social embarrassment or surprise. It is also notable that this activity gradually disappears from the records about later *mutawwi'at* in the first decades of the twentieth century.

Other *mutawwi'at* are reputed to this day to have tutored prominent men from the elite, or even royalty. Sharifa Husayn al-'Ali Al 'Umar (b. 1831), for example, is known to have schooled several generations in Kuwait and the Arabian Peninsula, including King 'Abd al-'Aziz Ibn Sa'ud (Khurafi 451). Among the students of Mozah bint Hamada (b. 1836) was Princess al-Jazi, the sister of King 'Abd al-'Aziz Al Sa'ud. It is reported that Mozah was especially interested in the Qur'anic sciences,

such as *tafsir* and the Hadith tradition, and that she owned a private
library. The source does not specify whether she taught these religious
sciences at an advanced level, or how exactly she accessed such specialized knowledge. It seems, however, that she was quite the intellectual in
her time, practicing a wide range of cultural activities, for she loved
poetry and recited it—especially religious poetry—to her visitors. She
was also well versed in folk ballads and popular, historical tales, which
she used in storytelling.

One noticeable phenomenon is the development of a line of female
educators, consisting of mothers and daughters who passed on the profession. An example is Saliha Muhammad 'Ali al-Ramzi (b. 1849), who
received her Qur'anic education at the *kuttab* of her cousin, Latifa
al-Shamali, and then raised her twin daughters, Khayriyya and Amina, to
teach with her. She was also assisted by her nieces, Asma' Rashid
al-Shamali and Sukayna Rashid al-Shamali, and had boys as well as girls
in her *kuttab*. It is mentioned that, besides the rules of Qu'ranic recitation,
teaching also involved understanding its meanings and *ahkam* (rules,
commands). Notable men and women of Kuwaiti society at the time, such
as poets and writers, are named in the source material as her students,
which confirms her memorable influential role. Another example is Hissa
al-Hanif (b. 1858), who established a school in her home, teaching around
fifty girls from various classes of Kuwaiti society, the most famous being
Munira al-'Ayar, the mother of Shaykh Sabah al-Ahmad al-Jabir Al Sabah.

These women teachers, it appears, were not completely isolated from
the male circles in their communities. One *mutawwi'a*, Lulwa Hilal Al
'Utaybi (b. 1865), is said to have possessed a 'strong personality in her
dealings with men' and a reputation for having a wise temperament
(Khurafi 468). Maryam Hamad Al Budi (b. 1865) mainly received her
education through her father, Mulla Hamad bin 'Abd al-Rahman al-Budi,
who trained her from her early years to assist him in teaching. Later she
also specialized in the teaching of *fiqh* and *'ibadat*. Fatima bint Husayn
al-Shihab (b. 1870) was also assisted by her daughter, Asma' bint Shaykh
'Ali Ramadan and also had boys in her school. Boys would often accompany their sisters to the same *kuttab*, and, especially if no boys' school was
available in the area, it was customary for women teachers to step in and
fulfill this educational role for the boys. As for Lulwa Sayyid Ahmad
Husayn al-Rifa'i (b. 1878), she was known for chanting religious

invocations (*ad'iya*) and lyrical ballads with her students; her husband, Shaykh Muhammad Ibrahim bin Nuh, who was the imam and muezzin of the Khalifa mosque at the time, used to participate with them in these recitations and chanting. Once again we note the overlapping realms of the religious and the aesthetic, the sacred and the artistic.

Hence, it can be said that women *mutawwi'at* in this region, more than being merely teachers of primary religious education or of the most basic achievement of memorizing the Qur'an, contributed actively to the dissemination of knowledge and the passing on of religious traditions within their contexts. Studies of the intellectual and cultural life of the eastern Arabian Peninsula during the Ottoman period of the second half of the nineteenth century show that both geographical and sociological factors played a role in shaping all aspects of life in these societies (al-'Idraws 194–95). Distance from the busy cosmopolitan urban and trade centers of the middle and western regions of the Arab Muslim world at the time (such as Baghdad, Damascus, Jerusalem and Cairo), as well as the unique circumstances of an economy and social life based on pearl diving and other marine activities, created societies that depended for the preservation of their traditions on communal efforts suited to the nature of the environment and local customs. If no formal or wide-ranging learning centers existed (comparable to Zaytuna in Tunis or al-Azhar in Cairo), it was the practice of this informal religious training that represented the highest form of education available at the time. For example, sources that trace the early evolution of learning in Kuwait refer to 'houses of learning' (al-Farhan, cited in al-Khurafi 486), of which three were significant. The foremost was the House of the al-'Umar family, to which Kuwaitis gave the name *Bayt al-mutaww'at* ('house of teaching women'), because this house or family in particular produced a mother, Tarifa al-'Umar, and her six daughters, who assisted her and eventually inherited her profession. Tarifa, it is said, used to teach the girls 'in the indoor marketplace in the town center, near the market mosque' (Farhan, cited in al-Khurafi 486). Once again, the aspect of visibility in the public sphere should not go unnoticed. In addition to the Qur'an, 'Tarifa taught her students to memorize famous poems and lyrics, such as the poetry of al-Barzanji (1690–1766)', who composed verses narrating the Prophet's birth and childhood and was an imam at the Prophet's holy shrine in Medina. Another teacher, Amina Sayyid 'Ali Salih Zalzala, who will be referred to again below, is said to have been an 'important source in the field of *fiqhi* knowledge in everyday problems, hence answering the queries of those who came seeking answers' (al-Khurafi 499). The biographer, interestingly, writes *al-sa'ilin wa-al-sa'ilat*, indicating that both men and women came to ask her questions and consult her on religious matters.

Turn of the twentieth century

Two particular changes documented in the sources on *mutawwi'at* in this region are worth noting. One has to do with the content of teaching and learning, and the other with the historical discourse itself. As these women teachers enter the twentieth century, subjects such as sewing, embroidery, and cookery begin to be introduced as important 'gendered' skills to be learned specifically by girls. The emphasis begins to shift from learning rules of Qur'anic *tilawa*, *fiqh*, *'ibadat*, *tafsir*, Arabic language and poetry, and arithmetic, to domestic skills. Chronological tracking of the *mutawwi'ats*' biographies and their educational/learning interests shows this pattern. Whereas someone like Munira Muhammad bin 'Ali al-Dukhan (b. 1870) concentrated on teaching the rules of Arabic language and grammar using wooden boards to be distributed to her students as teaching aids, we find that Amina Sayyid 'Ali Salih Zalzala (b. 1898), although she learned the *Sunna*, *fiqh*, and Islamic history from her father's private library, added to her teaching 'housework, setting the table and table manners, cleanliness of the home, principles of sewing, and on using the newly-available sewing machines of the time' (al-Khurafi 498). As further examples, the teachers Lulwa Ahmad Birak Al 'Usaymi (b. 1892) was so interested in learning *fiqh* that she borrowed important books and reference works from the private libraries of the scholars in her community, such as Ibn Yasin, and Haya 'Abd al-Rahman Al Jasim (b. 1893) regularly attended the local mosque to hear the Friday sermons and other daily lectures delivered by Shaykh Ahmad al-Khamis. Nevertheless, we find that, in the first formal school established in Kuwait along modern lines in 1926, embroidery and sewing cotton and woolen clothes dominated the curriculum ('Abd al-Ghafur, cited in al-Khurafi 449). This was a school established by a Turkish woman, 'A'isha al-Izmiri, and, while her own educational background is not known, it is evident that she brought to this first official girls' school a new 'modernized' and 'secularized' vision centered on middle-class domesticity and 'feminine' skills. (One *mutawwi'a* born in 1920, Shaykha Ahmad Fahd al-Nashmi, began to teach her girls, in addition to Qur'an and arithmetic, sewing, embroidery, and handcrafts.) This was followed by the first national school to be established by the Kuwaiti Council of Knowledge (*Da'irat al-Ma'arif al-Kuwaytiyya*) in 1937, where girls' education continued to follow 'modern methods and standards' (al-Salih, cited in al-Khurafi 514). The new curricula contained the following subjects: geometry, mathematics, geography, history, English, health sciences, drawing, handcrafts, needlework, nursing and first aid, sewing and embroidery. These diverse additions manifest the dilution of religious sciences, which women had mastered and managed freely, following the state's taking control and assuming the normative authority in religious education.

The reporting on, or examination of, this kind of development exhibits the typical 'modernist' discourse that views this shift in the focus of education to gendered domesticity as a form of positive progress and modernization. Al-Khurafi praises this developed curriculum because it differentiated between the content of boys' and girls' education and reflected social needs: in these modern curricula, girls learn 'everything related to housework, the art of managing the marital home, family affairs, and sound treatment of their husbands' (500). (By association and unsurprisingly, he further digresses into a short section that extols the virtues of motherhood and wifehood.) It is interesting that the very nature of his comments changes, from the earlier references to the *mutawwi'ats'* 'strength of character' (449) and 'wise, intelligent opinions' (468) to praising the awareness of the special role of wife, nurturer, and mother.

Traditional *kuttab*s continued to exist, but gradually diminished in number until around the 1950s. We have record of women *mutawwi'at* working in the early decades of the twentieth century and continuing the practice. 'A'isha 'Abd al-Rahman al-Mudahika (b. 1900) devoted her life to teaching and died unmarried. She had a 'beautiful voice' in Qur'anic recitation (Khurafi 506). Haya 'Abullah Sayf 'Abdullah (b. 1901) was famous for her Thursday afternoon outings to the desert with women relatives and neighbors, and she also took up making traditional clothes, such as the *dishdasha*, to supplement the family income while her husband and sons were away trading most of the year. Other teachers who also found themselves in this situation used their incomes from teaching or other related activities to support their families included Zaynab 'Abd al-Husayn Yusuf al-Sarraf (b. 1913), who initially received her Qur'anic education in the *kuttab* of the Mulla 'Ali Buland, and Sarra 'Isa 'Ali al-Shamali (b. 1915). Thus, women maintained both the economic stability and educational tradition of the community by preserving, transmitting, and disseminating religious knowledge in the absence of a large section of the male population. Furthermore, women teachers continued to utilize their household circumstances and extended families to refine their teaching and enhance their socially prestigious status. Zahra al-Sayyid 'Umar 'Asim (b. 1914) worked in her mother's *kuttab*, and Mozah bin Salih bin Jasim Al Misbah (b. 1902) worked in what developed to be a 'family *kuttab*'. She first started teaching her blind brother at home and then he was joined by her other brothers and sisters, then male and female cousins and other relatives. The source mentions three brothers in particular who were her students, 'Abdullah, Zuman, and Muhammad, as well as the other male relatives. This is a good indication that the cultural notion of supposed male superiority or gender distinction did not apply in the context of religious learning, or when the specialized training of a female family member was acknowledged and respected. Mozah held *'majlis 'ilm wa-hikma'* (517), sessions for disseminating knowledge and wisdom.

In a major work of oral history published in 1995, which documents the collective memory of the older generation in today's United Arab Emirates (those born approximately in the mid-1920s), information can be found about similar women religious teachers active in the 1920s, 1930s, and 1940s. The most prominent figure in the area, as recalled by one Shaykh Ahmad Muhammad bin Hashil, was 'Aliya bint Hamid, who established the first school of its kind in Ras al-Khaimah. The *shaykh* proudly states that he was one of her students, along with a number of others whom he names. In fact, he says that all in all there must have been around 150 male students in 'Aliya's school. She started by hiring two teachers from Najd and providing them with food, while taking minimal fees from the parents. During the *shaykh*'s three-year stay at the school, he learned the Qur'an, *fiqh* of *'ibadat*, grammar, and poetry, and finally says, 'We did not hear of a school similar to 'Aliya bint Hamid's at the time' ('Abd al-Rahman 131). However, he remembers more *mutawwi'at* teaching Qur'an and religion to the girls, such as Khadija, 'A'isha bint al-Sharif, Lulwa, 'A'isha bint Muhammad 'Ubayd, and others.

As for Shaykh Ahmad 'Abd al-Rahman bin Hafiz, an imam and *khatib* from Dubai, he remembers the local festivities of the *tomina,* a religious celebration held on the occasion of a girl's successful completion of memorizing and learning the Qur'an. This is how he describes it:

> Girls dressed in their prettiest clothes and toured the houses of the neighborhood to collect donations of money, food, and sweets to give to the girl's *mutawwi'a.* As they went around, they recited and sang religious poems and mystical lyrics in praise of the Prophet. It was an opportunity for the young men to choose their future brides and later send their mothers to propose marriage, so this was an accepted custom. (Ibid. 151)

Not only was this a proud event of public acknowledgement of both female teacher and student, but it was also a community entertainment and social activity that facilitated spontaneous mixing of the sexes. This traditional *tomina* is no longer practiced.

In relation to this phenomenon of women educators and women of culture or knowledge interacting with their male peers, there is mention in an interview with the renowned Emirati poet, Rashid bin 'Ali Al Maktum, of a famous school in the village of Umm al-Qaywin, by the name of *madrasat al-Baghdadi*, where male poets and one female poet, Munwa, used to gather following the *'isha* (night prayer) to recite their poetry to each other. He remembers this woman poet in particular participating in their meetings and composing mostly satirical poetry (*hija'*). He also remembers 'Aliya bint al-Kharji, who used to teach Qur'an to the girls by day, and whose house at night would fill with large numbers of village women, spilling out into the yard outside, in order to perform the Sufi *dhikr* (spiritual ceremony). 'Aliya would lead the sessions by reciting Hadiths and invocations, and the women would respond and chant after her. These instances recorded from the memories of today's elderly people have great value for attempts at historical re-construction and the re-imaging of the life of Gulf women in the pre-oil decades, before the accompanying economic and socio-cultural changes in these societies. Against the view that such instances are exceptional and not indicative of normative social practices, one can argue that the mere existence of a few examples, together with the absence of the narrator's comments on their strangeness, illustrates possible precedents or other similar events not necessarily documented or remembered.

In short, women *mutawwi'at* of the eastern Peninsula or the Gulf region enjoyed a certain level of authoritative and privileged social status derived from the authority and power of religious knowledge in traditional societies. The sources indicate that they were held in great respect; so much so that 'if a man met her in the street, he would hasten to greet her, despite customary social restraints on such public conversations between a man and a woman' (al-Khurafi 515).

Women in Najd

Dalal bint Mukhallad al-Harbi, the author of *Nisa' shahirat min Najd* (Famous Women from Najd), admits to the difficulty of gathering information on these women and the consequent non-comprehensiveness of her collection. She states that she used three criteria for including women in her book, none of which is directly related to religious activities: she selected women known for their poetry, or their charitable work, or because they were close relatives of a ruling personality. However, it will be noticed that the second category includes numerous women known for building mosques in their names, caring for and supporting poor imams and preachers, and paying for young people in their communities to learn the Qur'an and study religion. Furthermore, some of the women, following the defeat at Dar'iyya in 1818, had to leave Najd for a period of time and sought refuge in Egypt or Syria, where they were active in religious instruction, spreading Salafi ideas.

The women in the central Peninsula who belonged to or were associated with the House of Sa'ud, from the end of the nineteenth century and up to the death of King 'Abd al-'Aziz in 1953, were involved in one of the most interesting activities related to religious learning—*waqf* (religious bequests) of books. It seems that, for these women, being part of the elite class gave them the honor of learning and mastering the religious sciences and proudly sponsoring them. Al-Jawhara bint Faysal bin Turki Al Sa'ud (b. 1854) is said to have memorized the Qur'an, the Sira of the Prophet, and '*fiqhi* deductions' (al-Harbi 30). She collected reference books on the religious sciences, several of which are now in the National King Fahd Library in Riyadh, inscribed with her name and the declaration that the books are a *waqf* 'for the benefit of Muslims'. Al-Jawhara bint Musaʻid bin Jallawi Al Saʻud (b. 1891) has also endowed selected religious classics, such as books by Ibn al-Qayyim al-Jawziyya. The text of the *waqfiyya* on one of them reads as follows: 'Humble al-Jawhara bint Musaʻid bin Jallawi has made this book an endowment for the benefit of seekers of knowledge; whoever accesses it should not make it exclusive or prevent others from reading it.' Three sisters, Ruqayya, Shammaʻ, and Haya ʻAwad bin Muhammad al-Hijji, are known to have donated a large collection of major works and reference books on the religious sciences, which still carry their names. The source includes a list of them (al-Harbi 45).

Besides endowing books, it is reported that some women also organized and supervised the memorization of the Qurʼan by children, distributed prizes for it, built mosques, and dedicated specific *waqfs* for other *hafizat al-Qurʼan* (women who learned the Qurʼan by heart). An example is Hissa bint Ahmad bin Muhammad al-Dayri (b. 1900), who is also known for her book endowments, especially books on Hanbali *fiqh*. A written declaration on one of her books reads: 'This book has become the possession of Hissa bint Ahmad al-Dayri through legal purchase, and she has made it a special endowment for seekers of knowledge and so it is not to be sold, given away, or passed on as an inheritance.' Numerous books contain this 'documented claim of ownership' (*nass milkiyya*) with the full names of their owners. As for Sarra bint ʻAbdallah bin Faysal al-Saʻud (b. 1877), the sources state that, besides the Qurʼan and Hadith, she also studied 'several *fiqhi* texts', and established *waqfs* on books for the benefit of 'memorizers of the Qurʼan' (al-Harbi 48).

Another group of women focused on opening *kuttab*s in their homes. Tarfa bint Muhammad al-Kharif (b. 1927) learned the Qurʼan in the school of another teacher, Mudi bint Hamad bin Muhammad al-Hamad, then in 1942 opened a *kuttab* for girls in her own house in the area called ʻUqda, which lasted until 1956. Later, she moved to Riyadh and opened another from 1958 to 1961. Fatima bint Muhammad bin ʻAbd al-Wahhab (no specific birth date is given, but the source indicates roughly the beginning of the nineteenth century) taught both men and women, and it is reported that she used to draw a light curtain between her male students and herself. Al-Harbi claims that, strangely, this Fatima was not mentioned by another male researcher, Hamad al-Jasir, in his major work on women in the life of Muhammad bin ʻAbd al-Wahhab' (1991), although she is considered a

major figure and played an important role following the fall of the first
Sa'udi state in 1818. She first migrated to Ras al-Khaimah, and then to
Amman, where she contributed to promoting Salafi doctrine. With the
establishment of the second Saudi state in 1825 she returned to Riyadh.
She never married. Surprisingly, she seems to have led the life of a religious activist and independent woman, accommodating one of the most
conservative movements in modern Islam.

Other women known for their schools include Nura bin Sulayman bin
Fahd al-Rahayt (b. 1925), who opened a *kuttab* for girls when she was
sixteen in her house in 'Unayza to teach them Qur'an and *shar'i* (legal)
sciences, such as *tawhid* and *fiqh*. Nura bint 'Abd al-'Aziz bin Ibrahim
al-Hijji (b. 1891) opened a *kuttab* in 1928, which kept expanding, to the
extent that she employed her daughters and her former students as teachers.
It is said that she influenced her son, Muhammad, who also opened a
school and went on to be an imam and preacher. The last example to
include here is Haya bint Salih bin Nasir al-Sha'ir (b. 1887), whose school
gained fame as 'the *kuttab* of *khatiba* (preacher) Haya'. The title given to
her is usually reserved for male imams who traditionally deliver the
sermon or *khutba* during the Friday prayers.

Women from the elite class in the Arabian Peninsula were able to utilize
their social and economic position to enhance and sponsor religious learning.
Furthermore, their presence during the special historical circumstances of
founding and consolidating the House of Sa'ud allowed them, ironically,
and against expectations, to participate in advocating Salafi doctrines and to
become active in spreading conservative religious knowledge.

Conclusions

The above-mentioned presentation is not an exhaustive coverage of all the
women throughout the Arabian Peninsula who have worked in the religious arena, but it has set out to provide an overview of the historical
picture, highlight certain significant, representative cases, and to attempt
deductions and analysis based on the available textual sources. Furthermore,
it is hoped that the approach and theoretical framework adopted constitute
a paradigm shift in the study of women's cultural and social history in
large parts of the Arabian Peninsula, past and present. The following
general conclusions can be drawn:

(a) In form, the religious scholarly or educational activities of Arab Muslim women indicate that they had a public, performance role in occasionally gender-mixed environments.

(b) Working within their traditional contexts to preserve orthodox Islamic learning and pedagogy, women had a place within the dominant authority and power structures, competing with male hegemony, and carving a space for themselves in the religious sphere, and hence achieving self-empowerment. This is very striking when compared with the history of medieval Christian nuns and ascetics, who were subject to actual and conceptual alienation within their Christian contexts through the forbidding of female preaching or teaching and the taboos related to sin and notions of the body that were imposed on femininity and womanhood.

(c) Comparing women scholars of the classical pre-Ottoman period with those of early modern and modern pre-oil times demonstrates a slight diminishing in the nature and quality of the substance of their knowledge. Whereas pre-modern women possessed very specialized and profound knowledge of specific branches of the *shar'i* sciences, and so were *faqihat, muftiyat, muhaddithat*, or *sufiyyat*, no such clear-cut delineation exists in more recent time periods. Of course, this may be due to the overall historical context of the region, which underwent a stage of limitation in dynamic religious intellectual life, and so Arab women of the Peninsula were simply a part of that general framework, while managing to play important roles within it.

(d) We notice the creeping of the 'modernist' ideology of domesticity, strict gender role division, and seclusion—as well as the nation-state's assumption of control of educational and gender philosophies—into the historical social discourses, hence affecting the lives of women and the cultural construction of gender.

(e) In today's indigenous, cultural revival and post-modern awareness of the empowering potential of knowledge, and of the means of power structures and venues, Arab women in the Gulf region are making a comeback in the arena of religion, through accessing academia, research, and media. More study and analysis of this contemporary scene is therefore needed.

9. *Women and Education in the Gulf: Between the Modern and the Traditional*

RAMADAN AL-KHOULI

One day, His Excellency Prince 'Ali bin 'Abdullah al-Thani[1] invited the late Shaykh Muhammad bin Mani' to a meal along with some scholars, among whom were His Grace judge Shaykh 'Abdullah bin Zayd al-Mahmud,[2] the late Shaykh 'Abdullah Turki and Shaykh 'Ali bin Jabr al-Thani. During the meal, Shaykh Khalifa bin Hamad al-Thani posed a direct question to Shaykh Muhammad bin Mani': 'What is your opinion, Your Grace, about the education of girls, and those who ban it and call it a taboo?' Shaykh Bin Mani' answered: 'He who bans the education of girls is more than ignorant.' None of those present commented, though some of them were against educating girls. When they proceeded to wash their hands after the meal, Shaykh Khalifa said to Shaykh Bin Mani' 'Shaykh, release half the nation, I want a *fatwa* (an Islamic religious ruling).' Previously Shaykh 'Ali al-Thani, the deceased ruler of Qatar had sent a message to Shaykh Khalifa, known as 'the Chief of Education', informing him of Bin Mani''s opinion in regard to the education of girls and added that he, as governer, had no objection to the education of girls. After asking

---

[1] Shaykh 'Ali bin 'Abdullah was born around 1896 and became the governor of Qatar following the abdication of Shaykh 'Abdullah in his favor on 20 August 1948. He continued to govern the country until he abdicated in favor of his son HE Shaykh Ahmad bin 'Ali on 24 October 1960.

[2] One of the Ashraf of Najd; for more information, refer to http://www.alshreef.com.

his question and receiving Shaykh bin Mani''s response, Shaykh Khalifa
proceeded to ask him for an official letter and a *fatwa* stating the Shaykh's
response; these were issued and relayed to the 'Chief of Education' giving
religious support to the education of girls.[3]

Education is one of the fundamental pillars in building nations and civilizations. Contemporary international experience has proved that the real
beginning of progress is education. In fact, developed countries set education as a priority in their programs and policies. It is also natural that
transformations and changes in societies have a bearing on education, it
being a secondary social system within the framework of the collective
social system which also prompts the creation and re-structuring of that
shared social system. At times when nations undergo radical transformations in building an institutional system of governance, they usually make
the building of a modern educational institution one of their top priorities.
The Gulf states have passed through this foundational stage over similar
but not simultaneous periods, consistent with the emergence of oil wealth
as one of the most important determinants of the construction of the
modern state in the Arabian Gulf area.

More often than not, the construction of an institutional system is not
only related to the hierarchical structure within which it grows, but is also
a result of a specific philosophy that it aspires to achieve. The above story
gives some clear indications about the development of a view on the
education of 'half the nation'—as the state representative (Shaykh Khalifa
bin Hamad) calls it—and the controversy among religious leaders. How
then did this governing power that aspires to create a modern state deal
with building an educational system according to a certain philosophy and
vision for society (including both its male and female members)? How did
it manage to achieve its aim of including both parts of society in this structure by including, or excluding, males and females in this modern system,
or what it called modern education?

The conclusion expresses in one way or another, the view of the ruling
power rather than that of society. We should therefore go back a little to the
time that preceded the building of what we now call 'modern' education,

[3]This was a report written by Shaykh Muhammad bin Mani', education advisor to Qatar
in 1957 and sent to His Excellency the late 'Ali bin 'Abdullah al-Thani, governor of the
state at the time. I thank Shaykh 'Abdullah al-Mani' for providing me with a copy of the
report.

so that we can see, perhaps more clearly, the way society handled the education of males and females before the discovery of oil in the Gulf area.

It is difficult to identify accurately a specific time frame in this kind of study, especially if we want to fix specific years as start and end dates. Let the time frame therefore be between the beginning of the twentieth century, that is before the establishment of the first formal school in the Gulf—the Mubarakiyya school in Kuwait in 1912 (al-'Abdullah 19)—and the 1960s, that is to say after all the Gulf states adopted a modern educational system.

The study relies on a number of sources, the most important of which were personal interviews with the following:

- Mr 'Abdullah 'Ali al-Tabur from Ras al-Khaimah, who has several published works and is an active interviewer of senior citizens
- Mr 'Abd al-Rahman Yusuf al-'Ubaydan, director of the Radio and Television Organization in Qatar[4]
- Dr Mirza al-Sayigh, whose father was the owner of a school in Dubai before the state established a formal educational system
- Mr 'Abd al-Muhsin 'Abdullah al-Khourafi and Mrs Maryam al-Agruga from Kuwait[5]

In addition to these interviews, several books, research papers and statistics will be referred to. The study is divided into two sections. The first is about education in the Gulf in general, and the second is about the education of girls. Both sections are chronological.

Education in the Arab Gulf Emirates

This section aims to provide a general view of the history of education in the Gulf. More specifically the aim is to deconstruct the normative narrative that has dominated the history of education with a linear chronological approach without attention to the possibilities of alternative, conflicting

[4]The main purpose of the visit was to study archives of documentary programs and talk shows hosting elderly people. Fortunately for us, the director gave us a wealth of information that he had received from Mrs Amina al-Mahmud, by whom he had been taught as a child.
[5]I conducted the interview with them during a business trip to Kuwait (2008) to collect the required data for the research team.

and parallel narratives. The different analysis presented here explains the various consecutive, yet parallel stages, of the history of education experienced by the Gulf. As will be shown, this is particularly significant for unlocking the history of women. Re-reading critically these phases across the Gulf helps us understand the development of the educational process and frees us not only from terms and categorizations, but also from their negative and positive implications. Moreover, it allows us to examine the feminine presence within and outside this intellectual system in each of these phases.

'Education at a young age is like engraving stones' is a popular proverb in Arab countries, prompting parents to educate their children from a young age. Inherent in this educational paradigm is the educational concept salient today, which implies receiving education from a teacher. This is not a new notion; for the presence of an educator for children existed in most ancient civilizations, especially during times of stability. In the Arab world, the *kuttab* (an Islamic elementary school, usually attached to a mosque where the pupils learned the Qur'an) was the place for early education. The Emirate of Qatar, which witnessed a certain stability towards the end of the nineteenth century during the reign of Shaykh Qasim bin Muhammad al-Thani, knew the first form of education in the *katatib* (al-'Abdullah 307; cf. Naji 507) (plural of *kuttab*) system. Likewise, in Kuwait, education began in the *kuttab* (Husayn 264) as was the case in the villages of Najd[6]. The person responsible for a *kuttab* was called *sayyidna* (our master) in Egypt and *mutawwi'* (or the feminine *mutawwi'a*; teacher) in most of the Gulf region. In the district of al-Ihsa, before the establishment of modern education, religious education was the sole prerogative of the teachers (*mutawwa'a*) of the *katatib* (al-Milhim 28). Similarly, in the United Arab Emirates, we find that the educational process 'depends on the *mutawwi''* (al-Tabur 23), who in some places was also called the *mulla* (Jamal 389).

The *kuttab* was a one-room school with a single teacher. There were no specifications for the classroom and the teacher did not have to have any formal qualifications. In this room sat a number of students of different ages and levels (al-Amadi 16), and the focus of the *mutawwi'* or *mutawwa'a* was on teaching the Qur'an, although some of them used to add some

[6]http://www.g111g.com/vb/t146220.htm.

instruction in Hadith or grammar; but this differed from one *mutawwi'* to another and depended on his or her academic knowledge.

With regard to the teaching methodology, Ahmad bin Jasim Darwish says: 'We sat on sackcloth, and raised our Holy Books on wooden chairs that were called the *al-marafi'* (stands).' Amina al-Jayyida adds: 'I would sit opposite them reading and they repeated after me' (al-Amadi 35). Maryam 'Abd al-Malik al-Salih points out that this was the narrative method (*tariqat al-sard*), and that there was another technique which she calls *al-i'raba*, which is spelling out the alphabet in all its forms with dots, stress, intonation, vowel sounds and consonants, then spelling out the *suras* of the Qur'an until the pupil eventually spells out the whole *Amma* section (the first part) of the Quran, and thus she becomes an expert at reciting it and does not forget how to do it as she memorizes the whole Qur'an (al-Salih 38).

The *kuttab* teacher was paid a salary by the child's family, be it a boy or a girl:

> My salary was five paises, paid by the learner every Thursday. At the beginning of every month, I was given a 'nafela', which was half a kiran [the old currency of Qatar] and if the learner reached *Surat al-Bayyina* , I would be given a rupee, and if he/she learned *Surat al-Fajr*, I would be given another rupee, and after the learner finished a part, I would be given a rupee, until the completion of the Holy Qur'an. In the meantime, if the learner reached *Surat al-Kahf*, the parents would distribute nuts, and if he/she reached *Surat al-Anfal*, the parents would offer a *tarwiqa* [a breakfast of popular foods at the time], to the *mutawwi'a*, the students and neighbors. If the learner completed the Holy Qur'an, we would take him around the neighborhood reciting the prayer of thanks *al-tahmida*. Furthermore, the people gave the one who had completed the Qur'an what they could offer in food or money. On the third day after the completion of the Qur'an, the learner's parents hosted a lunch banquet for the family and neighbors, and sent some of the food to the *mutawwi'a* and her students. (Al-Amadi 37–8)

In the old days, a pupil who completed the memorization of the Qur'an was celebrated in a procession. The school decreed that all the other pupils should serve this accomplished learner and walk behind him/her along with the mother or one of the female relatives, visiting the houses of the well-to-do in the neighborhood, collecting a cash reward, a sum of which would be given to the *mulla* for his help in making the student learn the Qur'an (al-Ayub 114).

However, poorer families could not manage this, and the *mutawwi'* or *mutawwi'a* always took the financial status of the family into consideration. The system was similar in most of the Gulf area with perhaps a few differences in terminology. The system of payment was different for education with a Mullah or Mullayah. Studying with a Mullayah for example required the payment of 'a monthly salary ranging from one to two rupis depending on the girl's economic standard.'[7]

At first, this was the basic educational system and it has been variously described by historians: 'In Kuwait, education, like everything else, began modestly' (Husayn 264). Others saw that 'the Ihsa district, under the umbrella of this system, lives in a state of rampant illiteracy' (al-Milhim 28), and in the United Arab Emirates we find the educational process 'in tune with the simplicity of life' (al-Tabur 23). In these comments, the historians are perhaps projecting a judgment based on the state of education today. The question is, however, did education serve the needs of that period?

As soon as the second decade of the twentieth century began, rapid changes took place in the Gulf, such as the growth of trade, especially the pearl trade, the proliferation of diving ships in many parts of the Gulf, and the increase in travel and interaction with other societies, especially India. Consequently, the people began to feel that the *kuttab*, as it was at the time, was no longer able to address the needs of society, and that it could not offer more than it had offered so far. Thus, they felt the need to establish an educational tradition that would endeavor to spread structured education with a firm foundation, methodology and subject matter. 'The circumstances, as well as the social and economic atmosphere, helped crystallize the idea of the need to have a different type of education. In addition, the coastal environment prompted the people to take to the sea— before the appearance of oil—to earn their living, and they worked as traders and pearl divers. This meant that they traveled to other countries, where they were introduced to many aspects of life in general, and culture

[7]Maryam 'Abdal-Malik al-Salih, *Safahat min al-tatawur al-tarikhi li-ta'lim al-fatat fi al-Kuwait*, p. 55.

in particular that made them realize the extent of their need for education in their own societies' (al-'Abdullah 81). A new, alternative form of education thus emerged in conjunction with the *katatib* and, in 1912, the Mubarakiyya School was founded in Kuwait (Jamal 389), and the first school in Qatar, the Athariyya School, was founded in 1913 by Shaykh Bin Manea (Husayn 513–4). Many students from Qatar, Sharja, Najd, Kuwait and Iran joined this school upon the invitation of Shaykh bin Mani' (al-'Abdullah 308).

Education in Qatar remained limited to *katatib* during the closure of the Athariyya School (1938–1947). In 1947 oil was discovered in Qatar, although it was not yet exported. Shaykh Hamad bin 'Abdullah al-Thani, who was handling all government affairs on behalf of his aging father Shaykh 'Abdullah bin Qasim al-Thani, realized that modern education had become an inevitable necessity. He thus commissioned one of the notable Qataris to contact neighboring countries to find a competent and efficient educator who could establish a modern school in Doha. Muhammad bin 'Ali al-Mahmud, from Sharjah, was summoned to Qatar in 1947, where he rented a building in the al-Jasra district in Doha, and established a school which he called 'Al-Muhammadiyya Reform School' after Shaykh Hamad bin 'Abdullah, who commissioned and funded it. Fifty Qatari students joined the school in its first year; they were then joined by thirty students from Sharjah and formed two sections. Muhammad bin 'Ali al-Mahmud taught them until the end of the school year, and in the following year, he was joined by three other teachers (al-'Abdullah 311). It seems that this school attracted a number of students from other areas; for as Mirza al-Sayigh remarks, the clever students of Dubai were sent to Doha or Egypt.

There is a single reference to a regular school in the period that pre-dates modern education. This was the Rashidiyya School, which taught Islamic sciences in very much the same way as Ottoman schools, and it was made up of three elementary and three intermediate classes (al-Amadi 16).

The most prominent feature of this development in the type of education required was a functional change in keeping with the needs of society, which differed not only as time passed, but from state to state. In Kuwait, where the situation was similar in that education began in the *kuttab*, as a result of

the increase of commercial exchange with India and some European countries the need for bookkeeping and financial control emerged.

This encouraged some teachers to provide lessons while the number of students willing to learn this area increased since they found it could help them obtain an accounting job with one of the traders, which would bring them more money and raise their standard of living, or perhaps, should circumstances allow, help them venture into the world of commerce after obtaining enough knowledge in the field. (Jamal 392–3)

It is said that bookkeeping lessons were divided into three sections, taught in detail to anyone who desired to specialize in one of these subdivisions. The first section focused on commercial activity, income accounts, warehouse details, sales and procurement and the like, and this was called 'bookkeeping'. The second section was called 'album accounts', and dealt with everything about accounts for sailing ships traveling to India, such as expenses, and the crew's shares in the income. The third section was known as 'alshu'i accounts', and it was concerned with the accounts of diving ships and the methods of calculating expenses and income for this type of activity, as well as tesjam (advances offered to sailors by the owner/master of the ship). There were mutawwa'a and teachers who specialized in these accounting lessons, such as Mulla Murshid and Mulla Hamada (Jama 393).[8]

These schools spread throughout all the districts of Kuwait and are, therefore, difficult to enumerate. However, they started closing down in the early 1950s, when government schools were established and people preferred to send their children there because they provided free modern education, books, copybooks and clothes for the students (Jamal 398).

It is interesting to note here that this concurrence between katatib and school education strengthened the role of each, with the latter considered a phase that followed after the katatib, and 'the katatib were no longer a finalized or truncated stage, which encouraged a lot of Qataris to join the katatib and a number of mutawwa'a to establish their own private katatib' (al-Amadi 18).

After the drilling and selling of oil began, the Gulf emirates gave special and substantial care to education, spending generously until it became the

[8]From an interview with Ahmad 'Abd al-Latif 'Abd al-Jalil.

most favored sector, allowing it to more than double in size in most Gulf
societies. So much so that even the societies that did not have a financial
surplus managed to allocate considerable amounts from their budgets to
education (al-'Abdullah 81–2).

This has been a brief survey of education in the Gulf emirates up until
the state building stage, with all the institutions it comprises, including
the educational institutions. However, re-reading the events, with the
logical assessment of detail that historians always offer, leads to
different conclusions. Education in the Gulf area, according to the literature of the times, began as traditional education in the *kuttab* of the
mutawwi' or *mutawwi'a* (Jamal 389), a term that now has negative
connotations since it is almost always used to indicate the opposite of
modern education. Moreover, on the temporal level, it connotes the
times before the creation of the modern state. Modern education implies
formal education, under the auspices of the state and in accordance with
certain rules 'through which the development of the individual or the
group is directed by a person or a number of people by means of specific
methodologies and programs' ('Abd al-Rahman 11). This normative
approach which is consistently used as an introduction in historical
studies to compare between the past and the present, represents a methodology that demotes the former traditional, or popular, in favor of the
contemporary and modern.

Since there is always a need to create an 'other' to bear the responsibility for the traditional and popular, which connotes backwardness, the
creation of the 'other' is mandatory, and is forever alive in the Arab
consciousness as 'colonialism'. The historical literature on Egypt defines
the British occupation as responsible, while Morrocco blames the French
occupation and, by the same token, in the Gulf we find that Kamal Naji's
article, 'The History of Popular Education from the End of the Nineteenth
Century to the Middle of the Twentieth Century', indicates that Ottoman
and British occupation or presence deliberately fostered educational backwardness in the Gulf. Furthermore, even the selective educational policy
that Britain adopted in Egypt and India to build an elite class, did not
extend to the Gulf. In my view, the Ottoman Empire, which dominated the
Islamic world at the time, did not see education as one of the fundamental
duties of the state (Committee for the Documentation of Qatari History,
508).

These specific introductions to the methodology applied in historical studies prevent us from seeing clearly and deeply the details of the so-called traditional and popular education, and from knowing how it took place, and what were its features. We should therefore attempt to understand society at that time by comprehensively reviewing the history of the Arab provinces in Egypt and the Levant before the emergence of the modern state, and this shows that the system of services offered to society, such as health and education, were not the financial responsibility of the state, but were rather entrusted to charitable organizations, Islamic endowments (awqaf), or what may be referred to as civil society. It seems that the same applied to the Arabian Gulf area, where financial responsibility was borne by the wealthy merchants of each country. Indeed, they not only bore the costs of the schools, students and teachers, but also covered the expenses of exceptional students on scholarships from Sharjah to Doha to be educated under some of its prominent educators, such as Shaykh Muhammad 'Abd al-'Aziz al-Manea. Even the schools that were said to belong to the state, before formal education began, were in fact established by donations from sultans or governors, and were not under the auspices of the ruling establishment, as was the case in other parts of the Arab world. This phase was characterized by being traditional, and by the fact that its programs were mostly, if not always, imported from neighboring Arab countries, especially Egypt, which had begun a century earlier, and had witnessed changes and developments that matched the needs of society. This stage had the following specific features:

- It received its impetus from some of the notable men in the region, such as Shaykh al-Mahmud in Sharjah and some pearl traders in Kuwait.
- This phase did not replace the first stage, the *kuttab*, but ran parallel to it.
- This phase differed in extent from one area in the Gulf to another until the ruling establishments in these areas began to take the initiative and enforce a specific educational system that matched its own perspective on what was desirable in a modern state. We may thus consider that the first and second phases of education were the choice of society, whereas the third phase was decreed by the state.

- Amina Mahmud al-Jayyida was one of the pillars of the first phase, and helped bring in the second phase. In fact, it was she who advocated the move into the third phase, for she had lived between Doha and Bahrain during her marriage and had been introduced to other ventures, such as missionary schools. When she returned to Doha, she called for this kind of development there and even began implementing it herself.

The education of girls in the Gulf

The historian Yusuf al-'Abdullah remarks that Qatar was introduced to *katatib* in the last part of the nineteenth century, and considers that Amina al-Jayyida's *kuttab*, 'established in 1938, is the real beginning of girl's education' (al-'Abdullah 309). Dr Badriyya al-Amadi also adds: 'the *katatib* for the education of girls were not contemporaneous with those of boys, and therefore girls in Qatar did not get any *katatib* education until the end of the 1930s' (al-Amadi 25). Similarly, in Kuwait 'schools for girls were founded later than schools for boys' (Ja'far 360), and 'in Mecca, girls' schools were established half a century after boys' schools' ('Abd al-Rahman 288). Thus, historians of education in the Gulf have connected their documentation of girls' education with the creation of girls' educational establishments, whether *katatib* or schools, justifying this by the scarcity of the data about the number of literate males and females at the time. The question is, however, how methodologically correct is this connection? Another question is: at the time, did education in the Gulf begin with the sexes being taught separately? And how sure are we of the validity of the conclusions that have been reached? Indeed, how valid are the justifications for this delay? I will attempt to discuss this chronologically, following the stages of education in the Gulf area.

Historians of education in the Gulf indicate that 'Girls in the Gulf emirates remained outside the realm of education' although they learned some short Suras of the Holy Qur'an, and acquired its religious teachings from members of the family who went to the mosques and sat in on religious classes (al-'Abdullah 309), or from those who studied at the Athariya School in Qatar or the Mubarakiyya in Kuwait or al-Taymiyya al-Mahmudiyya in the United Arab Emirates. It seems, however, that some of these girls achieved remarkable progress in education, and that it was they who eventually contributed to the foundational stage of girls' education through the *katatib* of *mutawwi'at*. Therefore with regard to the pioneer *mutawwi'at*, according to their statements, they were educated unsystematically and privately at the hand of male members of their families. However, by looking at the biography of Amina Mahmud al-Jayyida, who says, 'I started learning to read the Holy Qur'an at the hands of Mulla Hamid bin Ahmad bin Muhammad, a Qatari shaykh, in the district of al-Jasra with the local children' (al-Amadi 28), which is similar to what happened to the mutawwi'a 'Alya' bint Jassim bin Hamad who studied at 'the hands of al-shaykh 'Abdalaziz bin 'Abdalrahman' from Ras al-Khaimah (Badriya 28), it becomes evident that family instruction was not the only option for girls and that they also learned at the hands of male *mutawwa'a* and *mullas*. In fact, the large number of significant *katatib* run by *mutawwi'at* in existence in the very same year that was considered by some as the real beginning of girls' education confirms the inaccuracy of connecting the history of *katatib* with that of girls' education: 'the most important girls' *katatib* in 1938 were those of Moza Slaybikh, Amina Mahmud al-Jayyida, Amina and Sbika al-Baharna, Amina Jasim al-Mas'ud, and Haya al-Zamami' (ibid. 25–6). Interestingly, al-'Abdullah also observes that 'the number of *katatib* reached twelve in 1938 for both boys and girls, and were mostly all located in Doha' (al- 'Abdullah 310). In other words, the number of schools run by women teachers was equal to that of those run by men, although 'Abd al-Aziz al-Rashid says that the number of *katatib* in Kuwait in 1926 amounted to more than seventeen schools for boys and eight for girls. Excluding the Mubarakiyya School, the Ahmadiyya School and the Sa'ada School, all the others were *katatib* where education was limited to reading, writing and arithmetic. We should take into account here Jamal's reservation (393) that he is referring to the big *katatib* with a large number of students, because there were tens of smaller ones and tens of *mutawwa'a*, since every neighborhood had one *mutawwi'* to teach the children. What is important here is the proportion of girls' *katatib* to boys' *katatib* in 1926, which was more than half. This long preceded the debate over the legitimacy of educating girls, and whether it was against religion and the traditions of the Gulf area or not, which should therefore be viewed in the context of the historical circumstances in which it emerged.

Consequently, even if we do follow the logic of connecting the historical progress of the *kuttab* and that of girls' education, it emerges that it is inaccurate to point to a great discrepancy between the education of boys and girls. The date used in this calculation was not the date of the beginning of education. Furthermore, the sources themselves do not indicate that date; rather, it is simply an estimated date according to Amina al-Jayyida, who was born in 1913 in al-Jasra district in Doha (al-Amadi 26), and who states: 'I was seven when I began to learn how to read the Holy Qur'an' (ibid. 28). This indicates that she started to attend Mulla Hamid bin Ahmad bin Muhammad's *kuttab* in al-Jasra regularly in 1920, a date very close to that of the beginning of the *kuttab* in Qatar. Moreover, she is not a unique case; there were others who had preceded her and had completed memorizing the Qur'an. She had also been instructed by a woman called Maryam, for it was customary that each woman who memorized the Qur'an would then instruct other girls in the neighborhood (ibid.). Despite the lack of information about this Maryam, the fact remains that she was educated before Amina—that is before 1920. Thus, if Amina was instructed in a *kuttab* with a male teacher, should we consider that there was mixed education? Did education start as co-education?

Once again Amina Mahmud al-Jayyida states: 'I had with me a number of the local students of al-Jasra district. The girls I remember are Sarra bint Muhammad al-Jawhara bint Nasir, Amina 'Abd al-Ghani, and the boys, Muhammad Jayyida, Nasir 'Ubaydan, 'Abd al-Latif al-Muslimani, Rashid 'Ubaydan, 'Abd al-Rahman Mulla Ibrahim, Hasan Murad, and there were many others that I cannot remember. We were a large group' (ibid.). Moreover, 'Abd al-Rahman Yusef Al 'Ubaydan, who himself studied at Amina Mahmud al-Jayyida's *kuttab*, confirms that both boys and girls went to some of the *katatib* run by women teachers.[9]

We can therefore conclude that the education of girls during the first period did not take place only within the family home and at the hands of relatives but took place on a wider scale outside of the family at the hands of the *mutawwi'* or the mullah and that it was in no way connected with — in this early period of girls' education — the *kuttab*s of *mutawi'at* and that it took place as mixed education involving both boys and girls.

[9]In an interview with Mr al-'Ubaydan.

As for the second stage of education, the stage undertaken by merchants who undertook financial support, and which took place parallel to the first stage without cancelling it, there are not enough details available to inform us of the inclusion of girls among this educational infrastructure, even though the education of girls continued densely within the *kuttab* structure. The only case about which we have some limited information is Qatar, through the efforts of Amna al-Jidda, whose call for the development of her *kuttab* received support from the ruling authority as was the case for the Athariyya School.

As for the period of modern education which took place in all countries of the Gulf under the full supervision and sponsorship of the ruling authorities, the statistical information produced by the Ministry of Education in Qatar, which provides information regarding the number of students according to gender, is of great significance, since it shows us these numbers from the point at which state education started. Thus, it makes clear that in 1972, the year modern education was first introduced, 240 male students were included but not a single female included in the modern education that the state adopted.

	Number of students		Year
Total	Girls	Boys	
240	0	240	1371/72
1050	50	1000	1375/76
5965	1942	4023	1380/81
12717	4811	7906	1385/86
18531	7827	10704	1390/91
29942	14087	15855	1395/96
39944	19356	20588	1400/01
52050	25525	26525	1405/06
56908	27971	28937	1407/08

Schedule according to Nura Nasser al-Thani, p. 244

Some of the studies written about education in the Gulf explained that this was due both to the religious belief that this was against the rules of Islam and the culture of the Arabian Gulf. However, a different reading of this schedule points to different conclusions; after all, until that date there was not a school dedicated specifically for girls and this gives the impression that there were no girls involved in the educational process when in fact the opposite was true. As to how this situation was corrected, it seems that Shaykh Khalifa was forced to have a *fatwa* issued from His Honor

al-Shaykh 'Abdalaziz al-Mani' that the education of girls does not contradict Islam. That year, fifty girls became enrolled in modern education and
a school was opened for them. At that time there were 1,000 boys in
modern education; in other words the proportion of boys to girls was one
to twenty. In five years, the number of girls caught up with that of the boys
to reach a total of 1,942 as compared with 4,023 boys. This increase in
female enrollment in modern educational institutions was explained by
some historians as being related to the religious fatwa. This phenomenon
however can be explained at various levels:

- First, with regard to the increase in the number of female students
  from fifty to 1,942, which is a significant increase in five years, it is
  unrealistic to expect that a society where women have been subjugated into ignorance and denied education and access to the public
  sphere could simply accept the education of girls so fast and in such
  significant numbers. The issue needs a different reading and can be
  explained by social readiness and acceptance of a woman's role in
  the public sphere; otherwise such a significant increase over a short
  time could not have taken place.
- Second, the comparisons between increases in ratios involving male
  and female numbers support the above conclusion, since while the
  ratio increase for female students was 20 students to each student,
  the increase in male students was approxiately one to two.

The fatwa on educating girls

When formal education began in Qatar and other Gulf areas, it began
solely with, and for, boys and men, whether students or teachers; and the
literature of the time states that giving official permission for girls' education was not 'an unproblematic or easy thing'.[10] In fact, Shaykh Khalifa
bin Hamad, the Chief of Education, according to the literature, had to
'exert great efforts to achieve this goal'.[11] At the time, Shaykh Muhammad
bin Manea was the advisor for educational affairs, and so Shaykh Khalifa
realized that the key to the solution of this issue lay in the opinion of

[10]From the report written by Shaykh Muhammad bin Mani', sent to 'Ali bin 'Abdullah
al-Thani, governor of the state at the time.
[11]Shaykh Khalifa bin Hamad in his own words.

Shaykh bin Manea, as related in the story presented at the beginning of this study, and Shaykh Mani''s response: 'He who bans the education of girls is more than ignorant.'

Educating Girls

12. This issue is controversial, some endorse their education and some prohibit it. The truth is that we should consider the rule of Shari'a and what it has allowed and decreed as a duty. Instructing girls about important religious matters is a duty; it will help a woman know about the pillars of Islam, about faith, about how her prayers should be and how she should manage her home and raise her children. However, this should be without violating *Shari'a*. She should not appear with her head uncovered in front of men who are unrelated to her; she should not leave her home without the legal *hijab*. A person who totally bans girls' education has invented his own ruling, a ruling that goes against the legal *Shari'a* decree which should be followed above everything else.

Following on the above, 'When His Grace the late Shaykh 'Ali contacted Shaykh Khalifa (as Chief of Education) to inform him of the late Shaykh bin Manea's opinion, and that he (the ruler) had no objection to the education of girls, Shaykh Khalifa asked for an official *fatwa*, which was issued'.

In light of what we have observed regarding girls' education in the early *katatib*, we might ask, who was this *fatwa* for? Why was it necessary? The question becomes even more pertinent when we examine the similar scenario for the decree on girls' education in Saudi Arabia. 'In the month of Rabi' Thani of the year 1379 AH, a royal proclamation was issued indicating the necessity of establishing schools for girls in the Kingdom of Saudi Arabia; it read: "Thanks be to Allah alone. We have resolved to carry out the wish of the scholars of true religion in the kingdom by establishing schools to educate girls"' ('Abd al-Rahman 288).

Did the ruling power need sanctified, religious support to force families to enroll girls in regular education that aimed to reshape society and its systems in a certain way? Was this necessary in order to convince a society that hid behind the dominant religious view about girls' education? Or was

ـ ٤ ـ

١ ـ مناهج الدراسة الابتدائية والثانوية ينبغي ان تكون مطابقة لمناهج معارف المملكة العربية السعودية لانها مناهج متعبرة حرة مقبولة في البلاد الخارجية

١٠ ـ الرياضة البدنية لا بد منها لطلاب المدارس فهي تقوي اعضاءهم وتنشطهم على الدراسة والطلب وتذهب عنهم الكسل والملل ولكن على وجه لا يخل بالدين فلا تفوت الصلاة وتخرج عن وقتها ويكون التلميذ سافرا لعورة وهي ما بين السرة والركبة ولو كان التلميذ صغيرا اخذ بالاحتياط .

١١ ـ التفتيش الفني ضروري لا بد منه في أنه ارسى ولكن المفتش لابد وان يكون عالما بالمقررات مراعيا حال الاساتذة والتلاميذ منتبها لما يقع من الخطأ حالة التدريس مبينا الوجه الصحيح بأسلوب حسن ولو أدى التفتيش الاداري في التفتيش الفني لكان حسنا وهذا امر المعول به في المعارف السعودية .

تعليم البنات

١٢ ـ هذه المسألة كثر الكلام فيها فمن مجيز لتعليمهن ومن مانع والحق في ذلك ما أوجبه الشرع وأباحه وتعليم البنات امور الدين الضرورية واجب فتعرف اركان الاسلام وأركان الايمان وتتعلم ما تصح به صلاتها وكذلك ما ينبغي لها ان تتعلم كيفية تدبير منزلها وتربية أولادها ولكن ذلك مشروط بعدم مخالفة شيء من الشرع فلا تبرز لارجال الاجانب سافرة ولا تخرج من بيتها الا ... الحجاب الشرعي فمن سد باب تعليم البنات مطلقا فقد جاء بشيء من عنده يخالف الدليل الشرعي الذي يجب اتباعه وترك ما سواه .

المدارس المسماة بالروضات

١٣ ـ يتعين الحاق جميع المدارس المسماة بالروضات بالمدارس الابتدائية والسنة الأولى من هذه الروضات في من الطلبة ... الابتدائيين فانفراد بعض الطلاب بهذا الاسم من الطلاب الابتدائيين تكليف للحكومة بزيادة مدرسين لا حاجة اليهم وفي الروضات عدد من الطلاب يبلغ الحد ويقرر التدريس فيها عدد من الاساتذة يحدون بالحجرات فاذا ألغيت هذه الروضات المدارس الابتدائية استغنت المعارف عن عدد كبير من المدرسين وفي ذلك الاقتصاد ما لا يخفى وفيه أيضا وضع للطلاب في صفوفهم اللائقة بهم وقد اشرنا الى ذلك سابقا واما القرى التي ليس فيها مدرسة ابتدائية وسميت مدرستها بالروضة فان هذا الاسم يلغى وتسمى تلك المدرسة الابتدائية وبالله التوفيق .

هذا ما أردت بيانه في هذا التقرير ارفعه لسموكم فان حاز منكم القبول فالأمل ارساله الى جهة الاختبار لاعتماده والعمل بشروطه والسلام .

The fatwa on educating girls by Shaykh Muhammad bin Mani‘
(above) and article 12, translated into English by Jehan Manei

it society that was refusing to allow females out of the private sphere into the public one, as studies reveal? What was the significance of issuing this decree, and the insistence on having it in writing? What is the implication of the manner in which it was issued? We do not have definitive or clear answers to these questions, except perhaps some explanations offered by the official power, that some members of society used to view education as corrupting for women (ibid.).

From what appears above, we note that families had a growing interest in educating girls in a *kuttab* at the hands of a male *mutawwi'*, as in the case of Amina al-Jayyida and many others. Indeed, it was often her mother who encouraged this, due to the absence of her father on long pearl diving trips:[12] 'My mother, God bless her soul, encouraged me a lot to learn the Holy Quran'. This was not strange, for the mother pushed her daughter to become like the other girls in the neighborhood' (al-Amadi 27). Her remark that the girls who completed the memorization of the Qur'an would instruct other girls in the neighborhood indicates that education was common among girls. Indeed, the issue of education was not alien to the members of society, and some wealthy families used to hire a *mutawwi'* to instruct the family's children of both sexes (ibid. 25). Moreover, in Kuwait, it was said that a *kuttab* existed in every quarter (*firij*). When Mahmud al-Jayyida opposed his daughter going out to work as a teacher when she was fourteen, it was not an objection to the educational process itself but rather a refusal of the idea 'of her leaving home to instruct women in their houses'. This is confirmed by his subsequent approval when the students came to her for instructions in her father's house (ibid. 32). Thus, it was not society that required a *fatwa* to settle the issue of women's right to education especially as education was not mandatory at the time. The most plausible explanation of the need for a *fatwa* would be that men wanted to be supported against some reactionary religious figures, who were opposed to women's education, as was mentioned in the opening anecdote.

Conclusion

There are many similarities between the developmental phases of education in the Gulf emirates throughout the three stages, and these are shared with many other Arab and Islamic regions. Although these phases were not concurrent in the Gulf area, the commonalities were many, while each emirate had its specific features. Despite the fact that the civil education

[12]Her father, Mahmud Yusuf al-Jayyida, a Qatari, God bless his soul, was known to have a very forceful personality, and was famous in Qatar for his diving trips and pearl trading. He was known to have a very prominent position in society (al-Amadi 26–7).

phase coincided with the period pre-dating the founding of the modern state, which decreed modern education in line with certain determinants, this stage in most Gulf countries materialized because of the enthusiasm and financial support of wealthy traders and important artisans—which is exactly what happened in Egypt earlier, in the nineteenth century. However, the Qatari model was an initiative of the ruling power, whether in 1913 when Shaykh Muhammad bin Manea was summoned, or in the second instance, when Shaykh al-Mahmud was brought in from Sharjah.

As we have seen in the second part of this article, it is not firmly established that girls' education was co-terminous with the *katatib* run by women teachers. What is evident is that the education of girls in the *katatib* pre-dated the emergence of *mutawwi'at*. In fact, during the first phase, when society had the power and freedom to choose, the fact that educating girls was already practiced became the persuasive and motivating force. Furthermore, it was the women themselves who played an active role, as we see in the example of Amina Mahmud al-Jayyida. With the beginning of state control and centralization and the building of state educational institutions, it began by constructing schools for boys alone. After the fatwa was issued, the state decided to build a school for girls and this is how the idea of separate and not mixed education started.

The logic followed by historians of education in the Gulf regarding the education of girls and the society's approach to it was based on how they themselves were raised and the social conditions they had become accustomed to according to the structure built by the state in Gulf countries. They traced the historical development of state-building of the educational structure without contextualizing the states' actions and the historical conditions that surrounded state-building, including the establishment of Wahhabism in Saudi Arabia and the nature of state structuralism.

10. *Women of the Gulf during the First Half of the Twentieth Century: A Comparative Study of American Missionary Archives and Local Memory*

FATMA AL-SAYEGH

Introduction

The position of women in the East in general, and in the Gulf in particular, has captured the interest of Westerners since the beginning of modern history when Western Europe recognized the economic, strategic and literary importance of the East. The East attracted the attention of Westerners with its wealth and commerce, and so they came to trade with it, travel in it and write about it. The Arabian Peninsula, in particular, was a source of inspiration for Orientalists and foreign travelers, and constituted a fertile source for literary artists. Its vast desert, the spirit of adventure that surrounds it, and its traditions have been a kind of magical inspiration for Europeans who came to the East in search of a transient adventure or pleasant literary enchantment. It was women, however, who represented a particular source of interest to Orientalists, an interest for which the stereotypical image of women in the East is largely responsible.

Women were objects secluded behind a black veil. These silent, meek, obedient creatures had no voice and no impact on public decisions, despite their great influence over their family and homes. If the aim was to delve deep into Eastern society with the intention of understanding it, recognizing its importance, and consequently influencing it, it is no wonder that women represented an integral theme in Orientalist writings.

The nineteenth century was a time when the East and its people were the focus of interest for Europeans. This was the age of 'Romanticism' in Europe, the age in which Byron, Lamartine and Goethe boasted of the region in their most famous poems and texts. It was their themes that increased Europeans' infatuation with the East, which ultimately reached its peak toward the end of the nineteenth century, and mobilized Europeans, both men and women, to come to the East and write in general about it and its people and what was happening there.[1]

In addition to trade, literary pleasure and the spirit of adventure, there was something else that prompted Westerners to come to the Arabian Peninsula and journey through it. This was the religious factor. Religious enthusiasm inflamed Christian societies and organizations, especially in the United States, and they began mobilizing volunteers and gathering donations to send missionaries regularly to the Arabian Peninsula, a place that had for centuries been thought of by Westerners as 'neglected Arabia'. Within the space of a few years, with the efforts of a limited number of individuals, an organization called 'The Wheel' was founded in 1889 in New Brunswick, New Jersey, whose aim was to evangelize the Arabian Peninsula. This later came to be known as the Arabian Mission (or as the American Mission). It had a strong impact on the attitude of the US toward the Peninsula, as well as in establishing US-Arabian relations in a way that remains evident in US policies until today.[2]

From its inception, the Arabian Mission set certain goals for itself, the most important of which was to infiltrate the Peninsula and preach among its people. To achieve this goal, it recruited a large group of missionaries, both men and women, qualified to do religious and humanitarian work such as medical treatment, teaching and social care. This team left behind a great wealth of personal memoirs, as well as daily and periodical reports that describe in intricate detail the life they led there, in addition to the salient traditions and social systems of the Gulf family unit. Furthermore, they left us the Mission journal, *Neglected Arabia*, previously known as *Arabia Calling*, a periodical journal published by the Arabian Mission, rich with

[1] Some of the women who were attracted by the magic and adventure of the East were Lady Hester Stanhope, Anne Blunt, Freya Stark, and Lucie Duff Gordon. For more information, see Stark.
[2] The mission began its work in the Protestant Dutch Reformed Church, and the mission that was established to work in the Arabian Peninsula was the Arabian Mission, which began work in the region in 1889 and was closed down in 1974.

details of their work and experiences, recounted to us through the reports of the male and female preachers in the Gulf. Similarly, the missionary reports that were sent from the mission to the headquarters, and which are now archived in New Brunswick and Connecticut, were replete with an enormous amount of information that provides us with an overview of social conditions in the Peninsula.[3]

Since missionary work largely depends on meeting people and communicating with them, the missionaries, despite their poor Arabic, managed to collect accurate details about the social reality they witnessed and lived in. Despite the objections of some historians to these reports as being unreliable and pious, since they were written for a specific purpose and to serve particular religious goals, they are nevertheless reports that reflect, to a great extent, the social reality of the time. Unlike the British reports, which were concerned with the political situation, the American reports focused on society and the social, financial and moral changes that were taking place within it. What makes these records so special is the fact that they represent the only written documentation of the social life of Gulf societies through which we can realistically visualize, to a great extent, the position of women at the time. As such, these records are important as the medium that documents an important part of the social history of the Gulf from 1892 (when the missionaries arrived there) up to the middle of the twentieth century.[4]

Conditions in the society that the missionaries dealt with were hard and rough. Poverty and ignorance were dominant, and medical services, as we know them, were non-existent; so people were deeply persuaded that cures from disease were to be found in traditional Arab medicine, which was based on communal prescriptions, and traditional and popular remedies. A group of women were responsible for medical care, and their treatments depended on cauterization, bloodletting (*hijama*) and herbal cures ('Abd al-Rahim 86). Treatment of mental illness depended largely on reading the Qur'an and some incantations or *zar* gatherings (for exorcism), because it was commonly believed that patients were possessed by evil spirits, demons or jinn.

---

[3]The Arabian Mission's records are deposited in New Brunswick Seminary, New Jersey and Hartford Seminary, Connecticut.

[4]The American mission in the Gulf closed down completely in 1974, ending with this a chapter in American/Gulf relations, which was followed by a new chapter based on economic and strategic interests.

The most common diseases at the time were malaria, smallpox, measles and eye diseases such as trachoma. Epidemics of illnesses such as cholera and the plague spread from time to time and wiped out large numbers of the population. As Lorimer observes in *Gazetteer of the Gulf*, cholera killed more than 1,200 people in Bahrain in May 1904; when the epidemic spread to the United Arab Emirates in July of that year, the number of victims reached 8,000, with deaths in the regions of the interior reaching around 14,000 before the disease reached the Sultanate of Oman (Lorimer 3667).

This was the situation in the society that the missionaries dealt with and which was the focus of their activities for almost a century: a primitive, simple society, based on firm beliefs and traditions inherited from the desert; a society that had no say over its destiny, unlike technologically and culturally developed societies. The people were poor and primitive and had nothing but their religious beliefs, compared with people who had everything, plus religious enthusiasm and a desire to radically change society. How these two societies interacted and how each dealt with women is the matter to be discussed.

This article aims to portray the social reality and the position of women in Gulf societies during the first half of the twentieth century through a comparative analysis of the American documents, records and reports, and the local documentation that is available. It also endeavors to throw some light on the development of the situation of women as a result of the cultural interaction that took place between female missionaries and Gulf women, and to highlight the effect of this on the future development of women in Gulf societies. The study's importance lies in its attempt to record the socio-economic changes that Gulf women underwent during the past century through a comparative study of the foreign perspective on the both familiar and unfamiliar reality, and popular memory conserved in local documents, *waqf* (charitable endowment) records, oral testimonies and photographs.[5] In addition, this research also answers a number of questions related to the status of women in society and their socio-economic position, and examines the effect of humanitarian missionary work on women in particular and Gulf societies in general. This article

---

[5]American documents contain many photographs of women in the Gulf, as do local archives such as those of Shaykh Dr Sultan al-Qassimi in Sharjah, some of which were obtained for the purposes of this article.

applies a descriptive analytical methodology, based on a comparative analysis of American missionary archives and local memory, with the purpose of arriving at an approximate representation of the social conditions and the position of women in that time frame.

This article is divided into five chronological stages. The first presents a historical background to the subject matter, explaining the establishment of missionary endeavors in the Gulf, which were channeled through Basra (in Iraq), which was the gateway to the Arabian Gulf region. The second stage covers missionary infiltration into Gulf societies in the early part of the twentieth century. In the third stage, the research examines evangelization efforts that targeted Gulf women, while the fourth stage considers women in the Gulf during World War I, in addition to the political changes experienced by Gulf societies, which eventually influenced the position of women. In the fifth and final stage, Christian influence in the inter-war period, and its cultural effect on women, are examined. This article concludes by analyzing missionary work and its many impacts on Gulf women.

First phase: Establishing missionary and evangelization endeavors: Basra the gateway to the Gulf

From its inception, the American Mission identified a goal and set out to achieve it: this was to infiltrate the Arabian Peninsula and evangelize it, on the basis that it was once an important part of the Christian world (see al-Tamimi).[6] At that time, we must note that the Levant, Egypt and Palestine were the only parts of the Arabian East known to Westerners — the 'East' they portrayed in their paintings, poems and other literature, and that they visited in their travels. Their knowledge of the Gulf region and the Arabian Peninsula was almost non-existent due to the absence of cultural interaction between the two areas.

From the end of the nineteenth century, however, Westerners began to be exposed to the Arabian Peninsula — an enchanting area of vast deserts, great mystery and sanctity, which was related to its holy cities of Mecca and Medina, which non-Muslims are prohibited from entering. All this added a certain aura to the place, and soon the activities of their new

[6]This book is considered one of the first important books to discuss the issue of missionary work in the Gulf and its influence on its societies.

Mission were primarily focused on the area. This added sanctity and magic
to their work and prompted benefactors to give money willingly. Why
not?—since the prime goal of the Arabian Mission was to reach the revered
Mecca, the seat of Islam and the focal point for Muslims worldwide, and
evangelize the Muslims there.

After several years of structured meetings and campaigns to collect both
financial assistance, books and in-kind donations in American churches, the
Mission began its first exploratory and practical trip to Basra in Iraq in 1889.
Basra was the foremost and closest place to the cities of the Gulf, and it was
from here that the missionaries studied the area and carried out several tours
of it. In addition, the British presence in Basra facilitated the work of
American missionaries in the Gulf, which they could not have carried out
without British protection, which was extended as a result of the political
treaties between the British and local rulers.[7]

During its early years, the Arabian Mission managed to establish major
stations in Basra, Bahrain, Kuwait and Muscat. The missionaries succeeded
in making regular trips inland, carrying a medicine bag in one hand, and
copies of the Bible in the other. Thus began the evangelization of the Gulf.
In 1891, the Reverend Samuel Zwemer, one of the founding fathers of the
Arabian Mission, made the first missionary trip to Jeddah in the Hijaz. The
following year, he travelled to the coastal areas of the Gulf, where he
visited al-Hasa and neighboring places. With the increasing number of
trips, stories began to be told, reports were sent, all to be published in the
above-mentioned Arabian Mission journal, *Neglected Arabia*, covering
the period from 1889 to 1973.[8] These reports were of various kinds: some
were descriptions of cities and villages, others relayed incidents that
happened to the missionaries themselves, and some simply presented their
hopes of reaching future goals not yet achieved. Women were a major
focus in these reports. Indeed, women missionaries worked for the Mission
and their aim was to work among Arab women and evangelize them.
Therefore reports abounded in accurate details of social life in the Gulf
and recorded what went on within the households there, and so they constitute a rich resource for the historian who seeks to examine the details of

[7]Basra was an important port and a calling place for British commercial ships on the
Europe-India route, hence its historic significance.
[8]The Arabian Peninsula was called 'neglected Arabia' because the missionaries claimed it
was neglected by Christianizing organizations (see 'Arabian Mission Field Reports' 68).

social life in the Gulf from the end of the nineteenth to the mid-twentieth century.

The Mission's activities were combined, and included Christian preaching and teaching, as well as medical, social and humanitarian work, all ultimately aimed at attaining one goal: evangelization and increasing the number of Christian converts under the influence of the Mission. However, the most important aspect of these reports is their precise description of daily life in Arab households in the villages and cities of the Gulf in the nineteenth and early twentieth centuries: what went on within these households, their secrets, relationships within the Gulf family, and the common traditions and customs. Unlike male travelers, the missionaries, especially the women, succeeded in entering these houses and describing them with great accuracy, because they were given access in a way that was generally forbidden to foreign men.

At the onset of the evangelizing activities of the American Mission in the Gulf and the Arabian Peninsula that began in 1890 from the city of Basra, which was still under Ottoman rule, the Mission encountered serious and diverse obstacles, especially when a confrontation took place between the Turkish government and the Mission. The animosity is quite evident in a report written by James Moerdyk, one of the most important of the Mission's missionaries, in December 1890, in which he describes the state of the Mission in Basra and the difficulties it was facing with the Turkish government:

At the beginning of our work in Basra, we were afraid that our endeavors would come up against real obstacles or be totally prohibited especially with the animosity that we have faced from the Turkish government . . . Although it is well known that the Turkish government was never friendly towards Protestant missions, missionary work depended, to a large extent, on the position of this government in this country or that city. The new Turkish governor was antagonistic to our missionary work . . . the increase in the sales of the Bible and other Christian booklets in our office in Basra attracted attention to the work and activity of the Mission and thus the Turkish book censor visited our office and announced that he had orders to look for destructive, anti-Islam and anti- Turkey books that are being sold. (Moerdyk Report)

He then goes on to state: 'In another unpleasant incident, a group of officers and soldiers came to search the Mission headquarters under the same pretext. However, this time we took our complaint to the British Consul in Basra' (al-Bassam 64).[9] This indicates Britain's protection of American missionary activities. The Turkish opposition to missionary activity continued to the extent that a member of the Mission observed: 'Despite the fact that former public preaching in the streets of Basra will currently be unwise and might threaten the future of our work, there are other opportunities for preaching through talking to some people in their homes or ours, and that is exactly what we are trying to do' (ibid. 65).

About the work of women missionaries in Basra, the missionary Elizabeth Cantine remarks:

> Although missionary work began early on, working among women was delayed for several reasons. Despite this delay, medical work was the oldest organized labor for the women of the Mission in Basra, for it began in 1901 and by time, became the largest medical care endeavor for women in the areas where the American Mission operated. If it were not for the female missionaries, Iraqi women would not have visited missionary medical units and female related medical efforts would not have achieved such obvious results; for medical care was not exclusive to Muslim women but also included Christian, Jewish and Armenian women who lived in Basra. The Lansing Memorial hospital, run by the Mission, was the only place in Basra where women, of all ethnic groups, religions and social classes met. Here, in the hospital, the colors, features and clothes of the women who come on a daily basis are blended. There are Christian, Protestant, and Catholic women together, Jewesses with their masks, and Christians with their ever changing attire, but they all share the black, long *Abbaya* (overcoat) that is worn over their clothes. Thus, you find among the ailing women a varied mix that is quite curious. The influence of Medical care does not stop there of course, but rather extends beyond Basra. Many of the women come from Al Nasserieh and Al Amarah and other cities on the banks of the Tigris. Indeed, some of them even came from Mahmara in Persia. In addition to curing women, the doctors and missionaries investigate all possible

---

[9]Al-Bassam collected different missionary archives between 1892 and 1925 and translated them into Arabic.

ways to lead them to Christ. However, missionary work is not as
enduring as medical care despite the fact that both emerge from one
place: the hospital. From my experience, I found out that there is nothing
better than spending some time in the morning with the women who
come for treatment in the hospital. (Ibid. 66)

These mission visits brought new results, and led to invitations to visit
new homes. Moreover, preaching Christianity in the hospital wards was,
to the missionaries, one of the most joyous tasks because it yielded good
results, and was often better than other traditional missionary methods.
According to the missionaries, visiting middle-class homes was far better
than visiting low-income or high-income families, since members of the
middle class were more intelligent than other classes and

> they are ready to listen to Biblical sermons whereas the rich do not care
> about the sermons despite the fact that they are more educated and have
> a higher social status. In addition, many of the middle class women
> work in the palm gardens that are scattered around Basra, and they
> spend time reading and chatting with the women when they visit them
> in the gardens. (Ibid. 90–2)

In addition to medical activities, there was another women-related activity
that the Mission in Basra undertook, and that was teaching in the girls'
school. As the report states, after much hope and waiting, a missionary
school was established in Basra towards the end of 1912. This school
carried out many important tasks besides daily instruction in both Arabic
and English. The girls learned sewing, embroidery and weaving. The
missionary Elizabeth Cantine says:

> A while back, some Turkish women expressed their desire to have their
> girls, already enrolled in the school, learn sewing and American fashion
> design. The truth is that when we see Turkish women in western attire
> with jarring and impossible colors, we feel that it is best to help them or
> teach their girls the way to dress, how to sew, and the art of modern
> embroidery as well as proper taste. Despite the fact that work in the
> hospital, school and nursery, which has just been opened, has achieved
> good results, our work with the women cannot develop or advance

without hiring local workers to address the shortage we suffer from in
that area. At the moment, we only have two workers and a single
missionary who does not work full time. (Ibid. 93)

With regard to educating girls in Basra, Dorothy Van Ess, herself a missionary
and the wife of missionary John Van Ess, comments on the status of education
in Basra. She describes the condition of the only available school for girls,
founded by the Ottoman authorities, to which a teacher was brought from
Istanbul, and how it came to compete with the American school. There was
also the Jewish school and the Catholic school, and there were thousands of
girls who enrolled in them. Mrs Van Ess, during one of her visits to the Turkish
school for girls in Basra, describes it thus:

> During our visit to one of the Turkish schools for girls we found a plain
> looking woman who was the Arabic teacher standing in front of twelve
> girls . . . teaching them in a traditional way . . . this is what the govern-
> ment of the Ottoman Empire (*Al Bab Al Aaly*) could do to teach women
> in one of the richest counties under its jurisdiction. When we asked
> about the syllabi, they told us that beside teaching the Quran, the girls
> study *Sunnah* (the teachings of Prophet Mohamed PBUH), mathematics
> and the like, and some subjects are taught in Turkish (which is Greek to
> the girls). In addition to these subjects the girls learn some simple crafts.
> These schools lack discipline and it seems that they are not yielding
> results.

She then continues to compare this school with the Mission school, which
was called the Hope School for Girls:

> Here, girls instead of reciting Quran verses, study the life of Christ, and
> instead of Sunnah, they learn about the anatomy of the human body and
> how to care for it. Girls study geography and how to become good
> mothers and housewives. We teach them how to use their minds and
> hands. In our school, there are around forty girls who all have the will-
> ingness and ability to learn and study. Some tell us that Islam suits the
> nature of Muslims and that Christian civilization is not compatible with
> Easterners, and that it is better for them to keep away from it. To these
> I say, come and take a look at the Turkish school in Basra and see how

the wives and mothers of the future are being prepared, come and compare this school to the School for Hope and you will see the difference. (Ibid. 9)

It was not only through education that bridges between women in Basra and women of the American Mission could be built. Medical treatment and social care represented another important means of communication between the Arabian Mission and Arab women, especially those of the middle and upper classes. In their reports, women missionaries describe the status of women and their ethnic origins and the various social classes. There were Jewesses, Persians, Arabs and Turks, who came from the middle class, upper class and other classes too. The missionaries also tell us how the simplest diseases took the women's lives and frightened and worried them because of the high death rate. Similarly, they tell us about the fear of mothers for their children because of the high mortality rate among infants under five. The simplest diseases such as measles, malaria and fever horrified mothers, and the shortage of inoculations and vaccines against disease was the cause of the prevalence of these illnesses and the high infant mortality rates. Basra became a center that attracted patients and women from nearby areas such as al-Zubayr, who came for treatment in the Mission hospital. As for the salient traditions, one of the missionaries says that upper-class women had more self-confidence than middle- or lower-class women, and that their obedience to their husbands was not blind compliance, as was the case among the other two classes, in contrast to Gulf societies, where the opposite is the norm. The slogan of the Arabian Mission was 'no listening to prayers, no medical services', so it was not surprising to find that missionary services were welcome among the people, especially in areas with a prevalence of illiteracy, poverty and disease—the three factors that facilitated the work of male and female missionaries equally.

Second phase: Missionary infiltration and the Mission's methods in the cities and villages of the Gulf

The nature of societies in the Gulf and the Peninsula was traditional and conservative, as was the case with all societies under the rule of the Ottoman Empire. This rendered isolation and poverty a pretext for the proliferation of ignorance, disease and harmful, archaic social habits. The status of women in these societies was degrading, and they were mostly treated badly and deprived of their simplest rights—rights that were granted them by Islam—and it was not intransigence, but rather ignorance that was the cause.

Furthermore, the inherited social and tribal traditions contributed to the demeaning of women. Child marriages were quite common: not marriages between children but rather marrying off a girl of seven, eight or nine to a much older man. For missionaries, this was the worst kind of exploitation and child abuse. In addition, diseases spread among women in general, they being the weaker sex as a result of pregnancy, childbirth and breastfeeding, which often threatened their lives. Some of the common practices among women in the Gulf area also caused harm to their health and endangered their lives, such as the use of rock salt as a natural contraceptive afterchild birth. The use of rock salt caused damage to their organs — this story was taken from the mouth of the late Marian Kennedy, herself a missionary doctor in the United Arab Emirates — and could often lead to death, chronic diseases or difficulty in subsequent pregnancies owing to the blockage of the cervix. Such practices ultimately led to an increase in female mortality and infertility. The incidence of disease is what led to the demand for missionary services, and missionaries used this weakness to infiltrate the local population under the pretext that the core of their work was to relieve people's suffering. Why not, indeed, when Christ himself was sent as a missionary and a healer?

When the people of the Mission began their work in the cities and villages of the Gulf and the Arabian Peninsula, they recognized two important factors: first, the importance of preaching among women because of their awareness of Arab women's role in raising the young, and their influence on their families and children, and second, the need to use female missionaries in order to have access to women. It was impossible for male preachers to contact Gulf women because of the prevailing customs and traditions, the absence of any concept of mixing between the sexes, and the *hijab*, which secluded women and distanced them from the male domain in a society where the two sexes inhabited largely different worlds. Thus, the idea of 'using women to reach women' was both logical and sensible.

Using female preachers began from the first moment the missionaries set foot in the Peninsula. Quite quickly, the American Mission recruited a group of women qualified to start evangelizing the women of the Arabian Peninsula. The Mission also initiated training programs in quick medical treatment for female missionaries and began to teach them Arabic to prepare them to enter the world of Arab women. At the time, Arab homes were out of bounds to foreigners, whether men or women, so the Mission began to pave the way into these homes by sending qualified women missionaries to teach Arab women sewing, reading, writing, and handicrafts, or to train them to work outside the home, in the American hospital as doctors' assistants, nurses or dispensary workers in order to create a kind of ongoing relationship between Arab women and female missionaries. The more the relationship grew, the closer the Mission came to its goal of spreading the principles of Christianity among women in the Arabian Peninsula. Female missionaries employed three methods to reach Arab women's hearts: education, medical care, and social work based on teaching handicrafts such as sewing and embroidery.

Education

Education was a cornerstone in the missionary operation; for without learning how to read and write, Arab women would not be able to read the Bible or understand its message, the Christian preachers claimed. The first girls' school was founded in the early twentieth century in Bahrain by the missionary Mrs Elizabeth Zwemer. The beginnings of the girls' school in Bahrain were humble: a handful of students, a few classes and hardly any full-time teachers. Nevertheless, the school continued to offer classes and, against all the odds, as Minnie Dykstra remarked in 1909:

> The first noticeable thing in the girls' school in Manama is the fact that not all the pupils are Arabs. Many of them were Persian women who enjoyed a relatively larger freedom than Arab women. Naturally, this presents many obstacles for the school since the teachers had to know Persian as well as Arabic so as to be able to communicate with the students. However, until now it is quite impossible since they hardly have enough time and are still studying Arabic, let alone the difficulty of finding a Persian language teacher. (Al-Bassam 96)

Describing the state of education in Bahrain in particular, and in the Gulf in general, Minnie Dykstra explains:

There is no such thing as compulsory education in Bahrain or in any part
of the Arabian Peninsula for that matter, and there is no law that prohibits
child labor either. Parents here are uneducated so why then would their
children get an education, especially their girls? (Ibid.)

Dykstra goes on to describe the educational conditions in the girls' Mission
school:

The school has many problems of course. To encourage the girls to come
to school regularly, gifts and prizes were handed out to them every Friday
especially to those who attended all days except Saturday and Sunday. Yet,
and in spite of all this, it seems that school attendance is quite a difficult
thing since most students have neither calendars nor watches or clocks in
their homes and thus all days are alike to them. To address this problem, the
school teachers explain about the days of the week and every Friday restate
that there will be no school tomorrow or the day after. It was difficult for
the students to understand the Christian weekend, Saturday and Sunday.

And thus, as Minnie Dykstra continued to remark:

many of the girls [are] standing in front of the school gate on Saturday
and Sunday mornings. Girls in Bahrain have special features and habits,
like American students, some are studious and others are lazy; some
good, others bad, and some with grim faces and others with smiley
faces. Furthermore, there are beautiful girls who have adoption and
poverty problems which force them to work after school and perform
household chores. (Al-Bassam, p. 96)

Another missionary continues to explain the position of children, saying:

One of them is called Fatima; she is eight years old and rarely comes to
school the reason being that she is very busy. In the morning, she sews
and brings timber to the house then goes off to the market to buy what the
family needs such as fish, vegetables and butter. When she finishes all
this, she brings some things to the school gate to sell to the students with
no care for the heat of summer or the cold of winter days. In addition,
Fatima makes dolls and toys and sells them in her small peddle cart.

Oftentimes, Fatima finds no buyers and so she plays with the children around her and gets to experience her childhood briefly. (Al-Bassam 99)

Dykstra goes on to talk about the children, saying: 'I remember a lot of stories about the girls who attended school as I watch daily episodes of girls I know well; my students used to carry pots and plates on their heads as they walked to and from the market every day.' At the end of her report, she continues to describe the husband/wife relationship, saying: 'Many of them (the students) married and became mothers with great responsibilities, and I often heard them telling one another "I must rush home otherwise my husband will beat me up"' (al-Bassam 99).

The relationships developed by the Mission were not restricted to marginalized and poor women, but extended to include ongoing relationships with women of the middle and upper classes too. Dykstra states that in 1910, a young woman married to a wealthy man in Manama wanted to learn English, but since the harem life that this woman led prevented her from practicing English, it seemed that learning the language was pointless as she would not be able to speak it with anyone. However, it seems that the desire to read was what prompted this young woman to learn English, and despite all the difficulties, the American Mission did not want to lose this opportunity; it would allow the Mission to read the Bible to this woman and to be in close contact with her family, and preach Christianity to them. This was important because such women had great influence over the family and the slaves, who were very close to the lady of the house. The desire to teach this woman increased, especially as it would allow daily contact with her, and provide a chance for them to record the details of daily life as they proceeded with their preaching. Dykstra was fortunate enough to stay all day and record all that went on in the Bahraini household among the women as they gathered and prepared what they needed for sewing and embroidery, activities that were necessary to pass the time for them when visiting one another. As Dykstra remarks, local women were interested in the Western women's embroidery and wool needlework and their lifestyle more than anything else. Local women often asked missionaries about the pattern of their daily life, conditions in their country, and the habits and traditions of the country they came from. The hymns and Bible readings used to cheer the women's hearts and they were pleased to hear them, without recognizing that these were religious hymns (Arabian Mission Field Report no. 75). This interest pleased the women missionaries because they felt that they had come close to achieving the aims delineated by the Mission: meeting daily with Arab women and preaching Christianity among them. The missionaries also seized this opportunity to record the details of all that they witnessed, such as habits, traditions, customs and daily rituals, and they sent in weekly or monthly reports that described the details of social life in Gulf societies during that period.

Gulf societies have been governed by habits, traditions and rituals, some of which persist until today. One of the observations documented by the women missionaries was the close relationship between father and children, often closer than that between husband and wife. The father often displayed a lot of affection and intimacy with his children, whereas he did not show the same affection to his wife, which seemed rather strange to the Western mind. This might be a result of the common idea in that society that what binds the husband to the wife is temporary (a marriage contract) while what binds him to his children is eternal. This way of thinking was also reflected in women's position in society, for a woman's presence in her husband's life was not always stable, but rather was determined by several factors, the most important of which were her ability to bear children, her acceptance by the husband's family, and his economic ability to take another wife.

The widespread social traditions in the Gulf prohibited a woman from leaving the house without a reason or without the permission of her husband. Therefore, these 'furtive visits caused much embarrassment' as one of the missionaries remarks: 'These poor women are not responsible for the scheming or conniving and deception that they disclose, for they need all the love and affection that we can give, and we must guide them to the right path, and teach them their mistakes' (*Neglected Arabia*).

One of the common stereotypical images about Gulf societies is the insistence of some that a woman should not receive an education because if she does, 'she will mix with men and thus become defiled' (al-Hamadi 169). The women missionaries thus took on a colossal task by starting to educate women because their ignorance was a scourge, and once a woman was educated, she was set on the right path. Consequently, missionaries made sure to enter homes and teach women reading and writing, and Christian organizations provided them with Biblical textbooks in Arabic.

Missionaries' duties were thus twofold: teaching and preaching. The women missionaries were housewives, mothers and wives of male missionaries, and so they gave examples from their own lives, presenting them as ideal: Christian homes are good homes that Arab women should regard as models.

Missionaries began their work in Basra in Iraq in 1892. The city had witnessed missionary visits around 1889, and from there the missionaries began to study the region and conduct expeditions in 'neglected Arabia'. In 1892, they managed to establish a subsidiary branch in Bahrain from which they could continue their regular visits to al-Ahsa, al-Qatif and Qatar. They also succeeded in establishing a station in Oman from where they managed to conduct regular visits to al-Buraimi and the Emirates, where the aim was to teach people reading and writing so that they could read the Biblical textbooks that were distributed to them. Education had a profound effect on the Arabian Peninsula and the number of students was to be counted in the hundreds. And although education was a means of preaching, in Bahrain it gained great importance as one of the factors of social change. There were two types of education in Bahrain: the Western type provided by the Mission and the Arab religious type known as the *kuttab* (plural: *katatib*) (Kritzeck and Bayly 310–11). Indeed, Bahrain is considered a pioneer in the education of girls. The first girls' school there, also the first school for girls in the Arabian Gulf, was established in 1895 by the American Mission, before the inauguration of the first government school in 1928. This step was widely opposed by parents since education for girls was considered to be against the customs and traditions that decreed that a girl, once she reached the age of six or seven, was to stay at home and wear the *hijab*. In addition, it was believed that teaching a girl how to write would tempt her to write love letters. In 1906, the Mission established two more schools in Bahrain, one for boys and another for girls, which had around twenty students. The girls' school was run by a missionary, Elizabeth Zwemer (wife of Samuel Zwemer, one of the founders of the Arabian Mission), although another teacher, Mrs L. Dame, was later appointed as her permanent assistant. Mrs Dame's appointment was a step toward confirming the presence of the school as a permanent educational establishment. In 1926, the school had curricula that included Arabic, English reading and writing, mathematics, and geography as well as Bible instruction. Moreover, in order not to lose the interest of the students, other subjects such as physical education, handicrafts such as sewing and embroidery, and scientific contests were added to the curricula. These programs captured the interest not only of the students but also of their families, and caused a substantial shift in Bahraini society by giving women a significant role in the program.

These missionary schools were opposed locally by Qur'an teachers who attacked them as competitors and opposed the idea of girls attending them. Some girls overcame this obstacle by going to the Qur'an schools (*katatib*) in the morning, and the missionary schools in the evening. It is worth noting here that the *katatib* played an important role in hampering evangelization for, while missionary education was alien to the society and its customs, *katatib* education was closely connected to the actuality of Gulf societies and their way of life ('Abd al-Rahim 106).

In addition to the American women missionaries, who taught girls reading and writing, a Bahraini woman teacher, who was trained to take on this mission, appeared at the Bahrain school in the mid-1920s. Her appearance was one of the factors that encouraged other Bahraini girls to venture into the area of teaching, education and work. In 1929, a girls' club was established in Bahrain to teach girls sports and the program also included various other kinds of entertainment aimed at attracting the girls to the club and, consequently, to the missionary establishments. Missionaries had a great influence on cultural development in Bahrain and so the government, in reaction to missionary organizations, founded a government girls' school and brought in a Syrian woman teacher to start formal education in Bahrain. Also, some of the missionary schools' outstanding students were chosen to work as teachers in the government school. This was a great stimulus for the work of missionaries, who saw this choice as a major step forward for their work and considered themselves pioneers in women's education.

In Muscat, the missionary Peter Zwemer, the brother of Samuel Zwemer, succeeded in establishing a school for freed slaves in 1896. Contrary to Samuel Zwemer's claims, this school was not a pre-planned project of the American Mission, for it began accidentally when Peter Zwemer managed to liberate around eighteen Omani boys and enroll them all as pupils in this school, where he taught them the Bible and gave them Western names such as Adrian and Henry.

The story of this school started in 1896, when a British battleship entered Muscat harbor. On board, beside the soldiers and seamen, there were eighteen black children, aged seven to eleven, who were said to have been rescued from a slave ship whose owner had intended to sell them in one of the Gulf ports. As soon as they arrived in Muscat, the British Consul brought them to the Mission and asked the missionaries to educate and look after them. Immediately, Peter Zwemer took them in and found that they were good material for evangelization. According to the Mission's report, the agreement between the Consul and the mission stated that the latter would be responsible for feeding, clothing and educating these children until they reached the age of sixteen, when they could depend on themselves and choose the life they wanted. Eventually, a few years later, those boys completed their education and became 'civilized' men 'all because of their sincerity, dedication and enthusiasm, as well as our constant prayers' (al-Bassam 25). The Mission remained in close contact with the boys, even after they came of age, and as one of the reports states: 'With regard to Nathan and Isaac, I know nothing about them in Bombay. However, I have recently heard rumors that they converted back to Islam, but I am positive that this is not true' (ibid. 26).

Education had a prominent role in the Arabian Mission's plans in Muscat. The school for freed slaves continued to work and recruit children from the date of its establishment, despite all the serious difficulties it came up against and which threatened its continuation. For example, the missionary James Cantine wrote in 1906 that the school was facing a problem: the demise of teachers. In spite of the fact that classes were regular and that the school was performing well, difficult weather conditions affected teachers' performance and caused a series of deaths. There was also another problem: the division of classes. Because of the diverse traditions, cultures and languages of the inhabitants of Muscat, and the presence of a mixture of different races and ethnic groups, such as Indians, Persians, Arabs and Balouchis, problems arose from the differences of language. Accordingly, the school opted for teaching Arabic, English, mathematics and geography, with the first and last lessons being Bible reading and Christian prayers, and the reports state: 'So far we have not heard about any objection from parents.' Here it should be noted that the school that started as a school for freed slaves soon became a school for all children (al-Bassam, 1993, 124). It is obvious, however, that parents were well aware of what their children were being taught at school, which would explain the marked fall in the number of students, as one of the reports observes: 'In fact, we cannot boast of having a large number of students. Last month they were only twelve, but we are hoping that when we move to the new school building in the Mission headquarters, which will render the school more attractive, the number of students will increase' (ibid. 25). The pupils who attended the school were the children of workers in the Mission and the children of Indians who worked in British establishments. In general, according to one report, most of the students were poor, so their attendance should be considered to represent a great sacrifice on the part of the parents, who preferred to educate their children rather than have them work with them or in the market, where some of them already worked, earning tiny amounts of money for doing strenuous jobs. On the other side of the building there was a section for girls. In Muscat the strong desire for modern education prompted the opening of a school to teach girls reading and writing as well as sewing and embroidery. Education was a way to engage in preaching, while teaching handicrafts gave mission- aries a chance to spend more time with the girls and to use this time to preach, instruct and pray, with the ultimate goal of opening up their ears and hearts to the Christian call.

Mission reports did not neglect the situation of children in Kuwait. In 1912, the American Mission inaugurated a small school in the city of Kuwait to teach English and some modern subjects using modern methods. There were around nine or ten Muslim students and three Jewish students in the school and they were taught Arabic and Turkish as well as mathe- matics and geography. However, when the parents heard that the students attended Sunday prayers, they realized the danger and the Muslims started collecting donations to build a new Muslim school for their children. Despite all these efforts to educate children, the young ones were convinced, as one missionary states, that 'we are infidels and do not pray' (ibid. 28). When a missionary was asked the reason for this interest in educating children despite the fact that they were very few in number, he answered: 'This is the only effective means for youth in Kuwait in the long run; besides, the small number gives an impression of power.' Thus, educa- tion was an effective tool used by missionaries to win over followers, but it was not successful with the people of the Gulf, for Islam was not only a religion but a way of life and a social system.

Health care and medicine

Medical treatment was considered one of the fields that would open doors that would otherwise remain closed to missionaries worldwide. Christ was sent as a missionary and a healer, and providing medical care was seen as the easiest way to reach Muslim hearts and make them listen to Christian prayers. Therefore, medical services were considered a fundamental pillar of missionary work in the world in general, and in the Gulf in particular. Missionaries focused on medical care and were keen to carry medicines with them even when they were lacking in medical expertise. According to the statistics published by the Arabian Mission in the Gulf, it appears that about 85,000 patients (Van Ess 22–23) were treated or offered medical services every year, a number that indicates the rate at which the mission saw itself as conveying Christ's message. If we take Muscat, for example, we find that the total number of people who received treatment at the hands of Dr Thoms and his wife was around 10,681 in 1901, of whom 1,631 were women who were treated by Mrs Thoms, despite the fact that she was not a qualified gynecologist.

Medical care began in Muscat in 1904 when Mrs Cantine, wife of the missionary James Cantine, opened the first women's clinic. She used their home as a clinic and a place for preaching, and women flocked there to receive treatment. When an official women's clinic was founded in 1913, with a qualified physician, it was considered a place for Christian preaching in the area, especially with the advent of Dr Sarah Hosman, one of the most enthusiastic Christian missionaries among women in the Gulf and the Arabian Peninsula. The missionaries encountered a number of diseases that they might otherwise be unfamiliar with. Elizabeth Zwemer wrote in 1913 about the American Mission's women's clinic in Bahrain, describing the spread of the plague:

Many poor men and women who challenged our presence came seeking our help and we were extremely happy to aid them . . . in the first few days three women under treatment passed away . . . we were often faced with this problem with the tough life of those women whose treatment became also very difficult especially those who live in small, suffo- cating, dirty and very hot huts devoid of ventilation. (Van Ess 22–3)

And as the missionary remarks in her report, 'the sojourn of those patients for a long time in the hospital is in fact a chance to read some Bible verses and talk about Christianity with the patients' (ibid. 23). As to the most common diseases, apart from the dangerous ones such as plague, eye diseases and smallpox,

> we are often faced with strange women's diseases that we have never encountered before. One day, a woman suffering from pains in the stomach came and, after examination, we found out that her back and stomach were full of wounds and purulence, and her body was totally disfigured, and she was given the necessary treatment and medication. (Influence of Christian Muslim Environment 84)

In addition to their concern for women, missionaries were also interested in children; for children were the nucleus of evangelization, and missionaries had great hope in them; they constituted an important asset for the mission in future terms.

Social work

Despite the great influence of the work of missionaries in Gulf societies in the early twentieth century, the position of women did not change dramatically, and that was because the missionaries could not change society's view of women which, according to the Mission reports, was characterized by injustice and social prejudice. In one report, a woman missionary states:

> During my stay in the Arab region, which was around sixteen years, I have not seen a single Arab house where the relationship between the man and woman was such that a Western woman could tolerate. The woman is always treated like a slave, she is beaten or divorced for the most trivial reasons and she has to tolerate all this without questioning anything and accept it as 'the will of Allah'. (*Neglected Arabia*, no.107)

It was therefore necessary for missionaries to provide examples of Christian homes as good homes where the relationship between husband and wife was one of equality, as they maintained.

While the work of Western missionaries may not have had much impact on women in the Gulf, the obvious and definite influence of missionary work on Gulf and Arabian Peninsula societies is expressed in the following report:

The influence of Western Christian influence on Gulf societies is evident in the cultural developments that appear from time to time, here and there, in Gulf cities and coastal areas. Basra has become a model modern city with its electric street lights, its distinctive government hospital and other aspects of Western culture, to which we have become accustomed. In Kuwait, roads have been widened; the city has been planned and is more secure. As for Bahrain, it has electricity, which has made people's lives more comfortable, especially with the use of electric fans which decrease the heat and humidity. Likewise, clean water has become available in houses in Bahrain so that people can use clean, running water. There has also been a call for the establishment of a government hospital. Even Musqat, that backward city, has not lagged behind in development; a road has been built between it and Matrah, where there is another mission. The government has also started building roads between Musqat and other neighboring towns and villages, so that we can now travel around 200 miles by car. Indeed, the accessibility of transportation has brought ease in missionary movement, especially to places they had not visited before, and the coming years will witness a revolution in our work in inland Oman. However, all this development does not mean that our work has become easier; for the more our satisfaction grows, the greater the difficulties become as we preach the Bible. (Influence of Christian Muslim Environment 24)

Third phase: The development of missionary work: women's work for women

This phase was characterized by the extensive use of women to gain access to women in the Gulf. The Mission's women succeeded in forming close relationships with women in the region, which played a great role in influencing the lives of both parties. Moreover, the relationships that Mission women formed were not exclusive to one class, but rather included women of all kinds and classes. The evangelization agenda was extensive, and was based on communicating with all sectors of society regardless of class. Missionaries therefore formed extended relationships with schoolgirls, their families and women from the middle and upper classes. They also succeeded in entering Arab homes and have conveyed to us an accurate description of women, their clothes and adornments, as well as the traditions that were familiar in these homes, so precisely that we have an overview of what went on there, as well as of the cultural reality of the times.

On the other hand, missionary women's lives were influenced by Arab life; they respected Arab customs and traditions and were never known to give any indication of lack of respect for them. On the contrary, they always expressed their admiration for these traditions and for Arab hospitality whenever they visited these homes.

The stereotypical Gulf house and the manner of receiving guests can be accurately envisioned through the report of missionary C. Stanley Mylrea who describes a visit to an upper-class woman in Kuwait in 1915. She says:

> When we entered the room, our hostess rose and received us cordially then pointed to some chairs which we noticed had been arranged especially for European visitors like ourselves, while the lady of the house herself sat on an exquisite carpet. There were a large number of cushions against the wall, in addition to other smaller and finer ones that were placed next to the lady. The hostess was young, and her beautiful costume made her even more stunning. Her dress was carefully tied with a fine silk scarf, and she wore a golden silk robe over it. Over her head she wore a black Hijab known as *Malfaa* (wrap), and over it a line of small golden pieces sewed into the Hijab. She wore her overcoat, made of black silk and embroidered with golden thread around the neck and shoulders, and which she pulled over her head so as to cover herself rapidly should a strange man appear unexpectedly. Opposite the lady there was a packet of cigarettes, matches and an ashtray. Immediately the hostess extended her hand to the packet, lit a cigarette and when she lit her second, one of the ladies sitting next to her approached us and asked if we wanted to smoke, and we answered that we don't smoke. (Arabian Mission Correspondence Box no. 754.5)

Although the report gives a realistic image of social life, it is quite strange to find this reference to women smoking, which was neither common nor even considered appropriate. Gulf societies were not introduced to cigarettes till a later stage, although tobacco was known and even grown in some Gulf countries.[10] As for Arab women's eating habits, this can be seen in the missionary's report of a conversation between herself and a woman sitting on the floor who said: 'We are not comfortable eating with forks and knives, especially when we are hungry', at this point, the lady of the house laughed and said: 'Don't worry, they know that we are Bedouins and that we use our hands to eat.' (Ibid.)

The missionary goes on to describe eating rituals and writes: 'After eating, we were offered glasses of milk and tea, and when we were done with it, rose water was sprinkled over our hands, and finally, time for the last ritual: offering coffee.' She continues:

> We finally heard the sound of small coffee cups loaded on top of each other, and a black maid appeared carrying a copper coffee pot in her left hand, and the cups in her right, and she began to pour a little coffee for each of us and we drank three cups. With the third cup, we signaled and said, 'Allah willing, your coffee will never be cold', a statement that indicates good wishes for the home owners. (Ibid.)

This enchanting and precise description of Arab hospitality would not have been possible had those women missionaries not infiltrated Gulf families and given us such accurate descriptions of these rituals, which have not changed to this day. They have remained an integral part of the acknowledged rituals of Arab hospitality in Gulf societies and have not been altered by civilization or the rapid developments that have affected many aspects of social behavior in the Gulf region.

In all the places in the Gulf where missionaries hoped to preach Christianity they focused on and attempted to deeply penetrate the local community. Missionary reports about what is today the United Arab Emirates, which was on the missionary map early on, contain important

---

[10]Smoking was not an acceptable habit in old Gulf societies, especially among women, except perhaps for smoking a pipe like today's hookah or water pipe. This was known as *al-qaduw*, and the tobacco used for it was grown in some areas of the Gulf such as Ras al-Khaimah, Bahrain and Basra.

information on aspects of social and economic life. The Emirates differed from other Gulf territories because it remained inaccessible to any foreign influence, as a result of British domination, which isolated it from its neighbors. According to the Exclusive Treaty of 1892, rulers were denied any rights to receive representatives from any foreign power other than the British. This made the development of social and general conditions extremely slow in the Emirates by comparison to other parts of the Gulf.

In the Emirates, which was open to male missionaries from 1895 and to female missionaries from the second decade of the twentieth century, the cultural impact of missionaries, especially on local women and children, was great. In this area, where poverty and illiteracy played a major role in lowering the standard of living, missionaries found fertile ground for preaching, especially through medical missionary work. Missionary reports recorded high mortality rates for women especially during child-birth. They also recorded alarming infant-mortality rates, especially for children under five. A high birth rate did not mean there were a lot of chil-dren, because many newborn infants were lost for lack of medical care. In these health conditions, missionaries found a fertile ground for their work, particularly among women.

In 1906, Dr Sharon Thoms, in a report to headquarters described the state of children's health from his observations as follows: 'What captured my attention most before I left the area was seeing some of the poor chil-dren in the villages near Sharjah sewing some proverbs and Wise Sulaiman's sayings on small leather sacks that they wore around their neck to protect them from "evil's eye".' As for the condition of women, Thoms' reports and those of others, revealed how terrible living conditions of women in this area were.

However, these frequent visits by missionaries to all parts of the Emirates, medical bag in one hand and Bible in another, did not mean missionary work was attractive or successful in the area. On the contrary, people there refused to listen to the missionaries. But, although women refused to listen to Christian prayers, they were drawn toward the mission-aries' medical services. This was one of the reasons that led Dr Sarah Hosman to make Sharjah the center in which she founded the American hospital known as Sarah Hosman's Hospital. This hospital, established in the 1930s, contributed to changing the lives of many Emirati women. It was the first modern hospital that offered advanced medical services to women, which alleviated their suffering and helped save many lives, as well as introducing modern medical treatment, which created health awareness among women throughout the Emirates (al-Sayegh, *Tabshir*).

American mission reports about al-Hasa and al-Qatif (in the eastern part of Saudi Arabia) are considered to be the most fascinating documentation of their kind for the reason that this area was not under any Western authority because of the dominance of the Ottomans and their prevention of any missionary involvement in the area. However, despite this Ottoman control, missionaries were not to be discouraged from visiting al-Hasa. The first of these visits was in 1893 by the Rev. Samuel Zwemer, who took the shortest route to al-Hasa, via Bahrain, the American Mission's base. Travel was by sea to the port of Ajir or al-Aqir and from there by land with commercial convoys to the capital al-Hafouf. The missionaries carried messages from the Mission in Bahrain to Turkish officers asking them for permission to carry out their work freely and wander about al-Hasa. In one of his reports, Zwemer describes the port of al-Aqir and the Turkish influence that was still very evident, including the Turkish customs building and al-Aqir port, which was a commercial harbour for the area where essential commodities such as rice and cloth arrived by sea from Bahrain destined for the cities of Arabia.

The first missionary visit did not pass without incident. The governor of the area ordered that the missionaries would have to leave immediately if they insisted on any overtly Christian practices before starting medical treatment. After the visit to al-Aqir ended, the missionary medical team visited the coastal area of al-Aqir, which was under the control of 'Abd al-'Aziz ibn Sa'ud. Then from al-Aqir they proceeded to al-Hasa using donkeys, horses and sailing boats. The medical team described al-Hasa as the paradise of the Arab Peninsula because it had sweet water, vegetation and palm trees, and they found that wheat, fruit and even rice could be grown. One of the most widespread conditions in this area was known as *ziran* (derived from the word *zar* [or *yazur*], a ritual thought to heal mental illnesses caused by spirit possession). It affected both men and women, although it was more widespread among women. According to missionaries, this condition was prevalent among women because Islam put a lot of pressure on them, while men enjoyed more freedom. Attending the *zar* was not socially accepted and a man would divorce his wife, or refuse to marry a woman, if he knew that she did so. One of the women missionaries tells of a man who bought a slave and when he found out that she had *ziran*, he resold her without regret because he was afraid that it would spread among the other women of his household. Missionaries also stated that many modern diseases such as fainting and epilepsy were diagnosed locally as *ziran* (*Neglected Arabia*, 25th Anniversary 23).

The missionaries also visited Riyadh, which was once called 'the capital of Muhammad's Empire' by the missionary Dr Paul Harrison, and the biggest city in the Arabian Peninsula. The opportunity to visit Riyadh presented itself when the Mission received a request from Ibn Sa'ud to visit his country to provide medical treatment, but with the proviso that they did not socialize with the people or preach to them. Dr Harrison gives an accurate account of the places he visited there and of the men and women he met in his book *Doctor in Arabia*. Although the Mission considered going into Arabia as a victory in itself, because they believed they were having access to the secrets of the empire, they did not achieve any missionary victories as such.

Fourth phase: The Gulf during the World War I period: political changes and their impact on women

In 1914, World War I broke out and Turkey was one of the parties involved. The war therefore affected the Arabian Gulf region and other areas under Ottoman control, especially al-Hasa, Basra and Kuwait, where Britain's influence and the failing Ottoman power were in conflict. Bahrain, where the Arabian Mission was based, was also a place that was affected by the war. According to one missionary, the Mission's headquarters became a center of attention, with visitors going to ask for newspapers, books and atlases, and to seek news of the war. The war also affected the economy; goods arrived in Bahrain from all over the world but when the war started, exports and imports declined by more that 50 percent. In addition, many commercial businesses declined, construction costs rose while workers' wages dropped from 33 cents to 20 cents a day, the pearl markets collapsed and divers suffered. Moreover, the economic situation affected provisions, and there were food shortages.

These conditions had a severe impact on the operation of the American Mission in Bahrain. When a missionary went to the market or to a village to preach, people ignored what he had to say and often asked: 'When will the great powers stop this war?' Missionaries also complained about the decline in sales of Bibles and Christian books, despite the fact that they were quite cheap, claiming that this was because people needed money to buy food and that even reading religious books was rejected, as if Bahrainis were saying, 'We have no time to bother with these books' (Harrison, 1924, 86–87). In parallel with the war, there was a recession in the economies of Gulf societies, which continued well into the mid-1930s and led to a decline in the pearl trade, which represented the backbone of the economy of the Gulf states prior to the discovery of oil.

Not only did these conditions influence missionary work in Gulf societies, but they also influenced all social classes. The trade of the upper class, mainly pearl merchants, was affected, and the middle and lower classes longed for the war to end because the international situation had overshadowed all aspects of life in Gulf societies. Women did not buy Christian books or Bibles, even if they were sold cheaply, because they were concentrating on providing for their families' daily needs and, even when missionaries attempted to give books away, the people refused to take them saying: 'We do not have time to waste on such books' (*Neglected Arabia*, 25th Anniversary, 5).

In addition to economic circumstances, the general situation also affected the missionaries' work. As soon as Turkey, whose influence extended to Basra, entered the war, it started a campaign to arouse Muslim public opinion against the Allies, with calls for *jihad* against foreigners. This prompted religious leaders to turn people against missionaries and the work that they were doing. In the summer of 1915, people were no longer visiting the Mission hospital in Basra as they had before, despite the fact that missionary Van Ess and his wife visited the Turkish governor in his quarters and offered him the use of the school and hospital to house wounded Turkish soldiers. This step was welcomed by the governor, but it did not alter the Muslims' attitude towards the Allies.

In general, Arab women viewed women missionaries with considerable respect and gratitude; they called them *khatun*, which means 'lady', and *hakima* (doctor), because to the local women, they were all *hakima*s who could give medication and relieve pain, and the relationships between them were based on superficial cordiality. Missionaries described the Arab homes they visited: both the extremely poor, where the furniture was dirty and plain; and those that reflected a higher social status, with Persian carpets and European furniture: simply the difference between poor houses and rich houses

Missionary reports always describe Gulf women's clothing. For example, Dr Sarah Hosman, describing Omani women, says: 'Women here are lucky, for they do not have to change the style of their clothes all the time. It is enough to wear the same model always since the styles here do not change although their colors and sources do. But if you travel from Bahrain to Basra, there will be a slight change in the costume.' She then goes on to say: 'In the beginning I could not accept Omani women's attire because it is a mixture of striking and mixed colors; however, after my stay in this stretch of desert land where you do not see any color, I learned to admire the color of women's clothes. But women here do not appear with their dresses outside home, they don a black piece of cloth called (*Abaya*) that covers their bodies and thus, they all look alike' (Hosman).

Arab women's clothes in the Gulf reflected their social status and their husbands' economic standing and was devoid of anything resembling Western style. In winter, for example, a woman's costume was made up of five pieces. She began by putting on the *serwal*, or trousers, ankle-length and usually made of silk or satin and embroidered with silver threads at the hem. The second piece, known as the *dishdasha*, which was brought from Bombay in India, was a fitted, knee-length dress with long sleeves usually embroidered with silver threads. The slit in the dress was also almost always embroidered with silver threads in four consecutive rows. The *dishdasha* was usually of a plain color, often dark red, while the *serwal* was often blue. Over the *dishdasha*, a woman wore a loose cape known as a *thawb*. It was long, with a hem embroidered in gold and silver thread, and was some-times worn over the head. Gulf women had a special way of wearing the *thawb* so as to cover their sleeves and the top of their head; it was usually multi-colored, unlike the *dishdasha*, with the colors mixing as they were sewn together, and then made into one dress usually of silk or chiffon. A Gulf woman's appearance was incomplete without combing her shiny black hair and plaiting it into several braids, sometimes ten or twenty, with a gold ornament at the end of each, and in the parting she always put henna. She also used henna on her hands, fingers, feet and heels, and kohl round her eyes, and dyed her eyebrows black. Her jewelry was made of pure gold, and she wore rings on all her fingers, with a particular ring for each. She wore bracelets on both wrists and anklets round her ankles, and she also wore a nose ring and several necklaces, usually three or four, around her neck, one of which was a choker while the rest fell to the waist. Her final piece was the *malfa*, a black wrap with which she covered her head, leaving a portion free to cover her face should she encounter a stranger. Finally, she would put one side of her colorful *thawb* over her head, that part covered by the *malfa*. It should be noted that this costume was dominant in middle-class households, but an upper-class woman wore an overcoat or cape (*abaya*) on top of all this, even when she was receiving guests in her home. As for middle- and lower-class women, they freed themselves of the *abaya* at home and wore it only outside. The *abaya*, still worn today, is made of black silk and embroidered at the hem with gold thread. Upper-class women and shaykhas wore a white *abaya*, and wealthy women would own several, costing between fifty and 2,000 dollars apiece. The missionary concludes by describing footwear and states that a woman 'does not wear stockings and doesn't know how to wear shoes but rather wears light slippers or sandals at home and more sturdy ones when she goes out' (al-Bassam 101–5). This accurate description of Gulf homes and costumes was not incidental but rather intentional, in order to show the American reader how successful the Mission was in getting close to the Arabs. Indeed, the success of Christian preachers in going into Gulf homes was a metaphor for their ability to break the privacy and seclusion that had always characterized the Arab home. To the missionaries, this was the fulfillment of a long-cherished desire.

However, this did not imply Gulf women's acceptance or trust of Christian missionaries and their work. Some women, for example, were afraid of medications, thinking that anyone who took them would become a Christian (Van Ess 15). Others were afraid of strangers, especially Christians. One woman tells how she met one of the missionaries, who was wearing a black hat, and says 'My heart started beating fast and I went to hide in my house, and my heart beat even faster till it was about to burst' (ibid.). Another Arab woman tells of her experience of visiting a Christian home:

I didn't dare enter this house before, but one time, during the holy month and Christmas, the lady of the house, or the Khatoun, as she was called, invited us to her home. I plucked up enough courage to enter the house;

a house I had long feared, my heart beating fast. As soon as I entered, my eyes fell on a tree full of lights and other baubles. My legs trembled with fear, and everything started dancing in front of my eyes. A few minutes later, I left the place, not knowing whether I was asleep or awake, dead or alive, and rushed home. I did not sleep a wink that night out of sheer fear, and I saw in my dreams the tree dancing with its lights as if they were flames. (Ibid.)

She then continues, 'I do not know if this kind of tree grows in London' (ibid.).

This communication between Gulf women and the American Mission women was the first cultural encounter for both, and both parties influenced each other. American women related to much that they found in Gulf women. They were given Arab names such as Latifa and Lu'lu'a, and they took on the title of 'Mother of so and so', like Arab women—Umm Yusuf for example, and other known titles. They also wore Arabian dress in order to be accepted by Arab society. Another significant factor was the Arabic language. Missionaries learned Arabic in order to facilitate contact with Arab women and to enable them to communicate in the Arab milieu where they were living. Moreover, some of them formed friendships with Arabs that continued even after the work of the Mission ended.

Fifth phase: The American Mission and women of the Gulf during the inter-war period (1918–1939)

In 1918, World War I ended, leaving extensive damage and many victims, not only on the human level, but also on the economic and developmental levels. It was not only the countries that started the war that were affected, but also all the other countries that joined in on one side or the other, including the Gulf states, which stood with the Allies during their long and expensive war against the Axis powers. As a result all Gulf societies were seriously affected economically, and women were perhaps the group most affected by the poverty, deprivation and disease that prevailed.

During World War I, the Arabian Mission stopped sending missionaries to the region, but when the war ended, mission activities resumed, and missionaries returned, this time in a serious attempt to win converts. In the inter-war period (1918–1939), church missionaries penetrated the whole of the Gulf and the Arabian Peninsula region, focusing their work mainly on the cities and their outskirts. They also used new preaching methods in their attempt to win converts, such as sending qualified doctors, teachers and social service experts. They failed, however, to achieve their primary aim of gaining converts. There were complaints in the United States, especially from donors, that missionaries were so engrossed in humanitarian work that they had no time to preach to the people (al-Sayegh, 'American Women Missionaries', 351), which prompted missionaries to exert enormous efforts to convey their main message to the people. Nevertheless, evangelization failed in this region because people were attached to their religion and Islam represented not only a religion but also a way of life and a set of values inspired by their desert environment. Accordingly, the only course open to the missionaries after World War II was to pack up and leave, admitting their failure to accomplish religious infiltration, despite their success in achieving positive results on the cultural and developmental fronts.

Despite their religious failure, the missionaries succeeded in disseminating a new educational culture that helped spread modernity and change the pattern of life in Gulf societies. Schools, especially those that were founded for girls, succeeded in drawing the attention of parents to a new type of education that would improve the lives of their daughters, an education that was different from the common religious *katatib*. As a result, a large number of girls began to opt for formal education. The Arabian Mission reports indicate that many of the girls that joined and benefited from its schools graduated to become leading women who have actively participated in the service of their communities — women such as Muna al-Mundari in Oman, who graduated to become the first woman television presenter and a civil rights activist, and in Bahrain, Mrs Lu'lu'a al-Khalifa, along with many others, who became an activist on the political and social fronts. Finally, one must say that missionary work, despite its failure on the religious front, succeeded in creating some kind of human contact between Arab and Western culture, and has greatly influenced the position of women in the Gulf. It also introduced new values to the lives of the people in the region in general, and to women's lives in particular.

Conclusion

In 1973, those in charge of the American Mission decided to close it down and suspend its work abroad, but despite this, and the halting of its religious work, the cultural influence of the Mission continued and could be seen in the bearing it had on the women who benefited from its non-religious services, and its great impact on their lives and societies. At that time, when the whole region had started to reap the benefits of development brought about by the oil boom, change was beginning to have a clear impact on Gulf women. Although the missionaries failed on the religious level, it can be said that they have achieved a marked success in the areas of service, humanitarian work and awareness.

Missionaries realized that the Arabian Peninsula and the Gulf region were not only full of villages and towns, but also of cultural mysteries and diverse rituals, traditions and customs, as well as cultural symbols that bewildered them and which at times they could not comprehend, decipher or analyze. Women missionaries therefore endeavored to observe and document the situation, recording it all with extreme accuracy in order to send details to the Mission headquarters. These observations included their impressions of the visits they made to Arab women, their customs and the traditions common in Arab households (Boersma).

These missionary reports were the only record of the position of women in the Gulf and the Arabian Peninsula from the end of the nineteenth century up to the mid-twentieth century. There are hardly any references to the situation of women in the region during this period in Arab or local sources, which means that historians have depended heavily on the American Church archives for relevant documentation. The photos taken by women missionaries, which were aimed at making their reports more effective and official, remain a vital source of social history in the area. They also illustrate the development of social and urban life in Gulf cities and villages.

It is important to note here that, much as the male missionaries were slandered, called heretics, rebuked and criticized for preaching and selling Christian books, no negative remarks were ever directed at a woman missionary by local Arabs. On the contrary, their work was met with appreciation and respect, especially when it was coupled with distributing clothes and sweets to children and reading religious hymns. Women missionaries were often invited into homes to teach women sewing, reading and writing, and local women liked to listen to their stories, songs and hymns, which gladdened their hearts. Their popularity among women was due to the fact that they did not sell religious books or preach in a direct manner, and the life of seclusion that Arab women led made the missionaries' visits an entertainment that broke their daily routine. It also seems clear that Arab women were not as suspicious of missionary intentions as Arab men, and so they enthusiastically received them and, for the most part, accepted their medications as beneficial and their presence as harmless.

On the other hand, the missionaries' traditions and customs, as well as their pattern of life and daily routine, were new to Gulf societies. Gulf women were always inquiring about the customs and traditions of the missionaries' native countries and often wondered about the distance these women had to travel to reach their homelands, which was very strange in a country where women were not used to traveling except for two purposes: pilgrimage (*Hajj*) or medical treatment in India. All these ideas were new to Gulf societies and, over time, contributed to the change that brought about the intellectual transformation of these societies, especially in the places where the missionaries lived permanently, such as Bahrain, Oman and Basra.

The style of missionary reports gives them a special quality. The reports were detailed, for they were directed to churches, missions and organizations in the United States to encourage them to donate the money that was needed. Expenses were detailed in order to give the donor a realistic, and emotional, image of the situation in the Gulf. The reports clarify that the missionaries' salaries were barely sufficient, and that a lot was being spent on hospitals, patients, religious books, and the rent of bookstores. The reports also explain, in detail, that all the religious books on display were being sold and that a number of Muslims had been evangelized. The reports were important for persuading donors to give willingly, and to convey the sense that their money was being well spent and that their efforts were not in vain.

Notwithstanding their real objective, missionary services were one of the factors of change in the life of Gulf women in the first half of the twentieth century. Women missionaries brought a way of life and a value system to the lives of Gulf women, the most important aspects of which were education, work and discipline, which all influenced the lives of Arab women who came into contact with Christian missionaries. Moreover, missionary services provided a solid basis upon which Arab women could accept the change that was taking place in their lives with better understanding and conviction. These services thus succeeded in becoming an effective tool for broadening women's horizons and introducing them to the positive aspects of modernity that could improve their own lives and those of their families.

Whereas popular culture suppressed women's determination and often degraded them, Western values have helped, to a great extent, in developing their understanding, affecting them positively, raising their spirits and motivating them to venture into the public and professional spheres with understanding and determination. It is no wonder that missionary services became one of the most influential factors for positive social change in Gulf societies in the first half of the twentieth century, and possibly the most daring in activating women's participation in public life from then on.

11. *Some Considerations on the Family in the Arabian Peninsula in the Late Ottoman and Early Post-Ottoman Period*

SORAYA ALTORKI

As a basic form of social organization, the family is closely related to the overall political, social, and economic contexts of society. In short, the ecological circumstances of a society—here understood as the sum total of cultural, economic, political and social contextual factors—have significant impacts upon the ways in which people in that society derive their norms and practices related to the family. Both stability and changes in those ecological circumstances may be expected to be reflected in patterns associated with the family, including solutions that members of the population bring to the problems of family life. These notions underscore the flexibility, rather than the rigidity, of family forms. Such forms in the Arabian Peninsula have taken various guises, depending on the mode of economic livelihood, the role of the state, the impact of international economic trends upon the local Arabian scene, and other external considerations.

In this study, I will mainly examine the family and women in Arabian society in the late Ottoman and early post-Ottoman period (ca 1860–1918, 1918–1924). To do this, I have surveyed what is available in both Arabic and English on pre-state Arabia. The information comes mainly from the memoirs of Western travelers to the region, such as John Lewis Burckhardt,[1]

---

[1]Burckhardt's book (1784–1817) was published posthumously in 1831, so the period covered by him is earlier than the time span covered in this paper. Thus, in references to his observations, I am being somewhat ahistorical. The reader should be aware that his

Charles M. Doughty, and Snouck Hurgronje, in addition to certain local histories, including those by Ahmad al-Siba'i, 'Abd al-Quddus al-Ansari, Sabira Mu'min Isma'il, and Tarfah 'Abd al-'Aziz al-'Ubaykan.

This study also examines the institution of the family in terms of the following themes: women in Mecca before the sixteenth-century Ottoman conquest of the Hijaz; state and society in Arabia from ca 1860s to 1924; the structure of the family; images of women; women's behavior; marriage and divorce; women's legal rights; women's participation in the economy; women's role in the world of spirits and cures; the state's impact on women.

Some preliminary evidence on the role of women in Mecca before the sixteenth-century Ottoman conquest of the Hijaz

Although the bulk of this study focuses on the late Ottoman to early post-Ottoman period, I would like to summarize some research on the role of women in Mecca in the pre-Ottoman period to provide some context for the later period. While it is true that information for the pre-Ottoman period is limited, it is worth presenting, pending further research by scholars that may broaden our understanding of this preliminary data and eventually permit comparisons and contrasts to be drawn.

In her research on pre-Ottoman Arabia (more specifically, the seventh and eighth centuries of the hijra, coinciding with the 1300s and 1400s of the Christian era), al-'Ubaykan reveals some trends regarding the role of women with regard to education, law, philanthropy, and the like that may appear somewhat surprising to those who have felt that role to have been greatly circumscribed by confinement to the domestic scene. For example, she notes that teaching was not confined to the mosque and *kuttab* (elementary religious school). Home schooling was practiced, where parents and relatives taught others—especially, women. At the same time, women were teachers of other women and even *maharim* men (that is, men whom they were not legally eligible to marry) (al-'Ubaykan 79).

She also relates that women attended mosques and listened to sermons given there, taking up positions behind the men present for prayers and homilies (ibid. 156). The mosque was also a site for learning and

attributions are to phenomena that might have undergone some change in the half century or so that passed subsequent to his having made them.

education. Women's educational concerns in this period focused upon the science of Hadith. It was not unusual for them both to learn these Hadith from others and also to obtain diplomas of learning (*ijazat*) from certain *shuyukh* among the ranks of the *'ulama'*. Some women were said to have taught 'honorable and pious men'. Indeed, according to al-'Ubaykan, certain women granted the diploma not only to other women but even to men (ibid. 157–9). We read, in fact, of students, not to mention prominent male *muhaddithun* (experts in the science of Hadith), flocking to the classes of some of these women (ibid. 160).

The reputation of some of these female instructors developed to the extent that individuals from other localities heard of their abilities and wrote to them, requesting diplomas of learning. Strikingly, among these individuals were both women and men, and the men, we are told, were just as keen to receive them as were the women. A certain Umm Hasan was just such a *muhaddidtha*, and important individuals studied under her. It was also the case that some women sought to obtain diplomas from the *'ulama'* residing in other localities (ibid. 161–4).

In addition to their role in education in the Mecca of the seventh and eighth centuries AH, they also were prominent in philanthropy, maintaining charities inside the city of Mecca. They also managed women's 'associations' (*rubat*, pl. *arbita*), some of which were founded as religious endowments (*awqaf*) for assisting pious but destitute women. Endowments also existed to assist widows, and one was dedicated to women seeking to withdraw from daily activities in order to focus their energies on worship. Al-'Ubaykan, in providing her descriptions of the various kinds of endowments, discusses one that was dedicated to widows of the Shafi'i rite (ibid. 226–7), one of the four legal schools in Sunni Islam. She details the case of one woman who founded an association for which she played the role of a *shaykha*. Her duties included supervision of certain religious devotions, such as *tasbih*, *dhikr*, and *wird*, as well as the provision of food (ibid.).

Al-'Ubaykan tells us that women's social status in Mecca resembled their status in other Islamic regions. Although their primary duty was to raise children, the pursuit of knowledge competed for their attention. Other functions that they performed included supervision of religious endowments. As such jobs were typically reserved for individuals of distinction and piety, this indicates the high status that these women achieved (ibid. 248–9).

In conclusion, if the role of women in various educational and cultural activities is an indicator, Meccan society was significantly less conservative than has been previously thought. The fact that women were often chosen as overseers or supervisors of devotions or of pious endowments indicates that they were adjudged to have sufficiently developed administrative skills and were perceived to enjoy the trust of others. Women therefore apparently had a significantly greater degree of freedom outside the home than is commonly believed, their activities ranging from those of venerable elder, overseer of associations, supervisor of endowments, and teacher of Hadith—to men as well as to other women (ibid. 249).

State and society in Arabia, ca 1860–1924

While the period from the 1860s to the early 1920s marks a time of Ottoman rule over the Arabian Peninsula, there was considerable local autonomy. The Ottoman presence in the Peninsula dates from the conquest of Egypt by Selim I (ruled 1512–1520), which led to the displacement of the previous Mamluk influence in the Hijaz by that of the Ottoman Empire. Although the Ottomans did not penetrate the interior of the Peninsula, they established a degree of control over the holy cities of Mecca and Medina from this early time until the collapse of the Empire in the aftermath of World War I. Watt (150) notes that the Ottomans extended patronage to the rulers of the Hijaz, known as the Sharifs, whose rule in the sixteenth century reached northward as far as Khaybar and to the east and south into Najd. The legal system adopted by the Ottomans was based on the Hanafi school, founded by Abu Hanifa (d. 767). The Sharifs, however, followed the school of al-Shafi'i (d. 820). The sources are somewhat contradictory on Ottoman policy regarding the legal system of the Hijaz. We are reasonably certain that the Ottomans interfered in the legal process in the territory. For example, Watt (144), without identifying the time period, argues that they intervened in the selection process of the Shafi'i judges there, writing:

A darker side of the Ottoman suzerainty was its intervention in the administration of justice. Since the Sharifs had adopted the Shafi'i madhhab, the Shafi'i qadi was the chief judge; this office had also remained for centuries in one family. Now the highest bidder for the office was sent every year from Istanbul to Mecca; the Meccans of course had to pay the price with interest.[2]

Hurgronje, however, maintains that Ottoman intervention went beyond these limited initiatives, although, like Watt, he fails to provide a time frame. He admits that in the early years of their rule the Ottomans appointed four judges for the Hijaz, one from each of the four Sunni schools. But this more liberal policy changed at a later point. He states:

> But later, perceiving that the administration of the Law was their affair, not that of their subjects, the government suppressed them all except the Hanafite one, who became the sole Judge in the Law of Religion and of family life, while all other matters were decided according to new secular Law (called al-Qanun al-Munif), which replaced the Shar' al-Sharif (Sacred Law). (182–3)

But he then contradicts himself by saying the Shafi'i, Maliki and Hanbali schools were not suppressed, as each community in Mecca did have its own *mufti*, and this plurality of *mufti*s to some extent acted as a brake on the power of the Hanafi judge. However, again contradicting himself, he seems to suggest that this really was not very meaningful by asserting that the authority of the judges from the other schools remained at the level of ritual only, and 'the power of the Ottoman Government tends to displace the non-Hanafite rites' (183).[3]

Accordingly, it is not clear what the Ottoman policy or behavior in fact was with regard to the legal system. Perhaps both policy and behavior

[2]It is worth noting that in this period—the era of the Tanzimat—Ottoman reform efforts in the Arab regions, among others, provoked opposition, including to Ottoman efforts to rationalize the legal system by imposing the Hanafi school of law. Whether the efforts in this direction in the Arabian Peninsula succeeded cannot be determined with certainty, but it may be said generally that Hanafi legal rulings with regard to women are more 'liberal' than those of the Shafi'i and Hanbali schools, which dominated Arabia. For example, Abu Hanifa permitted a free-born woman to marry without the need for a guardian's permission—although it is true that later Hanafi doctrine limited this entitlement to women who had already been married before. It is difficult to generalize from this to particular cases, however, without access to judicial records of the period.

[3]As noted earlier, the Ottoman preference for Hanafi law had its manifestation in Arabia in the form of appointment of judges. While no doubt it would be apposite to grasp the impact of Ottoman actions upon the law in Arabia during the period under review, providing details of that impact is difficult without access to the judicial records of the period. Perhaps this important topic can be examined in future research.

lacked consistency, and that is what lies behind Watt and Hurgronje's varying depictions of the legal situation in the Hijaz over the course of the Ottoman involvement in this territory.

On the whole, Ottoman conduct in the Hijaz could be characterized as refraining from direct efforts to control the region but taking initiatives at certain points in order to strengthen their influence there. For example, Sultan Murad IV (ruled 1623–1640) strove to expel the Shi'a from Mecca and to prevent them from making the pilgrimage to the holy city. The Sharifs objected to these interventions because they knew it would instigate disorder and complicate their administration of the region, so in fact they countermanded Murad's commands (ibid.).

In the main, the Ottomans did not meddle in the incessant rivalries between the Sharifian families of the Hijaz—the 'Abadila, the Dhawi Zayd, and the Dhawi Barakat—over the course of the seventeenth through the nineteenth centuries, although Murad IV (ruled 1623–1640) developed an antipathy toward the Dhawi Zayd and sought to remove them from Mecca.[4] However, by the early 1800s Ottoman patience with the turbulent power struggles in the Hijaz, complicated now by the Wahhabi invasion of the province from central Arabia, led them to order Muhammad 'Ali Pasha of Egypt (ruled 1805–1849) to intervene in order to restore stability. Muhammad 'Ali was not able to act until 1813, when he took Mecca from the Wahhabis. From 1813 to 1840, the Hijaz essentially became dependent upon Egypt, but in 1840, Muhammad 'Ali signed a treaty with the Ottoman government whereby the Hijaz was restored to Ottoman suzerainty, symbolized by the appointment by the Sublime Porte of the Wali (or governor) of the Hijaz, with his seat in the city of Jeddah.

The Ottoman state's presence in the Hijaz in the period after the 1840 agreement remained relatively unobtrusive. However, the Wali and the Sharif of Mecca carried on a rivalry, and the Ottomans were not loath occasionally to try to weaken the latter's power as a way of undermining the Hijaz's semi-autonomous status. One method that the Ottomans used to that end was to keep some of the members of the Sharifian families hostage in Istanbul (Isma'il 12–18). Sultan Abdul Hamid II (ruled

---

[4]To my knowledge, the power struggles among these Sharifian families have not been studied in close detail in the sources. Among those who pay some attention to the Amirs is Hogarth (48–50). There are some passing references to them in the later era of the Young Turks in the essay by Tell (41–52 and *passim*).

1876–1909) went beyond this restrained Ottoman policy in hopes of bringing control over Mecca and Medina more directly under Ottoman authority. As part of the new policy, the Wali of Jeddah moved his seat to Mecca, and replaced the then sitting Sharif with another individual.

This state of affairs was to reach a critical pass in the context of the outbreak of World War I, when the then Sharif, Husayn bin 'Ali (d. 1931), commenced negotiations with the British to overthrow Ottoman rule in exchange for British promises of help to recognize the Sharif as king of a future Arab state. For a few years the territory became subject to this Hashemite ruler. However, an invasion of the Hijaz in 1924 by the forces of Ibn 'Abd al-'Aziz Al Sa'ud of Najd unsettled the situation again.

There is little in the way of reliable documentation on the forms of the family and relationships between family members in any of the areas that 'Abd al-'Aziz conquered on the Peninsula, including Najd in 1902, al-Hasa in 1913, al-'Asir in 1918, and the Hijaz in 1924, leading to the formal establishment of the Kingdom of Saudi Arabia in 1932. One can infer, of course, that because the king had made an alliance with the Wahhabi leaders and constituted his forces as the 'Unitarians' (*Muwahhidun*), a more ideologically rigorous system was imposed on the family than had hitherto existed. We are told by European travelers, for example, that Shi'i influences in the Hijaz were not insignificant in the late Ottoman period (Hurgronje 41, 45, 124, 158, 183–4, 257),[5] which the new order established under Ibn 'Abd al-'Aziz suppressed. Similarly, the veneration of saints, a central institution in the Ottoman period in the Hijaz, also came to an end. These developments had major implications for the role of women, who were important actors in the commemorations of saints' days and the festivals associated with them.

Structure of the family

The extended family is considered to have been the central institution of Arabia in the late Ottoman period, but of course the term was not used by

[5]Hurgronje notes that on the tenth day of the month of Muharram, called 'Ashura, the people of Mecca voluntarily fast in honor of the third Imam; and out of respect for this Imam, the Ka'ba was opened up to the public (41). For an interesting analysis of the influence of Zaydi Shi'ism in the Hijaz, including the fact that the Hasanid Sharifs of Mecca into the fifteenth century were Zaydi Shi'ites, see Mortel. For the notion of Sunni and Shi'i participation in *mawlid*s, shrine visitations and public rituals, see Doumato (129). She relies on observations by Burton and St John Philby.

the Arabs themselves. It is rather a concept introduced in the nineteenth century by social scientists to refer to the phenomenon of several generations of affinal and agnatic relatives from a parental couple living in the same household, although the latter need not refer to a single dwelling but might include several abodes within a single compound. It might include the parents of a nuclear family, together with their children, their children's spouses, cousins, uncles, aunts, grandparents, grandchildren, adopted children, concubines, and slaves. In pastoral and agricultural societies, extended families constitute the optimum family size because of the various hands needed to maintain the existence of the unit. This may sometimes also be true for pastoralists and nomads when settled in periods of plenty. The nomads of the desert areas of Arabia often moved in small groups consisting of the *bayt* or nuclear family.[6] In towns, the need for large extended families typically would be less, but the presence of relatives beyond the conjugal pair and their immediate offspring within a household would continue to be relevant and important. Arabia in the late Ottoman period was a society characterized by pastoralism, agricultural settlements, and urban market towns. Life in these towns was shaped by festivals, pilgrimage, and commercial and business pursuits of various kinds.

When one speaks of the structure of the family, the reference is to its size, spatial arrangements, the role of its members, and the like. The European writers, Burckhardt, Doughty, and Hurgronje variously comment on family structure in late eighteenth- to early nineteenth-century Arabia. Hurgronje notes that Europeans have a distorted, stereotypical sense of spatial residence patterns in Arabia in this period. The stereotype of the urban Arabian family, for example, posits an inner sanctum (*harim*) located in the back of the domicile in which live four wives and numerous slaves, all reduced to abject servitude and at the mercy of the master. In fact, he reports that, at least around 1884–1885, the womenfolk of a household did not live in a fixed area of the home. Instead, wherever they were, that is where the *harim* was. It is true that the visitor usually did not have access to the area where the women happened to be, but he notes that Europeans

[6]What is referred to and defined as the 'nuclear family' in the social science literature will differ from the conception held in local areas and regions in a society such as Arabia in the period under review. We must be careful not to assume a homogenized conception of this term. To give just one example, the parents and children are considered to comprise a nuclear family in a society such as the UK, but in third world societies, perhaps an uncle or aunt or cousins could be accommodated by the rubric of 'nuclear family'.

also had little free access to the private quarters of their acquaintances' homes (Hurgronje 83).

At any rate, as Hurgronje tells it, in urban areas, partitions, screens, lattices, and veils divided the rooms in which the women happened to be from other areas of the residence. Sometimes, these dividers were to be found within a single room, in another part of which men might happen to be. By contrast, in the open country, Doughty reports that women 'have a liberty, as where all are kindred' (Doughty 280). This observation would appear very relevant to the concept of public space and the debates that are taking place over this issue among scholars. If accurate, it portrays an autonomy for women that contrasts with a more 'traditional' view, which relegates women to the private sphere. Burckhardt experienced a similar situation with Bedouin women, although he qualifies their more liberal behavior geographically by suggesting that it occurred only in a specific area, even though that area was rather extensive. He writes:

> In the mountains south of Mecca, towards Yemen, where manners appear very different from those in Najd and the northern plains of Arabia, women are said to entertain a guest in the absence of her husband, and to sit up with the stranger. (Burckhardt 1:349–50)

In the town of Khaybar, Doughty did experience a departure from the stricter segregation of women that was to be found in the desert areas, when he stayed in a home where his acquaintance's mother brought him his food, and refused payment for the victuals. She 'sat before me open-faced . . . treat[ing] me as her son'. However, he noted how rare this was, asserting 'hers was the only town-woman's face that I have seen in middle Nejd' (ibid., 2:404).

But Hurgronje implies that class or status differences might be significant with regard to outsider encounters with the women of the household. He offers the proposition that 'the simpler are the relations of life of the master of the house, the freer is the intercourse of the house friends with its women' (Hurgronje 83–4). Very wealthy men, however, were able to maintain more than one house. If they were merchants or officials, they would use the main or great house as the place for conducting their business, while the other house (or houses), which were smaller, they would maintain for the women. With this arrangement, the master was able to keep his *harim* sequestered and thus protected from the traffic of his male visitors (ibid. 84).

By way of contrast, chances were greater among the middle classes or strata of society for visitors to the house to at least be within earshot of the womenfolk. Thus, a male guest might find his host in the sitting room, and adjacent to that location might be an interior room, connected with that sitting room, with its door ajar, in which his wife is sitting. If the host believed his guest was trustworthy, he might draw his wife into the conversation, and in this way not only might a three-way conversation ensue but the guest and the wife might engage in verbal exchanges with one another. If the connecting door was open, a screen would be placed between the rooms, but 'various circumstances may even induce the husband to remove this last restriction' (ibid.).

Yet further variations were possible. In Mecca, for example a more liberal interpretation of the *mahram* rule was to be found. A *mahram* is a male relative, usually within one, two, or three degrees of relationship with a woman, who is thus not able to marry her. As a consequence, interaction with that woman is permitted. Hurgronje notes that even distant relations were considered *maharim* in Mecca, and they too were permitted such interaction. Finally, a husband who believed that his male friends did not have 'a roving eye' might even make them 'adoptive relations of a man's wife, and he introduces them according to circumstances as father, son or brother' (ibid.). In this way, outsiders were adopted into the family, and interaction with womenfolk in the family was enabled. The *Shari'a* is apparently silent on the possibility that one of these adopted relatives might somehow find himself in the position of seeking marriage with one of these women, but customary law considered it taboo.

The situation among the lower classes was yet again somewhat different. Hurgronje argues that a similarly more liberal attitude was adopted with regard to encounters between visitors to the household and its womenfolk as existed for the middle classes. But because the space available in these homes was more restricted, an even freer attitude might prevail, and 'the conversation between the sexes is in various ways facilitated' (ibid. 85).

Burckhardt, commenting on Bedouin women, notes that they actively participated with their male kinsmen in showing hospitality to strangers. He writes that these women grouped together in the female quarter of the tent and in loud voices commented approvingly on their husbands' right to show hospitality to guests. He further adds that women might attend to such visitors if their husbands were away, although he stipulates that in that event some male relative would play the host (Burckhardt 1:349). There were, to be sure, limits to the degree to which the Bedouin women Burckhardt encountered could show hospitality to visitors. He notes that among certain Syrian tribes the women were permitted by custom to drink coffee with strangers in the tent of the master, but only as long as the latter was present. In contrast, he states that such a practice was never followed 'among other Arabs in the Northern Desert [of Arabia], where a woman will never drink coffee nor eat before men' (ibid.). He also hypothesized that among the Bedouin tribes with which he interacted, 'the more a tribe is connected with the inhabitants of towns, the stricter they are with respect to the seclusion of women' (ibid. 353). This observation could mean one or both of two things. It could mean that urban women were segregated from men; or that rural women were supposed to be secluded when they went into town. Or both of these could be true, which I believe is the case.

With regard to the number of wives in a man's household, the sources seem to agree that it was highly unusual for a man to have more than one. Burckhardt, speaking about Bedouin, writes that most of the men he met had only one wife, and 'very few' had two, 'and I never met with any person who could recollect a Bedouin that had four wives at once in his tent' (ibid., 1:106–7). Hurgronje supports this point, maintaining that 'only very rich people, and they rarely, avail themselves of the legal permission to have four wives at once, and in general one finds only in the highest circles those who have more than one wife' (Hurgronje 86). However, men tended to have slaves and concubines, so these added to the size of the family, although financial constraints restricted the number of these a man could maintain, so concubines tended to be found in the wealthier homes. Another category of woman might also add to the size of the family: a divorced older wife might receive permission from her former spouse to live in his tent compound with her children (ibid. 111).

Images of women

The sources suggest that in Arabian society in the late Ottoman period there were basically two sets of images about women. The first emphasized the negative aspects: women were seen as inferior to men, gossipy, irrational, and the like; but the second stressed women's acumen, their ability to promote their own interests, and their capacity to maneuver their husbands into acknowledging their rights. Sometimes, the sources themselves adopt positions on these qualities, although an effort will be made to indicate this where relevant.[7]

Hurgronje's eyewitness account reveals that he encountered cases where two male friends, in the effort to preserve their friendship, kept their wives far apart from one another 'so that women's gossip may not disturb their good relations' (Hurgronje 84).

Burckhardt suggests that women were considered by the men he encountered to be inferior beings, on account of which the men constantly sought to instill in them the idea that their only function was to cook and to work (Burckhardt 1:350). However, at least among the poorer men of Mecca whom Hurgronje observed, cooking was something that they themselves did and would not allow their women to engage in. He attributes this preference to the fact that 'they cannot trust their wives enough', although why such trust should be lacking is unexamined (Hurgronje 90). Doughty, who focused on Bedouin, states that males considered females to be totally blameworthy and endowed with malevolent natures. He further observes that men behaved toward women as though granting them parity would permit 'her evil nature' to 'break forth' (Doughty 1:280). He comments: 'The Arabs are contrary to womankind, upon whom they would have God's curse' (Doughty 1:280). One townsman in Khaybar told Doughty that women must be kept in subjection because, if they were not, they would come to hold their husbands in contempt (ibid. 2:160). It is interesting that Doughty chooses not to comment on this remark, which indicates perhaps that he agrees with its tenor. But why women would hold their men in contempt unless they were subjugated by them is not self-evident and deserves to be investigated; the fact that Doughty neglected to do so may indicate his bias.

Beyond this, among the tribes with whom Doughty interacted, a general impression was held that the women folk were akin to 'wild creatures that suffer not in child-bearing', but he rejected this image and averred that, because of the constant need to be on the move and migrating, her lot is a hard one, and 'there is no indolent hope before her of comfort and repose'

[7]I did not have access to *fatwas* that could shed light on this issue. This is an important point, however, and I hope it may be investigated in future research.

(ibid. 1:281). He also reported that the death of female children went unlamented by their fathers, who, however, became 'overborne awhile with silent sorrow' upon the passing of their sons. The idea, which was validated by reference to no less than the Prophet himself by one of Doughty's informants, was that the best women were those who could keep silent (ibid. 281–2).

On the other hand, men valued women's mastery of certain arts and sciences, including the administration of massage and cures. In Mecca, women of Indian provenance had learned the skill of massage and practiced it as a profession, but slave girls acquired the skills and provided massages for their mistresses, who in turn provided them for their husbands. We are told that 'almost every woman, free or slave, has dabbled in the art, and many men are so accustomed to massage that they can hardly go to sleep without it' (Hurgronje 104). In addition to massage, women's abilities in the area of medication, drugs and healing were also highly admired by Meccan men. Husbands, who otherwise are presented as holding patronizing views of women, would seek their wives' advice in case of family illness because they considered women to be more knowledgeable in the field of medicine than even physicians themselves. 'Generally, [women] have their own little home drug store and always a knowledge of the healing virtue of some herbs and spices that can be got at any spice dealer' (ibid. 93).

Another positive trait that women were seen to possess, at least in the urban Hijazi scene, was sexual attractiveness. This was not, however, necessarily a characteristic with which the free-born woman was endowed. Quite the contrary; it inhered, according to the sources, especially in slave women (or slaves who had been freed by their masters after having had children by them). Apparently, black slaves in general and Ethiopians more specifically, at least among the Meccan population, held the highest degree of fascination for Meccan men. The image conjured up by men's enchantment with these categories of women is strongly advanced by Hurgronje in particular (ibid. 106–7). Why this should be the case, however, is left unexplained by the Dutch scholar and colonial official. Did he choose not to comment because he thought it was empirically obvious from his own experiences? Did he believe it was *outré* and he had no explanation for it? Does such a judgment reveal ethnocentrism and 'othering', reminiscent of descriptions of colonialized subjects?

Women's compliance and resistance

To a significant degree, the daily lives of women in the period under review revolved around visits and outings, including to the homes of friends and relatives, as well as to public places during festivals and holidays. With regard to wealthy families in Mecca, for example, the women paid visits to each other just as the men folk did, but, as mentioned earlier in connection with wealthy families, the sexes never commingled during these visits. The sources, being male, shed little light on the topics of conversation among these women during their reciprocal visits, but we are told that men who developed intimate friendships with one another talked about their women 'quite occasionally . . . without any reserve, unless there are some special grounds for reserve' (ibid. 84).

Women's behavior within the conjugal context generates varying commentaries in the sources. Generally speaking, Hurgronje, whose focus is on the urban scene, emphasizes the spouses' different interests and basically reduces their relationship to the husband's carnal motivations within the marriage and the wife's efforts to broaden the scope of her autonomy from him as much as possible. He observes: 'With the exception of the marriages in the highest and the poorest classes and of some rare happy cases, the husband and wife are . . . connected only by a loose concubinage' (ibid. 89). In short, the husband provides his wife with a dowry, lodging, clothing, and food, in exchange for sexual gratification. He admits that the spouses may harbor a 'nobler conception of the marriage relation', but he insists on his cynical interpretation. He does not spare the wife in his characterization, saying she 'does not for an instant lose sight of the financial basis of the [marital] contract and is even not ashamed to extort . . . extra gifts from her husband during their cohabitation' (ibid. 89–90).

It is important to be cautious about comments such as this. They may in fact tell us more about the source—in this case, the Dutch scholar—than about women in the homes of the Meccans in the 1880s. It is quite possible that he is gauging the situation on the basis of his own inclinations, beliefs and/or cultural values. It begs the question to make such a categorical statement about all marriages, although it accords with typical Orientalist perspectives that were dominant at that time. One need only ask, for instance, why marriage occurred if sexual gratification was the be-all and end-all of such unions? After all, concubines were available, if affection and love were not involved.

Doughty, whose focus is on rural settings, basically underscores the husband's tyranny and writes that it was common for Bedouin wives to flee that tyranny by taking refuge in their mothers' tribes. That these women were not helpless in the light of men's dominance can be seen in Doughty's characterization of unhappy Bedouin women, who would seek to publicize their grievances as a way of reproving their husbands' behavior, thus subjecting them to public scorn. The goal in this was to extract a divorce from them (Doughty 1:273). Of course, the husband, even when importuned in this manner, could withhold divorce and resort to punishing her for her 'indiscretions', which would prevent the wife from gaining her objective of separating from him. We do not know how frequently or successfully women were able to resort to this course of action. Yet, the fact that Doughty feels it was attempted and succeeded provides at least anecdotal evidence for its occurrence. It would also be interesting to find evidence of support by the woman's parents and other relatives for such courses of action. The implication is that some parents did not oppose it, but whether this could translate into positive support is another question.

Women had available to them certain 'weapons' of their own. These might include their complaints about food. It was the men who went to the market to purchase food for the table. Wealthier men would supervise the preparation of the food, although the wealthiest among them would delegate this task to a female servant whose domain was the kitchen. The connection between the men and food would give the opportunity to women to cavil about commensal matters 'without the smallest consideration for the husband's feelings, especially as [he] often takes his meals outside or if at home without her in the company of his friends' (Hurgronje 90–1). Another source of complaint by women was the spouse's house, to which she was brought upon their marriage. The reader is presented with the generalization that a woman will easily resort to criticism of the house—whether its size, its condition, or, presumably, even its location—all with the intent of inducing the husband to secure a new house more pleasing to her (ibid.). And more generally, it is stated that women who found themselves in unhappy relationships knew that they could pester their husbands and generally make themselves so unlikable that these men would seek relief and divorce them (ibid. 88). This suggests that these women believed that re-marriage was a viable option. And, indeed, pilgrims to Mecca, according to Hurgronje, were partly motivated by the desire to find wives, an issue taken up below.

But the constant point of contention, at least as observed by Hurgronje among Meccan spouses, was over the wife's clothes. He is even moved to assert, 'This subject of dress is a subject of terror to the husband.' The wife would berate him as a stingy man if he objected to her wishes to acquire new clothing and jewelry. The author even maintains that the jealousy a wife harbors toward her husband's mistress(es) is based not on the diminution or even loss of his affections as much as it is on their foregoing the clothing and jewelry that they otherwise might be acquiring were it not for the husband's lavishing these on the other women (ibid. 91).

The behavior of wives toward their husbands, according to Hurgronje, extended to their adultery, although one may take his reports about the extent of such extra-marital affairs with a grain of salt, given the severe punishments in Islamic law for such breaches. He notes that, on the one hand, women did not have a sound knowledge of the law so as to be deterred, but they might—and most likely did—know that their adultery was taboo; yet they shrugged it off by saying: 'I pray God for pardon.' He concludes by maintaining that Meccan society was indulgent toward women's indiscretions, 'as indulgent as that of Europe in regard to licentiousness of men' (ibid. 92).[8] A different picture, however, is provided by Burckhardt. In discussing tribal women and the possibility of adultery committed by them, he reports that, if a husband had clear proof of his spouse's philandering, he accused her before her father and/or brothers. If his accusation was proven (and Burckhardt does not specify how this may be so), then the father or brothers would kill her (Burckhardt 1:110).[9]

We know that contraception and abortion were options available to women in the period and location under review. Midwives, who were in any case important intermediaries in passing on knowledge of erotic practices to women, played an important role with regard to contraception and

---

[8]Hurgronje goes as far as to assert that, in Mecca, the sins of the men are 'much more severely judged' than those of women. How Hurgronje obtained the evidence on which to base his comments about adultery is not clear. Probably, he obtained anecdotal information, in the form of informal remarks in conversation with Meccans—men, to be sure.

[9]Future research should examine the literature on Arabian Bedouin law to see whether Hurgronje's milder version (albeit oriented to the urban scene) or Burckhardt's harsher version on women's indiscretions is more accurate.

abortion too. Contraceptive drugs were widely available, and while male physicians did have access to and dispensed them, it was primarily the midwives who played this part. They were considered to be so sure of the efficacy of their drugs that they agreed to refund the money for their medications in the event that pregnancy occurred.

As for abortion, a broad range of positions were held by the jurists of the four Sunni schools of law. While all held that abortion in the final four months is prohibited, differences across these schools may be found with regard to the earlier months. It is probably the case that stricter attitudes prevailed in the context of Arabian society at that time, which was mainly ruled by Shafi'i jurisprudence, although, as noted earlier, the Ottomans sought to impose Hanafi law. At any rate, midwives were known to offer abortion services to women who were further on in their pregnancies, although they would not carry them out on a Friday, because that would constitute a 'double sin'—that is, performing a late-term abortion and doing so on the day of prayer (ibid. 105).

Marriage and divorce

There is a consensus in literature on the family in Arabia during the period under review about the frequency of marriage and divorce. As already indicated, this is not a matter of polygyny but has to do with the inclination of men to marry and divorce repeatedly, as well as of women to seek marriage but also, at least among some of them, to prod their husbands into divorcing them so that they could remarry. Thus, Burckhardt categorically states that, although most of the Bedouin he met were monogamous, they tended to marry and divorce over and over again. 'Divorces are so common among the Aenezes [i.e., the members of the 'Aniza tribe] that they even take place during the wife's pregnancy' (Burckhardt 1:110–11). These women, he wrote, could initiate 'a kind of divorce' from their husbands through the simple tactic of fleeing their home to the abode of a relative. Although the husband could try to retrieve her through blandishments, he could not force her to return. As noted earlier, however, he did have the option of not divorcing her, thereby preventing her from remarrying. Burckhardt, himself, came across many cases of such women who were forced to live alone (ibid. 112).

We are told that paternal first cousins were customarily expected to marry each other. The male's claim upon his female paternal first cousin did not automatically mean that the two would be married. However, should it transpire that they did not, the woman would have to obtain his permission to marry someone else (ibid. 113).

Among Meccans, marriage was initiated by female relatives making inquiries with the kin of desirable matches. If these relatives reported back with positive news, the father or another older male would visit that family and finalize the arrangements. On the other hand, outsiders—for example, pilgrims—seeking marriage in Mecca were required to use marriage brokers, who constituted an important social group in the cities and towns of the Hijaz at that time (Hurgronje 85, 125–6).

It might be considered that Bedouin in that society and period might have felt fewer constraints than the townspeople with regard to whom they would give their daughters to in marriage. Although the sources do not provide details, it is generally well-known that certain tribes held other tribes in low esteem and would therefore be reluctant to enter into marital alliances with them. This might also have colored the attitude of tribesmen toward those who lived in the towns. In this connection, among the 'Aniza tribe, for example, fathers would not permit their daughters to marry artisans, peasants or even townspeople. Unlike the 'Aniza, however, this attitude did not pertain among the tribes of northern Arabia (Burckhardt 1:109–10).

Single women, whether previously unmarried or widows, were considered a burden on families who were not well-to-do. Such women might seek 'a position as temporary life-companion of a man', as that status would accrue to her a dower, housing, food, and clothes. The man, if he were wealthy, might even provide a slave for her (Hurgronje 85). If the woman were independently wealthy, she might seek marriage as a means to liberate herself from the control of a family whom she felt constrained her freedom too much. The advantage of such a match for the husband was the possibility that this spouse might make some of her assets available to her husband. However, if the new husband proved undesirable, she had the option of 'bring[ing] about a separation' (ibid.).

These comments by Hurgronje are somewhat puzzling. He does not explain what a 'temporary life-companion of a man' means. The 'position' seems to be that of marital status, with the difference that the woman is not serious about permanently remaining in the marriage. On the other hand, could it refer to prostitution? Yet, this seems highly unlikely, given the extreme punishment for that practice.

Although women might marry several times during their lifetimes, the suggested figure of between a dozen and two dozen times (ibid. 86) does not seem credible, and there were men in their mid-forties among the Bedouin who were reported to have married fifty times (Burckhardt 1: 111–12), which seems highly improbable. Men were constrained by several factors from marrying many times in their lives, including regard for the wife's family, the expense of a new marriage, the expense of divorcing, and, at times, regard for his wife (Hurgronje 86).

Despite these constraints, it is clear that men did repeatedly divorce their wives, 'while only in the rarest cases does the woman belong to but one man in her life' (ibid. 87). Discussing the situation among Meccans, Hurgronje puts it bluntly:

> So the man is glad to be continually changing his wife as he ever seeks for something better, while the woman knows how to make herself tolerably comfortable in most situations ... Let it be here expressly stated that also more favorable instances are not wanting, but the char-acteristic note of the usual Meccan marriage is the seamy-sidedness that we have above depicted. (Ibid. 92–3)

First paternal cousin marital ties were stated to be more durable, as divorcing one's first paternal cousin was considered by public opinion to be scandalous, unless the wife herself requested it (ibid. 86). Next to such marriages, the most durable were those among the very poor, because the spouses of such families, already close to destitute, would be made even poorer upon divorcing (ibid. 87).

Women seeking divorce could do so legally in certain circumstances, including severe ill treatment, failure of the husband to provide her with housing, clothing, or food, the husband's sexual impotence, or his mental infirmity. Hurgronje alleges that wealthy women might even purchase a divorce from their husbands, but perhaps the most common means was to make things 'so hot' for their husbands that they would willingly let them go. In other words, informal methods without recourse to the law were more frequently utilized than legal arguments before a judge based on entitlements provided by the *Shari'a* (ibid.). Alternatively, the couple might make certain oral statements at the time of their marriage that could serve as a basis of divorce. For example, the wife might get her husband to agree to give her a divorce in one or more of the following circumstances: (a) she would give up her right to be supported; (b) she would declare that she would be willing to have the husband's female relatives come to live with her; (c) she would declare that she was prepared to take over the direction of the affairs of the household. If the husband refused to grant divorce upon her making such pronouncements, he would be held in contempt by public opinion, even though the *Shari'a* contained no provisions compelling him to grant it (ibid.).

Shi'i influence was not insignificant in the Hijaz during the period under review in this study. The Shi'i practice of *mut'a* (temporary marriage, called by some legalized prostitution) was also a convention among some Sunnis of the region at that time, even though it was not permitted by the Sunni schools of law. Generally speaking the community ethos condemned *mut'a* marriage, but some Meccans told Hurgronje that opinions on it varied among those who hailed from the oldest community in the city. His wry comment on this situation was that although Sunni law forbids *mut'a*,

> the practice of the Sunnites in this as in many other cases is so divergent from the tenor of the law that while contractual time limits invalidate the marriage offer, verbal promises and agreements of all kinds outside the marriage contract are morally binding. (Ibid. 124–5)

Sunnis resorting to *mut'a* tended to be outsiders who were in Mecca temporarily. A man might propose a short-term marriage to a woman. If willing, the woman would calculate the amount of the marriage payment for the monthly subsistence stipend (including for the three month *'idda*— or period of waiting before she could remarry), and demand the total payment in advance. Should he agree, the *mut'a* is 'smuggled in by the Sunnites themselves', even though the institution was widely denounced as a heretical practice (ibid.).

Despite the frequency with which women were divorced in that society, the sources suggest that multiple divorces did not adversely impact on a woman's reputation (Burckhardt 1:111). Hurgronje in fact maintains several times that women expected to be divorced and sought divorce as a strategy to remarry in hopes of securing a better match. Doughty holds that Bedouin women ensnared in unhappy marriages publicly portrayed their alienation, being 'ready to forsake his wedlock and household, thus

putting upon him a common scorn, because he will not dismiss her'
(Doughty 1:273)[10]

Elopement as a drastic means of divorcing one's husband is also
discussed in the literature. Burckhardt gives an account of an Arab
tribesman who abducted and eloped with another man's wife and took
refuge in the tent of a third party. By killing a sheep, the third party was
considered by custom to have married the pair. Among the 'Aniza tribe,
the abducted woman then returned to the residence of her parents and
awaited her original husband's pronouncement of divorce. Meanwhile, the
abductor, in his capacity as the *dakhil* (literally, he who has entered) of the
family to whose tent he had taken his partner in elopement, remained safe
from the original husband's vengeance (Burckhardt 1:113). It would be of
interest for future research to investigate how closely these actions
conformed to the practices in the pre-Islamic and early Islamic periods
regarding men, women, and children taken captive (*saby*).

The situation was more serious among the Arab tribes of the Red Sea and
the Hijaz, however. There, an elopement, while a rare event, was treated
very severely. If the woman were unmarried, her relatives were legally
permitted to kill the abductor on the day of the elopement, without being
liable for blood money, although they had to pay it if they killed him after
that (ibid. 278–9). In one case related by Burckhardt, an Arab eloped with
a married woman of the tribe. Her husband's brother overtook the eloper
and severely wounded him. When the man recovered, the matter was
presented for arbitration. The eloper had to pay sixty camels, provide one
male and one female slave, one free girl, whom the original husband might
marry without having to pay her bride price, a fine dagger, and the drome-
dary upon which the couple had fled. The judgment was so severe that it
financially ruined not only the eloper but also his relatives (ibid. 279).

Women's legal rights

The *Shari'a* accords certain legal rights to women, some of which have
already been noted with regard to their initiating formal divorce proceedings before a judge. This was permitted by the original Hanafi understanding
of the law, albeit later Hanafi jurists altered this so that the right applied

---

[10]Doughty adds: 'The fugitive bedouin wife has good leave to run whethersoever she
would; she is free as the desert, there is none can detain her.'

only to a woman who had already been married. It will be remembered that the Ottomans sought to impose the Hanafi system of law. But customary law also must be considered when the matter of women's conduct is under review. Among the most significant features is women's ability to attend public festivals, feasts, and commemorations of various kinds. Women had to obtain their husbands' permission to attend such events, but if their husbands refused, they would be in for an unpleasant time for an extended period and would be subject to the mockery of their wives' friends and relatives (Hurgronje 49). Generally, they would find it wiser to yield to their wives' demands on these occasions. It should be stressed that the ability of women to attend these events and ceremonies was not necessarily a right, codified in law, but it appears to have become a norm or at least customarily expected.

Women's customary rights were also exercised when women wanted to make the pilgrimage. If the husband had the means, he had no right to deny his wife the costs of carrying out this religious obligation. Furthermore, visits to saints' tombs were also included among the customary rights of women, and a husband who denied his wife the means to make such visits would be considered a reprobate. The same applied, though to a lesser degree, to visits she might want to make to her female friends' homes (ibid. 77–8). Husbands, we are told, often sought to restrict their wives' hosting visits from friends and relatives because they feared that if they did not object to such visits, their wives would take it as a sign of weakness and escalate their demands over time. The wives 'become more impudent on the occasion of each concession made by him and the object of their visits is indeed merely exploitation in some form. So married couples share together neither joy nor sorrow, neither good nor bad, outside of the bed' (ibid. 91–2).

Women had rights to property and many feared their husband's efforts to control their assets. The *Shari'a* protects these rights, and the marriage contract, notes Hurgronje, 'grants a claim to money only to the wife' (ibid. 91). Women might waive their rights to their financial holdings in favor of their husbands, should the latter fall into poverty, but they had to be careful on this point, because some men would claim bankruptcy while being still solvent, in the hope that by this ruse they might gain control of their wife's property. Hurgronje concludes that 'the Meccan women prefer to bury their money underground or entrust it to good friends rather than bring it into the nuptial dwelling' (ibid.).

On the whole, the women of Mecca appear to have enjoyed more rights than women elsewhere, at least as far as other towns were concerned. We are told that Meccan women had 'a peculiar independent position which they could hardly win elsewhere'. This statement is presented in the context of Meccan women's customary rights, which in fact appeared to be in contravention of Islamic law. They apparently claimed the right to remain in Mecca when their husbands went abroad on business trips or other long journeys (ibid. 88).

Slave women also had certain legal entitlements. By law, a man who introduced a slave into his house had to wait a certain period of time before having relations with her in order for the paternity of any children to be clear, although Meccan men tended to honor this stipulation in the breach, rather than in the practice. On the other hand, pregnant slaves in deeply contentious relations with their masters over the paternity of the child could not be kept in limbo; as a matter of customary practice, the man was obliged to free her so that she could enter into a contract with someone else. If he denied paternity in order to be free to sell her to someone else, he would be denounced. 'Only scoundrels deny their children so as to be able again to sell the slave girl' (ibid. 108).

Another right of slaves, or rather of their offspring, related to how their children might be regarded. At least in theory, a child of a slave mother and her master was to be treated as an equal of the children of her master and a free-born Arab woman. 'In general . . . in every well-to-do family sons of both kinds of mothers, the free and the slave woman, are represented, but no difference in appearance or mutual behavior' (ibid. 109).

Women and the economy

We do not have a great deal of information on the participation of women in the economy for the period under review. The sources provide only a few observations. Hurgronje essentially relates Meccan women's work to the pilgrimage. He maintains that they assisted their husbands in whatever businesses they would engage in that served the pilgrimage economy. He then rather enigmatically adds: 'They not only help their husbands faithfully in their business, but also work on their own account' (ibid. 88). Since he does not specify his meaning, it is left to the reader to guess this. It could mean that some Meccan women had their own stalls, for example, and sold wares. But it could have another meaning, which may seem more likely in the light of Hurgronje's comment immediately after:

> We have already seen how easily a Meccan woman can get rid of distasteful marriage bonds: we can now understand why continued change in marriage is pleasing to most of them. Their wares in the pilgrim market are their charms; the oftener the charms are made the subject of new contracts, the better for business. The relation between demand and supply in Meccan society is strongly influenced by the concourse of strangers. A Meccan man . . . does not allow himself to be beguiled by the daughters of Mecca, as a stranger does, but the demand on the part of the strangers makes it easy for the Meccan woman to stipulate for great advantages for themselves. (Ibid. 89)[11]

The implication is participation in prostitution, although Hurgronje expresses it in terms of these women's marriages with the strangers who visit Mecca during pilgrimage. True to his overall view that the women of the town knew how to pursue their own interests, he relates that such marriages lasted until the husband's money ran out, which was the cue for the women to 'seek a new wedded position with the help of her friends' (ibid.).

It is worth noting here that this picture is very different from that presented by the Orientalists, who make women the object of men's sexual appetites. Hurgronje, while not denying that the men sexually exploited women, insists that women exploited men as well.

The employment of Bedouin women in smaller towns is something that anthropologists have commented upon. For the period and location under review in this study, evidence of female labor in the smaller towns and wilderness areas is provided by Doughty and Burckhardt. At one point in his travels, Doughty found himself in Burayda, in the Qasim in Najd. He expresses surprise at seeing women selling 'green stuff' (i.e., coffee) in the market. In addition, he reports 'a few poor saleswomen' in 'Unayza, another town in the Qasim region of Najd. And in Khaybar, he reports on

---

[11]He seems to be suggesting in this passage that women in the market were unveiled. We do not know, since he does not say so explicitly, but it is worth noting that veiling the face would not necessarily prevent women from 'showing their charms', which they might do by their behavior, for example.

a widow who 'held a small shop of all wares, where I sometimes bought bread' (Doughty 2:349, 404).

Women's role in the world of festivals, saints, spirits and cures

One of the most important social practices in the realm of festivals was the phenomenon of *al-Qis* [*al-Ges*], which took place during the four days of the annual pilgrimage to Mecca during which the pilgrims left the city to perform the rites at Arafat, Muzdalifa and Mina. The festival of *al-Qis* began in the eleventh century, so by the late Ottoman to early post-Ottoman period, it had become well-established in the community. It only disappeared, we are told, in the 1960s (Nasr and Bagader). The able-bodied male population of the city went with the pilgrims to serve them, and it was considered contemptible for any of their number to remain behind. Accordingly, the city was given over to the women, and the only males who stayed behind were the elderly and the young boys. The women dressed as men and processed from neighborhood to neighborhood, engaging in performances, playing instruments and singing songs. Each neighborhood would have its own procession, as well as spectators, with some boys joining the women.

Al-Qis (which etymologically comes from a root that has connotations of mimicry) essentially was an interlude in which women imitated male social conduct, but accompanied with verses in song, replete with innuendo and irony implying that men did not appreciate women as human beings but only as sexual objects. One of the women would dress up as the Sharif and others as members of the *'ulama'*, while yet others would play the parts of the shaykhs of the various quarters of the city, and even the policemen, complete with false beards and mustaches. Although imitation in general could theoretically proceed in some neutral manner, the behavior of the women during *al-Qis* certainly contained strong undertones of rebellion—which, however, was kept in check. The only female role was that of a gazelle, an animal that symbolized the Arab ideal of a beautiful maiden. The 'gazelle' was a wooden model, draped with fabric, the whole being incorporated into a costume that was worn by a woman who would take the lead in the procession. Individual actors' performances were evaluated and the entire four days thus had very much the aura of a carnival.

During the year, there were commemorations of saints' days, celebrations of festivals, participation in spirit sessions, cures and exorcisms.
These all provided opportunities for women to involve themselves in
public arenas. As a general rule, the three months following the end of the
annual *hajj* were a period when family life became livelier than before
because, with the end of the pilgrimage, businesses associated with it
slowed, providing scope for more attention to family matters. This was
apparently a period particularly popular for weddings and the feasts associated with them (Hurgronje 48).

Another important period on the calendar was the fifteenth to eighteenth
days of the sixth lunar month, Jumada al-Akhira, in which Meccans celebrated the anniversary of Shaykh Mahmud ibn Ibrahim al-Adham, a famous
revered sufi. The event was 'joyfully looked forward to by the daughters
of the Meccans and still more by their wives'. Shaykh Mahmud's tomb
was located along the western border of Jeddah, 'and for about three days
they [the women] occupy the entire precincts' (ibid. 48–9). These women
would insist that their spouses provide funds for their needs (clothing,
jewelry, food) to celebrate the occasion in due style. Husbands who refused
their permission for their wives to attend the ceremonies of the Shaykh
Mahmud festival would hear no end of it from their disappointed wives,
and also be the subject of ridicule by the other women (ibid. 49). Part of
the women's expenses included rental payments to Bedouin who would let
their huts to them, and additional expenses were incurred for the entertainment that would take place in these huts, including professional singers. In
an interesting evolution of the entertainment in honor of Shaykh Mahmud,
the observances gradually became transformed into occasions for sybaritic
displays, such as the recitation of poems, whose contents were almost
always erotic. As the women became more uninhibited in their conduct,
they substituted more vulgar language for the 'conventional amatory effu-
sions'. As they became caught up in events, they might even risk making
fun of the Ottoman Wali, as happened when he visited Jeddah in 1885
(ibid. 50). During the Shaykh Mahmud celebrations, women would drink
green and also black tea, smoke water pipes, and gossip. Lesbian liaisons
were part of the story, as reported by Hurgronje, who also notes that some
women also used the occasion for trysts with male lovers (ibid. 51).[12]

[12]It is not clear from the sources what the connection was between this saint and women's
activity in his lifetime.

Other feast days included the last Wednesday in the month of Safar, which was supposed to be a sad occasion because the month was believed to be a time of mischief, and people were meant to pray to avoid such mischief, but the common people came to commemorate the day as a joyous occasion, in a syncretistic transformation. Both men and women apparently spent that day riding, picnicking, and attending 'pleasure parties' (ibid. 46).[13]

On 12 Rabi' al-Awwal, considered the day of the death of the Prophet but retroactively also commemorated as his birthday, Meccans observed 'a great feast day'. The women not only wore fine dresses in the mosque, but they also took with them their children, similarly dressed up in even finer accoutrements, multi-colored and bedecked with gold and silver and many amulets that generated much tinkling. Although the devout in the mosque took umbrage, the ceremony nonetheless had been taking place for a long time. Hurgronje observes:

In the town chronicles we read how more than 300 years ago the feast was celebrated in like manner, and how certain rigorists declared themselves against it, because this procession and the unsupervised concourse of so many women out of doors excited rather immorality than pious thoughts. In this respect things have by no means changed. (Ibid. 47)

Hurgronje's evidence about women attending mosques wearing their finery should be considered in the light of the ongoing debates concerning women's presence there in earlier periods. His suggestion that they entered such spaces is of great interest, albeit this activity was restricted to the special ceremonial day of the Prophet's birthday.

The feast known as *sirara* similarly was an occasion for women (and men) to celebrate. It marked the return of a pilgrim from a visit to the Prophet's tomb in the mosque in Medina (the site of which has since been destroyed). The women apparently feasted more intensely than the men. The returning pilgrim waited outside the precincts of Mecca and entered the city the next day. The celebrations began after the post-sunset prayer and continued late into the night. On this occasion, the ladies 'enjoy countless cups of tea, glasses of sorbet, and hubble-bubble pipes, as well as . . .

[13]To the best of my knowledge, non-traveler accounts do not discuss these parties.

erotic songs' (ibid. 123).[14] Hurgronje notes that the pomp and circum-
stance of the celebrations is incommensurate with the sobriety required
when entering the city of God. The fine clothes worn by the returnee
contrast sharply with the custom of entering Mecca dressed in the simplest
clothing. However, even the *'ulama'* appeared to be resigned to this
flagrant violation of the code of ethics that required simplicity and humility
when entering God's house (ibid.).

Other occasions, not linked to the calendar, in which women would
participate included the purification ceremonies held forty days after childbirth, where mothers would invite their friends and eat and drink together.
The women took the infant to the mosque, where God's protection was
solicited, and after the ceremony at the mosque was completed, they
resumed their merrymaking. Similarly, women played a role in infants'
naming ceremonies as well as in the circumcision of children (ibid. 110–14).

On the issue of cures, it was the habit of husbands to seek their wife's
advice because women were considered to be more knowledgeable about
illness and medications. Male doctors would be invited in the event of the
more uncommon diseases, even though their 'recipes' for cures were
considered to be 'essentially the same' as the women's. Belief in evil
spirits and their targeting of expectant mothers especially led the latter to
wear belts over which a man with religious status had uttered some words
to avert their spells. Advice was acquired on the timing of conception and,
after the birth of children, mothers would try to ward off the evil spirits'
efforts to harm their infants (ibid. 93, 99).

One of the most important phenomena concerning spirits for women in
Arabia during the period under review was the *zar*. The *zar* was a form of
spirit that afflicted almost all women. Hurgronje relates that in days of yore, a
woman possessed by a *zar* was considered insane, whereas in his own time,
she was considered beset with hysteria. Among the symptoms of a woman
possessed by a *zar* were convulsions. Treatment was confided to an older
woman whom the community considered to be a specialist in dealing with *zar*.

The *zar* in Arabia apparently originated in Ethiopia. The migration of
Ethiopians to the Hijaz and other locations in the Peninsula brought the

---

[14]These activities were suppressed after 1924, but it is hard to say whether this occurred
because of the new Wahhabi administration's antipathy toward women's public role, its
opposition to *bid'a* (of which devotion to saints was a key example), or both. We cannot
read back from the present period to find evidence of motivations for an earlier era.

concept and cult of the *zar* there. All the ethnic groups in Mecca experienced *zar* possession, albeit they are believed to have had varying ways of exorcizing *zar*. The custom was to rely upon the *shaykhat al-zar*, an old woman who, attending the stricken woman, communicated with the *zar* directly. Hurgronje says that a successful outcome always ensued, and the spirit committed itself to abandon the body it had possessed provided that a new dress or trinket was given. Because the *zar* itself could not accept such gifts, they had to be presented to the possessed woman.

Given the importance of clothing and jewelry to women, it is not surprising that the *zar* ceremony of exorcism had become a key feature of the social scene. Women routinely said they must go to a *zar*, meaning to a gathering for an exorcism. Some women were known to tell their husbands: 'It is high time for me to give a Zar, for I have been to so many at my friends.' If the husband refused, she would throw tantrums, in the face of which the husband would either divorce her or yield. But, Hurgronje notes, the custom was so deeply rooted that his new wife would also eventually make the same demands. He concludes that the the *zar* could lead to the ruin of a family: 'It is no rare thing for all the prosperity and even the means of support of a middle class family to be sacrificed to the Zar' (ibid. 100–3).

The state's impact on the status of women

The Tanzimat reforms in the Ottoman Empire (1839–1876), which focused upon citizenship and the religious rights of that state's subjects, were not extended to the Arabian Peninsula. In the Hijaz, developments within the Ottoman Empire had relatively little impact. With regard to the role of women, we have evidence of the Sharif of Mecca organizing a major festival in which women participated, but this was in the nature of an isolated event, albeit an important one. He held a celebration on the occasion of the circumcision of his children, and on the final day of this celebration, he arranged for women singers—presumably professionals— to participate in the ceremonies. On the whole, however, the impact of the local state on Arabian women presumably was manifested in its not interfering in matters affecting their status in society as a whole or in their local communities within that society. The local state intervened on the occasion of what Hurgronje has termed 'All Souls' Day', which was commemorated annually in earlier times as an occasion when people would visit the Ma'la Cemetery in Mecca to say prayers for the dead. The occasion, however, became one where men and women would arrange illicit assignations. Accordingly, the Sharifian state prohibited the mixing of the sexes at the cemetery on that day, allowing women on Thursday afternoons until sunset and then clearing the area of women and allowing men to enter thereafter (ibid. 40–53).[15]

Conclusions

Our state of knowledge about the family and the role of women in Arabia in the late Ottoman and early post-Ottoman period remains sketchy. A number of issues remain unanswered, pending further research. The major discrepancy has to do with the repeated observation that women were considered inferior to men, while they also had a large degree of autonomy from men with regard to decisions directly affecting their lives.

It is a commonplace among scholars that women had no political power to speak of in that era, but a reconsideration of the available sources suggests that the matter is not so easily disposed of as this conventional view maintains. Burckhardt, speaking of the Begoum Arabs (whom he does not further identify), notes that they were led, at the time he encountered them, by a widow named Ghaliya. His description of her implies a woman of high status in her community.

> She herself possessed more wealth than any Arab family in the neighborhood. She distributed money and provisions among all the poor of her tribe, who were ready to fight the Turks. Her table was open to all faithful Wahabys, whose chiefs held their councils in her house . . . Her voice was not only heard, but generally prevailed. And she actually governed the Begoum, although they had a nominal chief, or sheikh . . . The Turkish soldiers' fears soon magnified her influence and importance; they regarded her as chief of the united Wahabys and reported the most absurd stories respecting her powers as a sorceress, bestowing her personal favors on all the Wahaby leaders, who, by her means, were rendered invincible. (Burckhardt 2:268–9)

[15]Incidentally, the state's interference did not prevent some 'lusty youths' nevertheless from continuing to accost women and to communicate with them in 'fairly elaborate conversation with gestures from a distance' (Hurgronje 53–4).

Obviously, this story of a single tribal woman cannot be the basis for any generalizations regarding women and political power. Anecdotal evidence, however, suggests that one should not be surprised to learn that they were mobile beyond the domestic scene. According to one source, for example, in the period 1885/86–1888/89 the municipal council of the town of Jeddah (*baladiyyat Jidda*) had a membership of seventeen persons, and among these was 'a Turkish mid-wife' (al-Ansari 288). This, of course, tells us nothing about any role in municipal affairs that may have been played by Arab women. The most that can be said is that one cannot rule out the possibility of one or maybe more of them serving in comparable positions in the area during the time under review in this study.

We have seen that both tribal and urban women were able to make demands upon men in order to promote their own interests. Presumably, if women were considered confined to 'a life of weary servitude' (Doughty 1:277), and if 'the women's sex is despised by the old nomad and divine law in Moses' (ibid. 280), there could be no question of companionship on the basis of some modicum of parity between male and female. But such companionship was evidenced earlier in this study in the discussion of husbands and their wives providing hospitality to guests, for example.

And it is also shown by no less a source than Doughty, who generally provides the darkest interpretation of the status of women in Arabian society in the late Ottoman to early post-Ottoman period. Thus, he recounts a narrative on the siege of 'Unayza. The story demonstrates the resolve of the town's women to assist their men in a battle with the forces of the Wahhabis, who were beleaguering that city with a very large force drawn from Eastern Najd, al-Hasa and even Amman. He writes that the 'Aniza women 'were come forth to the battle driving asses and girbies [water skins]. They poured out water for the thirsty fighters; and took up the wounded men' (ibid. 2:459–60). This story also accords with historical chronicles in earlier centuries of Islam, when women were known to play this role in the heat of battles between rival groups, though themselves, of course, not participating in the fighting.

The behavior of women, as discussed in this paper, was certainly influenced by social trends taking place in the wider society. The most outstanding example of this phenomenon is the annual pilgrimage to Mecca, which provided to such women opportunities to participate in the market to serve the pilgrims. As we have seen, on the testimony of

Hurgronje in particular, the market in question was both an economic market and a marriage market. It only remains to add that the marriage market cannot be separated from the economic context of the commodity market in which they sold wares to the pilgrims, since marriage with the latter was also to a very significant extent a matter of economic considerations.

The pilgrimage is also a period that provides striking evidence of women's criticism of men's tendencies to take them for granted, or even denigrate them. As we saw with regard to the *al-Qis* festival, 'the participants in *al-Qis* processions repeated songs that mocked the traditional norms of their society, its institutions, and its leading personalities' (Nasr and Bagader 254). Essentially, role reversals provided the ammunition for women seeking to send a message that they were just as capable as men.

A methodological issue that needs to be raised relates to the observations made by the sources upon which this article relies. It was not always possible to distinguish the writers' own personal opinions and biases from the cultural norms and values that they were commenting upon. For example, if the sources speak of the inferiority of women to men, to what extent does this characterization capture the ethos of the society? And to what extent is it rather colored by the writers' own commitment to this view, based on what would, in the end, have to be their outsider perspective on the role of women in that society? No matter how friendly the relations of these authors became with men, such friendship could not translate into their being able to access the innermost thoughts and feelings of the men's women. On that account, it would be very interesting to have available to us sources written by contemporary women, for example. It would be unusual if differences in perspective on the family and on women did not emerge between the observations and interpretations of European men and Arab women.

More broadly speaking, none of the sources suggests that relationships between husbands and wives were based on affectionate feelings or a spirit of mutuality and reciprocity. Since evidence of this latter has not been encountered, one cannot affirm that such feelings and spirit dominated the conjugal relationship. But, without trying to suggest that they were prevalent everywhere and at all times, the perspective that they were nearly totally absent in Arabia at that time seems to beg the question and must be rejected as Orientalist essentializing.

Who were the women we have been talking about? What did they want? What were the limits on their demands? They were probably not extremely indigent, but apart from that, we are speaking in general terms about large numbers of rural and urban women from various class, ethnic, and geographical backgrounds. What did they want? They wanted to be able to decide for themselves whether or not to go on visits and outings, to attend a festival, to go to parties, to listen to entertainers, and the like. Some wanted the authority to initiate divorce proceedings, others to have access to contraception or even abortion. Some were willing to risk public opprobrium by arranging assignations with their lovers. They clearly did not want (at least on the evidence available for this study) political power, the power to make decisions of a financial nature, parity with their husbands with regard to social intercourse in public arenas, and the like.

What were the limits upon their demands? They were a combination of customary and written law, as well as normative expectations in the community about what was possible and what was not. One is tempted to say that constraints on their behavior inhered more in the customs and traditions of the people of Arabia in the period under review than in the formal *Shari'a* provisions regulating any of these issues, and still less the power of the state to sanction them according to its interpretations of what was right and wrong.

Finally, it seems that the picture that has been drawn is at some variance with the standard depictions in a good deal of the literature about Arabian women in the period under review. In this regard, I draw the reader's attention back to the first section of this article, in which evidence on the role of women in the pre-Ottoman period, even though sketchy, provides depictions of women enjoying considerable autonomy in the realms of education, culture and philanthropy. On the other hand, as we saw in the main body of this study, signs of such autonomy continued to be seen in the late Ottoman to early post-Ottoman period. Further research is needed, however, to articulate the variations (and the continuities) beyond what has been shown here.

12. *The Family in Gulf History*

AMIRA EL-AZHARY SONBOL

Following worldwide trends, interest in Gulf family history has grown in popularity during the past few decades. Each year sees the publication of a number of tribal histories, illustrated with elaborate genealogical diagrams showing tribal ancestry and clan relationships. Curiosity about ancestors is perhaps natural and reflects the same avid quest for roots that has led thousands in Europe and America to search archives and family papers, and undertake the collection of oral histories to put together a narrative of their origins and who they are, in order to give themselves a sense of history and a space in a world that is becoming increasingly generic.

For people of the Arabian Gulf, interest in ancestry is nothing new; genealogical knowledge can almost be described as central to tribal discourses about clan and tribal alliances, upon which political relations and security in unfriendly desert environments are highly dependent. Drawing lines and connecting tribes to each other through blood or matrimonial links, or by building genealogies, confirms clans' origination from ever wider tribal configurations. Given the constant appearance of new kin formations as clans grow and split, keeping track of these relations constitutes part of tribal lore, about which poets wrote and tribal historians wove stories, some historical, others more imaginative.

What is new about this modern search for ancestry and construction of tribal family trees in Gulf countries is that they are taking place in an age of nation-state building and modernization; models used as a basis for historical research were adopted from the West and most of the early historians and political scientists writing about the Gulf focus on ruling families and the establishment of contending power centers. Even though interest in tribal genealogy was nothing new for these Arab countries, the differences are rather striking between what was a search for *nasab*, or relationships through ancestors, which was the focus of tribal genealogical memories, and the contemporary construction of genealogies based on a pyramidical approach, leading from an existing tribe/clan today and back to a particular point or points of legitimacy in the past. Earlier, pre-modern, interest in *nasab* is reflected in medieval literature that produced *tabaqat* works (biographical dictionaries), organized according to particular generations of important Muslims, ordered according to their proximity to the life of the Prophet Muhammad. The new contemporary tribal genealogical studies can be said to have begun with Western curiosity about the world of Islam, which focused on leaders and rulers and their families, a traditional method used to map out histories of Europe's nobility.[1]

Most important with regard to the historiography of the Gulf, while tribal narratives spoke consistently about clan affiliations through the mother and the father with equal pride (*madh*) or censure (*hija'*) depending on the context, modern genealogical trees all but eliminate any mention of women, except in rare cases. This is very problematic for women's history. Presenting history through diagrams and family trees gives the impression of unbiased facts, of 'truths' representing realities, when in fact such representation supports the deployment of discourses of patriarchy that obfuscate reality and construct images that in turn build new realities. This is particularly relevant, and at the same time effective for paradigm building, for societies that have been normatively understood to be patrilineal and patriarchal, as Arab society has always been presented. Models of 'patrilineality' and 'patriarchy' that have become the lenses through which particular societies all over the world are understood, no matter the subtleties of difference pointed out and elaborated on by social scientists, form a barrier to deconstructing representations in order to grasp the hidden realities of gender relations. When the starting point is belief in a

---

[1]Lane-Poole's *The Mohammedan Dynasties*, which first appeared in 1894, is perhaps the earliest, while von Zambaur's *Manuel de généalogie et de chronologie pour l'histoire de l'Islam* is the most used.

gendered division of society, that is the image one ends up with, and the paradigm becomes all-encompassing. Differentiating between relations within the home and relations outside the home further complicates the picture, although this division pushes further the dominant paradigm of women's seclusion, which has been successfully contested by scholars and researchers, but which continues to be accepted as a basis for under-standing how Arab Gulf families live and their members interact.

In other words, the construction of genealogical trees has helped in confirming and extending a model that becomes debatable once the reali-ties of Arab history are studied. Mapping or diagramming family ancestry has led to the establishment of new paradigms of gender relations because women are eliminated from these genealogies. The usual simplistic read-ings of these mappings become image-building representations of 'womenless communities', where women actually disappeared altogether from observed space. Once paradigms of 'womenless' public spheres were accepted, and as other modern technologies of representation were intro-duced, other forms of invisibility reinforced this image of womenlessness. The example of photography raises interesting questions. If the life of women in Gulf societies is to be studied through contemporary pictures, the absence of women (except for a few important personalities) in public pictures, would give the impression that women either do not exist in Arabia or are never allowed out of the home. A walk through the markets of any shopping center in any city in the Arabian Gulf today will show that such an image is totally false, as it is false in schools, universities, govern-ment offices and private businesses, where women constitute a significant proportion of students and workers. One question that could be asked here is why Arab women were consistently drawn and photographed by Western travelers early in the twentieth century while today this is an activity totally frowned upon. What changed during that century to bring about a more patriarchal and seclusionary attitude toward women in Gulf coun-tries, and what is the significance of this for the life of women today?

A survey of books written by Western travelers shows an array of sketches and photographs of women of various classes belonging to tribes dispersed throughout the Arabian Peninsula. Most of these pictures show women veiled (Nicholson 55)[2] in one way or another,

---

[2]Other pictures of women in other parts of Arabia show them completely veiled; for example, the pictures taken by Eleanor Nicholson in eastern Saudi Arabia in the 1950s and

often wearing the *batula* or the *burqaʻ*, but quite often the sketches and photographs are of unveiled women, sometimes pictured working with their men, herding camels or raising water from wells or carrying water back to their encampments (Thesiger 80). We also find images of women as buyers and sellers of fish in the fish market in Abu Dhabi or as 'vendors' and 'harberdashers' sitting in the market with their goods before them, or shopping in the *suq* for food and other items (Condrai 48). In one photograph taken by Ronald Condrai, a woman from the United Arab Emirates is pictured herding six camels, while other pictures show women undertaking the labor-intensive work of bringing up water from wells for the camels and donkeys they are herding (Condrai 84). Similar pictures show women actively involved in herding their clan's herds and caring for them, while others are taking goods to market by donkey, and still others are buying goods and carrying them home. Tribal women were very often photographed spinning and weaving, while pictures of family scenes of mothers and children, women doing domestic work, churning butter or taking down and setting up tents when tribes moved (Doughty 56), and taking care of children (Mauger 44), wives and husbands together, and new brides, were quite popular among Europeans traveling in Arabia. Women were also photographed traveling outside their home towns. In a series of such pictures, four women are shown traveling by camel from Abu Dhabi to Buraimi oasis to escape the summer heat, their luggage being carried by a fifth camel, all being protected by a group of Bedouin guards. As the author explains, the leader of the group of women, a *shaykha*, brought her camel closer to the men to listen to the news being brought by the foreigners (Condrai 60–61). As travelers describe and photograph their travels, they illustrate how Bedouin culture was not a monolith and that norms differed from one tribe to another. In his record of his travels in the Rubʻ al-Khali, Thierry Mauger illustrates how the women of Qahtan and Yam tribes covered half their faces to be photographed in all their tribal silver jewelry, while the Banu Faham did not cover their faces and had no problem with being photographed unveiled, whether alone or with their husbands and children (Mauger 44). Mingling

1960s show the author's daughter with two completely veiled Bedouin women outside their tent at al-Khobar, near Dhahran, where the ARAMCO oil operation was active (Nicholson 8).

between the sexes was also acceptable among these tribes, perhaps
because they were mostly related to each other, as one traveler described:

> In the Arabian small tribes and villages there is a perpetual mingling of
> kindred blood . . . Self-minded, a bold-faced wench, mistress Hirfa cast
> as she should not a pair of eyes upon their herdsman, a likely young
> man, whom in her husband's absence she wooed openly . . . but he was
> prudent, and faithful to his sheykh's service. Here, and though bordering
> the jealous Hejaz and the austere Wahaby Nejd, the Fukara women go
> open-faced, and (where all are kindred) I could never perceive amongst
> them any jealousy of the husbands. (Doughty 64–5)

This article focuses on the history of family in the Gulf; it required research
in records, and family genealogies, and also used oral history, government
records, travelers' accounts, missionary records, traditional histories and
other forms of *turath* (heritage) literature, as well as family law and legal
codes. To write the history of family is a major enterprise; this is but an
attempt that raises questions for further research and points out specific
issues and problems that need intensive investigation. The purpose is to
deconstruct the normative view of family in the Gulf. Because family is
central to the life of the people of the Gulf, as it is worldwide, it is taken
for granted that the family as we know it today has always had the same
structure, and that inter-family relations have therefore always been the
same. More problematic is the belief that the Muslim family today is the
product of, and response to, rules set by the Qur'an. As this study shows,
while the family has always been in existence and has historically constituted the main form of human organization, the structure of the family, as
well as relations between its members, has changed from one period to
another. Moreover, even though the modern Muslim family can be said to
be guided by the Islamic *Shari'a*, the laws by which the family is guided
today are different from the laws of yesterday. The legal systems by which
Muslims live today are the result of a hybridity of laws in which Islamic
principles play a central role, but in which modern laws have had a
dramatic input, including laws that discriminate against women, and that
interpret Islamic law through Victorian lenses. If tribal law fits the patriarchal model, the new legal codes have in fact added another level of
patriarchy.

The study begins with a discussion of family genealogies and focuses on the way women were depicted in early literature, with the intention of showing that descent from the mother was as much a source of tribal pride as descent from the father, and that this sense of family pride based on kinship through father and mother loses its value with the introduction of new philosophies and discourses regarding genealogies. It then discusses the genesis of family laws in their modern context. With the diffusion of law from one country to the other, a normal part of nation-state construction and development of the contemporary world system, a new, gendered division of labor, based on biological function, developed, which became established as part of social norms backed by state actions and new legal and court systems. Central to these gendered discourses is the idea that a woman's place is in the home, and so her role in the public sphere needs to be controlled; she should leave the home only for the sake of family needs and only with the approval of father, husband, brother or male guardian. The problem with this picture is that it takes models that may fit with urban settings and transposes them back to a different time and environment. In a desert environment, 'going out' is a non-issue. There were chores to be undertaken and clan members were kin who lived together and protected each other. Why would permission be needed for a Bedouin woman to leave her tent, for example, when her daily life was as much outside the tent as inside it? It is important to see women's history through the actual lived realities of their time and place; if medieval *fuqaha'* in towns such as Basra, Baghdad or Cairo discussed issues such as a woman's need for permission to leave the family home, their discussions were related to their particular time and place. It is a mistake to try to define the past through discourses valid for other places and times.

Put differently, paradigms and normative representations through which women and family in the Arabian Gulf are studied are inadequate for an understanding of gender relations in the past. Models and forms used by social scientists, particularly historians, construct a concentric model for Arab families, with the nuclear family at the center, with extensions to uncles, aunts and grandparents with whom the nuclear family forms an extended family. In this format, the father is the legal head of the nuclear family, which, as part of the wider extended family, is controlled by the traditions of the larger tribal community and of the nation-state, which gives legitimacy and recognition to the father as legal patriarch over his

wife and minor children. The latter, i.e. wife and children, were thereby
made into adjuncts of the persona of the father as head of the family, the
recognized legal unit at the heart of state-laws, their identity and citizenship rights subsumed under that of the father/husband. In this situation,
women are legally under the control of their husbands, and traditionally
under the control of their clans and the uncodified traditional laws of clan
and tribe. This model is real for today's women and is the reality against
which they have to exist and exert efforts for change. Traditionally,
husbands had power over wife and children, but marital relations were
guided and negotiated through tribal norms rather than through state codes
enforced by state power and authority. The differences are dramatic, as
this study will show. Much of the life of women in the Gulf today is the
result of the historical context in which they find themselves. That context
includes the changes brought about by oil-wealth and its impact on family
structure, socio-economic changes with their deep structural impact on
social relations, and the historical transformations that are taking place as
a consequence of nation-state building and the introduction of concepts of
citizenship involving the modernization of legal codes and the introduction of new legal systems with philosophies, structures and practices
different from those that existed before.

Women and family lineage

In his introduction to his history of Arab tribes, *Saba'ik al-dhahab fi
ma'rifat qaba'il al-'Arab'* in 1920, the Iraqi author Abu al-Fuz al-Baghdadi, explains that he wrote his book to correct Shihab al-Din
al-Qalqashandi's (1356–1418) *Nihayat al-irab fi ma'rifat ansab al-'Arab*,
considered the most important source on *ansab* (plural of *nasab*) produced
in medieval Islamic history.

> [it] is the best written about the science of *nasab* . . . [Qalqashandi]
> managed to gather [the names of] many *qaba'il* (tribes) and *shu'ub*
> (peoples); however, [he] organized [them] according to alphabetical
> order so that, if someone wanted to connect the relationship (*nasab*) of
> a recent tribe to an early tribe, he would have to look in many places and
> review multiple locations. For example, if he wants to connect the *nasab*
> of Bani al-'Abid to Qahtan, he would need to look first under the letters

'*alif*' and '*lam*' . . . then move to '*sin*' then to '*qaf*' then to '*hah*' then to '*shin*' . . . I wanted to organize things differently and use a different methodology (*uslub*) and that by *connecting the most recent tribe with its origins through clearly linked lines moving from father to son*, placing each name within a circle that surrounds it with details about tribes given by [Qalqashandi]. I went ahead and did this . . . removing some and adding much including the *ansab* of some kings and others *beginning with Adam*, the father of all humanity . . . (Al-Baghdadi, *Saba'ik*, 3–4 [emphasis added])

In this quotation, the author informs us that he found the organization of knowledge about tribes compiled by al-Qalqashandi[3] in the fourteenth century problematic because of the difficulty in determining tribal lineages. He proceeds to present a method for organizing tribes that departs significantly from earlier organizations undertaken by medieval historians. Through diagramming and linkages, he draws family trees of various larger tribes, *hama'il* (collections of tribes) and *fakha'idh* (sub-tribes), and down to clans with 'surrounding information' significant to specific ones. Following his methodology, the names of the tribes are all male and the lineage of kings and tribal leaders only includes the names of men, with no mention of associations through the mother. In other words, women are all but non-existent in his tribal diagrams, mentioned only in the rare case of a story about a particular woman included as part of the 'surrounding information'.

Ironically, al-Baghdadi agrees with al-Qalqashandi, and actually quotes him word for word, in that the original ancestors and 'founders' of tribes were not necessarily men; but that does not seem to make any difference to his construction of an exclusively male genealogy of Arab history.

Tribes are usually named after the original father of the tribe such as in the case of Rabi'a, Muddar, al-Aws and al-Khazraj. The tribe could also be named after the original mother of the tribe, such as Khandaf, Bajila

---

[3] Al-Qalqashandi's organization of his book of *ansab* was closely followed by other books of *ansab* of the medieval period. Al-Qalqashandi's interest was to show how tribes constructed their lineage, the various units in which they organized themselves, and the relations between these units. His alphabetical list covers every kin unit he could collect and how it was related to other larger units down to the period in which he lived.

and others; and sometimes it is named after a certain characteristic or a particular event . . .[4]

So, notwithstanding this clear statement, al-Baghdadi chose to construct a new paradigm which traces tribal lineages from father to son, a paradigm that eliminates any mention of women as founders of tribes, leaders of tribes, or the mothers and wives of important leaders after which various sub-groups were formed through marriage, break-up of the tribe or for any other reason.

It should be added that the fact that al-Baghdadi chooses to quote al-Qalqashandi about tribes being named after women shows the lack of intentionality in denying women a position in history; his paradigm is simply the result of particular concerns that resulted in a new organization of knowledge that seemed natural, i.e. emphasis on patriarchs and men, which seemed in accordance with historical changes involving the appearance of new monarchies and centralizing nation-states as modern structures following European monarchical models. Relating tribes to each other to establish the superiority of tribe and lineage, and ensuring that marriages are carried out between equal tribes, are quite familiar characteristics of nobility. Orientalist historians had already brought royal family-tree models, which were familiar to their political discourses, and applied them to countries of the Islamic world. These were brought to the Arabian Peninsula by travelers and missionaries, whose interests were mainly focused on political histories and new dynastic monarchies appearing in Gulf countries. A good example here is the work of Edward von Zambaur, which continues to be very widely used by Arab historians and which gives a list of all acknowledged dynasties in Islamic history, presented chronologically from one ruler to the next. Rarely is a woman's name mentioned and then usually in connection with a ruler's maternal relationship with the Prophet's family, mostly involving Shi'i dynasties, or when a woman is guardian of her minor royal son— for example, Dayfa Khatun, who was guardian of her grandson al-Nasir al-Yusuf al-Ayyubi (von Zambaur, Mu'jam, 53).

That changes in the political scene are the stimulus for the selection of

[4]The same words of this quote appear in al-Baghdadi (Saba'ik 9) and al-Qalqashandi, Nihayat al-irab (31).

new patriarchal models for tribal history is proven by the fact that al-Baghdadi follows these Western models in preference to earlier *ansab* literature, even though his concern for undertaking the effort was no different from what propelled early *ansab* compilers: he simply wanted to make the identification of connections easier. Quoting al-Qalqashandi, he explains that *nasab* must be established in order to ensure the determination of inheritance according to Islamic laws, the control of *awqaf* (religious endowments), and the contracting of marriages according to Islamic principles, which required *kafa'a* (parity)[5] for the marriage of women.

> If a genealogy consists of two or more levels, like Hashim, Quraysh, Muddar and 'Adnan, it is allowed to those who are in the line of Quraysh, line of Muddar and line of 'Adnan, it being said that *nasab* means belonging to all so that Bani Hashim can be related to Hashim and the 'Adnani . . . It is thus permitted to combine *nasab* between the upper level and the lower lever . . . some say that the lower should be given precedence over the higher . . .[6]

What this tells us is that Arab tribes trace their lineages toward what gives them greater power or prestige, how they relate one to the other in wider and more powerful configurations.

Kafa'a in marriage, the basis upon which tribal alliances are built, is given particular significance by all compilers of *ansab* in the medieval and modern periods,[7] who quote the Prophetic Hadith, 'a woman is married for four [reasons]: her religion, her *nasab*, her wealth, or her

---

[5]*Kafa'a* in marriage means that the husband and wife must be of equal background with regard to religion, class, and tribe.

[6]Al-Baghdadi, 8–9.

[7]The earliest recorded book of *nasab* is the incomplete work of Muhammad ibn Muslim al-Zuhri, who died in 124 AH, followed by the works of Abu al-Yaqzan Suhaym ibn Hifz al-Ikhbari (d. 190 AH) wrote several books, among which were *Al-nasab al-kabir* and *Nasab Khunduf wa-akhbaruha*. 'In Kufa there was Hisham b. Muhammad al-Kalbi who died in 204 AH. He left a major book on *ansab* known as *Al-nasab al-kabir* or *Jamharat al-nasab*. Ibn Hisham tells us that 'wherever a Companion of the Prophet was known by other than his father's name, "for example Sharik ibn al-Sahma", who was his mother, I mentioned him among those whose father's name began with "*sin*", then mentioned his father's name. I did that to make things easier' (al-Baghdadi 49).

beauty' (al-Baghdadi 4) as *shari'a* evidence for the requirement of *kafa'a*. Explanations of the Hadith focus on tribal lineage rather than on religious, class or national parity, as emphasized in modern books of *fiqh*; the differences in the approach to *kafa'a* illustrate changed social and legal concerns, the natural result of context, time, and place. While tribal *nasab* compilers accept the premise that *kafa'a* was essentially about tribal origins—and this belief continues to be a basis for marriages in Arabia today—a closer study of discourses on *kafa'a* shows divergent meanings. For example, another version of the *kafa'a* Hadith says: 'A Qurayshite woman is forbidden in marriage except to another Qurayshite, as there is no *kafa'a* for the Hashimi woman and the al-Mutalabiyya and other Qurayshites; and no other Arab who is not Qurayshite can be *kuf'* for a Qurayshite.' This Hadith gave mystical approbation to what became a tribal tradition requiring that women must marry men from equal tribes, particularly women of Quraysh and women of the Prophet's clan of Hashim, who were only allowed to marry men from Quraysh or Hashim respectively. This parity is extended by al-Qalqashandi and applied to the *'ajam* (non-Arab Muslims) and to slaves, stressing that *'ajam* should only marry *'ajam* and slaves slaves; in other words, marriage in Islam was to be based on ethnic group affiliation, and the purity of the Prophet's family in particular was to be guarded.

The questions raised above with regard to family trees and the construction of *nasab*, as well as the issue of *kafa'a*, are problematic when the life history of the Prophet, his Sunna as relayed by early *siyar* (biographies) of his life, is studied. Interpreting *kafa'a* for the bride has been explained in many ways over the course of Islamic history: similarity in religion, social background, wealth, education, even nationality, have all been used as possible bases for *kafa'a*. For the construction of tribal 'nobility', Hashim and Quraysh became central to the legitimacy of empires such as that of the Umayyads, who based their right to rule on their belonging to Quraysh. The Abbasids on the other hand, based their claim on being closer to the Prophet, since they were from Hashim, and the Shi'a claim an even closer link to the Prophet through the Prophet's daughter, Fatima. Early biographies, however, do not illustrate these concerns but speak of different types of relationship in equal terms: "Umar the slave of Ghafra said: "The mother of Ismail, the Prophet (PBUH) is from them and he is their in-law; and the Prophet (PBUH) *tasarar* (took a concubine) from among them." 'Ibn Lahi'a said: "The mother of Ismail, Hajir, is the mother of all Arabs . . . and the mother of Ibrahim is Mariya, the concubine of the Prophet (PBUH), who was gifted to him by al-Muqawqas . . . (Ibn Hisham vol.1, 44 –45).

Thus the Prophet's lineage was taken back to Hajar, 'mother of all Arabs', and his association with another slave-woman from Egypt, Maria, is celebrated for having produced a beloved son. Furthermore, the Prophet's history as presented in the various *siyar* is illustrative of the importance of the mother's lineage and the pride associated with it.

> [With regard to his father] . . . between 'Adnan and Isma'il ibn Ibrahim al-Khalil—PBUH—there is great disagreement regarding the number and the names, which are difficult to determine so we have left it alone. Then Muddar and Rabi'a, who were the children/descendants of Isma'il, as is agreed by all writers of *nasab*, though they differed a great deal about everything else. The Prophet's mother is Amna bint Wahb bin 'Abd Manaf bin Zahra bin Kilab bin Murra, the Qurayshite, al-Zuhriyya, and is joined together with 'Abdallah through Kilab. It is also said that they are joined through his uncles, since the mother of 'Abd al-Muttalib, Salma bint Zayd or daughter of 'Amru bin Zayd, of the Banu 'Adi bin al-Najjar. (Al-Baghdadi 4–5)

As regards the genealogy of the Prophet, Ibn Hisham first gives the Prophet's genealogy through his father all the way back to Adam and then does the same for his mother, again all the way back to Adam through the female line:

> 'Abdallah bin 'Abd al-Muttalib fathered Muhammad bin 'Abdullah, the Prophet of God (PBUH) . . . and his mother is Amna bint Wahb bin 'Abd Manaf bin Zahra bin Kilab bin Murra bin Ka'b bin Lu'ay bin Ghalib bin Fahr bin Malik bin al-Nadr; and her mother is Barra bint 'Abd al-'Aziyy bin 'Uthman bin [and so on] . . . and the mother of Barra is Umm Habib bint Asad [and so on] . . . and the mother of Umm Habib is Barra bint 'Awf [and so on] . . .[8]

---

[8](Ibn Hisham, http://www.al-eman.com/Islamlib/viewchp.asp?BID=249&CID=9#s2).

Ibn Hisham ends this lineage with: 'Then the Prophet of God is the noblest of all the children of Adam and the best of them in lineage through his father and through his mother, peace be upon him.'[9]

Ibn Hisham also gives particular importance to explaining the Prophet's repeated claim: 'I am the son of the 'Awatik and the son of the Fawatim, they are all pure women, mothers of Hashim ibn 'Abd al-Manaf, 'Atika bint Murra bin Hilal from Banu Salim.' Ibn Hisham then spends some time detailing the lineages of the Prophet's Companions, many of whom had 'Atikas or Fatimas in their lineage. For example, 'the mother of Umm Qasi, Fatima bint 'Awf bin Sa'd bin al-Azad', and 'the mother of Amna, the Prophet's grandmother, from her maternal side is Fatima bint 'Abdallah from the Banu Makhzoum . . .' In short, it was the norm to give details regarding the lineage of the mother as much as that of the father among early *siyar* and this continues into the medieval period, even though the detailing of female ancestors loses importance significantly with time to become all but forgotten in contemporary written genealogies. In oral history, however, women ancestors continue to be very important, and memories of the identity of mothers are part of historical memory and lore. This is found particularly among the older generation of Gulf women, but it seems to be dying out with younger generations.

Pride in relationship through the mother fits well with the life of women of the late *Jahiliyya* and early Islam. They were independent, they fought with their men in battle, even leading them as seers, and their *bay'a* (oath of allegiance) was required by political leaders, including the Prophet Muhammad. They fought alongside the Prophet and protected him at Uhud, and led their troops, as 'A'isha later did at the Battle of the Camel. Personal stories of women of that time show their independence and the equality they enjoyed with the male members of their tribe. A good example is found in Ibn Hisham, who tells the story of the marriage of the Prophet's father, 'Abdallah. He was on his way with his father, 'Abd al-Muttalib, to ask for Amna's hand in marriage. As he passed through the streets of Mecca on his way to Amna's house, he was stopped by a woman who was a stranger to him who proposed marriage to him. He refused her and went on to marry Amna.[10] This story is told to embroider the myths

[9](Ibn Hisham, http://www.al-eman.com/Islamlib/viewchp.asp?BID=249&CID=9#s2).
[10]Ibn Hisham, *Kitab al-sira al-nabawiyya*, vol. 1, pp. 111–16. http://www.al-eman.com/Islamlib/viewtoc.asp?BID=249.

about signs predicting the Prophet's birth; it also tells us of the belief in the power of women to foretell the future, and of a proposal of marriage by a woman to a man. The Prophet himself was offered marriage by Khadija, which he accepted. These are signs of the equal respect in which women and men held each other, rather than the later images used as representation of what is acceptable to Islam by those who saw relations between men and women on the basis of hierarchies of power.

Marriage and family

In the previous section, the material presented indicates the problems that arise from images of tribal lineages that peripheralized women and gave weight to paradigms of dismissal, seclusion and dependence that dominate our understanding of the life of Muslim women in the past and the present. In this section the intent is to deconstruct other aspects of the past with regard to family and inter-family relations. Here the aim is to discuss relations not only between husband and wife, but also between sister and brother, father and daughter, and the women of the family. While it is usual to focus on marital relations pertinent to the nuclear family of the modern period, for families that extend to clans and collections of clans living in joined settlements, which was the norm for pre-modern families, wider relations take on a significance that is often more important than the narrower relations between husband and wife. This is particularly so with regard to women and young girls and boys in locations where men were often absent from home, as was the case in regions bordering the Arabian Gulf where the men went out for weeks pearling or trading with Iraq, Najd or India. If we consider the life of women as it was lived within larger groupings whose members were interdependent, the realities of gender relations and women's social and economic place emerge. The changes in family structure brought about changes in gender relations and in the space occupied by women within the socio-economic system. Viewing the past through a prism of the present obfuscates realities and gives substance to paradigms of gender oppression that gain legitimacy from discourses conceptualizing the past in forms that are different from the reality. Here the sources are somewhat mixed; if for the earlier medieval period we are dependent on *ansab*, *tabaqat* and *siyar* literature to unlock the nature of family relations, for the pre-oil period in Arabia sources such as poetry,

travelers' accounts and oral memory are particularly useful. Widening the
geographical area under research to include surrounding territories in
which the tribes of Arabia moved and about which written records exist,
such as the Hijaz, Jordan and Yemen, enlarges our knowledge of tribal
relations and illustrates the great diversity that existed between tribes in
various parts of Arabia, as well as the importance of the political-economic
situation to inter-clan relations.

It is usual to divide the inhabitants of the Arabian Peninsula into two
groups: those settled close to oases throughout the Peninsula or in various
settlements and towns, and Bedouin who move from place to place but
who also have tribal areas known by their names. Settled tribes were at
one time nomadic Bedouin and, until very recently, they undertook
seasonal trips in search of food, water and grazing for their herds or to
trade with towns bordering their area. For much of the modern period,
many inhabitants of Arabia were actually somewhere between being
nomadic Bedouin and settled communities. Tribes were also known to
move together—to go into self-exile in acts of solidarity with their
members or when things became difficult for political reasons, or to
migrate in search of better living conditions. The important point here is
that tribes moved together and lived together, like extended families,
supporting each other in good and bad times, and considered their welfare
as well as their honor and allegiance to be related to other tribal entities as
a group. Tribal outcasts would soon attach themselves to tribal groups and
move around with them—otherwise they would not have the safety in
numbers necessary in the inhospitable environment of the desert. Women
formed an integral part of tribes, moving with them at times of war as well
as in migration or regular tribal movements. This type of tribe and clan
predominated before oil and before social transformations eroded the clan
system and began to replace it with the nuclear family. Among the Bedouin,
women constituted an integral part of the working family, undertaking
tasks necessary for the family's survival and working toward its economic
welfare. This included herding the clan's camels, sheep and goats, a task
which observers and travelers who spent time moving around with
Bedouin, or visiting their settlements, commented upon, calling these
women 'herdswomen' and commenting on their skill in handling and
working with cattle. Women were responsible for setting up, mending and
keeping tents and straw huts in areas where that was the main type of

dwelling. They also did the spinning and weaving, providing for the clan's needs for materials for constructing tents, and sewing camel saddles, transport bags, clothing, and items for trade and sale in markets. Given the nomadic life of many of the Bedouin, the work of women was constant and central not only to supporting the family and raising the children, but as an essential part of the tribe's economy (Nicholson 100–4).

The nature of the desert determined the life and function of its inhabitants. The constant search for water and food meant traveling long distances, which also meant traveling light, carrying only essential items and living in shelters, usually tents, that were easily assembled and collapsible. Their way of life also dictated their simple, basic approach to food. The general hardship of life necessitated a division of labor that demanded the cooperative effort of every member of the group, wherever he or she could contribute most. Bedouin society was structured accordingly, reflecting the hardships of life and the need for the unity of the group, who were ultimately totally dependent on each other for survival. This solidarity was strengthened by the relatively isolated life that Bedouin lived, for, although they communicated with other tribes and settled areas around their desert regions, there was still a wariness of strangers and a solidarity against outsiders, including intermarriage within the group or taking brides from other tribes to cement security alliances. When these groups began to settle, their family solidarity continued, and their approach to social relations remained endogamous and conservative, with cousins being taken as wives to keep the family line intact, thereby maintaining the solidarity of the desert in the settled areas. Other traditions besides marriage patterns included the recognition of the chief of the clan by his having a tent that stood apart from the rest, and was always larger and more prominent, well equipped and ready to receive guests when they appeared. This tradition translated itself in the *diwan*s and *majlis* (salons or meeting rooms), where the patriarch of an important clan held council and where visitors came to exchange information, undertake business, or to simply converse and negotiate. Another custom that found its way into settlements is the division of domiciles into areas for women and areas for men. The tents were divided this way to allow an area for men and another for the women, allowing the latter privacy in an environment where little privacy was available. A further tradition worth mentioning here concerns women's clothing. Women preferred to wear light fabrics in the heat of summer and heavy fabrics in winter to fight the severe cold of winter nights. Men followed the same pattern in selection of clothing, but while men preferred solid muted colors, women enjoyed bright colors, particularly red. They took these preferences into settled communities, with bright colors preferred. With time, the black 'abaya (mantle) gained in popularity, particularly with the increase in wealth following the oil boom, when it became affordable for women. Before the oil boom it was not the norm to have extra items of clothing, such as the 'abaya, which was mostly worn when a woman went out of the area in which she lived. Sometimes a whole family owned one 'abaya, which the women shared, and it was not uncommon to borrow an 'abaya from other households to undertake a trip.[11] Group solidarity was also evidenced in eating patterns. Food was prepared by the women together and the food was eaten in a group, the men separate from the women, all eating from the same dishes, perhaps because of the limited amount of food available. This same solidarity was transferred to settled communities, where the extended families prepared food together and ate major meals together.

> The family could thus be considered a single social unit built on relationship by blood, whose circle extended to include several marital units and therefore wide family relationships that most often lived together in one home or attached units. The family also represented a single economic unit, besides being a social unit, so that it undertook all economic responsibilities to provide for its own needs and the daily requirements of its members. The widening of the kinship group, strong feelings of solidarity, loyalty to the group, and the lack of independence, created a sort of social complementarity; this in turn made the individual feel safe and his family secure because of group strength, and he became thereby always sure of support from his kin group, regardless of his individual standing. This spirit of complementarity was guided and controlled by a number of moral codes and traditions that no individual from within the group could go against. (Haddad 57; my translation)

---

[11]Interview with Mrs Meera al-Misnad. The same information was confirmed in an interview with Shaykh Faysal bin Jasim al-Thani, who spoke of severe poverty in Qatar before the oil boom.

These solidarities, patterns, moral codes and traditions accompanied tribes when they settled; with time and socio-economic change, they would alter as the family began to move toward the nuclear family.

The life of women in the towns and settled communities of Arabia was somewhat different, depending on the size of the family, the presence of slaves and domestic servants to do heavy labor, and the wealth that the family commanded. But women continued to be central to the functioning and economic well-being of the family. The essential inter-dependency of clan-members and the cohesiveness of the extended family continued with the movement to urban environments. While towns and settled communities have always been a characteristic of life in Arabia, with well-known towns in the south in Yemen, in the Hijaz with its holy cities and Red Sea ports, and on the coast of the Arabian Gulf, the modern age has seen extensive sedentarization of the Bedouin, largely as a result of state-building efforts, particularly with the arrival of Wahhabism and the efforts of 'Abd al- 'Aziz bin Sa'ud (1876–1953). The latter sent Wahhabi missionaries among the tribes to correct what Wahhabis considered to be their faulty understanding of Islam, and then invited them to move into agricultural settlements to form religious brotherhoods, which supplied him with fighters to expand the territory under his power and bring about the establishment of Saudi Arabia. With the arrival of the oil age and oil wealth, the process of urbanization gained serious momentum and continues to escalate modernization, with multiple impacts on society and culture.

Traditionally, the economy of Arabian towns was based on internal trade and on external trade with the countries surrounding Arabia. The Hajj was particularly important for the western side of the Peninsula, while pearling, fishing, boat-building and other crafts were central to the economy of the eastern shores of Arabia. Some western and southern parts of Arabia were rich in agriculture, supported by rains, oases and water-holes, while the eastern coast had seasonal rains but few resources other than what the sea provided. Except for agricultural areas on the island of Bahrain, in Oman and in some of al-Ahsa's oases, the inhabitants of areas bordering the Arabian Gulf were highly dependent on importing most of their needs, from staples to supplies and weapons.

Until the 1930s, when Japanese cultured pearls began to win the market from the highly coveted Gulf pearls, pearling was the chief source of income for the people of the Gulf. The life of those living in Qatar, Bahrain, the Emirates and Najd revolved around it and involvement in pearl diving, trading in pearls and the industries connected with pearling not only provided the chief source of income, but also defined the life of the people of these countries, including their relations with each other, with other tribes with whom they dealt, and with outsiders with whom they had business. As a trade, pearling had existed since ancient times. It involved whole families and was passed on from father to son, the son apprenticing quite early, following in his father's footsteps onto the boats and learning the difficult and often dangerous skill of deep diving after the much-coveted oysters that yielded the highest quality pearls off the shores of the Gulf. Most of the men involved in pearling were employed, being paid by the owners of the boats, who were often merchants who stayed on shore and financed these trips. The divers were paid directly and enjoyed a share of the catch, while the boat-owners traded the pearls that were collected with merchants, who would then take them by boat sometimes to Iraq or India, or to trade with foreign merchants who came to the area.

Because pearling needed boats, boat-building and maintenance were important industries, providing employment for carpenters and sailmakers in various parts of the Gulf. While pearling occupied about five months of the year, the boats were also used for fishing, which provided the most important source of protein for the inhabitants of the Gulf. Fishing also took place from the shore, the Gulf waters containing a plentiful supply of a rich variety of fish.

There were several pearl seasons during the year, starting with early trips at the end of winter to investigate locations and check the potential harvest. Early harvesting took place in April, while a late harvesting was undertaken during November. The important season began in June and involved four months of seafaring and diving, sometimes in very deep waters. Different sizes of boat were used for these trips, some carrying sixteen and others up to a hundred men, the captain of the boat often also being its owner who may have put up the money himself or gone into partnership with a merchant who invested in the trip ('Abd al-Rahim 40). The hierarchy on board went from the boat-owner or merchant at the top, to the divers next, and then the men undertaking day-to-day services, such as cooking and cleaning.

With their men away a large part of the year pearling or on trade activities, as was the case with more important leaders and clans of the Gulf, women were left to maintain family life and the business of running their homes. Wealthier families had slaves to do shopping and other duties, but most families did not and women had to carry out most of the work of running the household, bringing in the water, raising and disciplining children, taking care of the home and its upkeep, caring for animals if they owned any, or crops, if they grew any, meeting with visitors, and all the other activities involved in running a home. To supplement their income, women took in sewing, although they mainly did the sewing for their own families, some became *mutawwi'at*, teaching in the local *kuttab*s, and a few even went out diving with the men to supplement their income when times were hard. Outside of the urban centers, in agricultural areas, women bore a heavy burden of work, including watering the crops or cattle, collecting date crops, and sometimes raising chickens and making cheese and ghee to sell in the market-place. For the families of men who came from areas far from the shore, such as Najd, the periods when they were alone were even longer and self-reliance was even more essential. With the collapse of pearling that hit the Gulf in the 1930s, women's contribution to the family's income became particularly important, and oral histories show that the memory of those years continues to be central to the community consciousness of people of the Gulf because of the depression and memories of hunger during that period. The efforts of women at that time, perhaps more than any other, helped in gaining the sense of gender respect that continues to mark family relations in the Gulf, although these relations are being transformed and clan solidarity is eroding.

A look at the shape of towns during the pre-oil period illustrates the type of relations that existed. Gulf society was tribal; the members of one family lived together in one house, and the father was the patriarch of the household with power over all who lived under its roof, married and unmarried. Good relations within the family and between members of the various households in the same quarter (*firij*) were necessary and were cultivated by the heads of the families, who were often away at sea pearling, fishing or trading. Clans of the same tribe tended to live close to each other, often in extended homes depending on how wealthy and powerful the family was. Each *firij* was named after the extended clan that lived in it and relations between these extended households were strong, although, as they grew in size and changes occurred, the direction was towards tribal mixing within the same *firij*, so that it was no longer inhabited only by the clan or tribe that originally formed it. When trouble occurred between members of different clans, it involved the clans as a whole, with disputes between them sometimes escalating to violence.

Traditions did not differ much between the settled tribes and unsettled Bedouin; they did business together and even inter-married. The unity of the family was evidenced in marriage patterns, since endogamy was the preferred form of marriage, the girl being destined to marry her cousin and only marrying outside the family if that was not possible. This pattern can be found all over the Middle East, wherever tribal modes predominate. The marriage was contracted by the family, with the father of the bride having the last word. Since marriages were within the family and intended to cement alliances, dowries were small, but when the bridegroom was from outside the tribe, the dowry (*mahr*) increased significantly as a sign of the bride's and her tribe's honor.

Living within this structure allowed for protection and family support. It also meant living within rules and traditions that took the collective good as a primary consideration. Presenting a united front, emphasizing clan solidarity and honor, was almost a necessity for survival in harsh environments as a form of mutual support and to deter would-be opportunistic predators. Negotiating from a position of strength was at the heart of clan solidarity. The well-known Arab proverb, 'My brother and I against my cousin and my cousin and I against the stranger', comes to mind here, showing the concentric system of layered solidarity. For women, living within their extended families meant abiding by its rules, but it also provided security and support and the work they undertook was part of the group economy, undertaken for the survival and welfare of the group as a whole. It is only in the modern period, with the development of new paradigms that have provided lenses colored with issues of women's rights and gender differences, that the past economic contributions of women have been dismissed or undermined. Seen from the perspective of the lived realities of the Arab past, women bore a substantial burden of the work and responsibility for the protection of their families and communities. In this they benefitted, like their male counterparts, and also suffered from the realities of their situation. A good example here is the issue of polygamy, which was never fully accepted by women, whether nomadic or settled, but which existed and was sanctioned by Islamic law as it was practiced throughout Arabia.

Development of the modern family

The Constitution of the United Arab Emirates points to the family as 'the basis of society, founded on religion, morals and love of country; its structure guarded by law, protected from deviation'. This statement is one that has appeared in one form or another in the constitutions of all Arab countries that have chosen to apply modern legal code formats to structure their legal systems. Codification requires the definition of central institutions around which the philosophy of the law is organized. The family, country, and religious affiliation provided such central core principles for all Arab countries. In the United Arab Emirates, as in all other countries of the Gulf Cooperation Council (GCC), the state religion is Islam, as Article 7 of the United Arab Emirates Constitution makes clear: 'Islam is the official religion of the union, and the Islamic *Shari'a* is a major source of its laws, and the official language of the Union is the Arabic language.'[12]

Like the Constitution of the United Arab Emirates, all the constitutions and laws of the other countries of the GCC contain statements about the Islamic nature of the state and the *Shari'a* as a main source of law. This includes Oman, which has followed Khariji Ibadist Islam since the eighth century; its 1996 Basic Law declared Islam the official religion of the state and the *Shari'a* the basis of its laws. The same goes for Saudi Arabia, which has no constitution but bases its laws on the Islamic *Shari'a*. The country's Basic Law of 1992 declares Islam the official religion and, following the Wahhabi *madhhab*, narrows the *Shari'a* to the Qur'an and Sunna as its sources of law. The law also includes an injunction that makes the decisions reached by the monarch a source of law in the Kingdom as long as these decisions do not contradict the *Shari'a*. As for the family, the Basic Law, like constitutions in other Muslim countries, declares the family to be 'the kernel of Saudi

---

[12]For the United Arab Emirates Constitution, see the GCC portal: http://www.gcc-legal.org/MojPortalPublic/DisplayLegislations.aspx?country=2&LawTreeSectionID=3938 (accessed 3 January 2011).

society and its members shall be brought up on the basis of the Islamic faith'.

This recognition of the centrality of the family in contemporary Gulf society is natural, for as explained earlier, families have been central to the communal health and productivity of the people of Arabia from time immemorial. The role played by women as part of these units was important and in fact central; the difficulties of life required that all hands participate in the running of daily life. The modern family continues the same principles, uniting family members in their loyalty to their clans and larger tribes. However, the modern context of nation-state building embarked upon by the countries of the Arabian Gulf, has provided a different context for the development of the family, as has the new economy that came into existence and continues to develop today as a result of the discovery and production of oil. While the dominant form of the family (*'a'ila*) that existed before the socio-economic transformations caused by oil can be described as an extended family, which included uncles, aunts, cousins, and grandparents, all living together in one large compound, today's family is different in many ways. For example, even though families may appear to be extended and living in large compounds, these compounds are increasingly being subdivided to house smaller nuclear families in separate housing units, even if within the same walls. This accommodates polygamy, which continues to be widely practiced if at an increasingly lower rate. The *'a'ila* is changing quickly in the Gulf and moving toward becoming an *usra*, the term used to refer to the smaller nuclear family that predominates in other Arab countries today. The *usra* is recognized as a legal entity and society's basic social unit; it has a male head and includes his wife/wives and children; the role of the male head is recognized by the state and powers are extended to him over other members within the unit. These powers include refusing to allow the wife to leave the home, travel or enter into employment. It also grants him the right to chastise his wife and the children, over whom he has almost complete control, both social and legal. Even though the smaller nuclear unit continues to be connected by traditions with the larger extended family, clan and tribe, the growth in size of the larger unit has led to a deterioration in relations and often to alienation between the various branches that make up the extended family, clan and the wider tribe. The fact that modern state borders have divided tribes and confined branches of them within state boundaries has also contributed to the deterioration of the tribal system as it functioned before modernity, when tribes moved freely over Arabia and could depend on reinforcement and replenishment from their original branches and homelands.

The new modern 'codified' family in the Gulf today is being shaped by legal codes that reflect the essence of tribal patriarchy and Islamic principles, but which also conform to imported legal structures. This has led to the creation of a new and different patriarchal order in which the husband's powers have been extended by law in many ways, some direct and others indirect and informal. While promulgated constitutions and laws have given women guarantees of equality and citizenship, the legal codes limit these rights and subsume them under the powers of the husband, father, brother or other male members of the immediate family and the wider clan. Women have found themselves gaining rights that may not have been defined clearly before — such as the right to education and citizenship — but they have also found that the laws limit these very rights by controlling their movements and making women peripheral to their male relatives.

This may not have been the spirit or the intention of the laws, but they certainly do not reflect the partnership culture that existed between husband and wife, sister and brother, before the introduction of legal modernity. As has happened elsewhere in the Arab world where the legal system changed from one that combined traditional, tribal and Islamic laws to focused legal codes compiled through a selection process aimed at the rationalization and homogenization of the legal system following Western models — all part of nation-state building — women lost space, perhaps not least because the agents of change were initially all male with a male perspective that saw the power of the state mirrored in the power of the head of the family.

Perhaps the example of Bahrain fills in some of the details regarding the genesis of new laws dealing with the family. It must first be noted that Bahrain has had long experience of British laws; following independence in 1971, the kingdom proceeded to promulgate new legal codes based on the *Shari'a* and modern law. In this, the Egyptian example proved useful since Egypt had been involved in the same process since the nineteenth century and had produced standardized codes which were based largely on French laws but which also observed the basic forms of *Shari'a* as interpreted through the Hanafi code. As in the case of the United Arab Emirates, the Bahraini Constitution of 1973 declared Bahrain to be an 'Arab Islamic State' and the *Shari'a* to be a main source of its laws. For some years now Bahrain worked on a personal status law for the Sunni section of its population based on sexual differences and social status; discussions of the law (passed as Law 19/2009 in May 2009) explained personal status law as being based on

> what differentiates one human being from another in natural or family characteristics . . . such as whether the human being is a male or female, married, widowed, or divorced, a father, or legitimate son, a full citizen or less by reason of age or imbecility or insanity, and whether he has full civil competence or is limited as to his competency for a legal reason. (Government of Bahrain 3)

This definition was based on Egyptian law, which was in turn extracted from French law (Government of Egypt 11).

This borrowing by Bahrain is not surprising given that the reformed Egyptian code compiled by Ahmad Qadri Pasha became the basis of the law formulated by the state of Kuwait and other Arab countries. The interconnectedness between Arab countries, and the similarity in the education received by lawyers, politicians, legislators and other professionals in these countries, has contributed to the diffusion of legal systems from one Arab state to another. At the same time, there are important differences in the personal status laws of these countries, which reflect their particular social make-up and cultural expectations.

> Personal status law is formed of a collection of legal rules that regulate relations between individuals with regard to *nasab*, marriage, relationship by marriage (*musahara*), and the rights and duties that are created through this relationship throughout its various phases and which are derived (*mustamadda*) from Islamic *Shari'a* laws. As such it regulates the marital relationship and relationships created through marriage, children, custody/guardianship (*hadana*) and mutual rights and the consequences of its demise with regard to rights to financial support (*nafaqa*), *hadana*, inheritance and wills (*wisaya*). (Government of Bahrain 3)

Nowhere in Egyptian personal status laws do we see *nasab* or *musahara* as defining relations of significance to personal status. These specifics fit with traditions in Bahrain, where tribalism and the extended family continue to be important to the social fabric. It should be added that, even though Bahraini law indicates that the law is 'derived from the Islamic *Shari'a* and does not go outside of it' (ibid. 6), it is clear that the law is actually a product of various types of laws that accord with what Bahrain considers to be acceptable.

The shape of the family and the laws that guide it in Gulf countries today can be said to differ from earlier laws in force before the modernization of the law in significant ways, not the least of which is their philosophical approach to gender and law. As the earlier quotation defining personal status illustrates, the laws applied by the modern state involve a particular philosophical approach to human relations which views human beings in terms of 'natural' characteristics and 'family' units. Notwithstanding claims that modern laws promote personal freedoms, in actuality they form new structures through which human society is perceived, organized and dealt with, both legally and otherwise. By defining personal status laws on the basis of natural qualifications—i.e., whether the individual is male or female, minor or major, sane or insane, etc.—and social needs—such as the state's responsibility to maintain the 'family' and its espousal of a moral discourse that sanctifies and fortifies the family—an unequal system developed that places some sectors of society (women and children) in the hands of the rest (adult males). Thus gender difference has come to define the law and biological differences have become a liability, denying women full legal competence, similar to an insane person or a minor who needs the protection of a 'guardian'. When arguments based on biological differences became normative, the impact of patriarchy on the interpretation of laws dealing with family became all the more obvious. While personal status laws implemented in Gulf countries immediately and comprehensively put the family at the center of the law—in that we can speak of the laws as a more or less finished product in structure if not in detail—the move towards placing the nuclear family (*usra*) at the center of the legal discourse actually took place incrementally in Arab history. Before the modernization of law began in parts of the Arab world in the nineteenth century, marriage was an open contract in which the individual partners included provisions they agreed upon within an Islamic framework that set a number of rules legitimating the marriage. As laws became codified, definitions of what constituted marriage began to emerge. We see a beginning of this process in an early reformed law regulating marriage dating from 1885 in Egypt. In this law the *mahr* (dowry) at the time of contracting the marriage and *nafaqa* (alimony) provisions upon divorce were central concerns, as were statements establishing rules that the legislators found it necessary to include. Thus, the right of a husband to take a second, third, or fourth wife without any rights for the wife to oppose this was included, as was his absolute right to divorce her at will.[13] The *Shari'a* was used as the basis for these rulings and such decisions can in fact be said to be contained in the *Shari'a* as interpreted through *fiqh*. In other words, it was the choice of the Egyptian legislators to apply certain *fiqh* rulings that emphasized patriarchal power, rather than use precedent followed in *Shari'a* courts in Egypt before the modernization of the law, when practice and lived realities were quite different from what was being established by the modern law. At that time it was true that men could divorce their wives whenever they wished, as evidenced by *Shari'a* court records; but the same records illustrate that women legally controlled their husband's ability to take a second wife and that they could go out of the house at will, unless not leaving the marital home without permission was included as a condition in their marriage contract or negotiated in court.

In other words, women's ability to negotiate and determine conditions that applied to their marriage was removed by the modern state and deliberately so. Thus Article 12 of the 1885 law states:

> A marriage that includes a condition or circumstance whose realization is uncertain is not valid. But a marriage that is contracted with a condition that is not legal will be considered legal, although the condition will be treated as nonexistent; this will be the case where the husband stipulates that he does not owe a dowry.[14]

---

[13] According to the Egyptian law of 1885 the government official responsible for officiating at the marriage (*ma'dhun*) is expected to explain the following to the bride and bridegroom contracting it: 'I am to explain to them that the *shari'a* includes the following dispositions: 1. The husband can validly, if no legal impediments exist, take at the same time two, three or four wives notwithstanding the opposition of the one he is already married to. 2. He can divorce his wife, whenever he wishes, without her consent. He can also forbid her from leaving the marital home without authorization . . .'

[14] The wife is considered to have the right to receive a dowry (*mahr*) from the husband at the time when the marriage is contracted.

This was a far cry from pre-modern marriages recorded in *Shariʻa* courts dating from as far back as the Ikhshidid period (935–969) and continuing until the last quarter of the nineteenth century, when modernization of the laws began. During that period, it was quite normative for wives to include a condition restricting the right of a husband to take a second wife, which might allow her to leave the marriage or re-negotiate it, or make any other stipulation that the husband agreed to. We see the above 1885 law reflected in personal status laws in Gulf countries; for example, Kuwait's personal status law contains almost the same meaning: 'A marriage is not valid that includes a condition that is not legal.'[15]

The 1885 law ended the earlier flexibility, putting an end to an important opportunity for women to be party to decisions regarding the conditions of their marriage and offering them a way out of the marriage if it became polygamous, if they so desired. By 1920, with the establishment of the first comprehensive personal status law in Egypt, the door closed further and a distinct difference from the 1885 law was introduced. The intention of the 1920 law was to regularize the family; the focus was no longer 'marriage' between two persons determining their contractual union, but rather the 'family', so that the marital union was situated within patriarchal power relations that reflected state patriarchal power, and was supported by it. The move from the one to the other is significant; the first presented a philosophy that looked for a contractual agreement involving rights and duties between two persons, while the latter focused on and was interested in the family and the laws defining relationships between its various members and determining who has the legal authority to take decisions, an authority backed, moreover, by the power of the state with its enforcing apparatuses. The husband/father was the recognized legal head of this nuclear family with almost absolute powers over his wife and children, the wife becoming an adjunct to the husband before the state.

While personal status laws began elsewhere in the Arab world, they moved to the Gulf along with efforts to establish centralized governments, a process which necessitated dependence on Arab legislators and laws, particularly from Egypt, Syria and Iraq—all countries that had undergone similar experiences with the modernization of law. The impact for women of the Gulf is significant and, as an example, one has but to point to nationality and

[15]http://www.gcc-legal.org/MojPortalPublic/LawAsPDF.aspx?opt&country=3&LawID=2736#Section_3770.

citizenship laws, which had to be formulated in the Gulf countries as part of national development following independence. Citizenship laws in all the Gulf countries, as in all Arab countries, consider a wife to be an adjunct of her husband; his citizenship can be extended to his foreign wife and his children from a foreign wife have automatic rights of citizenship, whereas these rights are denied to the foreign husband of a Gulf wife, and citizenship is denied to her children from a foreign husband. These discrepancies are attributed to the *Shari'a*, which describes a child as belonging to the marital bed, and this statement has been defined as meaning that the child 'belongs' to the father and hence acquires his citizenship. However, citizenship and nationality are modern concepts and creations, and it was the modern state that made the choice not to recognize a mother's full rights.

With regard to granting Qatari nationality to a non-Qatari, for example, Law 38 of 2005, Rule 2, states:

> . . . Consideration is given in granting nationality, according to these rules, to giving priority to a person whose mother is Qatari; a person born in Qatar or outside Qatar to a father who has been granted Qatari nationality. A person who is born in Qatar of unknown parentage is considered as having received Qatari nationality, and a *laqit* (abandoned child of unknown parentage) is considered born in Qatar unless otherwise proven.[16]

This statement reveals the law's basic lack of equality in its handling of male and female Qataris and their citizenship rights. The children of Qatari women do not have the automatic right to Qatari citizenship as do the children of male Qatari citizens.[17] They may have priority when consideration is given as to whether to grant citizenship, but that is not a guarantee and, since citizenship brings entitlement to other social and economic rights, they are clearly placed in a position of inferiority vis-à-vis the children of Qatari men. Most interesting is that the same law and conditions apply to illegitimate children. These rules seem to be consistent in all Gulf countries; different wordings may be used, but the same framework applies. Kuwait's laws thus declare:

---

[16]http://www.gcc-legal.org/MojPortalPublic/LawAsPDF.aspx?opt&country=3&LawID=2 736#Section_3770 (in Arabic).
[17]It is perhaps worth noting that UK laws were similar until the 1970s.

A Kuwaiti is one born inside or outside Kuwait of a Kuwaiti father. Anyone born in Kuwait of unknown parentage gains Kuwaiti nationality; a *laqit* is considered born in Kuwait unless otherwise proven. The Minister of the Interior may grant Kuwaiti nationality to a person born in Kuwait or outside Kuwait whose mother is a Kuwaiti national and whose father is of unknown identity or whose parentage is not established legally; and it is permitted, by a declaration of the Ministry of Interior, that *qusar* (minors) be treated in this way until they attain their majority.[18]

What is the connection between citizenship and gender? While the relationship may not be immediately obvious and may appear to be the consequence of long-standing traditions, structuring and defining citizenship is in fact a function of the modern state and part of its efforts to control its territory and mobilize its people. It should be remembered that nationality and citizenship are important instruments by which the modern nation-state exercises power and control over 'its' population within and beyond its geographical borders. The power of modern nation states over their territory and people has been determined by extending their jurisdiction over them and has been achieved by the mechanism of nationality and by defining people as citizens or protégés. All the Gulf countries have been involved in such processes since the 1920s, mapping out their borders and defining who belonged within them and who did not. Nationality is central to this, as is citizenship. Nationality determines who belongs and therefore has the right to live in a particular country and carry its passport when traveling abroad, while citizenship defines the rights and duties of the national as well as the laws that he or she is expected to abide by and the protection that the nation extends to him or her. In the process of working out these details, establishing and implementing rules included defining what citizenship meant.

The repercussions of adopting nationality and citizenship rules in the Gulf are traceable through official papers. The records of the Saudi village of al-'Ulya from 1945 to 1960, published by Muna al-Dukhayl, provide a glimpse into the process by which Saudi Arabia, once it was established as

---

[18]Ibid.

a kingdom, proceeded to define its borders and put in place increasingly stringent measures to control entry into the kingdom, mapping out the various provinces, who had the right to nationality, the specific conditions applied for entry into Saudi Arabia, and the forms that were developed by the state in its effort to control and standardize its rules and regulations. The records of al-'Ulya, which is 350 kilometers north-east of Riyadh[19] and considered a crossroads between Saudi Arabia and Kuwait and a passport and mail administrative center, contain forms for Saudis wishing to travel abroad and foreigners arriving in Saudi Arabia from Kuwait for a variety of purposes, including work and pilgrimage. Without going into great detail about these forms, the information required for travel into and out of the country illustrates a different attitude towards travelers from that we find in Saudi Arabia today. Here it is most interesting that the word *mihrim*[20] never appears anywhere on the forms regarding travel out of or into Saudi Arabia. It may be that the forms concerning work would not be expected to take women into consideration, since women seem not to have constituted a significant proportion of the manual laborers who accounted for most of those coming to work in Saudi Arabia. But those traveling to Saudi Arabia for the purpose of pilgrimage must have included women and children, who are only mentioned by al-Dukhayl in an explanatory note regarding 'accompanying persons', the heading of a box on the forms that applicants had to fill in. The form does not ask the gender of the applicant nor does it specify that the applicant should be male (al-Dukhayl 113–4). It may have been traditional that only males traveled, and if females did travel it would only be as accompanying family members traveling with men. However, such information would have been required as a matter of travel control, and no such forms or requirements would have been expected to be in place before the establishment of Saudi Arabia. As other articles in this collection show, women traveled in Arabia in earlier times without any need to be accompanied by a male family member, as is required by modern regulations regarding travel for women of all nationalities, which require that any woman must be accompanied by a *mihrim* in order to enter or leave Saudi Arabia. Egyptian regulations

---

[19]A port located 350 kilometers from the Saudi-Kuwaiti border.
[20]A *mihrim* is a male related to a woman in a degree of closeness that makes marriage between them inadmissible. Any woman of any nationality entering or leaving Saudi Arabia today must be accompanied by a *mihrim*.

regarding the annual pilgrimage organized in 1920 do not mention the word *mihrim* either, and actually require that separate passports be issued for women and children who go on pilgrimage. It was probably common practice that women accompanied their male relatives, given the difficulties of the journey, which was mostly by camel caravan at that time, but there do not seem to have been any set laws controlling the movement of women on pilgrimage as there are today.

As other chapters in this collection on law and the codification of law in the Gulf show, today's Gulf states are becoming increasingly guided by legal codes applied uniformly throughout the country. This has led to the extension of rights to women, including the right to vote, and rights regarding education, employment, and health support by the state. This has been a great benefit to women, and its results can be seen in the important advances women have made in Gulf countries, their increased presence in leadership positions and the posts they hold in schools and universities. The fact that they are leading the call for social change is also quite tangible in the role they are playing in building social services, cultural and educational facilities, and charities, and in their push for changes to the law.

At the same time, however, because of the basic philosophical inequalities that came into existence as part of nation-state construction and the rationalization of law, women are held back by serious legislative inequalities that often translate into handicaps when it comes to their lived realities. Many of these inequalities exist because of the laws governing and protecting the patriarchal family and placing it within a discourse that associates the laws determining power relations within the family with the *Shari'a*. This gives an almost holy solidity to the patriarchal family as it stands today, with the laws that define it. The common discourse describes the family in the Gulf and the Arab world today as 'the Islamic family', implying that, though its shape may have shifted, its laws have not.

As this study shows, the laws guiding personal relations have changed in the course of Islamic history, responding closely to the historical context with its definitive political structures and accompanying socio-economic changes. Laws in modern states, like the laws previously in force in the early modern and medieval periods, reflect the state-society and social relations of their particular communities. This reality needs to be understood, and the history of the genesis of family laws clarified, to allow for a freer understanding of the laws governing family relations today and hence for a wider approach to the problems the Gulf family faces. Personal status laws in force or in the process of being introduced in Gulf countries today strengthen the power of the patriarch and the family, and state modernity in practice promotes the nuclear family and control by the father and male relatives.

13. *Gender Rights and Islamic Legal Tradition: An Exploration*

This article explores constructions of gender rights in Islamic legal tradition.[1] It is a contribution to the emerging feminist scholarship in Islam that is both discovering a hidden history and re-reading the textual sources to unveil and argue for an egalitarian vision of gender relations.[2] I focus on two sets of legal rulings: those regulating marriage and divorce, and those relating to women's participation in society, specifically the notion of *hijab* as seclusion. These rulings form two sides of the same patriarchal coin that has legitimated and institutionalized the control and subjugation of women throughout the history of the Muslim world. By highlighting the theological and philosophical assumptions that underlie these rulings, I aim to reveal the genesis of gender inequality in Islamic legal tradition, which, as I shall argue, is rooted in the social, cultural and political conditions within which Islam's sacred texts were understood and turned into law.

[1]Earlier versions are Mir-Hosseini, 'Construction of Gender'; idem, 'Islam and Gender justice'; and idem, 'Towards Gender Equality'.
[2]The growing literature of feminist scholarship in Islam is too large to list here; for a useful collection, see Webb; other important works are Ahmed, *Women and Gender*; Al-Hibri, 'Study of Islamic Herstory'; idem, 'Islam, Law and Custom'; idem, 'Muslim Women's Rights'; idem, 'Islamic Perspective'; Ali, 'Progressive Muslims'; idem, *Sexual Ethics*; Barazangi; Barlas; Hassan, 'Equal before Allah?'; idem, 'Feminist Theology'; idem, 'Feminism in Islam'; Mernissi, *Women and Islam*; Shaikh, 'Exegetical Violence'; idem, 'Knowledge, Women and Gender'; Wadud, *Qur'an and Woman*; idem, 'Qur'an, Gender and Interpretive Possibilities'; idem, *Inside the Gender Jihad*.

I begin with a note on my own position and conceptual background, then proceed to an examination of notions of gender rights as constructed in classical jurisprudential texts, and as reproduced, modified and reconstructed in the course of the twentieth century. I end by considering the potential of an emerging discourse that aspires to an egalitarian construction of gender within an Islamic framework. There are three interconnected elements to my argument: First, assumptions about gender in Islam—as in any other religion—are necessarily social/cultural constructions, thus historically changing and subject to negotiation. Second, Islamic legal tradition contains neither a unitary nor a coherent concept of gender, but rather a variety of inconsistent concepts, each resting on different theological, juristic, social and sexual assumptions and theories. This, in part, reflects a tension in Islam's sacred texts between ethical egalitarianism as an essential part of its message and the patriarchal context in which this message was unfolded and implemented. This tension enables both proponents and opponents of gender equality to claim textual legitimacy for their respective positions and gender ideologies.[3] Finally, the idea of gender equality became inherent in conceptions of justice in the course of the twentieth century and acquired a clear legal mandate through international human rights instruments, notably the Convention on the Elimination of All Forms of Discrimination against Women (CEDAW). These philosophical and legal developments, coupled with the changed status of Muslim women and their growing demand for legal equality, face Islamic legal tradition with an epistemological crisis, as its patriarchal constructions of gender rights are becoming increasingly untenable and challenged from within.

Approach and conceptual framework

I approach Islamic legal tradition as a trained legal anthropologist, but also as a believing Muslim woman, and place my analysis within the tradition of Islamic legal thought by invoking two crucial distinctions in that tradition.[4] These distinctions are made by all classical Muslim jurists and

[3]As feminist scholarship on religion teaches us, such a tension is present in other scriptural religions. See Gross for this tension in Buddhism; Ruether and Schussler Fiorenza for Christianity; Herschel and Plaskow for Judaism.

[4]A clear statement of position is essential, as the literature on Islam and women is replete with polemic in the guise of scholarship (see Mir-Hosseini *Islam and Gender*, 3–6).

have been upheld in all schools of Islamic law, but they have been distorted and obscured in modern times, when modern nation-states have created uniform legal systems and selectively reformed and codified elements of Islamic family law, and when a new political Islam has emerged that uses *Shari'a* as an ideology.

The first distinction is between *Shari'a* (revealed law) and *fiqh* (the science of Islamic jurisprudence). This distinction underlies the emergence of various schools of Islamic law and within them a multiplicity of positions and opinions. In Muslim belief, *Shari'a*, which literally means 'the path or the road leading to the water', is the totality of God's will as revealed to the Prophet Muhammad. As Fazlur Rahman notes, 'in its religious usage, from the earliest period, it has meant "the highway of good life", i.e. religious values, expressed functionally and in concrete terms, to direct man's life' (*Islam*, 100). *Fiqh*, which literally means 'understanding', denotes the process of human endeavor to discern and extract legal rules from the sacred sources of Islam: that is, the Qur'an and the *Sunna* (the practice of the Prophet, as contained in Hadith [Traditions]). In other words, while the *Shari'a* in Muslim belief is sacred, eternal and universal, *fiqh*, consisting of the vast literature produced by Muslim jurists, is—like any other system of jurisprudence—human, mundane, temporal and local. Throughout the present study, then, the *Shari'a* is understood as a transcendent ideal that embodies the spirit and the trajectory of Islam's revealed texts, a path that guides us in the direction of justice; while *fiqh* includes not only the legal rulings (*ahkam*) and positive laws (enacted or legislated) that Muslim jurists claim to be rooted in the sacred texts, but also the vast corpus of jurisprudential and exegetical texts produced by the scholars.

The concept of justice is deeply rooted in Islam's teaching, and is integral to the basic outlook and philosophy of the *Shari'a*. This is where the juristic consensus ends. What justice requires and permits, its scope and its manifestation in laws, and its roots in Islam's sacred texts, have been the subject of contention and debate.[5] In brief, there are two main schools of theological thought. On the one hand, the prevailing Ash'ari school holds that our notion

[5]For a discussion of conceptions of justice in Islamic texts, see Khadduri and Lampe; for a discussion of the absence of theological debate in the work of contemporary jurists, see Abou El Fadl, 'Ethical Obligations'; for discussion of links between justice and Shari'a, see Kamali, *Freedom*.

of justice is contingent on revealed texts and is not subject to extra-religious rationality. The Mu'tazili school, on the other hand, argues that our notion of justice is innate and has a rational basis, and exists independently of revealed texts. I adhere to the second position, as developed by contemporary neo-rationalist Muslim thinkers, notably Abdolkarim Soroush and Nasr Hamid Abu Zayd.[6] In this perspective, our notion of justice, like our understanding of revealed texts, is contingent on the knowledge around us, and is shaped by extra-religious forces. In Soroush's words, 'Justice as a value cannot be religious, it is religion that has to be just' ('Islamic Revival', 132–3); any religious text or law that defies our notion of justice should be reinterpreted in the light of an ethical critique of its religious roots.

My second distinction, which I also take from Islamic jurisprudence, is between the two main categories of legal rulings (*ahkam*): between *'ibadat* (ritual/spiritual acts) and *mu'amalat* (social/contractual acts). Rulings in the first category, *'ibadat*, regulate relations between God and the believer, where jurists contend there is only limited scope for rationalization, explanation and change, since they pertain to the spiritual realm and divine mysteries. This is not the case with *mu'amalat*, which regulate relations between humans and remain open to rational considerations and social forces, and to which most rulings concerning women and gender relations belong. Since human affairs are in a state of constant change and evolution, there is always a need for new rulings, based on new interpretations of the sacred texts, in line with the changing realities of time and place. This is the very rationale for *ijtihad* (literally, 'self-exertion', 'endeavor'), which is the jurist's method of finding solutions to new issues in the light of the guidance of revelation (Kamali, 'Methodological Issues', 21).

I must stress that I am not attempting to emulate Muslim jurists (*fuqaha'*), who extract legal rules from the sacred sources by following juristic methodology (*usul al-fiqh*). Nor is my approach the same as that of the majority of Muslim feminists who go back to the sacred texts in order to 'unread patriarchy'.[7] Rather, I seek to engage with juristic constructs

---

[6]See Soroush, 'Islamic Revival'; idem, 'Beauty of Justice'; Abu Zayd, 'Concept of Justice'; idem, *Reformation*.

[7]For instance, Barlas; Barazangi; Hassan, 'Equal before Allah?'; idem, 'Feminist Theology'; idem, 'Feminism in Islam'; Jawad; Mernissi, *Women and Islam*; Shaikh, 'Exegetical Violence'; idem, 'Knowledge, Women and Gender'; Wadud, *Qur'an and Woman*; idem, 'Qur'an, Gender and Interpretive Possibilities'; idem, *Inside the Gender Jihad*; Al-Hibri, 'Islam, Law and Custom'; idem, 'Muslim Women's Rights; Ali,

and theories, to unveil the theological and rational arguments and legal theories that underlie them and, above all, to understand the conception of justice and the notion of gender that permeate family law in Islamic legal tradition. I contend that this family law is a social construction, like other laws in the realm of *mu'amalat*, and is shaped in interaction with political, economic, social and cultural forces and with those who have the power to represent and define interpretations of Islam's sacred texts.

Gender in classical *fiqh*: the sanctification of patriarchy

In classical *fiqh* texts,[8] gender inequality is an *a priori* principle that reflects the way in which their authors related to the sacred texts of Islam and the world in which they lived. In this world, inequality between men and women was the natural order of things, the only way to regulate relations between them. Classical *fiqh*'s assumptions about gender are encapsulated in two sets of legal rulings: on the one hand, those that define marriage and divorce, and on the other those that regulate women's covering and seclusion. In these matters, the various *fiqh* schools all share the same inner logic and patriarchal conception. If they differ, it is in the manner and extent to which they have translated this conception into legal rules.[9]

Marriage: from contract to control

Classical jurists defined marriage as a contract of exchange whose prime purpose is to render sexual relations between a man and a woman licit. The contract is called *'aqd al-nikah* (literally 'contract of coitus') and has three essential elements: the offer (*ijab*) by the woman or her guardian (*wali*), the acceptance (*qabul*) by the man, and the payment of dower (*mahr*), a sum of money or any valuable that the husband pays or undertakes to pay to the bride before or after consummation.

In discussing its legal structure and effects, classical jurists often used the analogy of the contract of sale and alluded to parallels between the status of wives and female slaves, to whose sexual services husbands/

'Progressive Muslims'; idem, *Sexual Ethics*.
[8]By 'classical', I mean dating from the formative period, before modern times.
[9]For differences between the *fiqh* schools, see Maghniyyah.

owners were entitled, and who were deprived of freedom of movement. Al-Ghazali, the great twelfth-century Muslim philosopher, in his monumental work *Revival of Religious Sciences*, devoted a book to marriage, where he echoed the prevalent view of his time:

> It is enough to say that marriage is a kind of slavery, for a wife is a slave to her husband. She owes her husband absolute obedience in whatever he may demand of her, where she herself is concerned, as long as no sin is involved. (89)[10]

Likewise, Muhaqqiq al-Hilli, the renowned thirteenth-century Shi'i jurist, wrote:

> Marriage etymologically is uniting one thing with another thing; it is also said to mean coitus and to mean sexual intercourse . . . it has been said that it is a contract whose object is that of dominion over *buz'* (vagina), without the right of its possession. It has also been said that it is a verbal contract that first establishes the right to sexual intercourse, that is to say: it is not like buying a female slave, when the man acquires the right of intercourse as a consequence of the possession of the slave. (428)

Khalil ibn Ishaq, the prominent fourteenth-century Maliki jurist, was equally explicit when it came to dower and its function in marriage:

> When a woman marries, she sells a part of her person. In the market one buys merchandise, in marriage the husband buys the genital *arvum mulieris*.[11] As in any other bargain and sale, only useful and ritually clean objects may be given in dower. (Ruxton 106)[12]

I am not suggesting that classical jurists conceptualized marriage either as a sale or as slavery.[13] Certainly there were significant differences and disa-

---

[10]For another rendering of this passage, see Farah (120).

[11]This Latin phrase—meaning 'woman's pasture'—is Ruxton's prudish rendering of the Arabic word *buz'* as used by Hilli, quoted above.

[12]Jorjani, another Maliki jurist, defines marriage in the following terms: 'a contract through which the husband acquires exclusive rights over the sexual organs of woman' (quoted in Pesle 20).

[13]For similarities in the juristic conceptions of slavery and marriage, see Marmon, and Willis.

greements about this among the schools, and debates within each, with legal and practical implications.[14] Even statements such as those quoted above distinguish between the right of access to the woman's sexual and reproductive faculties (which her husband acquires) and the right over her person (which he does not). Rather, what I want to communicate is that the notion and legal logic of 'ownership' (*tamlik*) and sale underlie their conception of marriage and define the parameters of laws and practices, where a woman's sexuality, if not her person, becomes a commodity, an object of exchange. It is also this logic, as we shall see, that defines the rights and duties of each spouse in marriage and, in al-Ghazali's words, makes marriage like slavery for women.

Aware of possible misunderstandings, classical jurists were careful to stress that marriage resembles sale only in form, not in spirit, and they drew a clear line between free and slave women in terms of rights and status.[15] The marriage contract is among the few contracts in *fiqh* that crosses the boundary between its two main divisions: *'ibadat* and *mu'amalat*. The jurists spoke of marriage as a religious duty, lauded its religious merit and enumerated the ethical injunctions that the contract entailed for the spouses. But these ethical injunctions were eclipsed by those elements in the contract that concerned the exchange and sanctioned men's control over women's sexuality. What jurists defined as the prime 'purposes of marriage' separated the legal from the moral in marriage; their consensus held these purposes to be: the gratification of sexual needs, procreation, and the preservation of morality.[16] Whatever served, or followed from, these purposes became compulsory duties incumbent on each spouse, which the jurists discussed under *ahkam al-zawaj* (laws of matrimony). The rest, though still morally incumbent, remained legally unenforceable and were left to the conscience of individuals.

For each party, the contract entails a set of defined rights and obligations, some with moral sanction and others with legal force. Those with

---

[14]For these disagreements see Ali ('Progressive Muslims', 70–82); for the impact of these disagreements on rulings related to *mahr* and the ways in which classical jurists discussed them, see Ibn Rushd (2:31–3).

[15]For differentiation by Hanafi jurists between social and commercial exchange, and the valorization of the human body, see Johansen, 'Commercial Exchange'; idem, 'Valorization'.

[16]For a discussion, see 'Abd Al 'Ati; the last purpose takes prime place in the writings of radical Islamists such as Maududi (see, for example, his *Laws of Marriage*, and *Purdah*).

legal force revolve around the twin themes of sexual access and compensation, embodied in the two concepts *tamkin* (obedience; also *ta'a*) and *nafaqa* (maintenance). *Tamkin*, defined in terms of sexual submission, is a man's right and thus a woman's duty; whereas *nafaqa*, defined as shelter, food and clothing, is a woman's right and a man's duty. A woman becomes entitled to *nafaqa* only after consummation of the marriage, and she loses her claim if she is in a state of *nushuz* (disobedience). There is no matrimonial regime: the husband is the sole owner of the matrimonial resources, and the wife remains the possessor of her dower and whatever she brings to or earns during the marriage. She has no legal duty to do housework and is entitled to demand wages if she does. The procreation of children is the only area the spouses share, but even here a wife is not legally required to suckle her child and can demand compensation if she does.

Among the default rights of the husband is his power to control his wife's movements and her 'excess piety'. She needs his permission to leave the house, to take up employment, or to engage in fasting or forms of worship other than what is obligatory (i.e. the fast of Ramadan). Such acts may infringe on the husband's right of 'unhampered sexual access'.

A man may enter into up to four marriages at a time,[17] and may terminate each contract at will: he needs neither grounds for termination nor the consent or presence of his wife. Legally speaking, *talaq*, repudiation of the wife, is a unilateral act (*iqa'*), which acquires legal effect by the husband's declaration. Likewise, a woman may not be released without her husband's consent, although she may secure her release through offering him inducements, by means of *khul'*, often referred to as 'divorce by mutual consent'. As defined by classical jurists, *khul'* is a separation claimed by the wife as a result of her extreme 'reluctance' or 'dislike' (*karahiyya*) towards her husband, and the essential element is the payment of compensation (*'iwad*) to the husband in return for her release. This can be the return of the dower, or any other form of compensation. Unlike *talaq*, *khul'* is not a unilateral but a bilateral act, as it cannot take legal effect without the consent of the husband. If the wife fails to secure his consent, her only recourse is the intervention of the court and the judge's power either to compel the husband to pronounce *talaq* or to pronounce it on his behalf. In defining *talaq* as the exclusive right of the husband, the classical jurists used the

---

[17]In Shi'a law a man may contract as many temporary marriages (*mut'a*) as he desires or can afford. For this form of marriage, see Haeri.

analogy of manumission—a right that exclusively rested with the master of a slave. In al-Ghazali's words, 'the man is the owner and he has, as it were, enslaved the woman through the dowry and . . . she has no discernment in her affairs' (cited in Marmon 19).[18]

Hijab: from covering to confinement

Unlike rulings on marriage, classical *fiqh* texts contain little on the dress code for women. The prominence of *hijab* in Islamic discourses is a recent phenomenon, dating to the nineteenth-century Muslim encounter with colonial powers. It is then that we see the emergence of a new genre of literature in which the veil acquires a civilizational dimension and becomes both a marker of Muslim identity and an element of faith.

Classical Islamic legal texts—at least the genre that sets out rulings (*ahkam*) or what we may call 'positive law'—contain no explicit rulings on women's dress, nor on how women should appear in public.[19] They do not use the term *hijab*,[20] and they use *sitr* (covering) to discuss the issue of dress for both men and women, but only in two contexts: first, rulings for covering the body during prayers, secondly, rulings that govern a man's 'gaze' at a woman prior to marriage.

The rules are minimal, but clear-cut. During prayer, both men and women must cover their *'awra*, their private parts; for men, this is the area between knees and navel, but for women it means all parts of the body apart from hands, feet and face. As regards the 'gaze', it is forbidden for men to look at the uncovered body of women to whom he is not closely related—a ban that may be removed when a man wants to contract a marriage and needs to inspect the woman he intends to marry. The rulings

[18]In classical *fiqh* texts, the *Book of Divorce* (*Kitab al-talaq*) is often followed by the *Book of Manumission* (*kitab al-itaq*); in the words of al-'Ayni, a fifteenth-century commentator: 'The reason for the analogy between the two books lies in the fact that divorce is the release of the individual from the subjugation of ownership of the sexual organ (*takhlis al-shakhs min dhull milk al-mut'a*) and manumission is the release of the individual from the subjugation ownership of the physical person (*takhlis al-shakhs min dhull milk al-raqaba*)' (quoted in Marmon, 18; q.v. for discussion).
[19]Clark shows there is little concern in the Hadith literature with women's covering, and no explicit reference to the covering of hair; there are more hadith on men's dress and covering their *'awra* than on women's dress.
[20]Other terms commonly used today in various countries, such as *parda* ('*purdah*'), *chador*, *burqa'*, are not found in classical *fiqh* texts.

on covering during prayer are discussed in the Book of Prayer and are among the *'ibadat* (ritual/worship acts), while those on 'gaze' come in the Book of Marriage, and fall under *mu'amalat* (social/contractual acts).[21]

There is, however, another notion of *hijab* that remains implicit in these texts: 'confinement'. This notion rests on two interrelated juristic constructs that cut across *fiqh*'s two divisions: *'ibadat* and *mu'amalat*. The first construct defines a woman's whole body as *'awra*, a sexual zone, that must be covered both during prayers (before God) and in society (before men). This is found in the Book of Prayer (*kitab al-salah*) under 'covering of private parts' (*sitr al-'awra*), the only place in the text that requires the covering of specific parts of the body. The second construct considers a woman's sexuality to be *fitna*, a source of danger to public order, and consequently grants men the right to control women's movements. The rulings on segregation (banning any kind of interaction between unrelated men and women) have their logic in the second construct.[22]

Unveiling patriarchal premises

These are, in a nutshell, the classical *fiqh* rulings on marriage and covering. Whether they ever have corresponded to actual practices of marriage and gender relations is, of course, another area of inquiry, and that, too, feminist scholarship in Islam has started to uncover.[23] Yet some scholars and Islamists continue to claim that they are immutable and divinely ordained, and therefore invoke them to legitimate patriarchy on religious grounds. Such claims must be challenged on their own terms. Among important questions to ask are: How far do these rulings reflect the principle of justice that is inherent in the *Shari'a*? Why and how does classical *fiqh* define marriage and covering in such a way that they deprive women of free will, confine them to the home and make them subject to male authority? These questions become even more crucial if we accept—as I do—the sincerity

[21]For these rulings and their rationale, see Mutahhari, *Islamic Modest Dress*, and Ibn Rushd (1: 125–30; 2:2).

[22]For a critical discussion of these two assumptions, see Abou El Fadl, *Speaking in God's Name*, 239–47.

[23]For an insightful discussion of the ways in which women in pre-modern times related to *fiqh* rulings, see Rapoport; Sonbol, *Women, Family and Divorce Laws*; and idem, 'Women in Shariah Courts'.

of the classical jurists' claim that they derive their ideal model of gender relations from Islam's sacred sources.

Feminist scholarship in Islam gives us two sets of related answers. The first set is ideological and political, and has to do with the strong patriarchal ethos that informed the classical jurists' readings of the sacred texts and the exclusion of women from production of religious knowledge, and their consequent inability to have their voices heard and their interests reflected in law. The second set of answers is more epistemological, and concerns the ways in which social norms, existing norms, marriage practices and gender ideologies were sanctified, and then turned into fixed entities in *fiqh*. That is, rather than considering them as social, and thus temporal, institutions and phenomena, the classical jurists treated them as 'divinely ordained', thus immutable.

The model of marriage and gender roles constructed in *fiqh* is grounded in the patriarchal ideology of pre-Islamic Arabia, which continued into the Islamic era, though in a modified form. There is an extensive debate in the literature on this, which I will not enter.[24] But there are two points of consensus among students of Islam and gender. The first is that the revelatory texts and the Prophet altered only some of the existing patriarchal practices of the time (such as burying infant girls alive, and coercing women into unwanted marriages) and left others intact (such as polygamy and men's right to unilateral divorce). The Qur'an and the Hadith set in motion a reform of family laws in the direction of justice that was halted after the Prophet's death. What the Prophet did was to rectify injustice and to introduce justice, as these were understood in his day. Second, the further we move from the time of revelation, the more women are marginalized and lose their political clout: their voices are silenced and their presence in public space is curtailed.

Many verses in the Qur'an condemn women's subjugation, affirm the principle of equality between genders, and aim to reform existing practices in that direction.[25] Yet this subjugation is reproduced in *fiqh*—though

---

[24]Some argue that the advent of Islam weakened the patriarchal structures of Arabian society, others that it reinforced them. The latter also maintain that, before the advent of Islam, society was undergoing a transition from matrilineal to patrilineal descent, that Islam facilitated this by giving patriarchy the seal of approval, and that the Qur'anic injunctions on marriage, divorce, inheritance, and whatever relates to women, both reflect and affirm such a transition. For concise accounts of the debate, see Smith, and Spellberg.

[25]Of more than 6,000 verses in the Qur'an, only a few treat men and women differently;

in a mitigated form. The classical *fiqh* model of marriage is based on one type of marriage agreement prevalent in pre-Islamic Arabia, known as 'marriage of dominion'; it closely resembled a sale, by which a woman became the property of her husband (Esposito 14–15). The jurists redefined and reformed certain aspects of the 'marriage of dominion' to accommodate the Qur'anic call to reform and to enhance women's status and to protect them in a patriarchal institution. Women became parties to, not subjects of, the contract, and recipients of the dower or marriage gift. Likewise, by modifying the regulations on polygamy and divorce, the jurists curtailed men's scope of dominion over women in the contract, without altering the essence of the contract or freeing women from the authority of men—whether fathers or husbands.[26]

In producing these rulings, the jurists based their theological arguments on a number of philosophical, metaphysical, social and legal assumptions. Salient assumptions that underlie *fiqh* rulings on marriage and gender rights are: 'women are created of and for men', 'God made men superior to women', 'women are defective in reason and faith'. While they are not substantiated in the Qur'an—as recent scholarship has shown[27]—they became the main theological assumptions for classical jurists seeking to discern legal rules from the sacred texts. The moral and social rationale for women's subjugation is found in the theory of difference in male and female sexuality, which goes as follows: God gave women greater sexual desire than men, but this is mitigated by two innate factors, men's *ghayra* (sexual honor and jealousy) and women's *haya* (modesty and shyness). What jurists concluded from this theory is that women's sexuality, if left uncontrolled by men, runs havoc, and is a real threat to social order. Feminist scholarship on Islam gives vivid accounts of the working of this theory in medieval legal and erotic texts, and its impact on women's lives in contemporary Muslim societies.[28] Women's *haya* and men's *ghayra*, seen as innate qualities defining femininity and masculinity, in this way became tools for controlling women and the rationale for their exclusion

four of these (2:222, 228 and 4:3, 34) are frequently cited as justifications for unequal gender rights in marriage. For a discussion, see Muhammad et al.
[26]For differences between classical schools on matrimonial guardianship or *wilaya*, see Maghniyyah (47–53).
[27]See Barlas; Hassan, 'Equal before Allah?'; idem, 'Feminist Theology'; Mernissi, *Women and Islam*; Wadud, *Qur'an and Woman*; idem, *Inside the Gender Jihad*, 186–216.
[28]See Mernissi, *Beyond the Veil*; and Mir-Hosseini, 'Sexuality, Rights and Islam'.

from public life.[29] The sale contract, as already discussed, provided the juristic basis for women's subjugation in marriage, and the legal construction of women's bodies as *'awra* (pudenda) and of their sexuality as a source of *fitna* (chaos) removed them from public space, and thus from political life in Muslim societies.

By the time the *fiqh* schools emerged, women's critical faculties were so far denigrated as to make their concerns irrelevant to law-making processes.[30] Women were among transmitters of prophetic Hadith, yet, as Sachedina reminds us:

> It is remarkable that even when women transmitters of hadith were admitted in the *'ilm al-rijal* ('Science dealing with the scrutiny of the reports'), and . . . even when their narratives were recognized as valid documentation for deducing various rulings, they were not participants in the intellectual process that produced the prejudicial rulings encroaching upon the personal status of women. More importantly, the revelatory text, regardless of its being extracted from the Qur'an or the Sunna, was casuistically extrapolated in order to disprove a woman's intellectual and emotional capacities to formulate independent decisions that would have been sensitive and more accurate in estimating her radically different life experience. ('Woman Half-the-Man', 149)

I do not suggest that there was a conspiracy among classical jurists to undermine women, or that they deliberately sought to ignore the voice of revelation. Rather I argue that, in their understanding of the sacred texts, these jurists were guided by their own outlook, and in discerning the terms of the *Shari'a*, they were constrained by a set of gender assumptions and legal theories that reflected the social and political realities of their age. These assumptions and theories, which reflected the state of knowledge and the normative values and patriarchal institutions of their time, came to be treated by subsequent generations as though they were immutable, and as part of the *Shari'a*. This is what

---

[29]This rationale is found in many contemporary texts on women in Islam; an explicit example is Maududi, *Purdah*.

[30]As Abou-Bakr shows, women remained active in transmitting religious knowledge, but their activities were limited to the informal arena of homes and mosques and their status as jurists was not officially recognized.

Sachedina calls the crisis of epistemology in traditional evaluation of Islamic legal heritage.

> The Muslim jurists, by exercise of their rational faculty to its utmost degree, recorded their reactions to the experiences of the community: *they created, rather than discovered, God's law.* What they created was a literary expression of their aspirations, their consensual interests, and their achievements; what they provided for Islamic society was an ideal, a symbol, a conscience, and a principle of order and identity. ('Ideal and Real', 29 [emphasis added])

In this way, essentially time-bound phenomena—patriarchal notions of marriage and gender rights—were turned into juridical principles of permanent validity. This was achieved, first by assimilating social norms into *Shari'a* ideals, and second by classifying rulings pertaining to family and gender relations under the category of *mu'amalat* (social / private contracts, where the rulings are subject to rationalization and change), while treating them as though they belonged to the category of *'ibadat* (acts of worship where the rulings are immutable and not open to rational discussion).

In short, *fiqh* rulings on the family are literal expressions of the classical jurists' consensual understanding of Islam's revealed texts and their notions of justice and gender relations, shaped in interaction with the values and norms, the social and economic and political realities, of the world in which they lived. In that world, patriarchy and slavery were part of the fabric of society, seen as the natural order of things, the way to regulate social relations. The idea of gender equality—as we mean it today—had no place and little relevance to the classical jurists' conceptions of justice, and thus was naturally absent in all pre-modern legal theories and systems.[31] They were, in Arkoun's terms, 'unthinkable' for pre-modern Muslim jurists, and remained 'unthought' in Islamic legal tradition.[32]

---

[31]Until the nineteenth century, the Islamic legal tradition granted women better rights than did its Western counterparts. For instance, Muslim women have always been able to retain their legal and economic autonomy in marriage, while in England it was not until 1882, with the passage of the Married Women's Property Act, that women acquired the right to retain ownership of property after marriage (see Wright); Wright's discussion of the assumptions that informed English family law in the eighteenth century reveals striking parallels with those of classical *fiqh*.

[32]For a discussion of these concepts in Arkoun's work, see Gunther.

Gender in twentieth-century legal discourses: a modification of patriarchy

With the rise of Western hegemony over the Muslim world and the spread of secular systems of education in the nineteenth century, the ideological hold of *fiqh* conceptions of gender relations began to wane. At the same time, the colonial encounter turned the 'status of women in Islam' into a contested issue, a symbolic political battleground between the forces of traditionalism and modernity, a situation that has continued ever since.

New gender discourses emerged and were aired in the vast literature on 'women in Islam' that dates from the start of the twentieth century. Produced by religious publishing houses in both Muslim and Western countries, this literature is available (much of it now on the Internet) in a variety of languages, including English.[33] It consists of highly varied texts, which range from outright polemic to sound scholarship, and which, in terms of their gender perspective, fall into two broad genres. The first, which comprises the majority of available texts and views, advocates a modified version of classical *fiqh* rulings. Authors in this genre, which I term 'Neo-Traditionalist', reject legal equality between the sexes as an imported 'Western' concept that has no place in an Islamic worldview. Instead they argue for 'complementarity of rights', sometimes called 'gender equity' or 'balance'. The second genre, which I call Reformist or Feminist, advocates gender equality on all fronts. It emerged in the last two decades of the twentieth century and is in the process of formation; it constitutes a small part of the literature.

Gender balance: inequality redefined

The roots of the first new discourse can be traced to the nineteenth century and the Muslim world's encounter with Western colonial powers, but its impact is linked with the emergence of modern nation-states in the twentieth century and the creation of modern legal systems inspired by Western models. In many such Muslim states, classical *fiqh* provisions on the

---

[33]For a discussion of such writings in the Arab world, see Haddad, and Stowasser; for Iran, see Mir-Hosseini, *Islam and Gender*; for Muslims living in Europe and North America, see Roald; texts in English include Badawi; Doi; Khan; Maududi, *Laws of Marriage*; idem, *Purdah*; Mutahhari, *Rights of Women*; idem, *Islamic Modest Dress*.

family were selectively reformed, codified and grafted onto unified legal systems inspired by Western models. With the exceptions of Turkey, which abandoned *fiqh* in all spheres of law and replaced it with Western-inspired codes, and Saudi Arabia, which preserved classical *fiqh* as a fundamental law and attempted to apply it in all spheres of law, the large majority of Muslim states retained *fiqh* only with respect to personal status law (family and inheritance). The extent and impetus for reform varied from one country to another, but those governments that codified family law introduced reforms through procedural rules (i.e. registration of marriages and divorces), which in most cases left the substance of the classical *fiqh* rulings more or less unchanged.[34]

In the process of adaptation, family law moved from being the concern of private scholars operating within a particular *fiqh* school, to the legislative assembly of a particular nation-state. Statute books took the place of *fiqh* manuals and texts in regulating the legal status of women in society. This led to the creation of a hybrid family law that is neither classical *fiqh* nor Western, and a new gender discourse that is ambivalent on the issue of equality in the family. Though commonly termed Islamic Modernism, I suggest that 'Neo-Traditionalism' is a more apt term for this discourse, as it shares the classical jurists' basic understanding of gender. Where it differs is that, unlike classical jurists, advocates of the new discourse are able to impose their notions through the machinery of a modern nation-state. This gave the patriarchal interpretations of the *Shari'a* a different legal force (see Mir-Hosseini , *Marriage on Trial*, 10–13).[35]

The Neo-Traditionalist gender discourse is found not only in the legal codes of Muslim countries, but in a new type of texts that, unlike classical *fiqh* texts, are neither necessarily produced by jurists nor strictly legal in their reasoning and arguments, which makes them more accessible to the general public. Published by religious houses and largely written by

---

[34]Tunisia was the exception, incorporating the principle of gender equity into its 1956 family law (see Nasir 125–42). For the codification of *fiqh* rulings and reforms, see Anderson, and Rahman, 'Survey of Modernization'; for their adoption by legal codes in Arab countries, see El Alami; for debates surrounding codification and further reforms, see Moors, and Welchman.

[35]Recent studies of medieval and Ottoman court archive materials and judgments show that, not only did judges generally take a liberal and protective attitude toward women, but also women could choose between legal schools and judges; see, for instance, Sonbol, *Women, Family and Divorce Laws*; idem, 'Women in Shariah Courts'; Rapoport; and Tucker.

men—at least until recently—the overt aims of these texts are to shed new
light on the status of women in Islam, and to clarify what they see as
'misunderstandings about the law of Islam'. The main themes through
which the authors of these texts address the issue of gender relations and
define a range of positions are women's covering, marriage and divorce
laws, and women's right to education and employment. Despite their
variety and diverse cultural origins, what these authors have in common is
an oppositional stance and a defensive or apologetic tone: oppositional,
because their concern is to resist change and suppress voices of dissent
from within, which they see as 'invasion of Western and alien values';
apologetic, because by going back to classical *fiqh* and upholding its
rulings they inadvertently expose—and have to defend—its inherent and
anachronistic gender biases.

Unwilling to accept that the aspiration for gender equality is not just an
imported (Western) concept but part of modern realities, these authors
often find themselves in a paradoxical position. On the one hand, they
adopt an uncritical approach to classical *fiqh* constructions of marriage and
gender relations, and on the other, aware of, and sensitive to, criticisms of
patriarchal bias, they begin their texts with abstract and general statements
such as 'Islam affirms the basic equality of men and women', 'Islam grants
women all their rights', and 'Islam protects and honors women'. It is
common to find a single text in which the author accepts the principle of
gender equality on one issue (usually on women's education and employment, where classical *fiqh* is more or less silent), but rejects it on matters
related to covering and marriage laws (where classical *fiqh* is strident).

Neo-Traditionalist texts lack the legal coherence and the sense of real
conviction that imbue classical *fiqh* texts. Keen to distance themselves
from overtly patriarchal language and concepts, their authors keep silent
on the juristic theories and theological and other assumptions that underlie
these rulings in classical *fiqh* texts. For instance, they ignore the parallels
in the legal structures of the contracts of marriage and sale, and views such
as those of al-Ghazali (quoted earlier), which see marriage as a type of
enslavement for women. Yet the patriarchal logic and the notion of possession (*tamlik*) implicit in their texts come to the surface when they resort to
legal arguments, as in Maududi's explanation of why women cannot have
equal rights to divorce:

If she were to be given this right, she would grow over-bold and easily violate the men's rights. It is evident that if a person buys something with money, he tries to keep it as long as he can. He parts with it only when he cannot help it. But when a thing is purchased by one individual, and the right to cast it away is given to another, there is little hope that the latter will protect the interest of the buyer, who invested the money. Investing man with the right to divorce amounts to the protection of his legitimate rights. This also checks the growth of the divorce rate. (*Laws of Marriage* 27)

A large majority of these Neo-Traditionalist texts focus on the ethical and moral rules that marriage entails for each spouse, drawing attention to those Qur'anic verses and Hadiths that affirm the essential equality of the sexes. Yet they fail to mention that these ethical rules, in effect, carry no legal sanction, nor do they offer any suggestions as to how they can be translated into legal imperatives. Likewise, while rejecting *fiqh* rulings on seclusion, Neo-Traditionalist texts defend the principle of gender segregation and speak of *hijab* as a religious duty that requires a woman to cover her hair and body (with the exception of face and hands) when in the presence of unrelated men and in public. A good example is Jamal Badawi's booklet, *Gender Equity in Islam: Basic Principles*. Marriage, Badawi states, 'is about peace, love and compassion, not just the satisfaction of men's needs', but then he goes on to reproduce all the *fiqh* rulings on marriage and divorce almost verbatim.[36] In line with other texts in this genre, Badawi is content with simply outlining what he calls 'normative teachings of Islam', glosses over male dominance, and imputes the injustices that women suffer in marriage and society to what he calls 'diverse cultural practices among Muslims'. He seems to be unaware that many of the *fiqh* rulings that he reproduces negate the 'basic principles' of 'gender equity' that he claims in his booklet are Islamic.

Among texts of this genre that offer a new rationalization and defense of classical *fiqh* rulings on marriage and *hijab*, and contain a theory of gender rights, are: Morteza Mutahhari's *System of Women's Rights in Islam* and Abul A'la Maududi's *Purdah and the Status of Women in Islam*.[37]

[36]A short version of the booklet is posted on several Islamist websites.

[37]Both books are available in English and Arabic and have gone through many editions; for a reading of their texts, see Shehadeh.

Both authors were Islamic ideologues, and their writings, rooted in anti-colonial and anti-Western discourses, have become seminal texts for Islamist groups and movements. Writing in Urdu in the 1930s, in the context of pre-partition India, Maududi's adamant rejection and condemnation of modernity and liberal values have made him more appealing to radical Islamists. For him, the problem with Muslims is that they have abandoned their own way of life and adopted secular (i.e. Western and to some extent Hindu) values that have corrupted them and are destroying their civilization. The solution he offers is an 'Islamic state' with the power and inclination to enforce the Islamic way of life, where women's seclusion and control by men are foundational. Mutahhari, writing in Persian in 1960s Iran as part of the religious opposition to the Shah's secularizing policies, is less adamant in his opposition to modernity and less overtly patriarchal: he is more popular with moderate Islamist groups.[38]

Though different in language and sophistication, Maududi and Mutahhari follow the same line of argument, based on the same premises of the 'naturalness' of laws in Islam and the 'innate difference' between men and women. These two premises become the pillars of a new defense of gender inequality, which goes as follows: though men and women are created equal and are equal in the eyes of God, the roles assigned to them in creation, and by implication in the social order, are different, and *fiqh* rules reflect this difference; if correctly understood, they are the very essence of justice. This is so, they argue, because these rulings not only reflect the *Shari'a*, the divine blueprint for society, but are also in line with 'human nature' (*fitra*) and take into consideration the biological and psychological differences between the sexes.

This new defense has, ironically, further accentuated the internal contradictions and anachronisms in classical *fiqh* rulings. For example, if, as the classical theory of sexuality holds, women's sexual desire is greater than men's, and if laws in Islam work with, not against, the grain of nature, how can they allow men but not women to contract more than one marriage at a time? Surely God would not give women greater sexual desire, and then allow men to be the polygamists and make covering obligatory for women? The Neo-Traditionalists resolve such contradictions by modifying the classical theory of sexuality, to eliminate its conflict with the newly

[38]For a discussion and analysis of Mutahhari's text, see Mir-Hosseini, *Islam and Gender*.

advocated theory of the naturalness of *fiqh*-based law. Women's sexuality, thus, is now explained as passive and responsive, and men's as active and aggressive—a theory that has indeed little precedent in classical texts.[39] In arguing for such a theory of sexuality, it is important to note that both Maududi and Mutahhari do not draw on Islam's sacred texts but on Western psychological and sociological studies. Their readings of these—now long outdated—sources are quite selective, and they cite as 'scientific evidence' only those that are in line with *fiqh* definitions of marriage. They are also selective in their readings of the sacred texts and in their usage of classical *fiqh* concepts and definitions.[40]

Gender equality: questioning patriarchal premises

With the rise of political Islam in the second part of the twentieth century, and the rallying cry of 'Return to the *Shari'a*' as embodied in *fiqh* rulings, Islamist political movements appropriated these Neo-Traditionalist texts and their gender discourse. Political Islam had its biggest triumph in 1979 with the popular revolution in Iran that brought Islamic clerics to power; women's covering and gender segregation in public space were soon mandatory. The same year saw the dismantling of reforms introduced earlier in the century by modernist governments in Iran and Egypt, and the introduction of *hudud* ordinances in Pakistan. Yet this was also the year when the United Nations adopted CEDAW.

Paradoxically, the Islamists' slogan of 'Return to *Shari'a*' and their attempt to translate *fiqh* notions of gender into policy became the catalyst for a critique of these notions and a spur to women's increased activism. Islamists' defense of pre-modern patriarchal interpretations of the *Shari'a* as 'God's Law', as the authentic 'Islamic' way of life, brought the classical *fiqh* books out of the closet and exposed them to critical scrutiny and public debate. A new phase in the politics of gender in Islam began, as growing numbers of women came to question whether there was an inherent or logical link between Islamic ideals and patriarchy. One crucial element of this new phase has been that it places women themselves—rather than the

[39]Allameh Tabataba'i, the renowned Shi'i philosopher, was the first to advance this theory in his monumental Qur'anic commentary known as *Al-Mizan*, written in Arabic between 1954 and 1972; see Mir-Hosseini, 'Women's Rights'.
[40]See also Ali, *Sexual Ethics*.

abstract notion of 'the status of woman in Islam' — at the heart of the battle between forces of traditionalism and modernism.

By the early 1990s, a new way of thinking about gender emerged, a discourse that is 'feminist' in its aspiration and demands, yet 'Islamic' in its language and sources of legitimacy. Some versions of this new discourse came to be labeled 'Islamic Feminism' — a conjunction that is unsettling to the majority of Islamists and some secular feminists. Among others, I have written and spoken at some length about this emerging feminism, which is quite diverse and speaks with many voices ('Muslim Women's Quest'). In my view, it is difficult and perhaps futile to put these voices into neat categories, and to try to generate a definition that reflects the diversity of positions and approaches of so-called 'Islamic feminists'. As with other feminists, their positions are local, multiple and evolving; many of them have difficulty with the label, and object to being called either 'Islamic' or 'feminist'. They all seek gender justice and equality for women, though they do not always agree on what constitutes 'justice' or 'equality', or the best ways of attaining them.

But what is important to stress is the potential of a brand of feminism that takes Islam as the source of its legitimacy to challenge both the hegemony of patriarchal interpretations of the *Shari'a* and the authority of those who speak in the name of Islam. This places so-called 'Islamic feminism' in a unique position to expose the inequalities embedded in current interpretations of the *Shari'a* as constructions by male jurists rather than manifestations of divine will. This exposure can have important epistemological and political consequences. Epistemological because, if it is taken to its logical conclusion, it can be argued that some rules that until now have been claimed as 'Islamic', and part of the *Shari'a*, are in fact only the views and perceptions of some Muslims, and are social practices and norms that are neither sacred nor immutable but human and changing. Political because it can both free Muslims from taking a defensive position and enable them to go beyond old jurisprudential dogmas in search of new questions and new answers.

'Islamic feminism' is part of a new trend of reformist religious thought that is consolidating a conception of Islam and modernity as compatible, not opposed. Reformist thinkers do not reject an idea simply because it is Western, nor do they see Islam as providing a blueprint, as having an in-built program of action for the social, economic, and political problems of the Muslim world. Following and building on the work of earlier reformers such as Muhammad 'Abduh, Muhammad Iqbal and Fazlur Rahman, they contend that the human understanding of Islam is flexible, that Islam's tenets can be interpreted to encourage both pluralism and democracy, and that Islam allows change in the face of time, space and experience.[41] Not only do they pose a serious challenge to legalistic and absolutist conceptions of Islam, but they are also carving a space within which Muslim women can achieve gender equality in law.

Instead of searching for an Islamic genealogy for modern concepts such as gender equality, human rights and democracy (the concern of earlier reformers), the new thinkers place the emphasis on how religion is understood and how religious knowledge is produced. Revisiting the old theological debates, they aim to revive the rationalist approach that was eclipsed when legalism took over as the dominant mode and gave precedence to the form of the law over its substance and spirit. In this respect, the works of the new wave of Muslim thinkers such as Mohammad Arkoun, Khaled Abu El Fadl, Nasr Hamid Abu Zayd, Mohammad Mojtahed Shabestari and Abdolkarim Soroush are of immense importance and relevance.[42] The questions they are now asking, and the assumptions that inform their readings of the sacred texts, are radically different from those of classical jurists. They are re-examining critically the older interpretations and epistemologies and exposing the contradictions inherent in the earlier discourses on family and gender rights.

Conclusions

Both feminist and reformist voices in Islam are still in a formative phase, and their future prospects are tied to political developments all over the Muslim world—and to global politics. But let me end this article with two observations that herald the emergence of an egalitarian gender paradigm in Islamic legal tradition, the catalyst for which has been the rise of political Islam.

[41]For the textual genealogy of this thinking, see Kurzman.
[42]For Arkoun, see Gunther; for Abou El Fadl, see his *Speaking in God's Name* and idem, 'Human Rights Commitment'; for Abu Zayd, see Kermani; for Soroush, see his 'Islamic Revival' and the articles available on his website (http://www.drsoroush.com/English. htm), and for his ideas on gender, see Mir-Hosseini, *Islam and Gender*, ch 7; for Shabestari, see Vahdat and articles and interviews at Qantara.de (http://qantara.de/webcom/show_ article.php/_c-575/i.html).

First, as the twentieth century came to a close, for many Muslims the patriarchal dogmas and constructs that informed the pre-modern notions of marriage in Islamic legal tradition lost their theological validity and their power to convince. In their place, the discourses of feminism and human rights have combined to bring a new consciousness and a new point of reference for Muslim women and reformist thinkers. The growing body of texts under the rubric of 'women in Islam', the intensity of the debate, and the diametrically opposed positions taken by some authors, are indications of a radical change in thinking about gender rights, Islamic legal theory and politics. Significantly, even those who see classical *fiqh* rulings on marriage and gender roles as immutable, as part of the *Shari'a*, use titles such as 'Women's Rights in Islam' and 'Gender Equity in Islam', and are silent on the juristic theories and theological assumptions that underlie them, which I have outlined above. Such theories and assumptions are so repugnant to modern sensibilities and ethics, so alien to the experience of marriage among contemporary Muslims, that no one can afford to acknowledge them. This is clear proof that the classical *fiqh* definition of marriage has already become irrelevant to the contemporary experiences and ethical values of Muslims, and that a 'paradigm shift' in Islamic legal tradition and politics is well underway. We become aware of the old paradigm only when the shift has already taken place, when the old rationale and logic, previously undisputed, lose their power to convince and cannot be defended on ethical grounds.

My second observation is that legal systems and jurisprudential theories must be understood in the cultural, political and social contexts in which they operate. The old *fiqh* paradigm, with its strong patriarchal ethos, as well as the new feminist readings of the *Shari'a*, should be understood in this complex double image, as both expressing and moulding social norms and practice. We must not forget that legal theory or jurisprudence is often reactive, in that it reacts to social practices, political, economic and ideological forces, and people's experiences and expectations. Islamic legal tradition is no exception—as attested by the way both legal systems and women's lives and social experiences have been transformed in the course of the twentieth century. The earlier part of the century, in spite of the retreat of religion from politics and the secularization of law and legal systems, did not see the formation of an egalitarian family law. Putting aside *fiqh* as the source in all areas of law except the family reinforced the religious tone of provisions that related to gender rights, turning them into the last bastion of Islamic legal tradition. At the same time, deprived of the power to define and administer family law, *fiqh* and its practitioners were confined to the ivory tower of seminaries; they lost touch with changing political realities and were unable to meet the epistemological challenges of modernity. The rise of political Islam in the 1970s reversed this process, bringing religion back into politics and law, but had the paradoxical and unintended consequences that patriarchal interpretations of the *Shari'a* were desanctified, and that women gained both the reason to demand equality and the language to argue for it from within the tradition. In the new century, Islamic legal tradition can no longer ignore this egalitarian challenge.

14. *Gulf Women and the Codification of Muslim Family Law*

LYNN WELCHMAN

This article provides a preliminary examination of the recent processes and outcomes of family law codification in three Gulf states: the United Arab Emirates (UAE) (2005), Qatar (2006) and most recently Bahrain, where in May 2009 a codified family law was passed for the Sunni section of Bahraini society. The promulgation of these three first-time Muslim family law codes is a significant development in family law codification in the Arab region more generally and in the Gulf in particular. Scholars, lawyers and women's rights activists are presented with an unusual opportunity for comparative empirical and theoretical research with a view to the examination of both the impact of women's contribution to these processes and the impact on women of the results.

In members of the League of Arab States (LAS), women's contribution to and participation in these national debates and legislative and political processes come in various forms. Women participate as members of legislatures and political parties; as lawyers; as members of governmental commissions of women's (and family) affairs and of non-governmental associations and societies. In future research in the Gulf states, uncovering the role of women in these debates and processes will involve exploring the different spaces in which women work to ensure the greater protection of women's (and children's) rights in the family. It will mean tracking the objectives and strategies articulated and worked for by different groupings of women in different contexts, and investigating women's assessment of the processes and their results. It will mean looking at women's agency in court and through the new laws. The recent codification processes offer potentially rich ground for such investigations.

This preliminary consideration seeks to lay some of the groundwork for such investigations and is informed by a close reading of the statutory provisions in question, along with—when they were available—the official commentaries on them and the analyses of non-state actors, particularly specific interventions by women. I begin with a short introduction to the first codification of Muslim family law by the Ottomans with a view to introducing the projected aims and critiques of the idea and process of codification of family law in this first phase. I then briefly consider the recent Gulf codifications in a comparative analysis that includes codifications in other Arab states, with a focus on process, actors, and antecedents. This section includes a short review of the results of a public opinion poll in Bahrain which elicited respondents' attitudes to a number of these same questions: what kind of law, who should draft it, who should promulgate it, where should it be drawn from and—fundamentally—is there a need for one? In the third section, I seek to situate the approaches taken to particular issues of Muslim family law in the Emirati, Qatari and Bahraini Sunni codes in the context of regional Gulf patterns, as well as the somewhat divergent trajectories being taken elsewhere, notably in North Africa. The fourth section points forward in a concluding comment.

Context: codification of Muslim family law in the Middle East

The enactment of codifications of Muslim family law began in the Middle East with the Ottoman Law of Family Rights (OLFR) of 1917. Prior to this, the uncodified jurisprudence of the schools of law, guided mostly by the prevailing opinions of the school of the relevant *qadi* (judge), had been applied to questions of Muslim family law—and often to non-Muslims too. Manuals, compilations and commentaries on the opinions of earlier prominent jurists guided the judges in the application of the law. The OLFR took as its basis the dominant opinions of the Hanafi school, the Ottomans' preferred school, while bringing in minority opinions from the school, and also drew on rules from the other Sunni schools and, on occasion, individual views of prominent jurists, in order to implement and standardize legal approaches to issues of particular interest to the legislator at the start of the twentieth century.

The Ottoman law was abandoned shortly after its promulgation by the new Turkish state, but elsewhere it was applied to varying extents in various Arab successor states under the political arrangements established at the end of World War I (1914–1918) (including mandatory powers held by Britain and France). It was not applied in the three states under consideration here. In Egypt, where the OLFR had not been applied either, significant legislation was issued in the 1920s and 1940s which, while not constituting an overall 'code', addressed a number of areas of family law with approaches that were similarly incorporated into later national codifications elsewhere in the region. In the 1950s, in a second phase of Muslim family law reform, first codifications were issued after independence in Jordan, Syria, Tunisia, and Morocco, and after the overthrow of the monarchy in Iraq; since then, all these countries have either issued substantive amendments or new laws—in some cases, both. Other states followed in succeeding decades. The best-known example in recent years—and a signal 'third phase' development—is Morocco, whose 2004 law is widely regarded as a model of progressive family law reform in the region. The most recent codifications in the Arab world have come in the Gulf.

Paralleling third phase developments in statute and practice in Arab states has been a set of writings by scholars examining the impact on women of the original codification in the OLFR and in early Egyptian legislation, by comparison with pre-existing practice as evidenced by court records and juristic opinions of the sixteenth to nineteenth centuries. As Judith Tucker notes in a relatively early contribution to this debate ('Revisiting Reform', 3), 'We are predisposed to think of reform in general as a good thing, as the key to correcting past abuses and undermining the forces of reaction.' Questioning the extent to which the drafters of the OLFR in fact 'reformed' existing practice unsettles assumptions of uniform 'progress' for all women in the promulgation of every code. The centrality of the state is key; in her most recent work, *Women, Family and Gender in Islamic Law*, Tucker tells the reader that in each area she covers, she seeks to confront:

> . . . the epistemological break in the law of the late nineteenth century
> and the entrance of the state as a central figure in modern legal systems;

this was a watershed period that had far-reaching effects, for better and
worse, on women and gender issues. (36–7)

The Ottomans of the late nineteenth and early twentieth centuries came
to the codification of family law after the extensive re-structuring of the
legal system in the Tanzimat reforms and the introduction, in the newly
established *nizamiyya* courts (state courts), of codes inspired by
European models. The first state-issued codification of Islamic law in
the particular sense in which such codifications came to be 'recognized'
(Messick 57) describes it as initiating 'the transformation of the *Shari'a*
into law') came in the *Majalla*, the collection of civil law principles and
directives that had a lasting impact in several of the Arab states that had
been under Ottoman rule. The *Majalla* included rulings drawn from
minority as well as majority Hanafi opinions in the process of 'selection' (*takhayyur*) that came to constitute the principal methodological
approach of legislators in the Arab states approaching Muslim family
law codification. The *Majalla* set the scene and gave the justification for
the intervention of the state in this manner. In the OLFR, as noted above,
the Ottoman legislators expanded their approach to include rules from
outside the Hanafi school. The binding of the *qadi*s, within the reduced
jurisdiction of the *Shari'a* courts, by a particular juristic opinion, across
the wide range of family law matters of concern to Ottoman subjects,
was a qualitatively—and politically—enhanced leap from the occasional centrally-issued circulars on particular issues that had previously
constituted state intervention in the administration of family law (see,
for example, Imber).

The political impetus of a centralizing state in extending its reach to
family law was, as Tucker points out, 'one subtext of reform'; another was
'the need to improve conditions for women' ('Revisiting Reform' 1996,
4–5). All in all, in examining the text of the OLFR on the specific subjects
of a woman's rights within marriage and access to divorce, Tucker finds
that this first codification was 'a project of modest proportions' and notes
that 'what we experience in reading the Ottoman law is an overall contrac-
tion of the sense of vast possibilities that inhabited the many and varied
texts of the *Shari'a*' (ibid. 16). Amira Sonbol (1998) reaches a similar
finding in Egypt, with regard to practice before the advent of statutory
intervention in family law.

There is much more to be said on this debate, which cannot be covered in this study. Suffice it to say here that scholars of women's history examining court records and other sources on the practice of Muslim family law pre-codification dispute the picture painted of the pre-existing system in both contemporary justifications for state-centered change and subsequent commentaries focused on the benefits of a positivist approach to family law. Since codification is nowadays the rule rather than the exception, these observations serve to inform those considering current approaches to law as a tool for the greater protection of women's rights in the family, particularly with regard to the issues of state patriarchy, judicial discretion and the role of individual judges, and women's agency.

In the twentieth century, socio-economic circumstances combined with political aspirations and the exigencies of the modern state went hand-in-hand with the promulgation of codes in their impact on the work of the courts. The tendency toward national codification that began in earnest in the 1950s continues today in Arab states. Codification—and its associated bureaucratic and procedural regimes—is clearly regarded as the form of state intervention most readily available for the political authorities in most Arab states to address the issue of women's rights within the family, and as the key to the implementation by the state of its commitments with regard to family law reform. In Bahrain, where there was until recently no codification, there has been significant activism from women's groups advocating the adoption of a code. Beyond the Gulf, where a code has been previously legislated, the text and application of the law are subjected to examination, with demands often made for expanded and more detailed intervention from the legislature through amendments, directives, guidelines and the establishment of particular fora for dispute processing in family law matters. Women's rights activists have sought greater input into and participation in the formulation of these state interventions. This may be on specific issues, or more broadly in seeking the participation of women in drafting committees. In the UAE, Qatar and Bahrain, the involvement of governmental and quasi-governmental women's councils already provides a particular mechanism for monitoring and intervention. In Bahrain, women's civil society associations have been actively involved in the debate on codification for over two decades. Munira Fakhro's consideration of women's civil society activism and engagement on the drafting of personal status laws surveys efforts in Bahrain, the UAE,

Kuwait, Oman and Qatar ('Personal Status Laws' 38–41). Her finding is that the space for such intervention and impact is limited by a number of factors, including the limitations on funding of civil society organizations imposed by governments in the region and other legislated constraints on non-governmental organizations (NGOs). On the other hand, as the debates in Bahrain show, resistance to codification takes place in specifically contingent political circumstances that may not immediately be related to the content *per se* of the law.

Codification in the Gulf

The first Muslim family law codification in the states grouped in the Gulf Cooperation Council (GCC) came in Kuwait in 1984. Others have followed the adoption, in 1996, of the 'Muscat Document of the GCC Common Law of Personal Status'. The Muscat document was adopted 'as a reference' for an initial four years, extended for another four years in 2000.[1] It is one of two inter-governmental 'model texts' produced in the Arab region on Muslim personal status law; the earlier (the Draft Unified Arab Law of Personal Status) was drawn up by the LAS in the late 1980s. The official commentary to the UAE codification explicitly cites the Muscat document as one of its sources.

Developments in the Gulf countries are illustrative of the different political contexts and legislative approaches in various states. In the case of Kuwait, Fakhro holds that the 1984 law 'does not offer many rights for Kuwaiti women' ('Gulf Women' 256). The Omani codification is closely modeled on the 1996 Muscat document; elsewhere in the Gulf, discussions on drafts had been ongoing for several years in Qatar as well as in the UAE before the laws were promulgated. In Qatar, the draft was apparently tested out in the courts in advance of promulgation; in Bahrain the codification debate has included wide public debates and at one point the trading of libel allegations in court battles between certain members of the *shar'i* judiciary and women active in the pro-codification debate.

In the first twentieth-century codifications, the drafting committees were frequently headed by the Chief Islamic Justice (*Qadi al-Qudah*) or

---

[1]The GCC website (http://www.gccsg.org/eng/) describes this document as consultative. It was adopted at the 7th session of the Supreme Council of the GCC in accordance with a recommendation from the GCC Justice Ministers, in October 1996.

equivalent, with other senior members of the *shar'i* judiciary and *'ulama'* as members. One of the changes in some more recent processes of codification, such as that in Morocco leading to the new law in 2004, and the temporary amendments in Jordan in 2001, is the inclusion in drafting committees made up of individuals with expertise outside the *shar'i* system, including women. The processes of democratization and increased participation have led women's movements in various Arab states to seek inclusion in such drafting processes and, while arguments are still made for the exclusivity of *shar'i* expertise, it is increasingly usual to find members of the *shar'i* judiciary and other *'ulama'* being joined in these appointed committees by experts in other fields, such as sociologists and psychologists. In Qatar, where the drafting committee was constituted of judges, the circulation of the resulting draft provided a forum for review and intervention *inter alia* by Qatari women, with the governmental National Committee for Women's Affairs submitting amendments for the consideration of the drafting committee (al-Thani 24). As for the 2005 UAE codification, this was drawn up by a committee of nine male scholars established by a 2002 Decision of the Minister of Justice, Islamic Affairs and *Waqf*. According to the Explanatory Memorandum to the UAE law, in drawing up the law, the committee reviewed earlier drafts (the first having been completed in 1978), as well as the Muscat document and edicts from the UAE authorities regarding 'the preparation of a draft law including the four schools of *fiqh*, selecting the soundest and most beneficial of their opinions'. Mention is made of consultation with, and consideration of feedback from, over twenty other parties in the UAE concerned with the matter, although no further information is given as to which of these may have comprised governmental, quasi-governmental or non-governmental women's associations.

In Bahrain, among the findings of the 2004 public opinion survey discussed further below was that a majority of respondents preferred that the drafting committee for a personal status code should include members of civil society associations as well as the more established sources of *shar'i* expertise. A number of women lawyers were added to the membership of the Committee established by the Ministry of Justice in 2002 to prepare a draft codification after an intervention from the Supreme Council of Women (SCW) (SCW & BCSR 56, 22). The original Popular Personal Status Committee set up in Bahrain by three women's associations was developed as a quasi-official forum from 1982 and now comprises some ten associations as well as a number of individuals (ANDA 82).

In the Gulf, as elsewhere in the Middle East and North Africa, there is a consensus among legislators that when (and if) codified, Muslim family law should be '*Shari'a*-based'. Opinion polls among the public concur; in Bahrain in 2004, 97 percent of survey respondents 'agreed strongly' that codification should be drawn from the rulings of *Shari'a* (SCW & BCSR 49), and in Palestine in 2000 a survey deduced a 'profound commitment to *Shari'a* as the basis for family law . . . especially by women' (Hammami 141). What exactly is meant, understood or expected from '*Shari'a*' is not however uniform, and a gender difference shows up in surveys that probe more deeply issues of the protection of women's rights in '*Shari'a*-based' family law (Hammami; Fawzi). This is where the activism and advocacy of those who support greater protection of women's rights in the family are aimed; and this is the focus of criticisms of 'state patriarchy' and the choices made by nation-states, and the interpretations of statutory provisions by the judiciary.

In Arab states generally, the codifications of family law explicitly invoke the '*shar'i* postulate' by directing the judge to a residual reference in the event of a specific subject not covered in the text. This comes in a variety of formulations, which themselves indicate jurisprudential, legislative (and political) history and aspiration. In the Gulf codifications, there are a number of different approaches. The 2005 UAE law includes a detailed provision stressing that 'the provisions in this law are taken from and to be interpreted according to Islamic jurisprudence and its principles', with interpretative recourse to the jurisprudential school to which any particular provision is sourced, and in the event of there being no text, ruling to be made in accordance with the prevailing opinion in the Sunni schools in the following order: Maliki, Hanbali, Shafi'i and Hanafi. The Qatari law offers the first codification to have the dominant opinion of the Hanbali school as the residual source, 'unless the court decides to apply a different opinion for reasons set out in its ruling'; in the absence of a Hanbali text, the court is directed to 'another of the four schools' and failing this to the 'general principles of the Islamic *Shari'a*'. The Bahraini Sunni law directs the *qadi* to prevalent Maliki opinion, thence to the other Sunni schools and then the general jurisprudential principles of the *Shari'a*.

Another distinctive feature in two of the new Gulf codifications is the variation from the idea of a single national code to govern Muslim personal status matters. The main comparator elsewhere in the Middle East is Lebanon, where separate codified laws have long been the basis of family law regulation for different Muslim sects and other religious communities. More recently, Iraq has seen challenges to the existing national codification from those who wish to re-institute communal Sunni/Shiʻi jurisdiction; women's rights groups have rallied behind the code. One of the key issues in the Bahraini debate has been whether a codification should present one unified law to govern both Sunni and Shiʻi communities, one unified law with distinctions made on particular issues of difference between the sects, or two separate codifications to govern the two communities. Eventually, in 2009, the government submitted a draft of the Sunni section for ratification in the lower house, after the latter rejected an earlier draft that included the Shiʻi section (Toumi); the Sunni law retains the title 'First Part', presumably in anticipation of a second part to eventually govern rulings in the Shiʻi departments. Under the 2002 Law of the Judicial Authority, jurisdiction in cases arising from contracts of marriage is assigned to the Sunni or Jaʻfari departments of the *Shariʻa* court system according to the school under which the contract was concluded, which is determined 'according to the *Shariʻa* department or its *maʼdhun* that documented the marriage contract.' If there is no documented contract, jurisdiction follows the school of the husband.

A different approach has been taken in Oman, where the majority of the population is Ibadi, and in Qatar where the majority is Hanbali. In Oman, the 1997 law makes two specific exceptions to the application of the provisions of the code to all Muslims regardless of sect, one in divorce and one in inheritance. The Qatari code is more extensive in its jurisdictional exception, providing that the Law of the Family will apply to 'all those subject to the Hanbali *madhhab*' and that, along with non-Muslims, Muslims adhering to other schools of law may apply their own rules, or may opt for application of the state's codification. Research in the courts would throw valuable light on the extent to which those identifying with other schools of law would opt out of the state codification, and whether women in particular seek the application of non-Hanbali rules in their litigation or proceedings before the courts. The UAE code, on the other hand, is more insistent on inclusion: it applies 'to all UAE citizens so long as the non-Muslims among them do not have special rulings of their sect and *milla*; and to non-citizens in so far as one of them does not adhere to the application of his [personal] law.'

In Bahrain, a study published in 2005 by the SCW and the Bahrain Centre for Studies and Research (BCSR) notes that it was in light of the polarization of Bahraini society over the codification issue that the SCW decided in 2004 to charge the BCSR with undertaking a public opinion survey on the matter (SCW & BCSR 25).[2] The results were strongly in favor of codification (73.7 percent), with more females in agreement than males (56.8 percent: 43.92 percent) (ibid. 46–7). Strong majorities anticipated that codification of the law would have an impact in limiting the effects of family break-down (72.4 percent) and in expediting the process of obtaining rulings on personal status issues (67.35 percent) (ibid. 50); criticism of the *Shari'a* courts had been a major focus in the campaigns for codification.

On the form such codification should take, the results were more divided. The largest number of respondents (34.6 percent) opted for a unified law that would make allowance for areas of particular difference between Sunnis and Shi'is; the second largest proportion (30.1 percent) indicated a preference for one unified law to apply to both sects. In third place, although not far behind (29.8 percent), came preference for the path ultimately taken by the government, promulgation of separate laws for the two sects. A gender difference showed in relation to the first choice, with more females (57 percent) than males (43 percent) selecting this option (ibid. 51). Another interesting finding related to the social status of respondents: while among married respondents most (74.1 percent) opted for one unified law or one law with consideration for differences between the sects (73.9 percent), among unmarried respondents most (35.9 percent) either did not support the promulgation of a codified law or preferred separate laws for each community (35.9 percent); the study suggests (ibid. 55) that this indicates a greater awareness among married persons of the potential impact of the law on their lives. Finally, as already noted, the survey showed a preference on the part of the majority (53.6 percent) of

---

[2]The methodology is set out in pp. 27–39 of the study. It included 1,300 respondents on a random/cluster sampling basis, over the period February-April 2004; a total of 1,261 responses were analyzed (see pp. 39–44 on the sample and challenges to implementation of the survey).

respondents for the drafting committee of a family law codification to be comprised of *shar'i* jurists and scholars of the two schools, along with lawyers and members of civil society associations (ibid. 56). A higher proportion of women respondents (57.8 percent) made this choice than males (42.2 percent). A lower percentage (45.9 percent) opted for such a committee to be made up of *shar'i* jurists and *'ulama'* only.[3]

Those in support of codification in Bahrain raise a set of arguments, including a perceived increase in 'family problems' that could be more effectively addressed by the codification of family law, and the problems posed by different rulings issued by the courts in cases involving similar facts, leading to a lack of confidence in the courts (ibid.; ANDA; Bahrain NGOs Shadow Report to CEDAW). The process of codification is presented as intended to assist the judges and other actors in the *Shari'a* court system by providing clarity, reducing the need to consult *fiqh* sources in the majority of cases, and removing the possibility of pressure from external sources (such as litigants). Another point made here is that a code would make the law accessible and 'knowable' to the general public or more specifically to potential litigants; it is argued that when individual spouses are more aware of their rights and obligations under the law, the potential for dispute and litigation would be reduced (ANDA 13).

On the drafting and promulgation processes, *shar'i qadis* and *'ulama'* from both the Bahraini Sunni and Ja'fari communities have vigorously asserted their singular expertise to the exclusion of the legislative process. This point was made not only in support of the anti-codification position, but also by those who conceded the principle of codification but opposed the involvement of the legislature in the process. At various points in the debate, there were warnings that allowing the legislature, the National Council, to vote on drafts and promulgate a law would render *shar'i* rulings on personal status 'hostage to the Deputies', and that a parliamentary process could result in serious violations of the *Shari'a* (Jamshir). The codification debate in Bahrain continues. To date, it has involved a depth and breadth of discussion over the principles and processes of codification that offer a wealth of material for the researcher to examine the 'transformation of *Shari'a* into law' in a decidedly contemporary and extremely complex setting.

---

[3]The study notes that more than one answer was available to respondents for this question, accounting for a total of more than 100 percent.

While Bahrain has seen vigorous campaigns to achieve a codification, as well as vehement opposition to the same, among the features of campaigns where codes are already in place are proposals for increasingly detailed legislation. In light of experiences of failed legislative projects as well as more successful ones, the argument here is that if women's rights in the family are to be protected by the submission of various acts (such as early marriage, polygynous marriage, divorce, etc.) to judicial scrutiny, then judicial discretion must be (increasingly) directed from the legislature in order to secure the intended impact of the desired legislative changes, and to avoid their being subverted by the exercise or abuse of judicial discretion. The attention that Amira Sonbol and other scholars have given to the risks posed to women by the choices made by states in their codifications of Muslim family law, through infusion of the laws with 'state patriarchy', and their comparisons with pre-modern applications of *Shari'a*, provide vital perspectives in the questioning, as Sonbol (1998: 285) puts it, of the 'holiness' and 'untouchability' attributed to these codifications. If senior clerics in Bahrain and elsewhere worry that there is no risk-free process in codifying Muslim family law, women's rights activists have equally challenging concerns in seeking to enhance rights protection through legislation on the family.

Family law provisions in the new Gulf codes

The codes of Qatar and the UAE are quite lengthy documents, with 301 articles in the former and 363 in the latter. They cover a wide range of issues considered to be within the jurisdiction of family law: marriage and divorce and issues arising within and after marriage, rules governing children and the maintenance of other family members, and the various rules governing disposal of property (gift, legacy [*wasiyya*], succession). The Bahraini Sunni law is shorter (145 articles) and does not cover these last issues. The UAE law is unusual in being accompanied by a detailed, article-by-article Explanatory Memorandum composed by the same committee that drafted the provisions of the code.

Before commencing an overview of the provisions of these codes, it is worth noting that some Gulf states are following a relatively recent practice of seeking to encourage—or require—recourse to pre-court procedures by would-be litigants. Before the promulgation of its family law codification, the UAE had already instituted a practice of pre-litigation mediation or family guidance procedures in a state-regulated forum, the Committee of Family Guidance. The 2005 law institutionalizes this practice, requiring that parties be referred to the Committee before their claim can be heard by the court; exceptions to this rule include cases of inheritance and wills, provisional and accelerated petitions including urgent provisional orders for maintenance and custody, and 'claims where reconciliation is not in issue', such as the establishment of marriage and divorce.

Such initiatives may be presented as explicit efforts to reduce the incidence of divorce as well as the workload of the courts and the impact on the parties to the litigation. The Explanatory Memorandum to the UAE law states that this mandatory procedure is 'out of respect for the family, in preservation of its cohesion, and in protection of the secrets of the home' (139). They can also be read as the state seeking to extend further its involvement in the regulation of 'private' disputes and conflict resolution (Bernard-Maugiron 95). Further research would be needed in the UAE to ascertain whether women find this a helpful intervention by the state. The phrasing of the exceptions in the UAE provision suggests that, for example, all claims by a woman for *khul'* or for divorce on the grounds of injury will have to pass through the Committee as well as, subsequently, being the subject of mediation efforts by the judge. A serious criticism that is made of such statutory requirements in relation to such mediation or reconciliation procedures, and particularly with regard to divorce, is the daunting prospect they are likely to pose to a woman seeking divorce from an abusive husband. A particularly interesting and effective study might be made of how judges, for their part, deal with such situations.

The following sections deal with a number of issues in the Emirati, Qatari and Bahraini Sunni laws in comparison with patterns established in Muslim family law codifications promulgated by other Arab states.

Registration

The issue of registration of marriage, as a bureaucratic procedure, has been supported by women's rights groups across the region because of the opportunity it offers for protection of the rights of women in marriage: specifically, it allows for the enforcement of rules on the minimum age of marriage, consent of the parties, judicial oversight of statutory conditions related to polygyny and a woman's rights on divorce. Since the traditional jurisprudential consensus required no form of registration of marriage for these acts to have *shar'i* validity, and since unregistered marriage continues as a social practice in many states, women's rights groups also concern themselves with the rights of women involved in undocumented marriages and the children they may have borne in them.

Different approaches have been taken to encourage registration and to deal with the issue of unregistered marriages. These include the Egyptian approach of precluding the courts from hearing any claim arising from a marriage that was not officially documented in the event that one of the parties denied the marriage. The impact of this approach on women involved in unregistered *'urfi* marriages subsequently denied by their husbands was widely debated before the law was amended in 2000 to allow claims for judicial divorce or dissolution to be heard where there is no official document and one party is denying the marriage. The 2004 Moroccan family law envisages a five-year period during which those involved in unregistered marriages—including where one party denies the marriage—should regularize their situation, suggesting that thereafter marriage would have to be established by production of the official certificate.

A less radical approach is to establish the official certificate of marriage as the standard form of evidence of a marriage for the purposes of the courts, with various formulations allowing for the recognition of a marriage by a court ruling in the event that the statutory administrative procedures have not been complied with but the marriage fulfils the *shar'i* requirements for validity. All three laws have followed this approach, with the UAE and Bahrain allowing recognition of marriage by '*shar'i* proof' and Qatar allowing recognition of marriage 'exceptionally . . . in cases in the discretion of the judge'. In Bahrain, the government noted in its 2008 report to the Committee on the Elimination of Discrimination against Women (CEDAW) that a marriage can be recognized on the evidence of testimony, but that 'in practice, a marriage contract is written by an authorized, legal marriage official'.[4]

Note might also be taken of a further element in registration procedures that features in all three states, as well as elsewhere. This is the

[4]UN Doc. CEDAW/C/BHR/2 12 November 2007, combined initial and second periodic report of Bahrain, para. 328.

requirement that couples intending to marry submit medical certificates as part of the documentation needed by the official charged with registering or notarizing the marriage. The tests on which such medical certificates are based may cover both physical and mental diseases and disorders and may be regulated by detailed directives under the authority of government health agencies. In the UAE, the law requires attestation from the 'appropriate committee established by the Ministry of Health' that the parties are free of 'conditions on the basis of which this law allows a petition for judicial divorce' (see further below), while the Explanatory Memorandum refers to genetic disorders, conditions preventing consummation, or those that stand to 'affect future generations'. In Qatar, the law makes tests for inherited conditions mandatory. In Bahrain, a fine is stipulated for those violating the requirements of the 2004 law on medical tests for certain 'hereditary and contagious diseases'.[5] The texts require that the results of each party's tests are made known to the other. The objective is to ensure that neither party marries in ignorance of a particular health condition existing in the other. Less common are texts that address what should happen in the event that the test results are potentially problematic; Qatar's law, however, states explicitly that the official who registers the marriage 'is not permitted to refuse to document the contract because of the results of the medical test, in the event that the two parties desire to conclude it'.

Age of marriage

Issues of capacity for and consent to marriage have long attracted the attention of legislatures and activists in the region; the establishment of a minimum age of marriage by the legislature has been a feature of national legislation from the earliest promulgations, is supported by women's rights activists (who may continue to seek an increase in the minimum age), and is firmly in line with international norms and expectations. Advocacy tends to argue for the setting of the age of legal majority as the minimum age for marriage, and for the informed scrutiny of the court for any exceptions. As well as the attitude of judges and notaries, attention is focused on the procedures required for the contract, including the production and

[5]Law no.11/2004 pertaining to Medical Tests for those of Both Sexes Intending to Marry, *Official Gazette* no.2640, 23 June 2004; Minister of Heath Decision no.3/2004, *Official Gazette* no.2667, 29 December 2004.

availability of the various administrative certificates, and the availability and use of penal sanctions to support the requirement of consent as well as age.

All three Gulf laws under consideration here follow the pattern established in a number of other Arab personal status codes in setting an age of full capacity for marriage, while allowing marriage below this age under certain conditions, including the achievement of puberty and the permission of the court as well as that of the guardian. In the process leading up to promulgation of Qatar's law, al-Thani notes that particular concern was raised at the draft law's proposal that marriage under the set ages of capacity (sixteen for females, eighteen for males) could be concluded if both the parties to the marriage and the guardian agreed, and that it was the intervention of the National Commission for Women's Affairs that produced the inclusion in the final text of the additional need for the court's permission. This addition brought the Qatari law into accordance with the majority positions elsewhere. The Qatari law thus stipulates actual puberty as a condition for capacity for marriage, while documentation of marriage below the ages of sixteen for females and eighteen for males needs the consent of both the guardian and the court, with emphasis on the need to ascertain consent.

The UAE law sets a presumption of puberty at eighteen lunar years for both parties, at which point a woman may seek the *qadi*'s permission to marry in the event that her guardian refuses permission; marriage is, however, allowed at the attainment of actual puberty with the permission of both the judge and the guardian. As for the Bahraini Sunni law, the only explicit provision requires a female under sixteen to have the court's permission (as well as her guardian's) as to 'the appropriateness of the marriage'—which will presumably include achievement of puberty. A 2007 Regulation by the Minister of Justice already provides that:

> No marriage contract may be concluded or ratified unless the age of the wife is fifteen years and the age of the husband is eighteen years at the time of concluding the contract, unless an urgent necessity exists, justifying marriage for people less than this age. A court permission is mandatory in this case . . . (Article 10: Bahrain NGOs Shadow Report 22)

The issue here, besides the difference in marriageable ages between males and females, is the judicial interpretation of 'urgent necessity' for under-age marriage (see Welchman, *Women and Muslim Family Laws*, 65–8, on this debate in Jordan). In Bahrain, civil society organizations criticized this provision in the 2007 law as discriminatory in setting a lower age for women, and also criticized the lack of specification of the exceptional clause 'which leaves the doors open for circling around it'(Bahrain NGOs Shadow Report 22; see also ANDA 70). The government, for its part, in its report to CEDAW (para. 326) claims that '[i]n reality, girls and boys under 16 and 18 respectively rarely marry'.[6]

Guardianship in marriage

Women's rights activists in many Arab states continue to focus attention on the authority in a woman's marriage of the male family guardian or that of the court acting as a guardian. On the one hand, the battle against statutory recognition of the guardian's exercise of coercive guardianship over a female ward has been won: here, reform efforts focus on social practice and the need for judges to be aware of the complexities of 'consent' in under-age marriages. On the other hand, the issue of a woman's need for permission for her marriage (from the guardian or the court), and in some cases for the guardian to actually conclude the contract, remains an issue in many states. The 2004 law in Morocco may be seen to stand at one end of the spectrum on this, identifying guardianship as 'the right of the woman' to be exercised by her own choice, and allowing any woman of legal majority to conclude her own contract of marriage. At the other end come the provisions in the laws under consideration here, all three of which require consent from the family guardian or the court, and the conclusion of a woman's contract of marriage by the guardian.

The 2005 UAE law justifies its requirement that a woman's marriage contract is carried out by her guardian on the majority juristic view and in view of the 'potential hazards' of a woman undertaking her own marriage; however, the Explanatory Memorandum stresses (on p. 162) that the wife's consent is necessary and that it is to ensure that this consent has been given that the law requires the notary to have the wife sign the contract after its conclusion by her guardian. The UAE law is unequivocal on the need for

[6]UN Doc CEDAW/C/BHR/2, 12 November 2007 (Bahrain's combined initial and second periodic reports to the Committee on the Elimination of All Forms of Discrimination Against Women), para. 326.

the guardian, voiding contracts concluded without the woman's *wali* and
ordering the separation of the spouses, although establishing the paternity
of any children from such a marriage to the husband; the 'two contracting
parties' to the marriage contract are 'the husband and the *wali*'. An article
in the UAE's *Khaleej Times* some years earlier had quoted scholars and
judges in Dubai insisting on the juristic basis for the requirement of the
guardian, while setting their concern in a social context that clearly
revolves around *'urfi* marriage. One of the sources referred to the public
prosecution offices being 'packed' with cases of 'illegal' marriages
concluded without the consent of the guardian due to 'the ignorance of
Muslim couples' and underlined 'the common mistake among young
couples who tend to challenge their parents' will and get married without
their approval': 'Islam has set this rule to protect women, who are known
for being sentimental, from falling for the wrong men and ruining their
lives' (Raafat).

This gives some indication of the social practice targeted by the UAE
law, which clearly empowers the woman's male family guardian in the
matter of her marriage. It also indicates the common wisdom of the protective intention behind the institution of guardianship, suggesting that
women are prone to being swayed by emotional factors and in need of the
rational guidance of their male relatives. At the same time, the fact that the
laws allow a woman to take her case to the judge allows for the possibility
that the guardian cannot unexceptionally be relied upon to decide solely in
the woman's best interest; this interest can, in such circumstances, be
decided upon by the (male) judge. The Bahraini Sunni law is quicker than
either the UAE or Qatari laws to pass guardianship to the *qadi* in cases
where the family guardian's permission is not forthcoming. However, the
absolute requirement of the recognized *wali* in the marriage of a Bahraini
woman is underlined in rather unusual rules addressing the establishment
(*ithbat*) in Bahraini courts of a marriage concluded without the involvement of the *wali*. This provision first sets a general rule that such a marriage
'will be considered established by consummation provided the contract is
valid under the law of the place where it was concluded'; then it adds that
if the wife is Bahraini, the consent of her guardian is required to confirm
the contract of marriage.

Other powers of scrutiny given to the court in the Bahraini law involve
issues of nationality and age groups and reflect particular domestic

preoccupations. Thus the court's consent is needed for the documentation of a marriage between a man aged over sixty and a woman who is not a citizen of a GCC state; and for the marriage of a Bahraini female aged under twenty to a non-Bahraini man aged over fifty (in both cases, 'to ensure realization of benefit and adequacy of guarantees'). In other Arab family laws, this court scrutiny is exercised over marriages involving partners of substantially different ages, without regard to nationalities—usually, a younger woman marrying a much older man—where the legislator is aiming at strengthening the court's authority to investigate the authenticity of the young woman's consent. Such provisions reflect at least in part a concern that penurious fathers or other male guardians may marry off young female wards against their interests in return for a substantial dower from a considerably older and richer man. Besides concerns for the welfare of the young women involved, states worry about the ability of their young male citizens to find brides. Thus, the 2005 UAE codification (article 49) invokes existing legislation setting a maximum limit on the dower, with the Explanatory Memorandum referring to 'social problems and corruption caused by inflated dowers that prevent the youth from getting married' (180).

Polygyny

Muslim personal status codifications in Arab states have followed a number of patterns in regulating the institution of polygyny; Tunisia is the only one to have prohibited it. The codes promulgated in the UAE, Qatar and Bahrain show awareness of these developments but take very little from them; following the earlier Gulf codifications in Kuwait and Oman, they demonstrate an approach that is either unwilling to institute any statutory regulation or extremely cautious in doing so. This is particularly the case with the UAE code, which reiterates the established rights of co-wives, and in an expanded commentary takes on some of the arguments of the reformists, albeit not referring to them directly. The commentary examines the Qur'anic texts to conclude that, since control over matters of the heart is not within human capability, 'a husband is not required to be equal to his wives in respect of his heart's affection' although 'the heart's inclination must remain between the created and his Creator, and no evident inclination towards one wife may arise therefrom' (187). The focus of the only provisions regulating polygyny in the UAE codification (as in the Kuwaiti and Omani codes previously) is the requirement of 'equity' or 'just treatment' towards co-wives, which includes not obliging co-wives to share accommodation.

Elsewhere, legislative approaches to constraining polygyny have involved a combination of judicial scrutiny and bureaucratic procedure prior to the conclusion of a polygynous union, an approach which revolves around registration procedures and requires the court's consent, under specified conditions, to the conclusion of a polygynous marriage. The two elements on which the court's consent is most commonly conditioned in the codes are the husband's financial ability to provide for a new wife in addition to his existing wife and family, and the existence of what is termed a 'lawful benefit' from the polygynous union. These conditions, in various phrasings, are now common in the Mashreq and North Africa. The first (financial ability) is less controversial than the second. In Qatar, an initial draft which had omitted any regulation of polygyny was amended after public consultations and interventions to include a very restrained reference to the husband's financial circumstances. The Bahraini law adds the 'classical' entitlement of the wives to a just share of nights with the husband.

The other issue is remedy — the explicit acknowledgement in law that a woman may be injured by her husband taking another wife, and that she may have cause to seek dissolution of her marriage accordingly. While this is quite rare, most Arab states explicitly allow a wife to retain a remedy against polygyny by the insertion of a stipulation in her marriage contract entitling her to seek divorce if the husband marries another wife. All three laws deal with stipulations in general and do not explicitly address a stipulation against polygyny, although the Bahraini law does make express mention of such a stipulation when addressing the matter of notification of the existing wife in the event that the husband does marry again. Elsewhere, recent laws have focused on whether such notification is included in the requirements for the conclusion of a polygynous contract, and, if so, whether the existing wife is to be informed prior to the polygynous marriage (as in Morocco) or after its conclusion. In Bahrain, in a slightly unusual construction, the Sunni law requires a man marrying polygynously to notify his existing wife of his subsequent marriage (by registered letter, within sixty days) if that wife has inserted a stipulation in their marriage contract against such a marriage. Presumably a wife who has not inserted such a stipulation would not be so notified. While this is more empowering to the first wife than the other Gulf laws, it can also be compared with the 2004 Moroccan law, which takes the unusual position of disallowing a subsequent marriage by a man whose existing wife included a stipulation against polygyny in her marriage contract. Elsewhere, however, there continues to be resistance to this statutory measure, as shown during the Jordanian parliamentary debates on the 2001 'temporary' legislation, which provided for a wife to be notified after her husband's conclusion of a polygynous contract. 'No judge,' one deputy was reported as saying, 'has the right to inform a wife of her husband's decision to remarry should the husband decide to keep it secret' — sometimes it was necessary to wait for 'the right time' (*Jordan Times*, 29 June 2004). Similarly in Qatar, objections were reportedly made by the Legal Committee of the Qatari legislature to the draft law's requirement that an existing wife (or wives) be notified of a husband's polygynous marriage after it has been documented, declaring that it could find no *shar'i* basis for this requirement, that it was not local practice, and that such a requirement 'could lead to problems'.[7] The requirement remained in the law, but the objections are significant. One way of viewing this resistance is as an acknowledgement of the substantial challenge that can be posed to a man's decision if the existing wife is empowered with knowledge of it; it may also express a resentment at the further reach of state law and bureaucracy into the 'private sphere' of the family.

Spousal relationship

When the laws turn to articulate the nature of the relationship between husband and wife, all three laws follow the earlier model of Oman in introducing extended lists of rights and duties: one list relates to those shared by the spouses (including lawful sexual relations, cohabitation, mutual respect and bringing up children from the marriage), one to the rights of the wife and one to the rights of the husband. The wife's rights include maintenance, and the husband's include his wife's obedience and her stewardship of the marital home and its contents. The wife's

[7]From www.awfarab.org/page/qt/2004/pl.htm. Last accessed 13 August 2005.

obedience is to be 'in accordance with custom'. The Explanatory Memorandum to the UAE law (186–8) adduces a detailed jurisprudential justification for this provision, focusing on the *qiwama* (in this context, authority) of the man in the family, arguing that the man is 'more able to allow reason to rule and to control his emotions' and observing that 'all laws—civil or religious—put men a degree over women'. Nevertheless, as is the case in the other codes, the UAE law specifically rules out the forcible implementation of rulings for obedience, with the Memorandum (268, 100) explaining that such action would violate the woman's dignity, and that coercion cannot be a basis for marital life. In their listings of separate rights and duties for husband and wife, and the articulation of the principle of obedience, the codifications stand in contrast to two other recent pieces of Arab state legislation, in Morocco and Algeria. These have removed references to 'disobedience', while leaving the husband's obligation to maintain his wife, and replaced pre-existing lists of gender-specific rights and duties with single provisions on mutual rights and duties of the spouses.

All three laws address the issue of the wife's employment outside the home. The Qatari law includes this in a negative provision when dealing with situations in which the wife is to be held disobedient (*nashiz*), including 'if she goes out to work without the approval of her husband', although adding 'so long as the husband is not being arbitrary in forbidding her'. In something of a contrast, the UAE law has a longer clause on this, regulating the wife's right to go out to work without being held 'disobedient', 'if she was working when she got married, or if [her husband] consented to her working after the marriage, or if she stipulated this in the contract'. Unusually, the law instructs the marriage notary to 'inquire about' the insertion of a stipulation into the marriage contract on this matter, although it does subject even the implementation of such a stipulation to the 'interest of the family'. The Bahraini law has a lengthy article in similar vein. The UAE and Qatari codifications also address the wife's education; the UAE law includes in the list of the wife's rights her 'not being prevented from completing her education'. The Qatari code has a separate article on this, requiring the husband to provide his wife with the opportunity to complete the compulsory stage of her education and to facilitate her pursuit of university education 'inside the country, in so far as this does not conflict with her family duties'.

As already noted, the three codifications explicitly allow for stipulations to be inserted in the contract of marriage by either spouse, a facility that is referred to in later provisions, notably regarding the wife's employment outside the home and, in the Bahraini law, a subsequent polygynous marriage. In addition, in Bahrain, the marriage contract document has been amended, according to a speech by the head of delegation to CEDAW, to ensure that stipulations can be included at the request of the parties.[8] Scholars and activists in the last decades of the twentieth century focused considerable efforts on the option to insert stipulations in the marriage contract, on the basis that the parameters of the marital relationship could be negotiated and clarified between the spouses, with the prospect of legal remedy in the event of breach. Prior to codification, this was already a practice among certain socio-economic classes, at various times and places, whether carried out in the marriage contract itself or in other parallel documents agreed to by the spouses (Sonbol 291; (listed in) Shaham 464; Dennerlein 125). Egyptian activists invested years of effort into having certain stipulations included in the standard marriage contract document, a campaign that after a number of years gained the cooperation of the Ministry of Justice. The Egyptian campaign aimed at shifting the burden of initiative in the pre-marital negotiations from the party wishing to insert stipulations that altered the terms of the established framework (usually the wife) to the party wishing to retain the more traditional parameters under the existing law (usually the husband), by obliging the latter to take the initiative of refusal (by having the pre-worded conditions struck out, for example) and relieving the former of the often socially awkward burden of proposal (Zulficar and al-Sadda; Shaham; Singermann). Such campaigns also seek to make more women aware of the possibility of using such stipulations, through 'know-your-rights' activities, and to counteract prevailing social attitudes disapproving of such initiatives except in certain circumstances. On the other hand, activists have criticized states for leaving the greater legal protection of women's rights to the initiative of the individual woman (and her family), rather than themselves shouldering the burden of modifying the substantive law. In Bahrain,

---

[8]Speech by Her Excellency Dr Shaikha Mariam bint Hassan al-Khalifa, Deputy President of the Supreme Council for Women, Head of the Kingdom of Bahrain's delegation, to discuss Bahrain's report of the Convention on the Elimination of All Forms of Discrimination against Women', Geneva, 30 October 2008.

one of the proposals made by a Shi'i authority to women activists seeking a codified law was that they might start work on a 'marriage contract document' in the form of a pamphlet containing nearly fifty special stipulations that spouses could agree upon to govern their relationship, 'such as is done in some Islamic countries'—possibly in this case with the stipulations in the Iranian marriage contract in mind (Jamshir 140–5).

Another area of interest here is the separate property regime that applies to the spouses under Muslim personal status law. While this protects a married woman's independent property, in practice it can work against her in the event of a divorce, as explained in Bahrain's 2008 CEDAW report:

> [S]ome married women, especially those who work or own property, are exposed to tangible losses upon separating from their husbands after sharing in the expenses of purchasing or building a matrimonial home, which is usually recorded in the husband's name . . . [N]othing in Islamic law prevents the two spouses from agreeing in the marriage contract to share financial liability, whereby any property acquired by any of the two spouses during their marriage is considered jointly held by both of them. (Para. 330)

The Bahraini law does not include reference to this concern, however, although the legislator might have followed the model in the 2004 Moroccan law, which sets out the principle of separate spousal property, while also allowing the couple to agree on other terms for the management and investment of property acquired during the marriage in a document separate from the marriage contract. The Algerian amendments of 2005 followed suit, and Tunisia has had since 1998 a separate law providing the option for spouses to adopt a joint property regime for such goods.

Finally, another issue that has been of concern specifically in the Gulf, is that of *misyar* marriage. While various women's rights activists have advocated the inclusion of stipulations as a mechanism through which particular rights can be protected for the wife, the institution of *misyar* marriage rests on mutually agreed binding conditions that are regarded by such activists as compromising the rights of the wife and more broadly the institution of marriage. Arabi (*Modern Islamic Law* 157) observes that the legitimacy accorded to contracts of 'ambulant (*misyar*) marriage' is based on the principle of consent to these contractual terms, which significantly alter the assumptions traditionally arising from the contract (see also Wynn 115). Specifically, the wife waives her rights to maintenance, accommodation and cohabitation, and generally accepts a condition requiring lack of publicity of the marriage, a sort of 'strategic secrecy' that is aimed at concealing a man's polygynous marriage from his existing wife and family. The husband 'visits' his wife by day or night, without setting up home with her.

Women's rights activists in the Gulf have been vocal in their opposition to the apparent spread of this institution and its accommodation in law. In the UAE, the Arab Women's Forum reported that the 2003 draft of the personal status codification originally made specific provision for the formal registration of *misyar* marriages, requiring 'limited publicity' or declaration of the marriage and noting that 'full publicity' was not essential for validity. The limited publicity stood to protect the role of the wife's family, involving the knowledge of the guardian (who was to conclude the marriage) and the family of the woman involved, but not requiring notification of anyone on the husband's side—meaning that the existing wife would not be made aware through formal procedures that her husband had contracted this type of marriage with another woman.[9] This proposal did not survive into the final text of the 2005 law. The Explanatory Memorandum to the provision, when discussing examples of void stipulations that 'conflict with the requirements of the contract', includes those to the effect that the husband stipulates he will not pay maintenance (139). This does not mean that *misyar* marriage as such would be regarded as unlawful in the UAE; it might mean that women undertaking such marriages would not be held to their agreement to waive maintenance, for example, should they pursue a claim in court. Nevertheless, the explicit lack of male commitment under the *misyar* contract might mean a woman contracted in such a marriage would be unlikely to pursue her rights in court, being either personally persuaded of the benefits of the arrangement, or expecting divorce if she sought to challenge the mutually agreed conditions and bind the husband to responsibilities he explicitly sought to avoid.

[9]See www.awfarab.org/page/mrt/2004/lo.htm (last accessed 11 August 2005).

Divorce

A number of issues are raised by the approaches taken in the Gulf codifications to the matter of divorce, mostly in common with other Arab states.
There is a general concern at a perceived increase in the divorce rate, and
the fate of divorcées, including, for example, accommodation rights.
Munira Fakhro (259) has attributed the high rate of divorce in certain Gulf
states in the mid-1990s, when Kuwait was the only GCC state to have a
codification of Muslim personal status law, to a lack of statutory regulation
of the power of *talaq*. More recently a shadow report to CEDAW by the
Bahrain Human Rights Watch Society (4) notes 'an alarming increase of
divorce among Bahrainis'.

Across the region, making divorce a wholly judicial procedure remains
an aim for many women's rights activists, with considerable success being
achieved in this area in states in North Africa, but little in the Gulf states
in recent laws. The UAE codification states that '*talaq* occurs by declaration from the husband and is documented by the judge'. The Qatari and
Bahraini laws have the same wording, although adding a requirement for
the *qadi* to attempt reconciliation prior to hearing the husband's divorce
pronouncement. All three laws then provide that a *talaq* pronounced out of
court can be recognized by means of acknowledgement or proof. With
regard to this clause, the Explanatory Memorandum to the UAE law
(article 106) states the following:

> The conditions governing *talaq* and its occurrence do not require that it
> occur before the judge or before two just witnesses (unless it is by deputi-
> zation) because divorce is an expression of the husband's will. Accordingly,
> and given that *talaq* is one of the matters related to the right of God
> Almighty, if the husband causes *talaq* to occur outside the court and then
> he takes the matter to the judge and establishes that it has occurred in a
> manner that fulfils the [*shar'i*] conditions, then the judge rules for its occur-
> rence as of the date it happened. This is because not granting its occurrence
> leads to the continuation of an unlawful marital life in which illegitimate
> children proliferate in society, which must be protected therefrom. (223)

The focus on the lawful parentage of children at the end of this explanatory passage is repeated when the UAE Explanatory Memorandum deals

with paternity and modern reproductive technologies. As a whole, the passage implicitly rejects the approaches taken in other Arab states to the matter of out-of-court *talaq*, whether in terms of conditioning validity or recognition of a *talaq* or regarding the implementation of its effects by a judicial or registration process. Bolstering the statute with such arguments, in an official explanation of the law, complicates the prospects for successful advocacy for change. Nevertheless, the UAE law provides that, in the case of an extra-judicial *talaq*, the divorce is attributed to the date of the husband's subsequent acknowledgement of the *talaq* in court, or its establishment by proof, if a previous date is not found to be established.

Other than this, the codes in Qatar, the UAE and Bahrain follow practice elsewhere in Arab states by regulating the effects of *talaq* pronounced by the husband in certain physical and psychological circumstances, which mostly undermine the presumption of intent on the part of the husband. In such circumstances, the statutory laws provide that either no divorce takes effect, or a single revocable divorce is effected in place of what dominant Sunni *fiqh* (with some differences between the schools) would have ruled a three-fold and irrevocable *talaq*. The laws disallow *talaq* postponed to a future date, or pronounced as an oath, or any form of suspended or conditional *talaq* used as a threat to compel someone to do or not do something (rather than actually intended to bring about a divorce), and take up the generally codified position that a *talaq* accompanied in word or sign by a number gives rise only to a single revocable *talaq*. They also provide that no divorce occurs when *talaq* is pronounced under duress, and the Qatari and Bahraini texts add another widely codified position to the effect that no divorce occurs if a man pronounces it when intoxicated or overwhelmed by rage. The UAE law differs slightly but significantly here, providing that *talaq* does occur when pronounced by a man who has voluntarily lost his power of reason through a forbidden means. The Explanatory Memorandum explains this as a 'penalty for [the husband's] intentional violation of the prohibition [on drink]'.

As for judicial divorce, based on grounds that must be proven in court, the codes follow general patterns in specifying circumstances that are considered to cause harm or injury under the existing description of the husband's obligations: the wife can thus petition for divorce on the specific grounds of the husband's failure to pay maintenance, his disappearance or his unjustified absence or effective (and sexual) desertion of his wife for a specified period, or his being sentenced to a custodial term of more than a specified period. Both spouses may petition for divorce on the grounds of breach of a stipulation in the marriage contract, or of their spouse having or later developing a chronic mental or physical illness or condition that would (or could) cause harm were the marriage to continue, or prevent consummation or sexual relations. The UAE law is unusual in referring explicitly to 'AIDS and similar illnesses' (the Explanatory Memorandum refers also to herpes) requiring that the judge divorce a couple where such a condition is proved to exist in one spouse and there is a fear that it will be passed to the other, or to offspring. The wording here implies that the judge is not to attempt to reconcile the couple or otherwise seek continuation of the marriage in these circumstances, but is obliged to rule for the divorce. The UAE law also establishes marital infidelity by either spouse as grounds for divorce. Furthermore, in a fairly unusual provision, the UAE law deals explicitly with the issue of the infertility of either spouse as grounds for divorce, allowing a wife or husband under the age of forty and without her or his own children to seek dissolution in the event that the other spouse, in a marriage that has lasted more than five years, has been medically proved to be infertile and has undergone whatever treatment is possible for the condition.

At the time of the drafting of the codifications, the debate on the statutory regulation of 'judicial *khul'*' was ongoing in the region. A common form of divorce is consensual *khul'*, with the two parties agreeing to a *talaq* by the husband pronounced in exchange for certain compensation (often the waiving of remaining financial rights—notably the deferred dower) by the wife. The difference in the new statutory provisions on judicial *khul'* lies in the court having the authority, after attempts at reconciliation, to pronounce *talaq* for the set compensation without the consent of the husband. A few texts already allowed a procedure similar to judicial *khul'* in a marriage before consummation, including the Draft Unified Arab Law, in provisions that in essence allow a wife to withdraw unilaterally from the contract before cohabitation has commenced. This provision is taken up in all three of the laws under examination here.

The perspective changes substantially, however, when it is a matter of a consummated marriage where the wife seeks divorce without applying on a specified and statutorily recognized ground. Egypt led here in 2000 with a law that allows a wife to petition the court to grant a divorce without proving grounds, with the return of the dower and other conditions. Jordan followed suit in its 2001 amendments, and Algeria also introduced this possibility in 2005, but the controversy over 'women divorcing at will' has continued (Arabi, 'Dawning'; Welchman, 'Egypt'; Singermann); in its 2010 personal status law, Jordan re-worked the controversial article to remove the term *khul'*. In the UAE, it was reported that lawyers working on the draft law had lobbied for the inclusion of a provision for judicial *khul'*, and there appeared to be some confusion over the result. In the end, the 2005 text established the mutual consent of the spouses to *khul'* as the norm, with the Explanatory Memorandum noting explicitly that 'this law has not taken up what certain Arab personal status codes have done—such as Egypt and Jordan—in considering *khul'* an individual act on the part of the wife'. Nevertheless, in a final clause in the same article, the law does in fact allow the court to rule for *khul'* for an appropriate exchange in the event that the husband is being vexatious in his refusal and where there is 'fear that they [husband and wife] will not live in the limits of God'. Here, the UAE Explanatory Memorandum stresses that this provision applies where there is a fear regarding the conduct of both spouses 'if the relationship continues despite there being no desire on the part of either spouse for it to continue' (226–8). The Bahraini law adopts similar wording, although disallowing an exchange greater than the dower, while by contrast, and despite some reported opposition to this provision, the Qatari law stays somewhat closer to the Egyptian model. If the spouses fail to agree on divorce by *khul'*, the court appoints arbitrators to seek to reconcile them for a period of not more than six months. If this attempt is unsuccessful 'and the wife seeks *khul'* in exchange for her renunciation of all her *shar'i* financial rights, and returns to him the dower that he gave her, the court shall rule for their divorce'.

A final issue in the matter of divorce is compensation for the wife divorced injuriously. Statutory protection by way of compensation for a divorcée divorced unilaterally by her husband without 'cause' on her part was first included in the Syrian codification of 1953, and it has become a standard feature of Arab state codifications, sometimes termed *ta'wid* and sometimes *mut'a* from the provision in jurisprudential texts of a 'gift of consolation' for a divorced wife. Differences between the various texts include whether there are maximum or minimum limits on the amount of compensation that may be awarded, and how it is to be paid; whether the provision applies only to cases of unilateral *talaq* by the husband or also applies to injury by the husband established in a claim for divorce initiated by the wife; and whether the text focuses on the husband's abuse of his power of divorce, the wife's subsequent material position, or indeed the husband's financial circumstances, and/or specifically requires the court to take into consideration the length of the marriage. The variables here can make a substantial difference to the wife divorced against her will and arbitrarily.

The UAE and Bahraini Sunni codes are less generous to the divorcée on these matters than the Qatari. Both limit the maximum amount of any award to the sum of one year's maintenance. In the UAE, the provision appears to constrain the entitlement to cases of *talaq* only, and subjects the entitlement to the circumstances of the husband, while requiring the 'prejudice suffered by the woman' to be taken into account in the assessment. Bahrain adds the length of the marriage and the circumstances of the *talaq* as factors to be taken into account, along with the financial situation of the divorcer. The Qatari code, however, allows an entitlement to *mut'a* to every woman divorced on the grounds of the husband's behavior, with the exception of divorce for lack of maintenance by reason of the husband's poverty, and sets an upper limit of three years' maintenance.

Child custody

The Gulf laws follow the general regional approach of dividing the functions of parenting between those of custodian and guardian, and identifying the former with the mother and the latter with the father, in the first instance. In this description of the relationship, the custodian has duties of physical care and upbringing of minor children, while the guardian has duties and authority with regard to their financial affairs, their education, travel and other areas where the wards meet the 'public' world outside the home, as well as being financially responsible for them. The distinct duties of mother (custodian) and father (guardian) reflect gendered assumptions of 'ideal-type' social and familial roles in the upbringing of children, during marriage as well as after divorce. The UAE law reflects these assumptions in its description of custody as 'caring for the child and bringing him [/her] up and looking after him [/her] to the extent that this does not conflict with the guardian's right in guardianship over the person [of the ward]'. The Qatari law, after a similar description of the function of custody, adds, significantly, that 'custody is a right shared between the custodian and the minor, and the minor's right is the stronger'.

Developments in Arab personal status laws have tended generally to extend the period of custody of the children normally assigned to their mother following divorce beyond the age limits contemplated in the majority of *fiqh* rules. In addition, they have increasingly included statutory references to the concept of the 'interest of the child' on the basis of which the judge may modify this and other related parts of the law, including primary allocation of custody rights. The three new Gulf laws are part of more recent patterns that tend in this direction. In the draft UAE codification approved by cabinet in 2005, a provision ending the mother's custody over girls at thirteen and boys at eleven provoked public condemnation by lawyers who had consulted on previous drafts and held these ages to be a curtailment of existing custody rights.[10] The intervention appears to have had some impact: while the text of the law as passed maintained this position, it allows the court to extend a woman's custody until the male ward reaches puberty and the female marries. Addressing the selection of the ages of thirteen and eleven, the UAE Explanatory Memorandum makes the following observation:

> It is not up to the legislators to work out which of the schools [of law] best befits the love of mothers, or the love of fathers. Rather, they have to look at which most responds to the interests of proper social upbringing and education of the child. Thus the law holds in this regard that the age for males shall be eleven years, and for females thirteen. After this stage, the boy goes to his father to learn the bases of masculinity and men's counsel. The girl goes to her father in view of the circumstances of society that make it difficult for women to control girls. (256)

The UAE law allows the set extensions beyond these ages to be made by the court in the ward's interest. The Qatari law provides for a woman's custody to end in the case of male children at thirteen and females at fifteen, while allowing extension (in the ward's interest) to fifteen for males and until a female's consummation of her marriage. The Bahraini

---

[10]www.gulfnews.com/Articles/NationNF.asp?ArticleID=172793 (accessed 9 August 2005).

law goes further, setting a woman's custody to end at fifteen for the male ward and for the female at seventeen or upon consummation of marriage, while wards who reach those ages—and in the case of females have not married—are allowed to choose to be under the care (*damm*) of either parent or of another person with the right of custody. As is the case in the 2004 Moroccan law, the UAE and Qatari codes also provide that the woman's custody continues indefinitely if the ward is mentally or physically disabled, again subject to the best interest of the child, presumably on the assumption that such a ward will remain in need of the functions of care normatively assigned to the mother.

The court's consideration of the interest of the child is also increasingly required in codifications across the region in assessing the otherwise normative assignment of custody to an identified succession of relatives. The Qatari law is unusual in setting out what qualities the *qadi* is to consider in making such an assessment of the interest of the child. These include the custodian's affection for the child and ability to raise him or her, the provision of a sound environment in which the child can be brought up and 'protected from delinquency', the ability to provide the best education and medical care, and the ability to prepare the child in terms of morals and customs for the time that he or she is ready to 'leave the custody of women'.

The three laws follow the majority pattern in the region of enshrining in legislation the gendered assumption of the functions of custody as normatively assigned to women rather than men—and in requiring that, in the event that custody is assigned to a man, he must have 'a woman with him who can undertake the functions of custody'. However, the UAE and Qatari laws are also part of a quite recent trend towards establishing the father as following the mother in the presumptive order of entitled custodians, before the maternal (or in the Qatari case paternal) grandmother and other female relatives. The UAE law explicitly provides that the succession of relatives to custody is followed 'unless the judge decides otherwise in the interest of the child'; the Qatari code is more constrained here, allowing the interest of the child to be considered when a closer relative waives the right of custody in favor of a more distant custodian. However, as noted above, the Qatari treatment of custody already establishes that the interest of the child is paramount. Apart from this, both codes take a detailed 'listing' approach, with some seventeen individuals or categories of relatives successively entitled to claim custody of a minor child under the UAE law, and eighteen under the Qatari law. The Bahraini law norma-tively assigns custody to the mother followed by maternal and paternal grandmothers and ascendants, only then followed by the father and other relatives. It specifically allows the court to 'seek assistance from experts in psychology and sociology in determining [assignment of] *hadana*, taking into account the best interest of the child'.

On another contested issue, all three legislatures appear to have responded to women's advocacy across the region with regard to the general rule that a mother stands to lose her right to custody if she remar-ries a man who is not a close relative (usually *mahram*) of the ward (Jamshir 39). The specific issue of remarriage remains an advocacy target in various countries, *inter alia* on the grounds of discrimination (the father not being subject to such restrictions) and of the decision it imposes on women, whose ability to remarry may be constrained by the threat of losing custody of their children. The three laws explicitly allow the judge to consider the interest of the child in allowing custody to remain with the mother (or other female custodian) in the event that she has consummated a new marriage with a man who is not a close relative of the ward.

Finally, another pattern of Arab codifications where the Gulf laws under consideration here have tended to remain consistent concerns the rules applied to the non-Muslim custodian of the children of a Muslim father. Here, the texts tend to set shorter periods of custody—particularly if the custodian is not the mother—or not to allow the extension of the statutory period, sometimes subjecting this to the best interest of the child; they may explicitly allow for custody to be terminated if it is established that the mother (or female custodian) is bringing the child up to believe in a faith other than Islam. Thus the UAE law stipulates that a mother of a different religion loses custody of her child unless the *qadi* decides otherwise in the interest of the child, and in all cases that her custody ends when the child is five years old. The Qatari law allows a non-Muslim mother to have custody until the child is seven, provided she is not an apostate from Islam, and unless there is a concern that the ward is acquiring a different religion. The Bahraini law does not address this explicitly, although an earlier Sunni draft was comparatively generous to the non-Muslim mother; specific consideration is however again given to the issue of citizenship, with the law providing residency rights during the period of custody for the (non-Bahraini) custodian of a Bahraini ward.

Paternity/maternity

The rules governing paternity and the legal affiliation of a child to her or
his father (and thus the establishment of the child's paternal *nasab* or
lineage), and those governing adoption, continue to present challenges to
those seeking modifications of the rules related to parents and children in
Arab state codifications, and the Gulf state laws are no exception. With
regard to paternity, attention focuses on the obstacles that remain in law to
establishing the paternity of children born to a woman who is not in a
recognized or provable marital relationship with the biological father.
Established *fiqh* principles assume that 'the child is [affiliated] to the
conjugal bed' and award legitimate filiation to the husband of the woman
who has given birth to the child, unless it is otherwise claimed by the
husband and proven through the traditional process of *li'an*. In the *li'an*
procedure, the man denies on oath that the child is his and the woman
denies his allegation and the process results in a final divorce between the
couple with paternity not established. The three laws codify rules on *li'an*;
the UAE law in a final clause allows the court to 'seek the assistance of
scientific methods for refutation of *nasab* provided that it has not been
previously established', although the Explanatory Memorandum subjects
this procedure to the previous clauses of the paragraph describing the *li'an*
procedure. The Bahraini Sunni law has an interesting addition, requiring
DNA tests to be carried out on all parties before the process of *li'an*, and
disallowing the refutation of *nasab* by *li'an* in the event that paternity is
established. The statutory legitimation—and sometimes requirement—of
contemporary testing techniques alongside rules drawn from *fiqh* is
included in other rules on the establishment of paternity, as noted below.

The Gulf codes under consideration here follow, like other Arab codifications, established *fiqh* rules in requiring that to have a 'legitimate' *nasab*,
the child must be not only born but also conceived in the framework of
marriage or of what the couple believe to be a marriage. The jurists thus
looked to minimum and maximum periods of gestation to uphold or undermine the presumption of legitimacy of children born to a married couple.
While there was generally consensus on the minimum period of gestation
at six months, the jurists differed as to the maximum. Failing the presumption of paternity through a known marriage, paternity (and indeed maternity
for a child of unknown parentage) can also be established by

acknowledgement, provided certain conditions of feasibility are met, and '*shar'i* evidence' is available.

Among the rules of Muslim family law introduced in various Arab states in the twentieth century were limits to the maximum period of gestation, introducing a one-year rule either as a substantive rule or as a rule of procedure. All three new Gulf codifications establish one year as the maximum period of gestation and six months as the minimum as a substantive rule, although the UAE adds 'unless a medical committee established for this purpose decides otherwise'. As well as citing an individual view in the body of traditional Sunni *fiqh* in support of the one-year limit on the period of gestation, legislators in other Arab states have also referred to the consensus of '*shar'i* medicine'. While relying on scientific consensus to limit the period of maximum gestation recognized in law, which removed the assumption of legitimate filiation that previously worked in exceptional cases to the benefit of women and children, Arab legislatures have been somewhat slower to legislate explicitly on other methods now available to establish paternity, and the UAE exceptional clause (discussed further below) is an interesting addition in this regard, in line with some of the more recent laws in the region.

The key issue here is the difference in law between a father's paternity and a child's 'lineage' (*nasab*). While paternity is a biological fact, 'lineage' denotes the legally established filiation of the child to the parents and the subsequent establishment of legal rights and claims. In the case of the mother, *nasab* is established by the fact of her giving birth to the child. For the father, on the other hand, the laws generally require proof of an established *shar'i* relationship between the parents (*al-firash*, the 'conjugal bed') and, as the Explanatory Memorandum to the UAE law notes, 'this is the fundamental [relationship] because the child follows his [/her] father in *nasab*' (200). The UAE, Qatari and Bahraini Sunni laws follow the dominant pattern in that biological paternity alone does not give rise to the father's legal and financial responsibilities towards his child; biological maternity, on the other hand, gives rise to a mother's duties to her child whether the child was born in or out of a recognized marital relationship. This brings in the matter of statutory rules for the recognition of marriages. In general, the establishment of paternity and *nasab* is an exception to rules that might otherwise exclude state recognition of rights and claims arising from a marriage not conforming to the procedures legislated as mandatory by the state. In an undocumented and unregistered marriage, for example, the couple may decide to regularize their status *vis-à-vis* the central authorities when the time comes to register children from the marriage; the principle generally holds that establishing lineage works to establish the marriage, rather than the formalities of the marriage working to establish lineage. However, serious problems arise when one party, usually the man, denies the existence of the marriage, and the woman is unable to prove it to the satisfaction of the state. The Bahraini law includes an explicit provision regarding circumstances in which the parties have become 'engaged' with the knowledge of their families and agreement of the wife's guardian, but when there is no documented marriage, and the woman becomes pregnant; if the husband denies he is the father, 'all *shar'i* means may be resorted to in order to establish lineage'. This wording is similar to that used in the 2004 Moroccan law as a result of advocacy from women's and children's rights activists, and has been used there (albeit apparently not very frequently) to empower the court to require DNA testing of the man in certain circumstances of disputed paternity.

The UAE wording on how *nasab* on the father's side is to be established adds, after the conjugal bed, acknowledgement, and (*shar'i*) evidence, that it can be done 'through scientific methods where the conjugal bed is estab-lished'. The Explanatory Memorandum, quoted below, sets out the relationship between the envisaged use of methods such as DNA testing and the rules on 'the existence of the conjugal bed'. In the arguments for the need to establish *nasab* (rather than only biological paternity), refer-ences are made not only to the range of rights and responsibilities that arise for individuals through filiation, but also to the wider societal context:

> This article refers to establishing paternity through modern scientific methods such as DNA testing, which are scientific means of establishing the definite relationship between the child and his [/her] father; but in order not to make a mockery of the issues involved in establishment of paternity, by making it a matter simply of establishing this relationship through a medical test, the article has linked its ruling to the existence of the conjugal bed in accordance with article 90. This is to prevent what has happened in a number of cases, with sperm being taken from a man and implanted into a woman without there being any *shar'i* tie between them. Then medical tests establish the paternal relationship, while it is

not possible for the child to be attributed to the father in terms of lineage (*nasab*) in such circumstances. These means have developed in our time, and now there are laboratories and sperm banks . . . And there are several criminal cases involving such matters . . . It is known that recently in another country a wife saved sperm from her husband in a sperm bank and some time after he died the sperm was sown in her womb after implantation of an egg from her and she fell pregnant from that. If we were to allow *nasab* to be established in such cases, it would be problematic with regard, for example, to inheritance, and the impediment of affinity. And the woman might be married to another man, so lineage is mixed and corruption appears . . . (200–1)

Here, the need to properly assign lineage is linked to the entitlements of those related by *nasab* to proportions of each other's estate under the law of succession, and to the rules prohibiting marriage between a range of persons related through *nasab* and through marriage. The concerns raised at the prospect of 'mixing lineage' move from the more traditional requirement of a 'conjugal bed' and lawful sexual relations to new reproductive technologies in so far as the latter involve sperm (or eggs) provided by third parties.

Similar preoccupations with the 'mixing of lineage', as well as the established *fiqh* position, can be seen to underlie the general attitude towards adoption in Arab states. This issue is not dealt with in the UAE or Qatari codes, while the Bahraini law clarifies that adoption is not allowed to give rise to the establishment of paternity or its *shar'i* effects. Elsewhere, the Algerian family law of 1984 is unusual in including a separate section on the Islamic institution of *kafala*. Broadly speaking, *kafala* is a system of care that allows a child to be looked after and brought up in a family not his or her own, with similar rights of maintenance, education and so on that pertain to minors, but without key attributes of *nasab* (family name, fractional inheritance rights). The institution of *kafala* is explicitly referred to in the United Nations Convention on the Rights of the Child (CRC), in the same article as fostering and adoption, regarding the care of a child 'temporarily or permanently deprived of his or her family environment'. The UAE entered an explicit reservation to this article, stating that the UAE does not permit this system (adoption) 'given its commitment to the principles of Islamic law'. In the case of Qatar, prior to the announcement of a 'partial withdrawal' of its general reservation on the CRC in 2009, Qatar had already clarified in its initial report to the CRC's monitoring body that it did not recognize adoption as a system.[11] Bahrain entered no reservations on the CRC, but clarified in its first report in 2001 that, while it did not apply the system of adoption as understood in the CRC, Bahrain's then Cabinet had approved 'the Fosterage Act' (a law on *kafala*) to regulate this system of care.[12]

Concluding comment

The first-time codifications of Muslim family law in the UAE, Qatar and Bahrain offer a range of opportunities for researchers interested in the process, as well as the substance, of these laws. The substance is broadly similar to, but by no means identical with, some significant differences between the three laws—and here, as ever, what was omitted, and why, is as important as what was included. While on key issues such as guardianship and 'obedience', these three laws (along with other Gulf codifications) stand apart from recent developments, particularly in North Africa, the legislatures have at the same time tackled many issues in a manner comparable to Arab states with a longer history of Muslim family law codification. In most cases they build on the approaches taken in earlier Arab state codifications, while on some issues specific domestic concerns prompt a more individual approach. As for the processes, these have, variously, seen: a series of ministerial committees successively seized with the task of drafting personal status codifications, over a period of decades; a wide-ranging and at times acrimonious civil society debate involving the judiciary and women's rights groups; the interventions of official, national women's councils from a position outside the drafting process; the mobilization of practitioners and women's rights activists on a regional basis against certain reported positions in an upcoming piece of legislation; and studied engagement with the international human rights system on the issue of women's rights in the family.

In the same period, the first decade of the twenty-first century, all three states have also become parties to CEDAW: Bahrain was the first in 2002,

[11]UN Doc CRC/C/51/Add.5, 11 January 2001 (Qatar's initial report to the Committee on the Rights of the Child).
[12]UN Doc CRC/C/11/Add.24, 23 July 2001 (Bahrain's initial report to the Committee on the Rights of the Child).

with the UAE following in 2004 and Qatar becoming the most recent in 2009. This development signals an engagement with the international system most closely concerned with the protection of women's rights, and opens up the process of monitoring and debate that surrounds the submission of periodic reports to the monitoring committee in the United Nations. The pressure generated from participatory discussion in external—as distinct from domestic—advocacy on women's rights in the family, and regional dynamics is a relatively new factor. Ann Elizabeth Mayer has explored the impact of the process of preparing these reports by states, the role of non-state actors in providing parallel reports, and the discussions on (or defense of) these reports in CEDAW.

Bahrain submitted its first report to CEDAW in 2007. Of significance is the fact that its report was prepared by SCW, which was established in 2001 and chaired by the King's wife; as explained by the head of the delegation to CEDAW, SCW reports directly to the King, making it an 'official' body, although not a governmental one. The delegation to CEDAW was led by the deputy president of SCW, and lists several women's associations among entities that participated in the production of the report. The report clearly identified the 'promulgation of a family code' as a 'basic demand essential to achieving family stability for women and ensuring women's rights, especially in the area of family relations'. In its Concluding Observations issued in 2008, CEDAW agreed.[13]

Also of note is the fact that two 'shadow reports' were submitted by civil society organizations, including one by a national committee formed in 2003, following Bahrain's accession to the Convention, and comprising nine member associations of the Bahrain Women's Union and eleven 'other national parties' (Bahraini NGOs). Both shadow reports called for the promulgation of a codification of family law. The active engagement of women's associations and other civil society groups in this process is indicative of the mobilization of a significant sector of civil society around the issue, utilizing the space provided by CEDAW's consideration of the governmental report to submit their analyses to an international forum. The initial impetus, in the early 1980s, for codification of family law

[13]UN Doc. CEDAW/C/BHR/2, 12 November 2007, combined initial and second periodic report of Bahrain to the CEDAW, para. 91; and CEDAW/C/BHR//2, 14 November 2008, Concluding Observations of the Committee on the Elimination of Discrimination against Women: Bahrain, para. 39.

rulings in Bahrain came from women's civil society associations and women's rights activists and practitioners, including some of those involved in the preparation of the shadow reports. By the time Bahrain's report was submitted to the Committee, the government was already committed to codification, although not in the form called for by these civil society organizations.

Official women's councils also operate in the UAE and in Qatar, although not at the same apparent level of prominence as the SCW in Bahrain; in the UAE, the General Union of Women was one of the members of the Committee convened by the Ministry of Foreign Affairs that prepared the UAE's first report to CEDAW, while in Qatar the Supreme Council for Family Affairs has a Women's Committee. In addition, the international processes around CEDAW widen the opportunities for women's NGOs; one of the procedural questions put to the UAE delegation by CEDAW in consideration of the UAE's first report was the extent of women's civil society engagement with the process of compiling the report, a very pertinent question given that the record shows no equivalent of the Bahraini NGOs' domestic mobilization around the reporting process.[14] In addition, as noted in the previous sections, interventions on specific issues by various women's associations, lawyers and others have clearly had an impact during the family law drafting processes in the UAE and Qatar, as well as in the Bahraini debates. For the researcher, the directions of civil society associations as they work around the family laws, including region-wide exchange of experience, will be one focus of attention. Another should be the law in practice—how it is deployed and with what impact; and it is here, as the courts, legislatures and litigants learn from the experience of applying the new laws, that research in the 'real time' of the implementation process will be particularly enriching for the field.

[14]UNN Doc. CEDAW/C/ARE/Q/1, 13 March 2009 at para. 1. Available at http://daccess-dds-ny.un.org/doc/UNDOC/GEN/N09/265/89/PDF/N0926589.pdf?OpenElement (accessed 30 January 2010).

Bibliography

'Abbud, Shadi. *Al-'Ashiqun*. Lebanon: al-Mitn, 2007.

'Abd al-'Ati, Hammudah. *The Family Structure in Islam*. Indianapolis: American Trust Publications, 1997.

'Abd al Rahman. *The History of Education in Mecca* (n.p., n.d.).

'Abd al-Rahim, 'Abd al-Rahman 'Abd al-Rahim, *Al-Khalifj: ru'ya ijtima 'iyya wa hadariyya. The Gulf: A View of the Economic, Social and Cultural Reality 1900–1930*. Cairo: Dar al-Kitab al-Jami'i, 1994.

'Abd al-Rahim, 'Abd al-Rahim 'Abd al-Rahman. *Al-Khalij al-'Arabi: ru'ya fi al-waqi' al-iqtisadi wa-al-ijtima'i wa-al-thaqafi, marhalat ma qabl al-bitrul 1900–1930*. Al-'Ayn, United Arab Emirates: n.p. 1994.

'Abd al-Rahman, 'A'isha. *Sukaynah bint al-Husayn*. Beirut: Dar al-Kitab al-Lubnani, n.d.

'Abd al-Rahman, 'Abdallah. *Al-Imara fi dhakirat abna'iha*. Al-Sharqa: Manshurat Ittihad Kuttab wa-Udaba' al-Imarat, 1995.

'Abd al-Rahman, 'Abdallah. *Al-Imarat fi dhakirat abna'iha: al-haya' al-ijtima'iyya*. Dubai: Nadwat al Thaqafa wa'l 'Ulum, 1998.

'Atallah, Samir. *Qāfilat al-hibr: al-rahhala al-gharbiyyun ila al-Jazira 1762–1950* [The Ink Caravan: Western Travelers to the Arabian Peninsula 1762–1950]. Beirut: Al-Saqi, 1994.

'Atawi, Rafiq Khalil. *Surat al-mar'a fi shi'r al-ghazal al-Umawi*. Beirut: Dar al-'Ilm li-al-Malayin, 1986.

Abbott, Nabia. 'Women and the State on the Eve of Islam'. *American Journal of Semitic Languages and Literatures* 58(3), July 1941: 262–84.

Abou El Fadl, Khaled. 'The Human Rights Commitment in Modern Islam' in Joseph Runzo, Nancy Martin and Arvind Sharma (eds), *Human Rights and Responsibilities in the World Religions*. Oxford: Oneworld, 2003, 301–64.

Abou El Fadl, Khaled. 'The Place of Ethical Obligations in Islamic Law'. *UCLA Journal of Islamic and Near Eastern Law* 4 (1), 2004–2005: 1–40.

Abou El Fadl, Khaled. *Speaking in God's Name: Islamic Law, Authority and Women*. Oxford: Oneworld, 2001.

Abou Saud, Abeer. *Qatari Women Past and Present*. London, New York: Longman 1984.

Abou-Bakr, Omaima. 'Teaching the Words of the Prophet: Women Instructors of the Hadith (Fourteenth and Fifteenth Centuries)'. *Hawwa: Journal of Women of the Middle East and the Islamic World* 1 (3), 2003: 306–28.

Abou-Bakr, Omaima. *Al-Nisa' wa-mihnat al-tibb fi al-tarikh al-Islami* (Women and the Medical Profession in Islamic History), *Awraq al-dhakirah* Series (Occasional Papers), no. 1,. Cairo: Women & Memory Forum, 1999.

Abou-Bakr, Omaima.'*Qira'ah fi tarikh 'abidat al-Islam*' (A Reading in the History of Islam's Women Worshippers/Mystics), in *Zaman al-nisa' wa-al-dhakirah al-badilah* (Women's Time and Alternative Memory), eds. Hoda Elsadda & Omaima Abou-Bakr. Cairo: The Women & Memory Forum, 1998.

Abu 'Izza, A. *Al-khaleej al-Aarabi fi al-'asr al-'Islami*. al-'Ayn, UAE: Maktabat al-Falah li-al-Nashr wa-al-Tawzi', 2001.

Abu Rihab, Hasan. *al-Ghazal 'inda al-'Arab*. Cairo: Matba'at Misr, 1947.

Abu Zayd, Nasr Hamid. 'The Qur'anic Concept of Justice' [2001], available online at http://polylog.org/3fan-en.htm. accessed 24 July 2008.

Abu Zayd, Nasr Hamid. *Reformation of Islamic Thought: A Critical Analysis*. Amsterdam: Amsterdam University Press, 2006.

Abugideiri, Hibba E. 'Egyptian Woman and the Science Question: Gender in the Making of Colonized Medicine, 1893–1929' (PhD diss., Georgetown University, 2001.

Abugideiri, Hibba E. 'Off to Work at Home: Egyptian Midwives Blur Public-Private Boundaries'. *Hawwa: Journal of Women of the Middle East and Islamic World* 6(3), 2008: 254–83.

Abu-Lughod, Lila. *Veiled Sentiments*. Berkeley: University of California Press, 1986).

Abu-Lughod, Lila. *Writing Women's Worlds*. Berkeley and Los Angeles: University of California Press, 1993.

Afsaruddin, Asma. 'Reconstituting Women's Lives: Gender and the Poetics of Narrative in Medieval Biographical Collections'. *Muslim World* 92, fall 2002: 461–80.

Ahmed, Leila. 'Women and the Advent of Islam'. *Signs: Journal of Women in Culture and Society* 11(4), Summer 1986: 665–91.

Ahmed, Leila. *Women and Gender in Islam: Historical Roots of a Modern Debate*. New Haven, CT: Yale University Press, 1992.

Al-'Abdullah, Yusuf. *The History of Education in the Gulf* (n.p., n.d.).

Al-Ayoub, Ayoub Hussein. *Kuwaiti Heritage in Paintings* (n.p., n.d.).

Al-Milhim, Muhammad bin 'Abd al-Latif bin Muhammad. *It was More Like a University* (n.p., n.d.).

Al-Rashid, 'Abd al-'Aziz. *The History of Kuwait* (n.p., n.d.).

Al-Salih, Maryam 'Abd al-Malik. *Pages from the History of the Development of Girls' Education in Kuwait*. Kuwait: Ministry of Media and Popular Culture in Kuwait, 2002.

Al-Tabur, 'Abdullah. *Mutawwi'* (n.p., n.d.).

Al-Thani, Nura Nasir Jasim. 'Al-Mar'a al-Qatariyya wa-al-ta'lim' in 'Adil Hasan Ghunaym (ed.), *al-Tarikh al-ijtima'i li-al-mar'a al-Qatariyya al-mu'asira*. Doha: Qatar University, 1989, 117–76.

Al-'Adli, Faruq Muhammad. *Dirasat anthrupulujiyya fi al-mujtama' al-Qatari*. Cairo: Dar al-Kitab al-Jam'i, 1981.

Al-'Aqqad, 'Abbas Mahmud. *Sha'ir al-ghazal: 'Umar ibn Abi Rabi'a*. Iqra' 6. Cairo: Dar al-Ma'rif, 1965.

Al-'Idraws, Muhammad Hasan. *Dirasat fi al-Khalij al-'Arabi*. Kuwait: Dar al-Kitab al-Hadith, (n.d.).

Al-'Izzi, Najla' Isma'il. *Sina'at al-dhahab al-taqlidiyya fi Qatar, al-Doha*. Qatar: 1988.

Al-'Ubaykan, Tarfa 'Abd al-'Aziz. *Al-Hayat al-'ilmiyya wa-al-ijtima'iyya fi Makka fi al-qarnayn al-sabi' wa-al-thamin li-al-hijra*. Riyadh: Maktabat al-Malik Fahd al-Wataniyyah, 1996.

Al-Ahmad, S.S. *Ancient Iraq until the Akkadian Period*. Baghdad: National Library, 1978.

Al-Amadi, Badriyya Mubarak Sultan. *Amina Mahmud al- Jayyida: The Pioneer of Girls' Education and Feminism in Qatar 1913–2000*. Qatar: National Council for Culture, Arts and Heritage, 2004.

Al-Amd , I.S. 'Harakat laqeet bin malik al-'azdi fi 'Oman fi sadr al-'Islam', in *al-Dhikra wa al-tareekh, buhuth tarikhiyyah muhdat min 'a'dha' hay'at al-tadrees bi-qism al-tareekh 'la jami'at al-Kuwait bi-munasabat murur khamsah wa 'ushrun 'aman 'ala ta'seesaha'*, no editor. Kuwait: Jami'at al-Kuwait, 1990, 91–114.

Al-Andalusi, Ibn 'Abd al-Barr. *Al-Intiqa' fi fada'il al-a'imma al-thalatha al-fuqaha', Malik wa-al-Shafi'i wa-Abi Hanifa rahamahum Allah*. Aleppo: Maktab al-Matbu'at al-Islamiyya, 1997.

Al-Ansari, 'Abd al-Quddus. *Ta'rikh madinat Jidda*. Jeddah: Dar al-Isfahani wa-Shuraka'ihi, 1383 AH/1963.

Al-Ansary, A.R.T. 'Al-Gerrha: The Port of 'Qaryat' al-Fau', in J.F. Healey and V. Porte (eds), *Studies on Arabia in Honour of G. Rex Smith*. Oxford: Oxford University Press on behalf of the University of Manchester, 2002, 7–17.

Al-Asfahani, Abu al-Faraj. *Kitab al-aghani*. 23 vols. Cairo: Dar al-Fikr, (n.d.).

Al-Babatayn, Ilham. *Al-Haya al-ijtimaiyya fi Makka mundhu zuhur al-Islam hatta nihayat al-'asr al-Umawi*. Riyadh: University Press of King Saud, 1419 AH).

Al-Badr, S.S. *Mantiqat al-khaleej al-'Arabi khilal al-'alfayn al-rabi' wa al-thalith qabl al-milad*. Kuwait: Matba'at Dawlat al-Kuwayt, 1974.

Al-Badr, S.S. *Mantiqat al-khaleej al-'Arabi khilal al-'alfayn al-thani wa al-'awal qabl al-milad*. Kuwait: Matba'at Dawlat al-Kuwayt, 1978.

Al-Baghdadi, A. *Al-Farq bayn al-firaq*. 2nd ed. Beirut: Dar al-Afaq al-Jadida, 1977.

Al-Baghdadi, Abu al-Fuz Muhammad Amin. *Saba'ik al-dhahab fi ma'rifat qaba'il al-'Arab*. Baghdad: 1339 AH.

Al-Baladhuri, Ahmad ibn Yahya. *Futuh al-buldan*, ed. Radwan Muhammad Radwan. Beirut: Dar al-Kutub al-'Ilmiyya, 1983.

Al-Bassam, Khalid. *Sadmat al-ihtikak: hikayat al-irsaliyya al-Amrikiyya fi al-Khalij wa-al-Jazira al-'Arabiyya, 1892–1925* [The Shock of Interaction: Stories of the American Mission in the Gulf and the Arabian Peninsula 1892–1925]. London: Saqi 1988.

Al-Bassam, Khalid. *Al-Qawafil*. Bahrain: 1993

Al-Bunni, A. 'Ebla from A to Z'. *Bulletin of Arab and World History*, Aug 1984: 21–62.

Al-Dhahabi, Shams al-Din Muhammad Ahmad (d. 1347 AD). *Siyar a'lam al-nubala'* [Biographies of prominent noble figures]. Beirut: Mu'assasat al-Risala, 1996.

Al-Dukhayl, Muna bint 'Abdullah bin Hamad. *Watha'iq qaryat al-'Ulya: 1365–1380/1960–1945*. Riyadh: Maktabat al-Malik Fahd al-Wataniyya, 2005.

Al-Faraj, Khalid. *Diwan 'Abdullah al-Faraj*. Bombay, 1920.

Al-Faraj, Khalid. *Diwan al-Nabat*. Damascus: Matba'at al-Tararqqi, 1952.

Al-Fassi, H.A. *Women in Pre-Islamic Arabia: Nabataea*. British Archaeological Reports). Oxford: Archaeopress, 2007.

Al-Ghadeer, Moneera. *Desert Voices*. London: I.B. Tauris, Academic Series, 2009.

Al-Ghanim, Kaltham. 'Violence against Women in Qatari Society,' *Middle East Women's Studies*, vol.5, no.1,. Winter, 2009.

Al-Ghazali, Imam Abu Hamid. *The Proper Conduct of Marriage in Islam* (Adab an-Nikah). *Book Twelve of* Ihya 'Ulum ad-Din *[Revival of Religious Sciences]*, trans. Muhtar Holland. Hollywood, FA: Al-Baz, 1998.

Al-Hamadi, Muhammad 'Ali al-Shurafa'. *Nayl al-rutab fi jawami' al-adab*, ed. Falih Hanzal. Abu Dhabi: 1994.

Al-Harbi, Dalal bint Mukhallad. *Nisa' Shahirat min Najd* [Famous women from Najd]. Riyadh: Darat al-Malik Abdel Aziz, 1999.

Al-Hasan, Ghassan. *Al-Sh'ir al-Nabati fi mintaqat al-Khalij wa-al-Jazira al-'Arabiyya*. Dubai:Wizarat al-I'lam wa-al-Thaqafa fi Dawlat al-Imarat al-'Arabiyya al-Muttahida, 1998.

Al-Hatim, 'Abdullah. *Khiyar ma yultaqat min al-shi'r al-Nabati*. Damascus: al-Matba'a al-Umumiyya, 1952.

Al-Hibri, Aziza. 'A Study of Islamic Herstory; Or How Did We Get into This Mess' in *Islam and Women*, special issue of *Women's Studies International Forum* 5(2), 1982: 207–19.

Al-Hibri, Aziza. 'An Islamic Perspective on Domestic Violence'. *Fordham International Law Journal* 27, 2003–2004: 195–224.

Al-Hibri, Aziza. 'Islam, Law and Custom: Redefining Muslim Women's Rights'. *American University Journal of International Law and Policy* 12, 1997: 1–44.

Al-Hibri, Aziza. 'Muslim Women's Rights in the Global Village: Challenges and Opportunities'. *Journal of Law and Religion* 15(1 & 2), 2001: 37–66.

Al-Hilli, Muhaqqiq. *Sharayi' al-Islam*, Persian trans. A.A. Yazdi, compiled by Muhammad Taqi Danish-Pazhuh. Vol. 2. Tehran: Tehran University Press, 1985.

Ali, Jawad. *Al-mufassal fi tarikh al-'Arab qabl al-islam*, 2nd printing. Beirut: Dar al-'Ilm li al-Malayin, 1980. Available electronically in *Encyclopedia of Coptic History* http://www.coptichistory.org/new page 1994.htm.

Ali, Kecia. 'Progressive Muslims and Islamic Jurisprudence: The Necessity for Critical Engagement with Marriage and Divorce Law' in Omid Safi (ed.), *Progressive Muslims: On Justice, Gender, and Pluralism*. Oxford: Oneworld, 2003, 163–89.

Ali, Kecia. *Sexual Ethics and Islam: Feminist Reflections on Quran, Hadith and Jurisprudence*. Oxford: Oneworld, 2006.

Al-Ikri al-Hanbali, A. *Shadharat al-dhahab fi akhbar man dhahab*, ed. A.Arna'ut. 10 vols. Damascus: Dar Ibn Katheer, 1986.

Al-Isbahani, Abu al Faraj. *Al-qiyan*, ed. Jalil al-Atiyya. London: Riyad al-Rayyes, 1989.

Al-Isbahani, Abu al Faraj. *Kitab al-aghani*. Cairo: Dar al-sha'b, 1982.

Al-Isfahani, Abu al-Faraj. *Kitab al-aghani*, ed. Ihsan 'Abbas et al. Beirut: Dar Sadr, 2003.

Al-Ja'fari, A.A. 'Eastern Arabia in the Description of Moroccan and Andalusian Accounts in the Islamic Period'. *Journal of the Saudi Historical Association* 7(14), 2006: 5–43.

Al-Janbi, A.A. *Hajar wa qasabatuha al-thalath: al-Mushaqqar, al-Safa, al-Shab'an, wa nahruha Muhallam*. Beirut: Dar al-Mahajja al-Bayda', 2004.

Al-Jasir, Hamad. *Al-mar'a fi hayat imam al-da'wa al-Shaykh Muhammad ibn*

'Abd al-Wahhab. Riyadh: 'Imadat al-bahth al-'ilmi bijami'at al-imam Muhammad bin Sa'ud al-islamiya, 1991.

Al-Jawzi, Jamal al-Din Abu-al-Faraj 'Abd al-Rahman. *Sifat al-safwa*. Cairo: Dar al-Safa, 1991.

Al-Juhany, Uwidah. *Najd before the Salafi Reform Movement*. Ithaca, NY: Ithaca Press, 2002.

Al-Kamali, Shafiq. *Al-Sh'ir 'inda al-Badu*. Beirut: Kutub, 1964.

Al-Khalifa, Khalid Khalifa. 'Bahraini Trade from the 'Utoob Conquest until the Appearance of Oil' in Sheikh Abdullah al-Khalifa and Michael Rice (eds), *Bahrain through the Ages: The History*. London: Kegan Paul, 1993, 335–59.

Al-Khurafi, 'Abd al-Muhsin 'Abdullah. *Murabbun min baladi* [Educators from the Homeland]. Kuwait: Al-Shamiyya, 1998.

Al-Kitab al-dhahabi lil-mahakim al-ahliyya: 1883–1933. Bulaq: Al-Matba'a al-Amiriyya, 1937.

Al-Laziqani, M. *Thulathiyyat al-hulm al-qurmuti*. Cairo: Maktabat Madbuli, 1993.

Allen, Belle J. *A Crusade of Compassion for the Healing of the Nations: A Study of Medical Missions for Women and Children*, ed. Caroline Atwater Mason. West Medford MA: Central Committee on the United Study of Foreign Missions, 1919.

Allison, Mary Bruins. *Doctor Mary in Arabia: Memoirs by Mary Bruins Allison, M.D.*, ed Sandra Shaw. Austin: University of Texas, 1994.

Al-Manaa, Suad A. *Sukaynah bint al-Husayn: Women and Poetry Criticism in the Early Days of Poetry Criticism. The Case of the Literary Critical Texts Ascribed to Sukaynah bint al Husayn*. Kuwait: Kuwait University Press, 1999.

Al-Maqrizi, A. *'Itti'az al-hunafa bi 'akhbar al-'a'immah al-fatimiyeen al-khulafa*, vol 1: ed. J.D.al-Shayyal, vol 2: ed. M.H.M.Ahmad. Cairo: al-majlis al-'a'la lilshu'un al-'islamiyyah, lajnat 'ihya' al-turath al-'islami, 1967–1971.

Al-Mas'udi, A. *Muruj al-dhahab wa-ma'adin al-jawhar*, ed. M. 'Abd al-Hamid. 5 vols. Riyadh: Maktabat al-Riyadh al-Haditha, 1973.

Al-Misnad, Sheikha. *The Development of Modern Education in the Gulf*. London: Ithaca Press, 1985.

Al-Mughni, Haya. *Women in Kuwait: The Politics of Gender*. London: Saqi, 2001.

Al-Mulla, A. *Tarkih hajar*. 2 vols. al-Ahsa: Al-Jawad, 1991.

Al-Muraikhi, Khalil. *Glimpses of Bahrain from the Past*. Bahrain: Government Press, 1991.

Al-Nafzawi, Muhammad ibn Muhammad [Cheikh Nefzaoui]. *The Perfumed Garden of the Cheikh Nefzaoui: A Manual of Arabian Erotology*, trans. Sir Richard F. Burton. New York: Signet Classics, 1999.

Al-Nafzawi, Muhammad ibn Muhammad. *The Perfumed Garden of Sensual Delight*, trans. Jim Colville. London: Kegan Paul, 1999.

Al-Qalqashandi, A.A. *Nihayat al-irab fi ma'rifat ansab al-'Arab*. Dan-al-Kitab al-Libnani, 1980.

Al-Qalqashandi, A.A. *Subh al-a'sha? fi sina'at al-insha*, ed. A.Q. Zakka. 14 vols. Damascus: Ministry of Culture, 1981.

Al-Qaradawi, Yusuf. *Nisa' mu'minat*. Cairo: Maktabat Wahba, 1979.

Al-Rawi, 'Abd al-Jabbar. *Al-Badiya*. Baghdad: Dar Dejla li-al-Tiba'a wa-al-Nashr, 1947.

Al-Sa'di Hoda and Omaima Abou-Bakr. *Al-Mar'ah wa-al-hayah al-diniyah fi al-'usur al-wusta'* [Women and Religious Life in the Middle Ages between

Islam and the West]. Occasional Papers, no. 2. Cairo: Women & Memory Forum, 2001.

Al-Sa'id, Talal. *Al-Mawsu'a al-Nabatiyya al-kamila*. Kuwait: Dhat al-Salasil, 1987.

Al-Safadi, H. *Al-wajeez fi tarkih hadarat Asia al-gharbiyyah, bilad al-rafedayn hatta 'awakhir al-'alf al-thalith qabl al-milad*. Damascus: Matba'at Tarabeen, 1984.

Al-Safadi, Salah al-Din Khalil bin Aybak. *Al-Wafi bi-al-wafiyyat*. Istanbul: Matba'at al-Dawla, 1931.

Al-Sarraj, Ja'far. *Masari' al-'ushshaq*. Beirut: Dar Sadir, 1958.

Al-Sayegh, Fatima. *Al-tabshir fi mantiqat al-Imarat: al-khidma al-tibbiyya ka-wasila li-al-tabshir* [Evangelism in the Emirates: Medical Service as a Missionary Strategy]. Al-Majalla al-'Arabiyya li-al-'Ulum al-Insaniyya 53, Year 14, Autumn 1995:63–96.

Al-Sayegh, Fatima. 'American Women Missionaries in the Gulf: Agents for Cultural Change'. *Islam and Christian-Muslim Relations* 9(3), October 1998: 339–56.

Al-Sayegh, Fatima, 'Women and Economic Changes in the Gulf: The Case of the United Arab Emirates'. *Domes* 10(2) (2001): 3–10.

Al-Shayb, Qazim. *Al-'Unf al-usari: Qira'a fi al-zahira min ajl mujtama' salim* [Family Violence: A Reading of the Phenomenon with a View to a Healthy Society]. Beirut: Al-Markaz al-Thaqafi al-'Arabi, 2007.

Al-Shaybani, Sultan Mubarak. *Mu'jam al-nisa' al-'Umaniyyat: dalil tarikhi ila tarajim ashhar al-nisa' fi tarikh 'Uman al-majid*. Muscat: Matabi' al-Nahda, 2004).

Al-Shayib, Ahmad. *Tarikh al-Naqa'id fi al-shi'r al-'arabi*. Cairo, 1946.

Al-Siba'i, Ahmad. *Ta'rikh Makka* (1380AH/1960) Jidda: Tihama, 1960.

Al-Sindi, Khalid. *Dilmuni Seals*, trans. Mohammed al-Khoza. Bahrain: Bahrain National Museum, 1999.

Al-Suyuti, Jalal al-Din 'Abd al-Rahman. *Muwatta'al-imam Malik wa-sharhuh tanwir al-hawalik*. Egypt: *Matba'at Mustafa al-Halabi*, 1951.

Al-Tabari, M.J. *Tarikh al-umam wa-al-muluk,* ed. M.A.F. Ibrahim. 5 vols. Beirut: Dar al-Kutub al-'Ilmiyya, 1987.

Al-Tamimi, 'Abd al-Malik Khalaf. *Al-tabshir fi mantiqat al-Khalij al-'Arabi: Dirasa fi tarikh al-ijtam'i wa-al-siyasi* [Evangelism in the Arabian Gulf Region: a Study in Social and Political History]. Kuwait: Manshirat Sharikat Kazma lil-Nashr wal-Tawzi', 1982.

Al-Thani, Alya. 'The Realization of the Rights of the Girl Child in Qatar: Towards Ending the Traditional Practice of Early Marriage'. MA diss., School of Oriental and African Studies, University of London, 2006.

Al-Thani, Haya. *Al-khalij al-'arabi fi 'usur ma qabl al-tarikh*. Cairo: Markaz al-Kitab li-al-Nashr, 1997.

Al-Zahrani, Awad. *Thaj: dirasa athariyya maydaniyya*. Riyadh: King Saud University, 1996.

Amin, Jawdat. *Shu'ara' wa-tajarib fi al-'asr al-Umawi*. Cairo: Dar al-Thaqafa al-'Arabiyya, 1989.

Anderson, James Norman. *Law Reforms in the Muslim World*. London: Athlone, 1976.

Anonymous. 'Miscellaneous Archaeological News'. *Atlal* (6) 1980: 138–40.

Anthony, T.A. 'Documentation of the Modern History of Bahrain from American Sources (1900–1938)' in Sheikh Abdullah al-Khalifa and Michael Rice (eds),

Bahrain through the Ages: The History. London: Kegan Paul, 1993), 62–77.

Arabi, Oussama. 'The Dawning of the Third Millennium on Shariʻa: Egypt's Law no.1 of 2000, or Women May Divorce at Will'. *Arab Law Quarterly* 16(1), 2001: 2–21.

Arabi, Oussama. *Studies in Modern Islamic Law and Jurisprudence*. The Hague: Kluwer Law International, 2001.

Arabian Mission Correspondence, deposited at New Brunswick Seminary, Box no. 754.5

Arki, A. 'Nizam al-awzan fi Ibla', in *Ibla-ʻAblaa al-sakhrah al-baidha'*, ed. A.al-Bunni, tr. Q.Tuweir. Damascus: Matba'at Suriya, 143–162.

Arkoun, Mohammed. *Rethinking Islam: Common Questions, Uncommon Answers*. Boulder CO: Westview Press, 1994.

Arrian, F.X. *The Campaigns of Alexander*, trans. A. Sélincourt. London: Penguin Books, (n.d.)

Association of National Democratic Action—Waʻd (ANDA). *On the Codification of the Rules of the Family in Bahrain*. Farida Ghulam Ismaʻil (lead researcher), 'Abdullah al-Haddad and Sami Sayadi. In Arabic. Bahrain: Office of Women's Affairs, March 2008.

Badawi, Jamal. *Gender Equity in Islam: Basic Principles*. Indianapolis: American Trust Publication, 1995.

Bahrain Human Rights Watch Society. 'Shadow Report submitted to the United Nations Committee on the Elimination of Discrimination against Women (CEDAW) in response to the Kingdom of Bahrain Periodic Report' (Bahrain, August 2008). Available at: http://www2.ohchr.org/english/bodies/cedaw/docs/ngos/HRWS_Bahrain.pdf (accessed 30 January 2010).

Bahraini NGOs. 'The Shadow Report on Implementation of the Convention on the Elimination of all Forms of Discrimination against Women (CEDAW)' (Bahrain, September 2008). Available at: http://www2.ohchr.org/english/bodies/cedaw/docs/ngos/Bahrainwomenunion42.pdf (accessed 30 January 2010).

Bailey, Clinton. *Bedouin Poetry from Sinai and the Negev*. Oxford: Oxford University Press, 1991.

Bainbridge, Lucy S. *Women's Medical Work in Foreign Missions*. New York: Woman's Board of Foreign Missions, (n.d.).

Bamia, Aida Adib. *The Graying of the Raven*. Cairo: American University in Cairo Press, 2001.

Barazangi, Nimat Hafez. *Women's Identity and the Qur'an: A New Reading*. Gainsville: University of Florida Press, 2004.

Barlas, Asma. *Believing Women' in Islam: Unreading Patriarchal Interpretations of the Qur'an*. Austin: University of Texas Press, 2002.

Baron, Beth. 'Women, Honour, and the State: Evidence from Egypt'. *Middle Eastern Studies* 42(1), January 2006: 1–20.

Beeston, A.F.L. 'The So-Called Harlots of Hadramawt'. *Oriens* 5(1), July 1952: 16–22.

Bernard-Maugiron, Nathalie. 'Dissolution du marriage et persistance non juridictionnelle des conflits conjugaux en Égypte', in Baudouin Dupret and François Burgat (eds), *Le shaykh et le procureur: Systèmes coutumiers et pratiques juridiques au Yémen et en Égypte*. *Égypte/Monde Arabe* 3(1) (Paris: Centre d'Études et de Documentation Économiques, Juridiques et Sociales (Cedej), 2005), 73–100.

Bevan, A.A. *The Naqa'id of Jarir and al-Farazdaq*. 3 vols. Leiden: Brill, 1905–12.

Bibby, T.G. and H. Kapel. 'Preliminary Survey in East Arabia 1968'. *Reports of the Danish Archaeological Expedition to the Arabian Gulf*. 2 (Jutland Archeological society publications vol XII, 1973, in commission at Gyldendal, Copenhagen 1973).

Bin Serai, H. 'Al-sukkan al-qudamaa' li-shibh jazeerat Oman'. *Shu'un Ijtima'iyya* 43, 1994: 53–67.

Bin Serai. H. 'Al-'ilaqat al-hadhariyyah bayn mantiqat al-Khaleej al-'Arabi wa shibh al-qarrah al-hindiyyah wa janubi sharq Asia min al-qarn al-thalith qabl al-milad 'ila al-qarn al-sabi' miladi' (*Buhuth Tarikhiyya* 20) (Riyadh: al-jam'iyyah al-tarikhiyyah al-su'udiyyah, 2006.

Blachère, R. 'Al-Farazdak' in *Encyclopaedia of Islam*. Online edition, 2007.

Blunt, Lady Ann. *A Pilgrimage to Nejd: The Cradle of the Arab Race*. London: Murray, 1881; repr. London: Century, 1985.

Boersma, Jeanette. *Grace in the Gulf: The Autobiography of Jeanette Boersma, Missionary Nurse in Iraq and the Sultanate of Oman*. Historical Series of the Reformed Church in America 20. Grand Rapids, MI: Eerdmans, 1991.

Boucharlat, R. and J.F. Salles. 'The History and Archaeology of the Gulf from the Fifth Century BC to the Seventh Century AD: A Review of the Evidence'. *Seminar for Arabian Studies* 2, 1981: 65–94.

Bouhdiba, Abdelwahab. *Sexuality in Islam*. Translated from the French by Alan Sheridan. London: Saqi Books, 2004.

Brice, William. 'Traditional Techniques of Navigation in the Seas of Bahrain' in Sheikh Abdullah al-Khalifa and Michael Rice (eds), *Bahrain through the Ages: The History*. London: Kegan Paul, 1993, 135–43.

Buhl. F. 'Hind bint 'Utba B. Rabi'a' in *Encyclopaedia of Islam*. Leiden: Brill, 2007 and Brill Online.

Burckhardt, John Lewis. *Notes on the Bedouins and the Wahabys*. 2 vols. Reading, UK: Garnet, 1992 [1831]).

Burkhardt, John Lewis. *Travels in Arabia*. 2 vols. London: Henry Colburn, 1829.

Bynum, Caroline. *Gender and Religion: On the Complexity of Symbols*. Boston: Beacon Press, 1986.

Caetani, Leone. *Annali dell'Islam: Compilati da Leone Caetani*. Milan: Ulrico Hoeplie, 1907.

Calverley, Eleanor T. *My Arabian Days and Nights*. New York: Thomas Y. Crowell Company, 1958.

Calverley, Eleanor T., Mabel Ruth Nowlin, Alice B. Van Doren and E. Stanley Jones. *Christ Comes to the Village: A Study of Rural Life in Non-Christian Lands* (n.p., n.d.).

Chouin, Gerald. 'Seen, Said or Deduced? Travel Accounts, Historical Criticism, and Discourse: An "Archeology" of Dialogue in Seventeenth-Century Guinea'. *History of Africa* 28 (2001), 53–70.

Clark, Linda. 'Hijab According to Hadith: Text and Interpretation' in Sajida Alavi, Homa Hoodfar, and Sheila McDonough (eds), *The Muslim Veil in North America: Issues and Debates*. Toronto: Women's Press, 2003, 214–86.

Committee for the Documentation of Qatari History. Vol. 2 (n.p., n.d.).

Condrai, Ronald. *Abu Dhabi: An Arabian Album*. Abu Dhabi: Motivate Publishing, The Codrai Library, 1992.

Crone, Patricia. *Slaves on Horses: The Evolution of the Islamic Polity*. Cambridge: Cambridge University Press, 1980.

Dahir, Ahmad Jamal. *Al-Mar'a fi duwal al-Khalij al-'Arabi* [Women in the Arabian Gulf States]. Kuwait: Dirasat maydaniyya manshurat dhat al-salasil (n.d.).

Daw', Muhammad. *Al-'Unf didd al-mar'a fi Suriyya: abhath wa-maqalat* [Violence against Women in Syria: Studies and Articles, (n.d.)].

Dawes, James. *The Language of War*. Cambridge, MA: Harvard University Press, 2002.

Dayf, Shawqi. *Al-Shi'ir wa-al-ghina' fi al-Madina wa-Makka fi 'asr bani Umayya*. Cairo: Dar al-Ma'rif, 1976.

Dayf, Shawqi. *Al-'Asr al-Islami*. Cairo: Dar al-Ma'rif, 1963.

Dayf, Shawqi. *Al-Tatawwur wa-al-tajdid fi al-shi'r al-Umawi* 5th ed. Cairo: Dar al-Ma 'arif, 1965.

Dennerlein, Bettina, 'Changing Conceptions of Marriage in Algerian Personal Status Law' in R.S. Khare (ed.), *Perspectives on Islamic Law, Justice and Society*. Lanham, MD: Rowman and Littlefield, 1999, 123–41.

Dickson, H.R.P. *The Arab of the Desert: A Glimpse into Badawin Life in Kuwait and Sau'di Arabia*. London: George Allen & Unwin Ltd, 1949.

Dickson, Harold. *Kuwait and Her Neighbors*. London: Allen and Unwin, 1956.

Dickson, Harold. *The Arab of the Desert*, ed. Robert Wilson and Zahra Freeth. 3rd ed. London: Allen and Unwin, 1983.

Dickson, Violet. *Forty Years in Kuwait*. London: Allen and Unwin, 1971.

Dodd, Edward M. *How Far to the Nearest Doctor? Stories of Medical Missions around the World*. New York: Friendship Press, 1950.

Doi, Abdul Rahman. *Women in the Shari'a*. London: Ta-Ha, 1989.

Donner, Fred McGraw (trans.). *The History of al-Tabari*. Albany: State University of New York Press, 1993.

Donner, Fred McGraw. 'The Bakr b. Wa'il Tribes and Politics in Northeastern Arabia on the Eve of Islam'. *Studia Islamica* 51, 1980: 5–38.

Doughty, Charles M. *Travels in Arabia Deserta*. Gloucester, MA: Peter Smith, 1968.

Doughty, Charles M. *Travels in Arabia Deserta*. 2 vols. London: Jonathan Cape, 1936 [1888].

Doumato, Eleanor A. 'Hearing Other Voices: Christian Women and the Coming of Islam'. *International Journal of Middle East Studies* 23(2), May, 1991: 177–99.

Doumato, Eleanor Abdella. *Getting God's Ear: Women, Islam and Healing in Saudi Arabia and the Gulf*. New York: Columbia University Press, 2000.

Eickelman, Dale F. 'Musaylima: An Approach to the Social Anthropology of Seventh Century Arabia'. *Journal of the Economic and Social History of the Orient* 10(1), July 1967: 17–52.

El-Alami, Dawoud. *The Marriage Contract in Islamic Law in the Shari'ah and Personal Status Laws of Egypt and Morocco*. London: Graham and Trotman, 1992.

El-Zein, Amira. 'The Evolution of the Concept of the Jinn from pre-Islam to Islam'. diss. Georgetown University, 1994.

Esposito, John. *Women in Muslim Family Law*. New York: Syracuse University Press, 1982.

Fadel, Muhammad. 'Two Women, One Man: Knowledge, Power, and Gender in Medieval Sunni Legal Thought'. *IJMES*, 29 (1997), 185–204.

Fahmy, Khaled. 'Women, Medicine, and Power in Nineteenth-Century Egypt' in

Remaking Women: Feminism and Modernity in the Middle East, ed. Lila Abu-Lughod. Princeton NJ: Princeton University Press, 1998.

Fakhro, Munira. 'Gulf Women and Islamic Law' in Mai Yamani (ed.), *Feminism and Islam: Legal and Literary Perspectives*. Reading: Ithaca, 1996, 251–61.

Fakhro, Munira. 'Personal Status Laws and their Effects on Development in the Gulf Region' in papers from the Conference on Women and the Third Millennium. In Arabic. Bahrain: Nahda Association of Young Women of Bahrain, Bahrain Ministry of Information, 2006, 33–50.

Farah, Madelain. *Marriage and Sexuality in Islam: A Translation of Al-Ghazali's Book on the Etiquette of Marriage from the Ihya*. Salt Lake City: University of Utah Press, 1984.

Fares, Bichr. *L'honneur chez les Arabes avant l'Islam*. Paris: Librairie d'Amérique et d'Orient, 1932.

Fares, Bichr. 'Hidja' in *Encyclopaedia of Islam*. Online edition, 2007. Bichr was also the author of the article in the EI.

Fawzi, Essam. 'Muslim Personal Status Law in Egypt: The Current Situation and Possibilities of Reform through Internal Initiatives' in Lynn Welchman (ed.), *Women's Rights and Islamic Family Law: Perspectives on Reform*. London: Zed Books, 2004, 17–94.

Faysal, Shukri. *Tatawwur al-ghazal bayn al-jahiliyya wa-al-Islam*. Damascus: Matba'at Jami'at Dimashq, 1959.

Fishbein, Michael (trans.). *The History of al-Tabari*. Albany: State University of New York, 1997.

Foley, Sean. *The Arab Gulf States: Beyond Oil and Islam*. Boulder, CO: Lynne Rienner Publishers, 2010.

Foucault, Michel. *The Archaeology of Knowledge and the Discourse on Language*. Trans. A.M. Sheridan Smith. New York: Tavistock, 1972.

Frymer-Kensky, T. *In the Wake of the Goddesses: Women, Culture, and the Biblical Transformation of Pagan Myth*. New York: Free Press, 1992.

Gaudefroy-Demombynes, M. *Le monde musulman et Byzantin jusqu'aux croisades*. Paris: E. De Boccard, 1931.

Gazdar, M.S., D.T. Potts and A. Livingstone. 'Excavations at Thaj'. *Atlal* 8, 1984: 55–108, Pl. 60–90.

Gelder, G. 'Naka'id' in *Encyclopaedia of Islam*. Online edition, 2007.

Geyer, R. 'Die arabischen Frauen in der Schlacht'. *Mitteilungen der anthropologischen Gesellschaft* 39, 1909, 1–14.

Ghunaym, 'Adil Hasan. 'Al-awda' al-iqtisadiyya wa-al-ijtima'iyya fi Qatar mundh al-harb al-'alamiyya al-ula' in 'Adil Husayn Ghunaym (ed.), *Al-tarikh al-ijtima'i li-al-mar'a al-Qatariyya al-mu'asira*. Doha: Qatar University, 1989, 81–113.

Ghunaym, 'Adil Hasan. 'al-Mar'a al-Qatariyya wa-al-zawaj' in 'Adil Hasan Ghunaym (ed.), *Al-tarikh al-ijtima'i li-al-mar'a al-Qatariyya al-mu'asira*. Doha: Qatar University, 1989, 177–218.

Ghurayyib, Jurgi. *Al-Ghazal: tarikuhu wa-a'lamuh*. Beirut: Dar al Thaqafa, (n.d.).

Gibb, H.A.R. and J.H. Kramers (eds). *Shorter Encyclopaedia of Islam*. Leiden: Brill, 1965.

Gordon, Murray. *Slavery in the Arab World*. New York: New Amsterdam, 1989).

Government of Bahrain. *Qanun al-Ahwal al-shaksiyya al-muqtarah* (Al-Hamla al-Wataniyya li-Isdar Qanun al-Ahkam al-Usariyya). Manama: Government of Bahrain, 2005.

Government of Egypt. *Al-Majmu'a al-Rasmiyya li-al-Mahakim al-Ahliyya, 1937*. Bulaq, Cairo: Al-Matba'a al-Amiriyya, 1937.

Groom, N.StJ. 'Gerrha, a "Lost" Arabian City'. *Atlal* (6)1982: 97–108, Pl. 98–9.

Gross, Rita. *Buddhism after Patriarchy*. Albany: State University of New York Press, 1993.

Guillaume, Alfred. *The Life of Muhammad: A Translation of Ibn Ishaq's Sirat Rasul Allah*. Third impression. Karachi: Oxford University Press, 1970.

Gunther, Ursula. 'Mohammad Arkoun: Towards a Radical Rethinking of Islamic Thought' in S. Taji-Farouki (ed.), *Modern Muslim Intellectuals and the Qur'an*. Oxford: Oxford University Press, 2004, 125–67.

Haddad , Muhammad. *Al-Taghyir wa-al-thabat fi thaqafat al-badiya*' in Ahmad Abu-Zayd (ed.), *Turath al-badiya: Muqaddima li-dirasat al-badiya fi al-Kuwayt*. Kuwait University, 1987, 23–65.

Haddad, Yvonne Yazbeck. 'Islam and Gender: Dilemmas in the Changing Arab World' in Yvonne Yazbeck Haddad and John Esposito (eds), *Islam, Gender and Social Change*. Oxford: Oxford University Press, 1988, 1–29.

Haddad, Yvonne Yazbeck. 'Traditional Affirmations Concerning the Role of Women as Found in Contemporary Arab Islamic Literature' in Jane I. Smith (ed.), *Women in Contemporary Muslim Societies*. London: Associated University Presses, 1980, 61–86.

Haeri, Shahla. *Law of Desire: Temporary Marriage in Iran*. London: I.B. Tauris, 1989.

Hafez, Sherine. *The Terms of Empowerment: Islamic Women Activists in Egypt*. Cairo: American University in Cairo Press, 2003.

Hallock, C. and P. Arrowsmith. *Desert Doctor: Harrison of Arabia*. London: Lutterworth, 1950.

Hammami, Rema. 'Attitudes towards Legal Reform of Personal Status Law in Palestine' in Lynn Welchman (ed.), *Women's Rights and Islamic Family Law: Perspectives on Reform*. London: Zed Books, 2004, 125–43.

Harrison, Paul. 'Arabia Calls for More Doctors'. New York: Woman's Board of Foreign Missions, RCA, 1940.

Harrison, Paul. *Doctor in Arabia*. New York: The John Day Company, c. 1940.

Harrison, Paul. *The Arab at Home*. New York: Thomas Crowell Company, 1924.

Hashim, S.A., *Terracotta Figurines from Thaj*. Riyadh: Directorate General of Antiquities and Museums, Ministry of Education, 1991.

Hassan, Riffat. 'Equal before Allah? Woman-Man Equality in the Islamic Tradition'. *Harvard Divinity Bulletin* 7(2), January-May 1987: 2–4; repr. in her *Selected Articles*. London: Women Living Under Muslim Laws, 1994, 26–9.

Hassan, Riffat. 'Feminism in Islam' in Arvind Sharma and Kate Young (eds), *Feminism and World Religions*. Albany: SUNY Press, 1999.

Hassan, Riffat. 'Feminist Theology: Challenges for Muslim Women'. *Critique: Journal for Critical Studies of the Middle East* 9, 1996: 53–65.

Hatem, Mervat F. 'The Professionalization of Health and the Control of Women's Bodies as Modern Governmentalities in Nineteenth-Century Egypt' in *Women in the Ottoman Empire: Middle Eastern Women in the Early Modern Era*, ed. Madeline C. Zilfi. New York: E.J. Brill, 1997.

Hay, Rupert. *The Persian Gulf States*. Washington, DC: Middle East Institute, 1959.

Herschel, Susannah. *On Being a Jewish Feminist*. New York: Schocken Books, 1983.

Hijab, Nadia. *Womanpower: The Arab Debate on Women at Work*. New York: Cambridge University Press, 1988.

Hilal bin Muhammad, 'Isa. *Al-Ayyam al-khawali fi akhbar al-nisa' wa-al-ima' wa-al-jawari*. Riyadh: Maktabat al-Malik Fahd, 2000.

Hilal, Naji Muhammad. *Al-'Unf al-usari fi al-mujtama' al-Imarati* [Family Violence in Emirates Society]. Sharjah: Al-Idara al-'Amma li-Shurtat al-Shariqa, Markaz Buhuth al-Shurta, 2007.

Hogarth, David George. *Hijaz before World War I*. 2nd ed. New York: Oleander Press, 1978 [1917].

Hosman, Sarah. 'Arabian Mission Field Report' 89, *Neglected Arabia*, April-June, (n.p., n.d).

Humphreys, R. Stephen. *Islamic History: A Framework for Inquiry*. Minneapolis MN: Bibliotheca Islamica, 1988.

Hurgronje, Snouck. *Mecca in the Latter Part of the Nineteenth Century*. Leiden: Brill, 1970 [1931; 1st ed. 2 vols. 1888–1889].

Husayn, 'Abd al-'Aziz. *Education in Kuwait: The Mission*. Vol. 6 (n.p., n.d.).

Husayn, Taha. *Al-Hayat al-adabiyya fi Jazirat al-'Arab*. Beirut: Dar al-Kitab al-Lubnani, 1973.

Husayn, Taha. *Fi al-adab al-jahili*. Cairo: Dar al-Ma'arif, 1981.

Husayn, Taha. *Fi al-shi'r al-jahili*. Cairo, 1927.

Husayn, Taha. *Hadith al-'arba'*. Cairo: Matba'at Mustapha al-Babi al-Halabi, 1937.

Husni, Husayn and Suhayl Sha'ban. *Muzakkarat dabit 'Uthmani fi Najd: Al-awda' al-'amma fi mantaqat Najd* [Memoirs of an Ottoman Officer in Najd: The General Situation in the Najd Region]. Beirut: 2003.

Ibn 'Abd Rabbuh, A.M. *Kitab al-'iqd al-farid*, ed. A. al-Zayn, I. al-Abyar and A. Amin. 7 vols. Beirut: Dar al-Kitab al-'Arabi, 1982.

Ibn Abi Rabi'a, 'Umar. *Diwan*. Cairo: Al-Hay'a al-Misriyya al-'Amma li-al-Kitab, 1978.

Ibn al-Athir, A.M. *Al-kamil fi al-tarikh*, no editor's name was given. 10 vols. Beirut: Dar al-Kitab al-'Arabi, 1983.

Ibn Athir, 'Izz al-Din Abu al-Hasan 'Ali ibn Muhammad. *Usd al-ghaba fi ma'rifat al-sahaba*. Cairo: Dar al-Sha'b, 1970.

Ibn Habib. *Kitab al-muhabbar*, ed. Ilse Lichtenstädter. Hyderabad, 1942.

Ibn Hajar al-Asqalani. *Al-isaba fi tamyiz al-sahaba*. Cairo: Maktabat al-Kulliyyat al-Azhariyya, 1977.

Ibn Hisham. *Kitab al-sira al-nabawiyya*. Available at http://www.al-eman.com/ Islamlib/viewtoc.asp?BID=249.

Ibn Junaydil, Sa'd. *'Aliyyat Najd*. Riyadh: Dar al-Yamama, 1978.

Ibn Khaldun, A. *Kitab al-'ibar wa diwan al-mubtada' wa al-khabar fi ayyam al-'arab wa al-'ajam wa al-barbar wa man 'asarahum min thawi al-sultan al-'akbar, Tarikh Ibn Khaldun*, n.ed., 8 vols. Cairo: Kitab al-Sha'b, n.d.).

Ibn Khaldun. *Al-muqaddima*. Beirut: Dar al-Qalam, 1992.

Ibn Khaldun. *Histoire des Berbères*, trans. De Slane. 4 vols. Algiers, 1832–56.

Ibn Khaldun. *The Muqaddimah*, trans. Franz Rosenthal, ed. N.J. Dawood. Princeton NJ: Princeton University Press, 1989.

Ibn Khamis, 'Abdullah. *Al-adab al-sha'bi fi al-Jazira*. Riyadh: Matabi' al-Farazdaq al-Tijariya, 1958.

Ibn Khayyat, Kh. *Tarkih Khalifah bin Khayyat*, ed. Akram Diya' al-Umari. Damascus, Beirut: Dar al-Qalam, Mu'assasat al-Risala, 1979.

Ibn Manzur. *Lisan al-'Arab*. Beirut: Dar Sadir, (n.d).

Ibn Manzur. *Lisan al-'Arab*. 6 vols. Cairo: Dar al-Ma'arif, n.d.

Ibn Raddas, 'Abdullah. *Sha'irat min al-badiya*. Riyadh: Matabi' al-Shabil li-al-Nasr wa-al-Tauzi' wa-al-Tiba'a, 1991.

Ibn Rushd. *The Distinguished Jurist's Primer (Bidayat al-mujtahid wa-nihayat al-muqtasid)*, trans. Imran Ahsan Khan Nyazee. 2 vols. Reading: Garnet, 1994–1996.

Ibn Sa'd, Muhammad. *Kitab al-tabaqat al-kabir*. Cairo: Maktabat al-Khanji, 2001.

Ibn Sa'd, Muhammad. *Kitab al-tabaqat al-kabir*, ed. Carl Brockelmann. Leiden: Brill, 1904.

Ibn Tumart. *'A'azz ma Yutlab*, ed. J.D. Luciani. Algiers, 1903.

Imber, Colin. *Ebu's-Su'ud, The Islamic Legal Tradition*. Edinburgh: Edinburgh University Press, 1997.

Inizan, M.-L. 'First Results of Prehistoric Site Excavations in Khor Area' in J.Tixier (ed.), *Mission Archéologique française à Qatar 1976–77/1977–78*. Vol. 1. Paris, Qatar: CNRS, Ministere de l'Information, 1980. French 51–97, English 171–8.

Isma'il, Sabira Mu'min. *Jidda khilal al-fatra 1286–1326 /1869–1908: Dirasa tarikhiyya wa-hadariyya fi al-masadir al-mu'asira*. Riyadh: Dar al-Malik 'Abd al-'Aziz, 1418 AH/1998.

Izzard, Molly. *The Gulf: Arabia's Western Approaches*. London: Murray, 1997.

Ja'far, Buthayna Muhammad. *The Development of Education in Kuwait: The Mission*. Vol. 6. *Year 6: 1952*. Kuwait: Center for Research and Studies, 1997).

Jackson, Sherman. 'Liberal/Progressive, Modern, and Modernized Islam: Muslim Americans and the American State' *Innovation in Islam: Traditions and Contributions* edited by Mehran Kamrava. California University Press, 2011.

Jacobi, R. 'Nasib' in *Encyclopaedia of Islam*. Online edition, 2008.

Jad al-Mawla Bek, M.A., A.M. al-Bajawi and I. Abu al-Fadl. *Ayyam al-'arab fi al-jahiliyya*. Mecca: Dar Ihya' al-Kutub al-'Arabiyya, Dar al-Baz, 1942.

Jagailloux, Serge. *La Médicalisation de l'egypte au XIXe Siècle (1798–1918)*. Paris: Éditions Recherche sur les Civilisations, 1986.

Jamal, Muhammad 'Abd al-Hadi. *Occupations, Crafts and Old Commercial Activities in Kuwait*. Kuwait: Kuwait Center for Research and Studies, 2003.

Jamshir, Ghada Yusuf (ed.). *Al-Jallad wa-al-dahiya fi al-mahakim al-shar'iyya*. Beirut: Dar al-Kunuz al-Adabiyya, 2005.

Jarshale, Ismail Haqi. *Ashraf Makka al-mukarrama*. Trans. Khalil Ali Murad. Beirut: Al-Dar al-'Arabiya li-al-Mawsu'at, 2003.

Jasim bin Muhammad Al Thani, Shaykh. *Diwan al-Shaykh Jasim bin Muhammad Al Thani*. Doha: Matba'a Qatar Al-Wataniyya, 1910.

Jawad, Haifaa. *The Rights of Women in Islam: An Authentic Approach*. London: MacMillan, 1998.

Jayyusi, Salma. *Arabic Literature to the End of the Umayyad Period*. Cambridge History of Arabic Literature 1). Cambridge: Cambridge University Press, 1983.

Jayyusi, Salma. 'Umayyad Poetry', in Beeston, Alfred, Johnstone, T.M., Sarjeant, R.B., Smith, G.R., eds, *Arabic Literature to the End of the Umayyad Period*, Cambridge:. Cambridge University Press, 1984), 387–482.

Johansen, Baber. 'Commercial Exchange and Social Order in Hanafite Law' in Christopher Poll and Jakob Skovgaard-Petersen (eds), *Law and the Islamic*

World: Past and Present. Copenhagen: Royal Danish Academy of Sciences and Letters, 1995.

Johansen, Baber. 'Valorization of the Human Body in Muslim Sunni Law' in Devin J. Stewart, Baber Johansen and Amy Singer (eds), *Law and Society in Islam*. Princeton, NJ: Markus Wiener, 1996.

Jones, Alan. *Early Arabic Poetry*. Vol. 2: *Selected Odes*. Reading UK: Ithaca Press, 1996.

Jum'a, Ahmad Khalil. *Nisa' min Asr al-Tabi'in*. Damascus and Beirut: Dar Ibn Kathir, 2002.

Kabbani, Sheikh Muhammad Hisham and Laleh Bakhtiar, *Encyclopedia of Muhammad's Women Companions*. Chicago: Kazi Publications, 1998.

Kahhala, Omar Rida. *A'lam al-nisa' fi 'Alamay al-'Arab wa-al-Islam*. Beirut: Mu'assasat al-Risala, 1991.

Kamali, Muhammad Hashim. 'Methodological Issues in Islamic Jurisprudence'. *Arab Law Quarterly* 11(1), 1996: 3–33.

Kamali, Muhammad Hashim. *Freedom, Equality and Justice in Islam*. Kuala Lumpur: Ilmiah Publishers, 1999.

Kermani, Navid. 'From Revelation to Interpretation: Nasr Hamid Abu Zayd and the Literary Study of the Qur'an' in Suha Taji-Farouki (ed.), *Modern Muslim Intellectuals and the Qur'an*. Oxford: Oxford University Press, 2004, 169–92.

Khadduri, Majid. *The Islamic Conception of Justice*. Baltimore, MD: John Hopkins University Press, 1984.

Khalidi, Tarif. *Classical Arab Islam: The Culture and Heritage of the Golden Age*. Princeton NJ: Darwin, 1985.

Khan, Maulana Wahiduddin. *Woman between Islam and Western Society*. New Delhi: The Islamic Centre, 1995.

Khoury, Nabi F. and Valentine M. Moghadam. *Gender and Development in the Arab World. Women's Economic Participation: Patterns and Policies*. Atlantic Highlands NJ: United Nations University, World Institute for Development Economics Research by Zed Books and United Nations University Press, 1995.

Kiyal, Basima. *Tatawwur al-mar'a 'abr al-tarīkh* [Woman's Development throughout History]. Beirut: 'Izz al-Din li-al-Tiba'a wa-al-nashr, 1981.

Kjaerum, Poul *The Stamp and Cylinder Seals, Failaka/Dilmun, The Second Millennium Settlements, Vol 1:1, Danish Archaeological Investigations on Failaka*. Kuwait, Arhus, Denmark: Jutland Archaeological Society Publications XVII:1, 1983.

Kramer, Samuel Noah. *Sumerian Mythology: A Study of Spiritual and Literary Achievement in the Third Millennium BC* [1944], 2007. Published by forgottenbooks.org in 2010 at http://www.forgottenbooks.org/info/9781605060491 .

Kramer, Samuel Noah. *The Sumerians: Their History, Culture and Character*. Chicago IL: University of Chicago Press, 1971 [1963].

Kritzeck, James and R Bayly. *The World of Islam*. London: Macmillan, 1959.

Kuhnke, Laverne. *Lives at Risk: Public Health in Nineteenth-Century Egypt*. Berkeley: University of California Press, 1990.

Kurpershoek, Marcel P. *Oral Poetry and Narrative from Central Arabia*. Leiden: Brill, 1994.

Kurzman, Charles (ed.). *Liberal Islam: A Sourcebook*. Oxford: Oxford University Press, 1998.

Lamberg-Karlovsky, C.C. 'Dilmun: Gateway to Immortality'. *Journal of Near Eastern Studies* 41, 1982: 45–50.

Lampe, Gerald E. (ed.). *Justice and Human Rights in Islamic Law*. Washington, DC: International Law Institute, 1997.

Lane-Poole, Stanley. *The Mohammedan Dynasties: Chronological and Genealogical Tables with Historical Introductions*. Whitefish, MT: Kessinger Publishing, 2004 [1894].

Lecker, M. 'Tamim b. Murr' in *Encyclopaedia of Islam*. Online edition, 2007.

Lecker, Michael. 'Judaism among Kinda and the Ridda of Kinda'. *Journal of the American Oriental Society* 115(4), October-December 1995: 635–50.

Lewis, I.M. *Ecstatic Religion*. Baltimore, MD: Penguin, 1971.

Lichtenstädter, Ilse. *Women in the Aiyam al-Arab*. London: Royal Asiatic Society, 1935.

Lombard, P. 'The Salt Mine Site and the Hasaean Period of Northeastern Arabia' in D.T. Potts (ed.), *Araby the Blest*. Copenhagen: Carsten Neibuhr Institute of Ancient Near Eastern Studies, University of Kopenhagen, 1988, 117–36.

Lorimer, J.G. *Gazetteer of the Persian Gulf, Oman and Central Arabia*, 6 Vols., 1986.

Lorimer, John Gordon. *Gazetteer of the Persian Gulf, Oman and Central Arabia*, Vol. 1, Part 1B. Fransborough: Gregg International Publishing Ltd, 1970.

Maciver, R.M. and C.H. Page. *Society: An Introductory Analysis*. London: Macmillan 1961.

Maghniyyah, Muhammad Jawad. *Marriage According to Five Schools of Islamic Law*. Vol. 5. Tehran: Department of Translation and Publication, Islamic Culture and Relations Organization, 1997.

Mahmood, Saba. *Politics of Piety: The Islamic Revival and the Feminist Subject*. Princeton NJ: Princeton University Press, 2005.

Majid, A. *The Political History of the Arab State: The Umayyad Period*. 7th ed. Cairo: The Anglo-Egyptian Library, 1982.

Marmon, Shaun. 'Domestic Slavery in the Mamluk Empire: A Preliminary Sketch' in Shaun Marmon (ed.), *Slavery in the Islamic Middle East*. Princeton, NJ: Princeton University Department of Near Eastern Studies, 1999), 1–23.

Mason, Alfred DeWitt. *History of the Arabian Mission*. New York: Board of Foreign Missions, RCA, 1926.

Masud, Mahmud Khaled, et al., (eds). *Islamic Legal Interpretation: Muftis and their Fatwas*. Cambridge, Mass.: Harvard University Press, 1996.

Maududi, Maulana Abul A'Ala. *Purdah and the Status of Women in Islam*. 16th edn. Lahore: Islamic Publications, 1998.

Maududi, Maulana Abul A'Ala. *The Laws of Marriage and Divorce in Islam*. Kuwait: Islamic Book Publishers, 1983.

Mauger, Thierry. *The Bedouins of Arabia*. Paris: Souffles, 1988.

Mayer, Ann Elizabeth. 'Internationalising the Conversation on Arab Women's Rights: Arab Countries Face the CEDAW Committee' in Yvonne Hadded and Barbara Freyer Stowasser (eds), *Islamic Law and the Challenges of Modernity*. Walnut Creek, CA: AltaMira Press, 2004, 133–60.

McClintock, Anne. 'Family Feuds: Gender, Nationalism and the Family'. *Feminist Review* 44, Summer 1993: 61–80.

McKenzie, John L. 'Mythological Allusions in Ezek. 28:12–18'. *Journal of Biblical Literature* 75(4), 1956: 322–7.

McLaughlin, Eleanor. 'The Christian Past: Does it Hold a Future for Women?' in

Carol Christ and Judith Plaskow (eds), *Woman Spirit Rising*. San Francisco: Harper & Row, 1989.

Mernissi, Fatima. *Beyond the Veil: Male-Female Dynamics in Modern Muslim Society*. Cambridge MA: Schenkman, 1975.

Mernissi, Fatima. *Beyond the Veil: Male-Female Dynamics in Muslim Society*. Rev. edn. London: Saqi, 1985.

Mernissi, Fatima. *Women and Islam: An Historical and Theological Enquiry*, trans. Mary Jo Lakeland. Oxford: Blackwell, 1991.

Messick, Brinkley. *The Calligraphic State. Textual Domination and History in a Muslim Society*. Berkeley CA: University of California Press, 1993.

Milik, J.T. 'Origines des Nabatéens'. *Studies in the History and Archaeology of Jordan* 1, 1982: 261–5.

Mir-Hosseini, Ziba. 'Islam and Gender Justice' in Vincent J. Cornell and Omid Safi (eds), *Voices of Islam*. Vol. 5. Westport, CT: Praeger, 2007, 85–113.

Mir-Hosseini, Ziba. 'Muslim Women's Quest for Equality: Between Islamic Law and Feminism'. *Critical Inquiry* 32(1), 2006: 629–45.

Mir-Hosseini, Ziba. 'Sexuality, Rights and Islam: Competing Gender Discourses in Post-Revolutionary Iran' in Guity Nashat and Lois Beck (eds), *Women in Iran from 1800 to the Islamic Republic*. Urbana and Chicago: University of Illinois Press, 2004, 204–17.

Mir-Hosseini, Ziba. 'The Construction of Gender in Islamic Legal Thought and Strategies for Reform'. *Hawwa: Journal of Women of the Middle East and the Islamic World* 1(1), 2003: 1–28.

Mir-Hosseini, Ziba. 'Towards Gender Equality: Muslim Family Laws and the Shari'a' in Zainah Anwar (ed.), *Wanted: Equality and Justice in the Muslim Family*. Kuala Lumpur: Musawah, 2009. Available at http://www.musawah. org/background_papers.asp (accessed 30 December 2010.

Mir-Hosseini, Ziba. 'Women's Rights and Clerical Discourses: The Legacy of Allameh Tabataba'i' in Negin Nabavi (ed.), *Intellectual Trends in Twentieth Century Iran*. Gainsville: University Press of Florida, 2003, 193–217.

Mir-Hosseini, Ziba. *Islam and Gender: The Religious Debate in Contemporary Iran*. Princeton, NJ: Princeton University Press, 1999.

Mir-Hosseini, Ziba. *Marriage on Trial: A Study of Islamic Family Law. Iran and Morocco Compared*. London: I.B. Tauris, 1993.

Moghadam, Valentine M. *Women, Work, and Economic Reform in the Middle East and North Africa*. Boulder, CO: Lynne Rienner, 1988.

Moloney, G.E. *A Doctor in Saudi Arabia*. London: Regency, 1985.

Montgomery, J. *The Vagaries of the Qasida*. Warminster UK: Aris and Philips, 1997.

Moors, Annelies. 'Debating Islamic Family law: Legal Texts and Social Practices' in Margaret Meriwether and Judith Tucker (eds), *Social History of Women and Gender in the Middle East*. Boulder, CO: Westview, 1999, 149–75.

Mortel, Richard T. 'Zaydi Shi'ism and the Hasanid Sharifs of Mecca'. *International Journal of Middle East Studies* 19(4). November 1987: 455–72.

Mubarak, Zaki. *Al-Asmar wa al-ahadith: hubb Ibn Abi Rabi'a*. Giza: Al-Sharikah al-Misriyya al-'Alamiyya li-al-Nashr, 1998.

Muhammad, Husein, Faqihuddin Abdul Kodir, Lies Marcoes Natsir and Marzuki Wahid. *Dawrah Fiqh Concerning Women: Manual for a Course on Islam and Gender*. Cirebon, Indonesia: Fahmina Institute, 2006.

Muslim Women's League. 'Women in Pre-Islamic Arabia'. www.mwlusa.org/
topics/history/herstory.html accessed 18 October 2007.

Mutahhari, Murtaza. *The Islamic Modest Dress*. Trans. Laleh Bakhtiar. 3rd edn.
Chicago. IL: Kazi Publications, 1992.

Mutahhari, Murtaza. *The Rights of Women in Islam*. 4th edn. Tehran: World
Organization for Islamic Services, 1991.

Naji, Kamal. *The History of Popular Education in Qatar* (n.p., n.d.).

Nasharty, Hala. *Al-mar'a al-'Ouda*. 'Women between Two Worlds: A Study of the
Changing Social World of Kuwaiti Women'. MA Thesis, American University
in Cairo, 332, 1976.

Nasir, Jamal J. *The Islamic Law of Personal Status*. 2nd edn. London: Graham
and Trotman, 1990.

Nasr, Ahmad A. and Abu Bakr A. Bagader. 'Al-Ges: Woman's Festival and Drama
in Mecca'. *Journal of Folklore Research* 38(3). September-December 2001:
243–62.

Neglected Arabia. Arabia Calling. 8 Vols., 1988.

Nicholson, Eleanor. *In the Footsteps of the Camel: A Portrait of the Bedouins of
Eastern Saudi Arabia in Mid-Century*. Riyadh/London: Transworld Arabian
Library/Stacey International, 1983.

Nicholson, Reynold. *A Literary History of the Arabs*. Cambridge: Cambridge
University Press, 1962.

Nugent, Jeffrey and Theodore Thomas (eds). *Bahrain and the Gulf: Past
Perspectives and Alternative Futures*. London/Sydney: Croom Helm, 1985.

O'Conner, June. 'Rereading, Re-conceiving, and Reconstructing Traditions:
Feminist Research in Religion', *Women's Studies,* 17(1989), 101–123.

Olsen, Tillie. *Silences*. New York: Delta, 1978.

Palgrave, W.G. *Personal Narrative of a Year's Journey through Central and
Eastern Arabia (1862–1863)*. London: Macmillan, 1868.

Pastner, Carroll McC. 'Englishmen in Arabia: Encounters with Middle Eastern
Women'. *Signs* 4(2) Winter 1978: 309–23.

Pellat, Ch. 'Hidja' in *Encyclopaedia of Islam*. Online edition, 2007.

Pesle, Octave. *Le Mariage chez les Malekites de l'Afrique du Nord*. Rabat:
Moncho, 1936.

Plaskow, Judith. *The Coming of Lilith: Essays on Feminism, Judaism, and Sexual
Ethics, 1972–2003*. Boston, MA: Beacon Press, 2005.

Polybius. *The Histories of Polybius*, trans. W. R. Paton. London: Loeb Classical
Library, 1922–1927.

Pomeroy, S.B. *Goddesses, Whores, Wives and Slaves: Women in Classical
Antiquity*. London: Pimlico, 1994.

Potts, D.T. 'Eastern Arabia and the Oman Peninsula during the Late Fourth and
Early Third Millennium BC' in Uwe Finkbeiner and Wolfgang Röllig (eds),
Gamdat Nasr Period or Regional Style (Reihe B Geisteswissenschaften 62).
Wiesbaden: Beihefter zum Tübingen Atlas des Vorderen Orients, 1986,
121–70.

Potts, D.T. *The Arabian Gulf in Antiquity: From Alexander the Great to the
Coming of Islam*. 2 vols. Oxford: Clarendon Press, 1992.

Pritchard, J.B. *Ancient Near Eastern Texts: Related to the Old Testament*. 2nd ed.
2 vols. Princeton, NJ: Princeton University Press, 1955.

Profession in Islamic History. *Awraq al-dhakirah* Series (Occasional Papers), no.
1. Cairo: Women & Memory Forum, 1999.

Pruitt, Lisa Joy. *A Looking-Glass for Ladies: American Protestant Women and the Orient in the Nineteenth Century*. Macon, GA: Mercer University Press, 2005.

Qassab, W.I. 'Qatari bin al-Fuja'a: study in his biography and poetry' in *Makanat al-Khalij al-'Arabi fi al-tarikh al-Islami*. Dubai: UAE University with al-Majma' al-Thaqafi, 1988), 291–342.

Raafat, Hassan. 'Marriage without Approval of Bride's Guardian Illegal'. *Khaleej Times*, 26 January 2001.

Rahman, Fazlur. 'A Survey of Modernization of Muslim Family Law'. *International Journal of Middle Eastern Studies* 11(4), 1980: 451–65.

Rahman, Fazlur. *Islam*. Chicago, IL: Chicago University Press, 2002.

Rapoport, Yossef. *Marriage, Money and Divorce in Medieval Islamic Society*. Cambridge: Cambridge University Press, 2005.

Reuther, Rosemary. *Women and Redemption: A Theological History*. Minneapolis: Fortress Press, 1998.

Rice, Deborah Ann. 'Maritime Legislation in the Arabian Gulf States'. *Arab Law Quarterly* 1(1) (November 1985: 69–82.

Rihani, Ameen. *Around the Coast of Arabia*. London: Constable, 1930.

Roald, Anne Sofie. *Women in Islam: The Western Experience*. London: Routledge, 2001.

Robson, James. *Ion Keith-Falconer of Arabia*. New York: George H. Doran Co., 1923.

Rodinson, Maxime. *Muhammad*, trans. Anne Carder. New York: New Press, 2002.

Ruether, Rosemary Radford. *Sexism and God-Talk: Toward a Feminist Theology*. Boston, MA: Beacon Press, 1983.

Ruwaqa, An'am. *Al-Hayat al iqtisadiyya fi al-shi'r al-Umawi*. Amman: al-Warraq, 2002.

Ruxton, F.H. *Maliki Law: A Summary from French Translations of Mukhtasar Sidi Khalil*. London: Luzac, 1916.

Ryckmans, J. 'A Three Generations' Matrilineal Genealogy in a Hasaean Inscription: Matrilineal Ancestry in Pre-Islamic Arabia. In 'Bahrain through the Ages. The Archaeology' in H. Al-Khalifa and M. Rice (eds), *Bahrain through the Ages*. London etc.: KPI, 1986, 407–17.

Sachedina, Abdulaziz. 'The Ideal and Real in Islamic Law' in R.S. Khare (ed.), *Perspectives on Islamic Law, Justice and Society*. New York: Rowman and Littlefield, 1999, 15–31.

Sachedina, Abdulaziz. 'Woman, Half-the-Man? Crisis of Male Epistemology in Islamic Jurisprudence' in R.S. Khare (ed.), *Perspectives on Islamic Law, Justice and Society*. New York: Rowman and Littlefield, 1999, 145–60. Available at http://people.virginia.edu/~aas/article/article1.htm (accessed 25 July 2008).

Said, Edward. *Orientalism*. New York: Vintage Books, 1979.

Samed, Amal. 'Palestinian Women: Entering the Proletariat'. *Journal of Palestine Studies* 6(1), Autumn 1976: 159–67.

Samed, Amal. 'The Proletarianization of Palestinian Women in Israel'. *MERIP Reports* 50, August 1976: 10–15.

Saqr, 'Abd al-Badi'. *A Report about Education in Qatar delivered to H.E Sheikh Khalifa Bin Hamad Al Thany 1376 (Hijrah)* (n.p., n.d.).

Schaade, A. 'Djarir' in *Encyclopaedia of Islam*. Online edition, 2007.

Schussler Fiorenza, Elizabeth. *Bread Not Stone: The Challenge of Feminist Biblical Interpretation*. Boston, MA: Beacon Press, 1995.

Seibert, Isle. *Woman in the Ancient Near East*, ed. and rev. G.A. Shepperson, trans. Marianne Herzfeld. London, Leipzig: George Prior Publishers Ltd, Druckerei Fortschritt Erfurt, 1974.

Semyonov, Moshe. 'Ethnic Labor Markets, Gender, and Socioeconomic Inequality: A Study of Arabs in the Israeli Labor Force'. *Sociological Quarterly* 35(1), February 1994: 51–68.

Shaham, Ron. 'State, Feminists and Islamists: The Debate over Stipulations in Marriage Contracts in Egypt'. *Bulletin of the School of Oriental and African Studies* 62, 1999: 462–83.

Shaikh, Sa'diyya. 'Exegetical Violence: Nushuz in Qur'anic Gender Ideology'. *Journal for Islamic Studies* 17, 1997: 49–73.

Shaikh, Sa'diyya. 'Knowledge, Women and Gender in the Hadith'. *Islam and Christian-Muslim Relations* 15(1), 2004: 99–108.

Sharkey, Heather J. 'Two Sudanese Midwives'. *Sudanic Africa: A Journal of Historical Sources* 9, 1998: 19–38.

Shehadeh, Lamia Rustum. *The Idea of Women in Fundamentalist Islam*. Gainesville: University of Florida Press, 2003.

Shuqayr, William Nicholas. *Al-'Arji wa-shi'r al-ghazal fi al-'asr al-Umawi*. Beirut: Dar al-Afaq al-Jadida, 1986.

Singermann, Diane. 'Rewriting Divorce in Egypt: Reclaiming Islamic, Legal Activism and Coalition Politics' in Robert Hefner (ed.), *Remaking Muslim Politics*. Princeton, NJ: Princeton University Press, 2005, 161–88.

Sinker, Robert. *Memorials of the Hon. Ion Keith-Falconer*. London: George Bell and Sons, 1903.

Smith, Jane. 'Women, Religion and Social Change in Early Islam' in Yvonne Yazbeck Haddad and Ellison Banks Findly (eds), *Women, Religion, and Social Change*. Albany: State University of New York Press, 1985, 19–36.

Smith, W. Robertson. *Kinship and Marriage in Early Arabia*. London: Black, 1903.

Smoor, Pieter. 'Al-Farazdaq's Reception by Contemporaries and Later Generations'. *Journal of Arabic Literature* 20, 1987: 115–27.

Sonbol, Amira El Azhary (ed.). *Women, Family and Divorce Laws in Islamic History*. New York: Syracuse University Press, 1996.

Sonbol, Amira El Azhary. 'Ta'a and Modern Legal Reform: A Rereading'. *Islam and Christian-Muslim Relations* 9(3), 1998: 285–94.

Sonbol, Amira El Azhary. 'Women in Shariah Courts: A Historical and Methodological Discussion'. *Fordham International Law Journal* 27, 2003–2004: 225–53.

Sonbol, Amira El-Azhary. 'Living and Working Together: Negotiating and Disputing Marriage and Business in Early Modern Egypt and Palestine'. *L'Homme. Europäische Zeitschrift für Feministische Geschichtswissenschaft* 17(2), 2006: 37–60.

Sonbol, Amira el-Azhary. *The Creation of a Medical Profession in Egypt, 1800–1922*. New York: Syracuse University Press, 1991.

Soroush, Abdolkarim. 'Islamic Revival and Reform: Theological Approaches' in Mahmoud Sadri and Ahmed Sadri (trans. and ed.), *Reason, Freedom, and Democracy in Islam: Essential Writings of 'Abdolkarim Soroush*. Oxford: Oxford University Press, 2000), 26–38.

Soroush, Abdolkarim. 'The Beauty of Justice'. *CSD Bulletin*, 14(1–2), Summer 2007: 8–12. Available at http://www.drsoroush.com/English.htm (accessed 25 July 2008.

Soroush, Abdolkarim. 'Tolerance and Governance: A Discourse on Religion and Democracy' in Mahmoud Sadri and Ahmed Sadri (trans. and ed.), *Reason, Freedom, and Democracy in Islam: Essential Writings of 'Abdolkarim Soroush*. Oxford: Oxford University Press, 2000, 131–55.

Souaiaia, Ahmed. 'On the Sources of Islamic Law and Practices'. *Law and Religion* 20(1), 2004–2005: 132–233.

Sowayan, Saad. *Al-shi'r al-Nabati: dha'iqat al-sha'b wa-sultat al-nass*. London: Saqi, 2000.

Sowayan, Saad. *Nabati Poetry*. 7th ed. Berkeley: University of California Press, 1985.

Speece, Mark. 'The Role of Eastern Arabia in the Gulf Trade of the Third and Second Millennia' in *Pre-Islamic Arabia*. Vol. 2 , ed. A.T.al-Ansary. Riyadh: King Saud University, 1984, 167–76.

Spellberg, Denise A. *Politics, Gender, and the Islamic Past: The Legacy of Aisha bint Abi Bakr*. New York: Columbia University Press, 1994.

Spellberg, Denise. 'Political Action and Public Example: 'A'isha and the Battle of the Camel' in Nikki Keddie and Beth Baron (eds), *Women in Middle Eastern History*. New Haven CT: Yale University Press, 1991, 45–57.

Spencer, Robert F. 'The Arabian Matriarchate: An Old Controversy'. *South Western Journal of Anthropology* 8, 1952: 478–502.

Stark, Freya. *Famous Women in the East*. In Arabic. Aden: Publishing House, 1940.

Stetkevych, J. *The Zephyrs of the Najd: The Poetics of Nostalgia in the Classical Arabic Nasib*. Chicago, IL: University of Chicago Press, 1993.

Stetkevych, Suzanne Pinckney. *The Mute Immortals Speak: Pre-Islamic Poetry and the Poetics of Ritual*. Ithaca, NY: Cornell University Press, 1993.

Stone, M. *When God Was a Woman*. San Diego etc.: Harvest Book, Harcourt Brace & Company, 1976.

Storm, W. Harold. *Whither Arabia? A Survey of Missionary Opportunity*. London: Founder's Lodge, 1938.

Stowasser, Barbara. 'Women's Issues in Modern Islamic Thought' in Judith E. Tucker (ed.), *Arab Women: Old Boundaries, New Frontiers*. Bloomington: Indiana University Press, 1993, 3–28.

Stowasser, Barbara. *Women in the Qur'an: Traditions, and Interpretation*. New York: Oxford University Press, 1994.

Strabo. *Geography*, trans. H.L. Jones. 8 vols. London: Loeb Classical Library, 1989).

Supreme Council for Women and Bahrain Centre for Studies and Research (SCW and BCSR). 'Opinion Survey on the Codification of Family Law Rulings in the Kingdom of Bahrain'. In Arabic. Bahrain: SCW and BCSR, 2005.

Sweet, L.E. '"Pirates or Polities": Arab Societies of the Persian Arabian Gulf, 18th Century'. *Ethnohistory* 11(3). Summer 1964: 262–80.

Teipen, Alfons. '*Jahilite* and Muslim Women: Questions of Continuity and Communal Identity'. *Muslim World* 92, fall 2002: 437–60.

Tell, Tariq. 'Guns, Gold and Grain: War and Food Supply in the Making of Transjordan' in Steven Heydemann (ed.), *War, Institutions and Social Change in the Middle East*. Berkeley: University of California Press, 2000, 33–58.

Thesiger, Wilfred. *A Vanished World*. New York: W.W. Norton, 2001.

Toumi, Habib. 'Bahrain Parliament Passes Family Law for Sunni Section', 14 May 2009. Available at http://gulfnews.com/news/gulf/bahrain/bahrain-parliament-passes-family-law-for-sunni-section-1.2005. accessed 23 November 2010.

Tucker, Judith. 'Introduction'. *MERIP Reports* 95, March 1981: 3–4.

Tucker, Judith. 'Revisiting Reform: Women and the Ottoman Law of Family Rights, 1917.' *Arab Studies Journal* 1, 1996: 4–17.

Tucker, Judith. *In the House of Law: Gender and Islamic Law in Ottoman Syria and Palestine*. Berkeley: University of California Press, 2000.

Tucker, Judith. *Women, Family and Gender in Islamic Law*. Cambridge: Cambridge University Press, 2008.

Ulrich, Laurel Thatcher. *A Midwife's Tale: The Life of Martha Ballard, Based on Her Diary, 1785–1812*. New York: Alfred A. Knopf, 1990.

Vahdat, Farzin. 'Post-Revolutionary Modernity in Iran: The Subjective Hermeneutics of Mohamad Mojtahed Shabestari' in Suha Taji-Farouki (ed.), *Modern Muslim Intellectuals and the Qur'an*. Oxford: Oxford University Press, 2004), 193–224.

Van Ess, Mrs. John [Dorothy Firman]. *Who's Who in the Arabian Mission*. New York: Women's Board of Foreign Missions, 1939.

Van Ess, Dorothy. *History of the Arabian Mission, 1926–1957*. Mimeographed: Publication of the Reformed Church in America, 1959.

Von Zambaur, Edward. *Manuel de généalogie et de chronologie pour l'histoire de l'islam*. Hanover: Libraire Orientaliste Heinz Lafaire, 1927.

Von Zambaur, Edward. *Mu'jam al-Ansab wa-al-usarat fi al-tarikh al-islami*. Beirut: Dar al-Ra'id al-'Arabi, 1980.

Wadud, Amina. 'Qur'an, Gender and Interpretive Possibilities'. *Hawwa: Journal of Women of the Middle East and the Islamic World* 2(3), 2004: 317–36.

Wadud, Amina. *Inside the Gender Jihad: Women's Reform in Islam*. Oxford: Oneworld, 2006.

Wadud, Amina. *Qur'an and Woman: Rereading of the Sacred Text from a Woman's Perspective*. New York: Oxford University Press, 1999.

Wahba, Hafiz. *Arabian Days*. London: Baker, 1964.

Wahba, Sheikh Hafiz. *Arabian Days*. London: Arthur Barker Limited, 1964.

Watt, W. Mongtomery. 'Makka' in *Encyclopedia of Islam*. Leiden: Brill, 1991.

Watt, W. Montgomery and M.V. McDonald (trans.). *The History of al-Tabari*. Albany: State University of New York Press, 1987.

Watt, W. Montgomery. *Muhammad at Medina*. London: Oxford University Press, 1962.

Webb, Gisela (ed.). *Windows of Faith: Muslim Women Scholar-Activists in North America*. New York: Syracuse University Press, 2000.

Weimann, Robert. '*Shakespeare After Theory* by David Scott Kastan [Review]'. Modern Language Quarterly 62(2), 2001: 189–92.

Welchman, Lynn. 'Egypt: New Deal on Divorce'. *International Survey of Family Law* 2004: 123–42.

Welchman, Lynn. *Women and Muslim Family Laws in Arab States. A Comparative Overview of Textual Development and Advocacy*. Amsterdam: Amsterdam University Press, 2007.

Wellhausen, Julius. *Reste arabischen Heidentums*. Berlin: Walter DeGruyter, 1927).

White, Hayden. *Metahistory: The Historical Imagination in Nineteenth-Century Europe*. Baltimore, MD: Johns Hopkins University Press, 1973.

Willis, John Ralph. 'The Ideology of Enslavement in Islam: Introduction' in John Ralph Willis (ed.), *Slaves and Slavery in Muslim Africa*. Vol. 1. London: Frank Cass, 1985, 1–15.

Wolff, Joseph. *Missionary Labours among the Jews, Mohammedans, and Other Sects*. Philadelphia PA: Orrin Rogers, 1837.

'Women Worshippers/Mystics'. In *Zaman al-nisa' wa-al-dhakirah al-badilah* [Women's Time and Alternative Memory], eds. Hoda Elsadda & Omaima Abou-Bakr. Cairo: *The Women & Memory Forum*, 1988.

Wormhoudt, Arthur (trans.). *The Naqaith of Jarir and al-Farazdaq*. Oskaloosa, IA: William Penn College, 1974.

Wright, Danaya. 'Legal Rights and Women's Autonomy: Can Family Law Reform in Muslim Countries Avoid the Contradictions of Victorian Domesticity?' *Hawwa: Journal of Women of the Middle East and the Islamic World* 5 (1), 2007: 33–54.

Wynn, Lisa. 'Marriage Contracts and Women's Rights in Saudi Arabia' in Homa Hoodfar (ed.), *Shifting Boundaries in Marriage and Divorce in Muslim Communities*. Grabels: Women Living Under Muslim Laws, 1996, 106–20.

Yamani, Mai Ahmad Zaki. 'Birth and Behavior in a Hospital in Saudi Arabia'. *Bulletin (British Society for Middle Eastern Studies)* 13(2), 1986: 169–76.

Yaqut, A. *Mu'jam al-buldan*. No editor mentioned. 5 vols. Beirut: Dar 'Ihya' al-Turath al-'Arabi, (n.d.).

Young, Elise G. 'Between Daya and Doctor; A History of the Impact of Modern Nation-State Building on Health East and West of the Jordan River'. PhD diss., University of Massachusetts Amherst, 1997.

Yusuf 'Ali, 'Abdallah, *The Meaning of the Holy Qur'an*. Beltsville, MD: Amana, 1989.

Zarins, J., J.S.M. Mughannum and M. Kamal. 'Excavations at Dhahran South: The Tumuli Field (208–92) 1403 AH/1983 AD, A Preliminary Report'. *Atlal* 8, 1984: 25–54, Pl. 18–59.

Zulficar, Mona and Hoda al-Sadda. 'Hawl mashru' tatawwur namudhaj 'aqd al-zawaj'. *Hagar* 3–4, 1996: 251–260.

Zwemer, Samuel M. *Sketch of the Arabian Mission*. New York: Board of Foreign Missions, RCA, 1901.

Glossary

abu	father (of)
adab	manners, literature
ad'iya'	see *du'a'*
ahkam	see *hukm*
'a'ila	family
'ajami	(pl. *'ajam*) non-Arab Muslims
'alim	(pl. *'ulama'*; fem. *'alima*; fem. pl. *'alimat*) religious scholar
amin	trustworthy, honest
ansab	see *nasab*
ansariyyat	see *nasir*
'aqd	(pl. *'uqud*) contract; *'aqd al-nikah* marriage contract
'Arabi	(pl. *'Arab*) Arab
asl	(pl. *usul*) origin, basis; specifically, *usul al-fiqh* the fundamentals of jurisprudence
awqaf	see *waqf*
'awra	private parts, the parts of the body that should be covered, especially during prayer
ayyam	see *yawm*
banu	see *ibn*
batula	form of veil
bay'a	oath of allegiance
bayt	house, household
bid'a	innovation, innovative idea, heresy
bin	see *ibn*
bint	(pl. *banat*) daughter (of)
burqa'	full-lenth veil worn by women, leaving only the eyes exposed
dakhil	intruder
dallala	(pl. *dallalat*) [female] peddler
damm	lit. embrace; specifically, custody (of a child after divorce)
daya	(pl. *dayat*) midwife
dhikr	(lit. remembrance) chant or ceremony of commemoration

dishdasha	traditional women's robe
diwan	gathering for discussion, the place where such gatherings took place, salon; collection of poetical or literary works
du'a'	(pl. *ad'iya'*) intercessory prayer
fakha'idh	see *fakhidh*
fakhidh	(pl. *fakha'idh*) subdivision of a tribe
faqih	(pl. *fuqaha'*; fem. *faqiha*; fem. pl. *faqihat*) exegetes, religious scholars
Fatiha	(lit. opener) first *sura* of the Qur'an
fatwa	(pl. *fatawa*) juridical opinion
fiqh	jurisprudence
fiqhi	pertaining to jurisprudence
firij	Khaliji colloquial for urban quarter or area
fitna	temptation, act of sedition
fitra	the natural order, human nature
fuqaha'	see: *faqih*
ghasila	(pl. *ghasilat*) [female] corpse washer
ghayra	jealousy, sense of honor
ghazal	love poetry
ghazawat	see *ghazwa*
ghazwa	raid, military expedition
hadana	guardianship, custody (of a child)
hadd	(pl. *hudud*) fixed limit; specifically, a punishment stipulated in the *Shari'a* for a particular crime
Hadith	Hadith recorded saying(s) of the Prophet, considered a source of Islamic law
hafiz	(pl. *huffaz*; fem. *hafiza*; fem. pl. *hafizat*) one who has memorized the whole Qur'an
hajib	chamberlain
hajj	pilgrimage; specifically, the pilgrimage to Mecca obligatory for all Muslims able to undertake it
hakam	(fem. *hakama*) judge
halal	permitted in Islamic law
halaqa	ring; study circle
hama'il	see *hamula*
hamula	(pl. *hama'il*) collection of tribes
haram	forbidden in Islamic law
al-haram	or *al-haram al-sharif* the mosque of the Ka'ba, in Mecca
harb	(pl. *hurub*) war
harim	women; specifically, the women in a particular household
hawwafa	beautician
haya	modesty, shyness
hija'	defamation; defamatory poetry
hijab	covering, screen; specifically, a woman's veil or headcovering
hijra	migration; specifically, the migration of the Prophet and his followers from Mecca to Medina, which became the starting point for the Islamic calender
hikma	wisdom
hisba	market inspection, standards
hudud	see *hadd*

hujja	proof, exemplar
hukm	(pl. *ahkam*) rule, commandment
hulwan	reward
hurr	(pl. *ahrar*; fem. *hurra*; fem. pl. *hara'ir*) free, free-born
hurub	see: *harb*
'ibadat	acts of religious devotion
ibn	(pl. *banu*) son (of); used in the plural to designate a tribe
'idda	three month period of waiting before a woman may remarry after a divorce
ifta'	pronouncing a legal opinion
ijaza	(pl. *ijazat*) diploma of learning, educational certificate
ijtihad	endeavor, exertion; specifically, independent interpretation of religious or legal texts
'ilm	(pl. *'ulum*) science, (branch of) knowledge
imam	(pl. *a'imma*; fem. *imama*) leader of prayers
inshad	chanted recitation
'ird	honor
isha'	night prayer
'iwad	compensation
Jahili	pertaining to the *Jahiliyya*
Jahiliyya	(lit. ignorance) the pre-Islamic period
jariya	(pl. *jawari*) female slave, courtesan
jawari	see *jarya*
jihad	religious striving
jinni	(pl. *jinn*) spirit, jinn, demon
juz'	(pl. *ajza'*) part, section; specifically, a section of the Qur'an
kabir	great, large
kafa'a	parity, comparableness
kafala	protection and support; specifically, fostering [a child]
kahin	(pl. *kuhhan, kahana*; fem. *kahina*; fem. pl. *kahinat*) priest/priestess
karahiyya	aversion, dislike, antipathy
katatib	see *kuttab*
khatba	matchmaker
khatib	(pl. *khutaba'*) preacher
khatima	recitation of the whole Qur'an
khatma	final part; specifically, the completion of memorizing the Qur'an
Khawarij	Kharijites; a grouping within Islam, beginning in the late seventh century, who rejected the concept of an inherited caliphate and supported the right of Muslims to rebel against any leader who deviated from what they saw as authentic Islam
khayrazana	cane
khul'	a form of divorce by consent
khutba	sermon preached at Friday noon prayers
kihana	soothsaying, divination
kitab	(pl. *kutub*) book
kuf'	parity, a match
kuttab	(pl. *katatib*) elementary school with a primary focus on

	teaching the Qur'an
laqit	foundling, abandoned infant
li'an	sworn allegation of adultery
madh	praise
madhhab	(pl. *madhahib*) school (of thought); specifically, one of the four orthodox Sunni schools of law
ma'dhun	registrar of marriages
madrasa	(pl. *madaris*) school
maghazi	see *maghza*
maghza	(pl. *maghazi*) foray, raid, military expedition
mahr	dower, often translated 'dowry', but paid by the bride's family to the bridegroom, usually returned if a divorce takes place
mahram	sometimes also *mihrim* (pl. *maharim*) a man related to a woman within the degrees of kinship that make marriage between them impermissible
majalis	see *majlis*
majlis	(pl. *majalis*) council, session, sitting
maqasid	see *maqsad*
maqsad	(pl. *maqasid*) intention, objective; specifically, higher intents and ideals behind the injunctions of the *Shari'a*
marathi	see *marthiya*
marthiya	(pl. *marathi*, *ritha'*) elegy
mawla	(pl. *mawali*) freed slave; familiar spirit
mawali	see *mawla*
mawlid	celebration of the birth (of the Prophet Muhammad or of a saint)
mihna	ordeal, inquisition
mihrim	see *mahram*
milkiyya	ownership
milla	religious minority community
misyar	ambulant; specifically, of a form of *'urfi* marriage in which the wife forgoes her rights to maintenance and accommodation
mu'adhdhin	caller to prayer
mu'allaqat	form of classical Arabic poetry
mu'amalat	conduct towards others, social or business relations
mufti	(pl. *muftiyun*; fem. *muftiya*; fem. pl. *muftiyat*) jurisconsult, one authorized to pronounce *fatawa*
muhaddith	(pl. *muhaddithun*; fem. *muhadditha*; fem. pl. *muhaddithat*) scholar of, or instructor in, Hadith
mukhadramun	famous classical thinker
mulla	(fem. *mullaya*) religious teacher or leader; Qur'an reader or reciter
murabbi	(pl. *murabbiyun*; fem. *murabbiya*; fem. pl. *murabbiyat*) educator
murshid	(pl. *murshidun*; fem. *murshida*; fem. pl. *murshidat*) guide, mentor
musahara	relationship by marriage
mut'a	temporary marriage; also consolation; specifically, compensation to a wife, e.g. when unilaterally divorced by her husband
mutafiqqih	(pl. *mutafiqqihun*; fem. *mutafiqqiha*; fem. pl. *mutafiqqihat*)

mutawwa'a	
mutawwi'	(pl. *mutawwi'un* or *mutawwa'a*; fem. *mutawwi'a*; fem. pl. *mutawwi'at*) volunteer; specifically, a teacher who volunteers his/her services, although not necessarily without being paid
muwahhidun	believers in *tawhid*, 'unitarians', monotheists
nafaqa	support (in terms of material provision), maintenance, alimony (paid by a man to his ex-wife after divorce)
naqa'id	satirical or invective poetry
nasab	(pl. *ansab*)lineage, blood line
nashiz	recalcitrant, disobedient; specifically, of a wife towards her husband
nasib	love poetry section in a classical Arabic ode; luck/fate
nasir	(pl. *ansar*; fem. *nasira*; fem. pl. *ansariyyat*) helper, supporter; specifically, a supporter of the Prophet Muhammad in Medina
nass	(pl. *nusus*) text; specifically, authoritative text
nizamiyya	courts
nushuz	recalcitrance, disobedience; specifically, of a wife towards her husband
nusus	see *nass*
qaba'il	see *qabila*
qabila	(pl. *qaba'il*) tribe
qadi	(pl. *qudah*) judge
qanun	(pl. *qawanin*) law
Qaramita	Qarmatians/Karmathians; a Shi'ite sect
qasida	form of classical Arabic poetry
qasir	(pl. *qisar* or *qusar*) minor
qiwama	standing, status, authority
qubba	dome, pavilion
ra'i	seer, diviner
rajaz	a classical Arabic poetical meter
rawi	(pl. *ruwa*) reciter
ridda	apostacy
ri'i	seer, diviner
ritha'	see *marthiya*
rubat,	pl. *arbita*, *rubut*) association, institution
ruwa	see *rawi*
sabaya	see *sabiy*
sabiy	(pl. *sabaya*) captive
saby	captivity
sadaqa	voluntary alms
sahib	(pl. *sahaba*; fem. *sahiba*; fem. pl. *sahibat*, *sahabiyyat*) companion; specifically, Companion of the Prophet Muhammad
saj'	rhymed prose
saqqa	water carrier
sard	recitation (from memory)
sha'b	(pl. *shu'ub*) people
shahid	(pl. *shuhada'*; fem. *shahida*; fem. pl. *shahidat*) martyr
shar'i	pertaining to the *Shari'a*, legal *Shari'a* Islamic law

sharif	(pl. *ashraf*) member of the noble class; specifically, local ruler in the Hijaz
shaykh	(pl. *shuyukh*; fem. *shaykha*; fem. pl. *shaykhat*) religious authority, elder, one respected for his/her maturity and wisdom
shaykha, shaykhat	see *shaykh*
shaytan	(pl. *shayatin*) devil, demon
Shi'a	originally followers of the party (*shi'a*) of 'Ali, the Prophet Muhammad's son-in-law; now the second largest grouping within Islam
Shi'i	belonging or pertaining to the Shi'a
shu'ub	see *sha'b*
shuyukh	see *shaykh*
sira, Sira	(pl. *siyar*) biography; specifically, the biography of the Prophet Muhammad
sirara	celebration for the return of a pilgrim from visiting the Prophet's tomb in Medina
sitr	covering
siyar	see *sira*
sufi	(pl. *sufiyyun*; fem. *sufiyya*; fem. pl. *sufiyyat*) mystic, member of one of many mystical groupings within Islam
Sunna	the authoritative tradition(s) regarding the practice and way of life of the Prophet Muhammad
Sunni	(lit. a follower of the *sunna*) Sunnis represent the largest grouping within Islam
suq	market
suq al-harim	women's market
sura	'chapter' of the Qur'an
ta'a	obedience; specifically, the required obedience of a wife to her husband
tabaqat	dictionary of historical biography
tabi', tabi'i	(pl. *tabi'un, tabi'iyyun*; fem. *tabi'a, tabi'iyya*; fem. pl. *tabi'at, tabi'iyyat*) follower; specifically, an early follower of the Prophet Muhammad
tafsir	exegesis, commentary (on the Qur'an)
tahrid	incitement (to revenge)
talaq	divorce; specifically, divorce pronounced by the husband
tamkin	capacitation; specifically, granting (a husband) rights over (his wife)
tamlik	possession, ownership
tasbih	praise sung to God
tawhid	belief in the absolute oneness of God
ta'wid	compensation; specifically, to a wife unilaterally divorced or harmed by her husband
tilawa	chanting of the Qur'an
turath	legacy, (cultural) heritage
'ulum	see *'ilm*
umm	mother (of)
umma	nation; specifically, the whole people of Islam
'urf	custom, traditional laws

'urfi	traditional, customary, 'common-law'
usra	(nuclear) family
ustadh	(fem. *ustadha*) teacher, master/mistress
usul	see *asl*
wa'iz	(pl. *wu'az*; fem. *wa'iza*; fem. pl. *wa'izat*) preacher
wali	(pl. *awliya'*) governor; guardian; familiar spirit
waqf	(pl. *awqaf*) charitable endowment given or established as an act of religious piety
waqfiyya	dedicatory inscription on a *waqf*
wasiyya	(pl. *wisaya*) legacy, will
wird	supererogatory prayer
yawm	(pl. *ayyam*) day; specifically, (day of) battle
zaffa	procession
zar	a spirit thought to possess a person; ritual to exorcise such spirits
zaraqa	blue-eyes, strong eyesight, blind
zawaj	marriage
zina	fornication, adultery

Acknowledgements

The vision to research and bring to light the history of women of the Arabian Gulf belongs to Sheikha Moza Bint Nasser, whose spirit and dedication to Qatar and the Arab world gives a glimpse into the true nature and contribution of the women of this area, contributions that have yet to be researched and written about. The authors of the articles included in this volume, and I, extend our appreciation to Her Highness for this vision and for her support in making this research possible.

Jacqueline O'Rourke initiated this project with me and was instrumental in getting it approved and moving forward. Researching the Gulf and looking for material about a subject that had yet to receive adequate attention was no easy matter and required a team of first-class researchers. This team was headed by Ramadan al-Khouli, whose dedication and expert understanding of historical records was one of the pillars of this project. Appreciation also goes to other members of the team, Jila Camden and Mervat Sami. No book succeeds without an editor, and Carol Rowe's copy-editing helped clear out problems and inconsistencies while Anne Renahan provided the editorial expertise to see this book through. Inaam Omari undertook the organization and running of administrative matters. Appreciation also goes to Professors Hatem al-Karanshawi, 'Aisha al-Manai, Barbara Freyer Stowasser, Lynn Welshman, Omaima Abou-Bakr, and Amina al-Kazem for their work on the Advisory Board of the Gulf Women's project. Working with Dr. Sheikha Abdulla al-Misnad at Qatar University and with the Advisory Board helped me to appreciate the seriousness and integrity with which Qatari women serve their community and the respect that they enjoy from their communities in return.

No project is a success without the help and advice of those with wisdom and knowledge about the subject at hand. A very special appreciation goes to Sheikh Faisal Bin Jassim Al Thani for the time and effort he spent with my students and I, discussing and explaining the history, culture, myth and realities of Qatar. His advice about Qatar's culture, past and present, constituted an important element in the philosophical approach of this book. The same appreciation goes to Sheikh Zaki al-Yamani for meeting with me to speak about Mecca – as he and his family had experienced it – and of the realities of life for women in the Hijaz in the past. His generosity with his time, books and materials has been very much appreciated. Lastly, a big thank you goes to my students at Georgetown University in Qatar, and at Qatar University, through whom I learned so much about Qatar and its women.

Amira El-Azhary Sonbol
Doha, July 2010

Index